"A clear-eyed, engaging, and deeply researched study of an industry and an argument we cannot afford to ignore." —**Amy Werbel, author of** *Lust on Trial*

"Kelsy Burke may have done the impossible. At a time when debates over pornography's production and consumption have never been more heated, Dr. Burke has written a book that combatants on either side of that fight would find accurate, fair, and enlightening. And that's because Dr. Burke invites both sides to explain their case. She interviews the activists, the experts, and the producers. She traces the history and crunches the numbers. Meticulously researched, yet sweeping in scope, *The Pornography Wars* is required reading for anyone interested in America's love-hate obsession with porn." —**Samuel L. Perry, co-author of** *The Flag and the Cross*

The Pornography Wars

The Pornography Wars

*The Past, Present, and Future of
America's Obscene Obsession*

Kelsy Burke

BLOOMSBURY PUBLISHING
NEW YORK · LONDON · OXFORD · NEW DELHI · SYDNEY

BLOOMSBURY PUBLISHING
Bloomsbury Publishing Inc.
1385 Broadway, New York, NY 10018, USA

BLOOMSBURY, BLOOMSBURY PUBLISHING, and the Diana logo are trademarks of
Bloomsbury Publishing Plc

First published in the United States 2023

ISBN: HB: 978-1-63557-736-5; EBOOK: 978-1-63557-737-2

LIBRARY OF CONGRESS CATALOGING-IN-PUBLICATION DATA IS AVAILABLE

2 4 6 8 10 9 7 5 3

Typeset by Westchester Publishing Services
Printed and bound in the U.S.A.

To find out more about our authors and books visit www.bloomsbury.com
and sign up for our newsletters.

Bloomsbury books may be purchased for business or promotional use. For information on
bulk purchases please contact Macmillan Corporate and Premium Sales Department at
specialmarkets@macmillan.com.

For Jacob, Sylvie, and Esme

CONTENTS

A NOTE TO THE READER

In this book, I tell the stories of groups and individuals using many different sources, including my direct research as a sociologist. For some interview participants, I use a pseudonym to protect their identities. When using a pseudonym, I use only a first name. Other interview participants have given me permission to use their real names. When using a person's real name, I use both their first name and surname or surname initial depending on my participants' preferences. I also use the first and last names of figures whom I did not interview but whose public platforms warrant their inclusion in the book.

I use pseudonyms to refer to most conferences and events I attended over the course of my research because I promised their organizers of these events that I would do so confidentiality. These include the "Freedom from Sexual Slavery" conference, Prairie Christian Church, the "Sex Workers United" conference, and the "True Intimacy" weekend retreat, which are all fictionally named. With permission, I refer to the Sex Down South conference by its real name. I use the following pseudonyms to refer to some porn addiction recovery groups used by my interview participants: "True Intimacy," "Redeemed!," and "Clean Life." I use the real names of organizations and events that have readily available public information online about their activities related to pornography debates.

PREFACE

When I was fifteen, I became a born-again Christian. Beside an ice-cold lake in the mountains in Wyoming, at a spot where there were still patches of snow on the ground even though it was July, I accepted Jesus into my heart as my Lord and Savior on a church-sponsored wilderness camping trip. Afterward, my youth group and I ran into the frigid waters in celebration—a shocking, spontaneous baptism. Then we changed into dry clothes and warmed ourselves by a campfire, singing praise and worship songs to acoustic guitar. When I returned down the mountain, I became a member of the only Baptist church in my small town and was baptized again, this time officially. This was in fact my *third* baptism, if the one at the lake counts, given that my parents had baptized me as an infant in the Methodist Church, in a small building accommodating a small congregation, which included my whole family, my parents, and me . . . until my teenage rebellion into the more conservative born-again variety of the Christian faith.

For the next four years, my religion took up my time and sense of self. I spent one year setting my alarm fifteen minutes early so I could follow a "Read the Bible in One Year" program. I bought a little canvas bag with a big Jesus fish embroidered on the front, to carry the Good Book, along with pens and highlighters I used liberally to mark the passages that *moved* me, which were a lot of the Psalms and the New Testament after the Gospels but before the Book of Revelation. I did not highlight much from the Old Testament genealogies, but I dutifully stayed awake for what seemed endless passages of "so-and-so begat so-and-so." Even though I wasn't an athlete, I was an officer in my school's Fellowship for Christian Athletes, because it was the only Christian group in the school. I went to youth group meetings every Wednesday night and Sunday morning. I listened to Christian music and sang in a church band called the Red Letter Edition.

A year after my lake baptism, I happened upon an unlabeled box in my family's basement storage room. We had recently moved, and I was looking for something that had not yet been unpacked. The box I found instead caused me to forget my original mission and sit down cross-legged on the cold cement floor. Feelings of surprise, wonder, and guilt rose in my chest. Neatly filed in the box were issues of *Playboy* magazine dating from the 1970s through the '80s. I saw that they were addressed to my dad, who was married to my mom for the duration of the subscription.

Everyone says they can't imagine their parents as sexual people, but mine were (and still are) especially wholesome and serious, people who scolded me if I said "suck" or "crap" and who fast-forwarded VHS tapes so I wouldn't see scenes of sexual innuendo in their favorite Western shoot-out movies.

My parents would not describe themselves as born-again Christians. My dad grew up going occasionally to a Methodist church, and my mom was from a family of Catholics in name only. My mom had made the decision that our family would be Methodists and had attempted to cajole my dad and me to church every Sunday. And so, my enthusiastic and sincere involvement with the Baptists in our town came as a surprise to my parents. I imagine they found it annoying when I pestered them, asking if they were *really* saved, worried that their souls might be condemned to hell. But they seemed to like that I spent evenings in the innocuous setting of a church.

I was first invited to the Baptist church after my freshman year in high school, a year during which I struggled to hold on to the few friends from middle school I had. As most of my peers seemed to naturally acclimate to the strange new land that was high school, accepting invitations to attend football games and parties and climb into the trucks of upper-class boys, I spent most afternoons and weekends alone. After finishing my homework, I watched television or read my mom's mystery paperbacks. One day

PREFACE

over the summer, an old friend from middle school asked if I wanted to tag along with her to help out at her church's Vacation Bible School, a free weeklong day camp for kids in the church. I agreed, as I had nothing better to do. And then, when the youth group leader invited me back to the church for their meeting, I said, "Sure, why not?" And I decided to go the week after, and the next. We played games and sang songs, and I found myself feeling confident and welcomed into a group of my peers, something that had not happened for a long time.

Ever since middle school, I had felt like an outsider. I was savvy enough to understand that I didn't fit in, but not savvy enough to chameleon my way to looking and acting like the other girls. For the seventh-grade Halloween Dance, other girls arrived in no costume at all or a subtle one, like felt cat ears glued to a headband and drawn-on whiskers. I wore a costume that I had proudly made myself: a trash can. I made a shirt by cutting three holes in a large plastic garbage bag for my arms and head. I then glued pieces of trash (a soup can, a spaghetti box) haphazardly onto the front and back. Over that I wore, attached to suspenders, a large piece of cardboard curved around my torso and spray-painted gray. My "hat" was a matching cardboard trash can lid, attached to my head by an elastic band I secured under my chin. I won Best Costume that year, an award desig-nated by teachers, but I remember mostly feeling sweaty and humiliated.

Part of my feelings of isolation had to do with being a sexual outsider, queer without yet having the label. That I had sexual feelings at all I knew to be inappropriate for a girl like me: white, middle class, and a "goody-goody." Surely, the other girls who were also "goody goodies" (mostly Latter-day Saint straight-A students) never had thoughts like mine. Surely, they never touched themselves or looked up the word *sex* or *masturbation* in the dictionary.

And then there were those copies of *Playboy* magazine and the fact that I really liked looking at them. I began stealing a few at a time and stashing them under my mattress to read before bed, which I knew was a cliché for boys, but not for a girl like me. I read them cover to cover, feeling like an excavator of some past world—1975, after all, felt utterly ancient—but also an onlooker to a present-day reality that existed just beyond my reach. As I watched the shows on MTV and was even allowed to watch all the PG-13

movies I wanted by then, I observed a sexual world that enticed and celebrated, rather than shamed or hid. It was not yet my world, but I was
excited about it.

I understood intellectually that my Baptist peers and pastor would have
told me it was wrong to read those magazines or to indulge in my carnal
fantasies. I was committing the sin of lust, given that sexual thoughts were
supposed to remain shut tightly away until I was married. I was also
committing the sin that my church made seem much worse: homosexual
perversion. I did feel different for liking those magazines, but not wrong.
In fact, I felt authentic and invigorated, similar to how I felt singing and
raising my hands during a particularly powerful rendition of "Our God Is
an Awesome God." I felt both small and big, vulnerable and honest. I felt
just right. Looking back at my life as a teenager, I can say that both Jesus
and *Playboy* saved me.

IN HER ADVICE column, Cheryl Strayed writes of "sister lives," the passing
ships of possibility, what our lives could have been had we altered our course.
My research often makes me feel like I am observing what my life could
have been had I only made a different choice in an earlier chapter. Like the
Choose Your Own Adventure books I read as a kid, I have thought about what
my life would have been like if I remained enrolled at a Baptist college
instead of transferring to a state school and telling my parents I was gay.
Would I have ended up among the group of Christian women I observed
as part of my research, the ones who gathered together on a Tuesday
morning for Bible study and prayer while their children were enrolled in
the church's Christian education program in the room next door? The irony
is that I *did* end up in that group of women, though not as a participant.

Sociology became the tool I used to make sense of my sexuality and
religious faith and the persistent ways that sex and religion collide more
broadly in American culture and politics—as in debates over *Playboy* magazine. Eventually, I found my spiritual home not among Baptists, but among
the notorious religious misfits, Unitarian Universalists. I found my friends,
lovers, and politics in women's and gender studies departments and gay bars.
But it's not a matter of simply saying I am an outsider to the evangelical

communities I have researched, that I and my peers of politically liberal, feminist queers are the "us" against the religious conservative "them." We are all more complex than these labels afford, as my own story attests.

I share these experiences because, in writing a book about the pornography wars, I do not pretend to be a neutral party. I am a social scientist, but I am a human being, too. Being a scientist means that I deploy specific methods to collect and analyze data—in this case, interviews with ninety people, more than one hundred hours of participant observation at events across the country, and content analysis of newspapers, government documents, and scientific studies. Being a human being means that I am a social creature, biased by my own experiences and position in the world. In the pages that follow, you will come to understand what I think about pornography—an opinion that I believe is both fair and informed, given the five years I have spent immersed in various stories and arguments about both its harms and its potential.

But this book is not about me. This book is about the many people, past and present, who believe they know the truth when it comes to pornography and who seek to shape both the culture and the law. My goal is not to prove one side right and one side wrong—there are other books for that—but rather, to investigate how these competing truths came into being, what they rest upon, and where they overlap. Sex in America is an example of what sociologist Arlie Hochschild calls a "deep story," one where our beliefs are *felt* more than rationalized. These are beliefs that don't come about after careful deduction, but rather, the reverse: they are beliefs we know to be true so deeply that we construct logical support and justification for them after the fact. It doesn't matter what evidence the "other side" might have to convince us that our perspective is wrong or ill-informed. We believe in its rightness at our core.

Consider your own beliefs about sex and porn. Here are some you might choose from, all quotes or paraphrases from interviews I conducted with people on the front lines of today's porn wars:

"No sex act is wrong so long as it's consensual."
"God created sex for one man and one woman in marriage."
"Don't yuck someone else's yum."

"Masturbation is good for your health."
"Masturbation is bad for your health."
"Porn can help you access hidden sexual desires."
"Porn creates deviant sexual desires."
"I am addicted to pornography."
"Pornography addiction is a myth."
"Sex workers are victims."
"Sex workers are workers."

What do you believe? Where did your beliefs come from? What could convince you to change them?

A common theme across my interviews was that participants acknowledged their beliefs about sex and pornography by articulating what they were *not*. "Moral judgment and the condemnation of others . . . is a universal and essential feature of human social life," writes psychologist Paul Rozin and his coauthors. This judgment includes "fictional others," people who have not actually harmed us and who may exist largely in our imagination. Scattered throughout my interviews were phrases like "I'm not one of those people who thinks pornography is harmless," or "I oppose the fundamentalists who are trying to control other people's sexuality." Both sides develop their own group identity by distancing themselves from others. Their emphasis is difference rather than sameness.

Yet I am trained in the sociological tradition that attempts to climb over what Hochschild calls the "empathy wall": "an obstacle to deep understanding of another person, one that can make us feel indifferent or even hostile to those who hold different beliefs." I climb this wall not because I am a particularly empathetic person. But as a sociologist, I do not assume that others, even when their beliefs appear so radically different from mine, are liars, dupes, or villains. I purposefully approach my research with curiosity rather than judgment. As Larry Flynt, the producer of the pornographic *Hustler* magazine, wrote in his eulogy of the late Jerry Falwell, the evangelical fundamentalist who took Flynt to court, "My mother always told me that no matter how repugnant you find a person, when you meet them face to face you will always find something about them to like." Flynt and Falwell would come to exchange Christmas cards after they hugged on

Larry King's TV talk show a decade after their epic courtroom battles over pornography and free speech.

I have come to understand that the different sides of the pornography wars are not in fact opposites. There are many important differences, including what counts as scientific fact, whose stories are told and prioritized, and which morals or ethical principles should guide us. After years of research, I have learned that this dividing line of anti- or pro-porn is a false dichotomy, one in which there appears to be only two mutually exclusive options when, in fact, overlap and alternatives do exist. Despite the polarizing rhetoric, those fighting the porn wars have a lot in common, including the fact that they believe sexuality is of utmost importance in the world in which we live. The attitude "If you're not with us, you're against us" is everywhere, but in fact, the raison d'être of both sides is essentially the same: to navigate the rough waters of American life—shaped by a sea of social inequality, predatory capitalism, and sexualized media—in order to find freedom and authenticity.

Introduction

In 1939, a German geologist named Otto Völzing walked out of spring sunshine and into damp and darkness—a fitting metaphor for the state of things, as the world was on the brink of war. He entered a cave tucked inside the Swabian Alps, the Hohle Fels (German for "Hollow Rock"), known to be a site of human life during the Stone Age. Völzing was likely acting on a direct order from the Schutzstaffel, or SS, the German police force whose expansive power included archaeology and the quest for physical evidence of the superiority of the Germanic race. Völzing had been on expeditions like this one before, and he expected to find nothing more now than flint and the inconsequential remains of prehistoric life. Instead, his hoe struck a hard object, and he unearthed the remains of a small statue that he inadvertently broke apart. He packed the pieces into a bag and sent them, along with his other discoveries of the day, to the Museum Ulm, in the south of Germany. Upon returning home, Völzing learned that the SS had terminated the excavation. Germany invaded Poland the following week. Völzing abandoned geology and joined the Nazi army.

Otto Völzing's disassembled statue remained untouched for decades. In 1982, a team of archaeologists rediscovered, and began piecing together, what they called the Löwenmensch, or "the Lion-man." They believed it to be the oldest piece of figurative art ever discovered, dating it back some

35,000 to 40,000 years ago, to the earliest phase of the Stone Age, the Paleolithic era. The Hohle Fels became a site of renewed archaeological interest, and in 2008, an American anthropologist, Dr. Nicholas Conard, discovered another small statue carved out of mammoth ivory. Conard named the figure the Venus of Hohle Fels, and went on to describe the anatomical details of the unmistakably female figure in scientific publications: "Beneath the shoulders, which are roughly as thick as they are wide, large breasts project forward." Below the abdomen, "The split between the two halves of the buttocks is deep and continuous without interruption to the front of the figurine, where the vulva with pronounced labia majora is visible between the open legs." Instead of a head, the figure has a carved ring above its shoulders, which Conard believes is suggestive that it was worn as a pendant. "There can be no doubt," he writes, "that the depiction of oversized breasts, accentuated buttocks and genitalia results from the deliberate exaggeration of the sexual features." News stories featuring the discovery enticed readers with headlines about the world's oldest pornography.

Conard's discovery suggests that visual representations of sex date back to the earliest humans on earth. Yet historians of pornography insist that it has a *pre*history, a time when it did not exist. The term *pornography* itself originated in the 1800s, when a Greek word, *pornographoi* (literally translating to "whore-painters"), was first used to describe erotic artwork, some of which was hundreds or even thousands of years old. Still, visual and literary representations of human sexuality became "pornographic" only when named as such. In the words of historian Walter Kendrick, "Pornography names an argument, not a thing." According to his reading of European history, it's the middle of the 1800s that marks the argument's beginning, when elites in Europe began cataloguing historic artwork and deeming some to be too sexually explicit for public viewing or consumption. "Those centuries before the nineteenth," Kendrick writes, "obscenity existed in plenty but did not yet go by its modern name. The development of the modern concept entailed the wholesale reorganization of the past to make room for a category the past had not recognized."

Today, pornography is most obviously a genre of sexually explicit media, but is also a way to describe "a specific kind of relationship," in the words of philosophers C. Thi Nguyen and Bekka Williams. Immediate gratification "without the complications of the real thing" is what food porn, real estate porn, organization porn, and porn porn have in common. With any kind of porn, "we get to skip the hard part," they write. With "organization porn," people lust after magazine photographs of kitchen pantries stocked only with glass bottles of Perrier and multicolored grains and legumes. With "real estate porn," the feelings one experiences while scrolling the Zillow app are quite different from those felt when one actually buys and moves into a house. And with online pornography, watching videos can offer pleasure while allowing us to momentarily avoid the hard work it takes to create and maintain a successful real-life sexual relationship.

Supreme Court justice Potter Stewart's famous definition of pornography—"I know it when I see it"—feels both dissatisfying and difficult to dispute. We do know it when we see it, but not because of *it*, that thing that is pornography, but rather, because we *see*, we collectively recognize. "*Being pornography* isn't an intrinsic property of anything," philosopher Michael Rea writes. Instead, pornography is best understood not as a noun but as a verb. It *does* something, and not just in the sense of an individual's arousal. Pornography does something for us as a society. It is a socially constructed concept, like money or the English language, and thus meaningless without collective agreement.

But consensus is not always so easy to come by. In 2016, artist Stephanie Sarley had her Instagram account suspended and restored three times in a single month because Instagram could not make up its mind as to whether she had violated its policy regarding sexual content. Instagram forbids "filmed sexual activities," "pornographic activities," and nudity. Sarley's series *Fruit Art Videos* and the still photographs that accompany it show a piece of fruit (or, in some cases, a vegetable) and a hand manipulating it. Giving a hand job to a cucumber with a small round hole cut at the end, so that gelatinous seeds spew out the top. Fingering a blood orange sliced in half so that its juices slide out and over the index and middle finger. Can food be pornographic? Instagram seems to think so. That same year, it suspended a British woman's account after she posted a picture of an Easter simnel cake, telling the user that her post violated the platform's standards related to content that is sexually suggestive or contains nudity. "IT'S NOT A BOOB," her daughter wrote furiously on Twitter. Instagram issued an apology and reinstated the offending account quickly, but by then the story had already gone viral.

In the same year as the fruit porn ban and the Easter cake fiasco, the European Union publicly criticized Instagram and other social media sites for their failure to remove hate speech. It was also the same year that Donald Trump was elected president when disinformation campaigns on Facebook and Twitter likely influenced the outcome of the election. Still, when Instagram suspended accounts in 2016, it included the message, "We understand that people have different ideas about what's okay to share on Instagram, but to keep Instagram safe, we require everyone to follow our guidelines." Sarley still uses her Instagram account, which in 2021 has nearly four hundred thousand followers, but she continues to have some of her posts flagged and removed for violating the site's guidelines related to "adult nudity and sexual activity."

What of the Venus of Hohle Fels, then? Stories about the world's first pornography make for sensational headlines, but labeling the relic as such risks imposing standards and values on a past very different from our reality today. The small statue may have ended up inadvertently banned on Instagram had it been created in the twenty-first century, but we can assume it did not spark moral outrage among the foraging groups for which it was made. The world's earliest humans had other things to do.

FORTY THOUSAND YEARS later, and there is no sexual bogeyman bigger than internet pornography. Porn panic comes from both the right and the left. The Republican Party insists that porn is "destroying the lives of millions." A *New York Times* columnist tells us, IT'S O.K., LIBERAL PARENTS, YOU CAN FREAK OUT ABOUT PORN. At the same time, other media stories act like pornography is no big deal. "Sexperts" normalize watching it, and magazines such as *Cosmopolitan* publish articles like "Everything You Need To Know About That 'Downton Abbey' Porn Parody."

To understand why pornography means so much and so many different things in the twenty-first century, we must look beyond pornography itself to who makes claims about it and why. As a sociologist, I have spent the past decade researching and writing about how sex matters in American politics and culture. I wrote my first book, about the Christian sex advice industry, after reading countless stories of evangelical men who struggled with what they described as a porn addiction. It surprised me that their language was medical rather than moral, and I wanted to learn more. As a follow-up study, I interviewed participants in porn addiction recovery programs. I thought it would wrap up any lingering questions I had. Instead, I was left with a trail of bread crumbs I followed over the next five years.

The research that emerged and became the basis for this book involved unprecedented access to claims makers on both sides of the pornography wars, from porn addicts to porn stars. On one side, which I refer to collectively as the antiporn movement, I have studied the strange alliance among religious conservatives, feminists, and secular Millennials concerned about the impact of pornography on contemporary society. Because the internet makes pornography instantly accessible and difficult to regulate on free online streaming sites, these groups point to widespread pornography addiction and sex trafficking as nothing short of a national crisis. I have observed events across the country, including lobbying efforts in Congress to end sexual exploitation in the porn industry, antiporn conferences, and a weekend retreat for Christian women whose lives have been harmed by sex and porn addiction.

On the other side, I have interviewed feminist and queer activists, sex workers, and sex educators who struggle to improve the pornography industry itself and people's understanding of it. This movement is more accurately "porn positive," rather than "pro-porn," because this is not a group that uniformly supports the commercial industry. Porn's potential, they insist, is found in independent production where two overlapping genres are on the rise: feminist pornography, which boasts real orgasms and pleasure by a diverse set of performers who are not typically showcased in mainstream porn; and ethical pornography, which prioritizes consent and adequate pay and labor rights for performers and transparency with regard to pornography as a form of entertainment, much like with movies or video games. My research took me to conferences on protecting porn performers' rights, workshops for "sex connoisseurs" to learn about creating their own porn and consuming better porn, and the shoot of an independent porn production.

I am trained in both quantitative and qualitative research methods but most often use the latter (a combination of interviews, participant observation, and content analysis) to answer my research questions. Though I include statistics from surveys and other quantitative measures in my analysis when appropriate, I am interested in stories more than numbers. And indeed, numbers have their own stories. As the book goes on to describe, activists on both sides have used research either to support or to counter the claim that porn is bad for us. When confronting inconclusive research findings, I return to the researchers themselves: the questions they ask, whom they ask them of, and how they draw conclusions. At other times throughout the book, I draw from survey data to offer context for the phenomenon I am describing. These data come from what I have determined to be the best possible sources—typically, surveys with national samples. Whenever I cite statistics or other research findings, I explain where they come from, what they tell us, and what they cannot tell us. All the research I personally conducted was approved by my university's Institutional Review Board, including my observation of a porn shoot where every performer and member of the crew gave their consent to my presence.

In total, I interviewed ninety people who, in varying capacities, engage in pornography debates. For the fifty-two people who were antiporn, the vast majority were white and identified as men. They ranged in age from nineteen to eighty-four. Slightly more than half were evangelical Protestants, but many were also Catholics and Latter-day Saints (Mormons). About 15 percent were not religious. The antiporn sample was evenly split when it came to political ideology; about 54 percent identified as conservative. Most (82 percent) participated in pornography addiction recovery programs as leaders, clinicians, or "addicts," and the remaining 18 percent were antipornography activists unaffiliated with pornography addiction treatment.

The group I call "porn positive" was made up of thirty-eight people, including sex workers, sex therapists, and sex educators and other academics. They ranged in age from twenty to seventy-six. Most identified as women, but 21 percent identified as men, and 13 percent identified as nonbinary, transgender, or gender fluid. About 70 percent identified as white, and 30 percent as Black or African American. None considered themselves politically conservative, and two thirds did not practice any religion. Those who did identified as Christian, Buddhist, New Age, or spiritual.

This interview sample is nonrandom—which means I cannot make generalizable claims about everyone who has strong opinions about pornography or who participates in activism surrounding porn. But this method offers two primary strengths. First, I systematically recruited interview participants from some of the largest organizations and events on both sides of the porn wars, ensuring that the loudest voices in public debates were included and analyzed in this book. Second, in-depth interviews allowed me to dig into, not gloss over, each person's story. Complexities, contradictions, and nuance are at the heart of this book.

In addition to the interviews and observations I conducted, I also draw from newspaper articles, government documents, and other primary sources, as well as the secondary work of historians, to trace pornography's significance throughout American history. The first part of the book tells this story, beginning in the nineteenth century and ending with the emergence of the internet. The second part examines contemporary debates over making porn; and the third, debates over watching it. In the final section, I bring together lessons from each battle fought in the porn wars, past and present, to propose a truce.

RATHER THAN DIRECT readers to a single truth about porn, this book instead challenges the myths that surround pornography itself and the people who have something to say about it. I challenge myths that the antipornography movement tells, including: people who defend or support pornography are not religious; all women who perform in porn are coerced and/or mistreated; you can't be a feminist if you support porn; people who support porn don't believe in porn addiction. Then there are the myths that the porn-positive movement tells about the other side: people who oppose pornography are all religious conservatives who are sexually repressed; you can't be a feminist if you oppose porn; pornography addiction isn't real.

Most important, this book tackles a myth that transcends either side of the debate and pervades contemporary culture. This is the myth that pornography debates are yet another example of polarizing culture wars, this us-versus-them mentality that is so ubiquitous in American life. This social divide is all around us. Journalist Bill Bishop calls it the "big sort," where Americans today cluster among others who think and live like they do, avoiding those who think and live otherwise. This narrows our perspective, affirms our assumptions as true even if they are false, and limits productive dialogue across differences.

As with our bipartisan and polarized political system, Americans' sexual beliefs are often described by public commentators and scholars as falling into one of two categories: sexual liberals or sexual conservatives. For conservatives, sex is sacred and, thus, should be protected against its watering down or misuse. Sexual liberals see sex as a natural source of pleasure and, thus, deserving of freedom. Although this dichotomy is grounded in empirical evidence, it perpetuates a misleading dualism that only one side is guided by religion and moral principles and the other by science and knowledge.

These are, in fact, only partial truths, and they gloss over complexities and shared ground. There's a scene in *The People vs. Larry Flynt*, the 1996 film starring Woody Harrelson as Larry Flynt, when Flynt's young fourth wife, Althea, played by Courtney Love, brainstorms ideas for future issues of their newly released and highly successful *Hustler* magazine. "*Wizard of Oz*?" Althea offers to a roomful of men who work for the magazine. "Some things are sacred, Althea," says a deadpan Larry, with no hint of irony, presumably to reject her idea. Later in the film, we see a spread of *Hustler* covers on the desk of obscenity laws crusader Charles Keating. His assistant flips through one and asks Keating, aghast, "Is that the Tin Man?" "It is," Keating says thinly. It was the November 1982 issue, and the cover story featured a photospread of the Tin Man along with Dorothy, the Scarecrow, and the Lion, all in various positions while engaged in group sex.

Perhaps it was the screenwriters' intent only to show the influence and leadership of the enigmatic Althea Flynt within the *Hustler* company, but the *Wizard of Oz* scenes also suggest that the two men, Flynt and Keating, had something in common: a shared reverence for a 1939 movie musical.

Not particularly notable, as *The Wizard of Oz* seems neither here nor there when it comes to political beliefs or attitudes about pornography. And yet, how is it that some cultural relics offer us common ground, while others deeply divide us? Sociologist John Levi Martin has proposed a theory of culture that explains not just how individuals within a social group share certain beliefs (that sexual conservatives agree that watching pornography is morally wrong, for example), but also how members of opposing groups may share an overlapping framework (that conservatives and liberals alike believe that conservativism is associated with opposition to pornography). It's not that the Flynts disagree with Keating on the nature of *The Wizard of Oz*. It's that their shared sense that it is wholesome is precisely what makes *The Wizard of Oz* the kind of object the Flynts want to transgress and that Keating and his assistant want to protect.

What is happening here is not simply opposition, but in fact a kind of consensus, an agreement on the rules of combat: that people like Flynt defile *The Wizard of Oz*, and people like Keating protect it; that liberals produce pornography, and religious conservatives oppose it. Across the pornography wars exists a recognition that certain beliefs go together and certain beliefs do not. These sets of beliefs provide the foundation for disputes that have been argued over for decades, even centuries. But they are flexible rather than fixed. People find common ground on the issue of pornography, but debates are never about pornography alone. Instead, they reveal a broader nexus of shared assumptions about the social world. These assumptions confront deep social dilemmas having to do with intimacy and authenticity, protection and safety, truth and knowledge, agency and autonomy. By tracing the history and contemporary contours of the pornography wars, we can see the steady but evolving pulse of American society itself.

PART I

The Hundred Years' War

L ike a long marriage, the details of America's fights over pornography may change, but each new dispute is a return to the same tensions. Debates center on the role of both religion and sexuality in public life, the boundaries of censorship and free speech, the autonomy and agency of those trying to make a living within a capitalist society, and gender inequality.

To fully understand the fight over pornography today, we must first understand its origins, which date back to the nineteenth century. This marks the emergence of the pornography industry and its opposition. The twentieth century saw a rise in U.S. court battles over obscenity, conservative Christian resistance to pornography and other progressive changes relating to sexuality, Hollywood and its intersection with pornographic films, antipornography feminism, and finally, the advent of the internet. Taken together, these mile markers in history explain who is fighting the pornography wars in the twenty-first century and what they are fighting for.

CHAPTER I

Comstockery

From the 1840s to the 1940s, pornography—a broad category that included drawings, photographs, performances, literature, objects, and eventually film—came to represent a changing America, for better or worse. For its distributors and proponents, it would stand for modernization and for liberation from oppressive religious practices and beliefs. For its critics and censors, pornography represented the indecency and secularity that threatened to crush the precarious power held by white Protestant men in an increasingly diverse society.

Before the 1840s, selling pornography wasn't exactly legal in the United States—it was considered a form of libel or injuring a person's reputation—but it was rarely prosecuted. Like tea or cacao, porn was a popular imported good. Early nineteenth-century periodicals noted at the time that obscene drawings and literature were readily available "across the land." *Fanny Hill*, for example, was an erotic novel that Americans could buy from select booksellers at city ports or in catalogues advertising the latest popular readings. First published in England in 1748 under its more formal title, *Memoirs of a Woman of Pleasure*, the novel is still available for purchase today, as it is too old to be protected by copyright. Amazon sells a Kindle edition for $0.99 and a paperback that looks like a Harlequin romance novel for $5.99. Reviews are mixed, though, with some purchasers disappointed that sex scenes are described primarily through euphemism and coy suggestion, while others applaud the novel as a match for the best of contemporary erotica. "Still great after all these years," one reviewer writes, as if they can recollect with fondness its eighteenth-century release.

The plot to *Fanny Hill* would become a cliché trajectory for smut novels for centuries to come: depravity followed by redemption. Young Fanny is orphaned and, thus, forced to turn to prostitution to survive. She does not willfully choose the occupation, but nor does she complain. The book presents a series of sexual encounters (sometimes violent, sometimes playful) between Fanny and her customers and Fanny and other women in the brothel where she works. The book's popularity was no doubt a result of its sense of the forbidden, but it also worked to push the moral agenda of the time. By the book's end, Fanny leaves the brothel for marriage and respectability.

In 1842, the U.S. Congress passed a customs law that explicitly prohibited the distribution of obscene material. The law didn't attract much fanfare, because its regulatory language focused on handling international mail, but it did mean that imports were riskier than illicit material made right in the U.S.A. Technically, there was nothing illegal about using U.S. mail to circulate smut, and so, dealers began to take advantage. The largest and most successful operations were out of New York City, where publishers printed illicit stories and sketches on cheap paper and sold them through street vendors.

Meanwhile, Americans took up the fad of making, buying, and sharing *cartes de visite* after a French photographer patented the technique in 1854. These iconic sepia portraits from the Civil War era glued to small pieces of cardstock also became a way for smut (a shorthand used at the time for any material signaling sexual impropriety) to evolve and expand its market. Similar to baseball trading cards, *cartes de visite* were cheap to produce in mass quantities, as they took advantage of a four-lensed camera to make eight small photographs from one large print. The technique gave way to the "beaver shot," a close-up image of a woman's genitals, which became a hit among male customers. Another French invention that became a popular American souvenir, the Stanhope or Stanho-scope, consisted of miniature photographs cleverly disguised in ordinary small objects, such as rings or watches, and magnified when viewed through a small peephole.

COMSTOCKERY   15

The new mass market for porn emerged just as America fell into civil war. Soldiers leaving home for battlefields could buy pornography from street markets or mail-order catalogues. *Fanny Hill* was a popular choice that was said to have been read aloud among soldiers at camp. As historian Judith Giesberg argues, pornography served a purpose beyond the sexual fantasies and satisfactions of individual soldiers. It also worked to shore up masculine camaraderie among the troops. "Pornography served as a means of social leveling," she writes, "working against class and army hierarchy, as officers and enlisted men bonded over erotic images and words that explicitly violated the terms of domesticity and that could also embrace violence or domination." Coercive sex and rape, alongside racist imagery, were as present in the nineteenth century as they are in today's porn. And as they do today, men used these images to feel emboldened in their entitlement, not just to women's bodies, but also to their supremacy and authority elsewhere in their lives.

While pornography may have been celebrated and heartily enjoyed by many within solider camps, it was feared by key and respected figures. In 1861, the Young Men's Christian Association (the YMCA) created the U.S. Christian Commission to send chaplains into Union Army camps to provide spiritual guidance. The YMCA was waging its own war against indecency and immorality among the troops, believing that sinful vices would corrupt not only a soldier's soul but also God's favor for the Union Army. Shocked at the prevalence of pornography in the camps, the YMCA began lobbying politicians to pass laws to explicitly outlaw and prosecute it.

In March 1865, amid stories of bloody battles and passionate congressional debates over how to win the war, newspapers across the country also reported on the Senate's passage of a bill amending the postal laws. Innocuous enough, it seemed, the law was originally intended to regulate the operation of the U.S. Postal Service and prevent Confederate soldiers from using the mail for espionage. There were seventeen sections of the law in total, and the final section made little fanfare at the time. One paper summarized it succinctly: "Section 17 relates to the exclusion of obscene publications, and the arrest of persons guilty of mailing such matter." No senator opposed the inclusion of Section 17, for they agreed that soldiers should uphold the strictest of moral standards and not be tempted by illicit mailings.

A month after the Senate passed An Act Relating to the Postal Laws, John Wilkes Booth shot Abraham Lincoln. In the news, the assassination eclipsed any bill that passed that spring in the Thirty-Eighth Congress. But the postal bill passed in the House and, thus, made it a crime to send porn via the U.S. Postal Service. The law officially stated that "no obscene book, pamphlet, picture print, or other publication of a vulgar and indecent character, shall be admitted into the mails of the United States, but all such obscene publications deposited in or received at any post office, or discovered in the mails, shall be seized and destroyed." To break this law was to commit a misdemeanor offense that resulted in up to one year in prison and a fine of up to $500 (or, roughly, $8,500 in today's currency). Over the next seven years, there were but a handful of arrests across the Midwest and New York City for violations of the law.

WHEN THE CIVIL War finally ended, twenty-one-year-old Anthony Comstock returned to his home in New England, disturbed not only by images of bloody battlefields and wounded soldiers, but also by the excessive profanity and pornography that saturated the camps of the Seventeenth Connecticut Infantry. But both the literal and symbolic wars over men's courage and decency were experienced for Comstock largely secondhand. He never made it onto the battlefield, and all smut sightings were furtive or involuntary. Instead, Comstock was stationed for eighteen months at an inactive occupation in Florida. As he describes in his diary at the time, boredom was among his greatest challenges.

Before volunteering for the Union Army, Comstock followed in his parents' footsteps in his devotion to his Congregationalist faith. A self-proclaimed "weeder in God's garden," a teenage Comstock called upon the local sheriff to investigate a saloon he believed was offering illegal drink to women and children. When the sheriff ignored his complaints, Comstock took it upon himself to empty the saloon's barrels of alcohol.

In 1871, Comstock moved to New York City to continue his efforts to weed God's garden, this time in a city with a reputation for vice. He joined forces with the YMCA, which was already leading efforts to outlaw obscenity in the city and beyond. In 1873, with the backing of the YMCA, Comstock successfully lobbied Congress to pass An Act for the Suppression of Trade in, and Circulation of, Obscene Literature and Articles of Immoral Use, which was referred to as the Comstock Act. The most notable difference between this law and the earlier Postal Act was obscenity's punishment: imprisonment in a labor camp or prison for no less than six months and no more than ten years, with a fine of no less than one hundred dollars and no more than five thousand dollars (over one hundred thousand dollars in today's currency).

Three days after the passage of the law, Comstock was named special agent of the U.S. Postal Service. His independent mission to rid the world of obscenity was now his government-appointed position. Near the end of his life, Comstock estimated that he was responsible for the convictions of more than 3,500 people on charges of obscenity and for destroying 160 tons of obscene literature. That's 320,000 pounds—or nearly thirty elephants' worth of dirty books.

"Comstockery" (as efforts to suppress sexual material would come to be called by critics) had always faced opposition. George Francis Train, a presidential candidate, was an early enemy of anti-obscenity laws. Having earned a small fortune as a founder of the Union Pacific Railroad, he dabbled in various other pursuits, including midwestern real estate and a record-setting trip sailing around the world. Just a few days before Christmas 1872 (the same year as his failed presidential bid), police arrested Train on charges of obscenity for publishing a periodical, the *Train Ligue*, which he started in Omaha, Nebraska. "This is just what Train wanted," one newspaper journalist speculated, as Train was well known for attracting outlandish attention. "He appeared in Court, fashionably attired, with hair wildly tumbled" and told the judge that all of the so-called obscenity his paper had published came from quotations in the Bible. Train's arrest, imprisonment, and trial made news across the country. His defense was ahead of its time, arguing that obscenity laws were subjective and vague. If Train's so-called obscene content came from the Hebrew Bible, was there anything obscenity laws could not touch? And if nothing was objectively sacred, then could it also be true that nothing was objectively obscene?

A doctor declared Train "of unsound mind," but ultimately, the judge declared him sane enough to face trial and ordered his release in the meantime. On the same day of his release, he boarded a ship to the Baltic Sea. His obscenity case was eventually dismissed, and Train spent the next several years traveling and being thrown in prison in every country in Europe for intentionally violating what he described as their "tyrannical laws." Eventually, he settled in New York City, where, on occasion, he gave public lectures about the dire state of politics and economics.

Train represented Comstock's early opponents, who were largely relegated to the margins of respectable society. He had the benefit of deep pockets, which meant his public opposition to obscenity laws caused him no serious repercussions. Though men made up the majority of obscenity prosecutions in the late nineteenth century, the arrests of women rose dramatically in the Comstock era, from only 3 percent of overall arrests in 1873 to 12 percent in 1913. One of these women was less fortunate than Train, though no less eccentric. Like Train, Ida Craddock was considered to be a "freethinker" and radical, but the public did not treat her with the same fondness; nor did the courts ultimately give her sympathy.

Craddock was born in Philadelphia and raised by her mother, who was a Spiritualist and obsessed with sexual purity. Spiritualism in the mid- and late nineteenth century was popular especially among progressive-thinking middle-class white women like Craddock and her mother. Mary Todd Lincoln famously practiced Spiritualism in the White House. Spiritualism appealed to American women who questioned their Christian faith as they witnessed tragedy after tragedy, from the Civil War to infant mortality. It required no blind faith but, rather, the practice of revealing the spiritual through a variety of rituals, including holding seances and using Ouija boards, allowing women to believe they were communicating with their deceased loved ones.

Craddock adopted her mother's Spiritualist practices but rejected her attitudes about sex and sexuality. She was well educated, middle class, and as a young adult, joined the women's movement, campaigning for women to be admitted to universities. She traveled to cities across the United States and Europe, supporting herself by working as a teacher or secretary, and in her spare time, she studied Spiritualism and the occult. She believed her

Ouija board connected her to spirits of the dead, and she eventually claimed to have married one of them, whom she called "Soph." For this, her mother committed her to an insane asylum. Craddock was eventually released, undeterred.

For her progressive thinking and strange curiosities, it's no wonder she was captivated by the Chicago World's Fair of 1893, the World's Columbian Exposition. In particular, she was absorbed by a dancer, Fahreda Mahzar, who went by the stage name "Little Egypt" and belly danced for huge crowds. The performance was criticized by Comstock himself, who called it a "hoochie-coochie dance" and attempted to shut down the performance. Later, Craddock wrote a letter defending Mahzar and her dance and admonishing Comstock, calling the dance a "solemn religious perfor-mance," one that emphasized the worship of sensuality and self-restraint. When she mailed the letter, Craddock was arrested for mailing obscenity but was never prosecuted in Chicago. Instead, she stayed in the city and continued to write about sex, claiming that her "spirit husband" had helped teach her about sexual relations. She began signing her writing as "Mrs. Craddock."

For ten dollars, she would mail a pamphlet on sexual instruction. For five dollars, she would answer written correspondence with questions about sexual matters. She promoted sex only in the context of marriage and believed that sex could be a spiritual union among husband, wife, and the divine. She promoted women's pleasure and instructed couples on how to achieve it. In 1901, in a direct challenge to Comstock, it seems, she moved to New York City, where she publicly advertised her pamphlets and services. Comstock himself wrote to her using an alias and requested a pamphlet. He then arranged her arrest on charges of breaking New York State's obscenity laws, for which she served three months in a workhouse prison. Upon release, she was immediately arrested again, over the same pamphlet, but this time on federal obscenity charges. She was tried and convicted again in the fall of 1902. Before beginning her five-year prison sentence, she took her own life.

By the time of Craddock's death, forty-two of forty-five U.S. states had passed anti-obscenity laws. Yet, at the same time, the attitudes of the American public were diverging from those of Comstock, who was increasingly mocked as a religious zealot. He opposed nudity in any form. He opposed anything that accentuated the human body in a way that could be read as sensual, including classical art and literature, dance, and theater. This posed a problem, given that the human body on display was precisely what was growing the entertainment industry from seedling to blossom. Vaudeville displayed bodies in all their strange, majestic, and indeed sensual forms. *Tableaux vivants*, or "living pictures," were popular in city theaters, with actors posing as if in a photograph or famous painting or statue. The curtain would come down, and the actors would quickly transition to another scene. In 1895, a group of performers and directors was arrested after putting on a show featuring bronze statues of Orpheus and Eurydice (actually, a man and woman painted from head to toe in luminous gold). Orpheus wore only a tight brief, and Eurydice, a brief and a cloth wrap exposing one of her breasts. In New York City, the penal code forbade "indecent exposures, obscene exhibitions, books and prints, and bawdy and other disorderly houses," thus justifying the arrest of the actors depicting the fateful lovers.

WHEN EARLY CINEMA emerged at the end of the nineteenth century, voyeurism was an American pastime. "Owning the right to look," in the words of porn studies scholar Mireille Miller-Young, was a direct result of white supremacy and slavery. African bodies had long been on display for white audiences, including the auction block spectacle where enslaved men, women, and children were often forced to perform in song and dance. Long after emancipation, Black Americans became the source of both entertainment and scientific experiment to satisfy whites' curiosity and pleasure. Thus, what film historian Linda Williams calls the "frenzy of the visible" that emerged out of the popular moving picture added to an already widespread practice of exploiting certain bodies.

The earliest form of American cinema—dating back to the 1870s zoopraxiscope, which took sequenced pictures to illustrate movement—normalized an obsession with looking at bodies close up and uncontrolled. Williams notes how one of the first moving picture films, the five-second *Fred Ott's Sneeze*, produced in 1894, was not intended to depict Mr. Ott at all but, rather, the filming of the spontaneous sneeze of a "pretty young woman." Ott was Thomas Edison's lab assistant and was the less desirable but more convenient choice. Still, the popularity of the film and others like it marked the excitement over the moving picture's new vantage point of human action and interaction. Early cinema, whose goal was to "maximize visibility," in the words of Williams, was not so different from the gritty pornography that emerged at the same time. These were two sides of the same coin.

In 1907, Chicago was the first city to outlaw the public viewing of obscene films. Many other cities followed suit, bolstering federal obscenity laws that focused on mail and distribution. Still, by the 1930s, illegal pornographic films made for a successful mass market, if one forced to operate underground. Despite a myth that pornography at the time was largely produced by the Mafia, or powerful criminal families, the FBI discovered that the industry was in fact made up of much smaller, disparate operations with little connection to one another.

These early pornography films were called "stags," named after the groups of men who would gather to view them. Like the vast majority of commercial porn that came after them, stag films focused on women's bodies in their entirety (including close-ups of faces, breasts, genitals, butts, legs, and feet) and men's bodies cropped to display only their penises. As remains true today in mainstream porn, male performers in stags served as "surrogates for the male audience," according to stag aficionados Al Di Lauro and Gerald Rabkin, who published an illustrated history of the genre in the 1970s. But unlike modern porn, stag films remained primitive even after motion pictures had expanded to sound and full-length features. Stags continued to be shot on a single reel of film, which limited their length to no more than fifteen minutes. They relied on crude techniques that impeded narrative flow, including the use of sound cards to indicate dialogue, given that the films were almost always silent. As with other early motion pictures, the pleasure for the viewer was in the snapshots and close-ups, often disjoined, but that nonetheless enticed. Not unlike "compilation" videos that are popular today on streaming websites like Pornhub, stag films often strung together a series of sexual scenes entirely unrelated to one another, with no attempt at narrative storytelling. The stag's grand finale was usually a genital shot, or proof that penetrative sex was indeed taking place. It was not until the 1970s that the "money shot" (a man's ejaculation) became the standard final scene.

Along with brothels, saloons, and nightclubs, smut films and cheap pulp paperbacks were frequent targets of the anti-vice efforts that outlasted Comstock, who died in 1915. Following World War II, the New York Society for the Suppression of Vice, which had led efforts to pass the Comstock Act, organized a campaign for greater crackdown on obscenity. It opposed, for example, that the U.S. military sanctioned paintings of nude women as decoration on fighter planes. Comstock's legacy also directed obscenity laws at unsuspecting and seemingly respectable citizens.

In 1929, the *New York Times* described a fifty-seven-year-old grandmother (a "gray-haired, kindly-looking matron") who was being tried on obscenity charges. Mrs. Mary Ware Dennett was arrested for writing a pamphlet about sex that she had shared with her adolescent sons nearly fifteen years earlier (then ages eleven and fourteen). At the time she wrote the pamphlet, Dennett was active in what was called the "social hygiene movement" and, thus, was acquainted with doctors and nurses who shared her belief that young people must be educated on the risks of sex, including unwanted pregnancy and venereal disease. She shared with them her pamphlet, which she called *The Sex Side of Life, an Explanation for Young People*, and eventually it was printed in a medical journal, used for a school curriculum, and even circulated by the YMCA, the organization that had led efforts to codify anti-obscenity measures some fifty years earlier.

In Mary Dennett's trial, her pamphlet was the single piece of evidence used against her. It included four images and explicit explanations of both practical and emotional elements of sex. Her lawyer told the jury the case was "absurd" and that a conviction would signal "silence on fundamental facts." According to the prosecuting attorney, however, the jury's task was to determine if the pamphlet was "capable of raising lewd, lascivious or libidinous thought." "This is pure and simple smut," he insisted. "If I can stand between this woman and the children of the land, I will have accomplished something." Dennett countered that her aim was not to harm children, but to help them. The jury deliberated for forty minutes and returned with a guilty verdict.

Though Dennett faced up to five years in prison, the judge sentenced her to only a three-hundred-dollar fine. Her lawyer appealed, and six months after her initial conviction, a federal court judge ruled that the pamphlet was *not* obscene, reasoning that intent was a necessary component. Dennett's intent was educational rather than salacious. Unlike Comstock, who had vehemently opposed any form of education that acknowledged the fact of sexual bodies, Dennett's case established in the courts that medical information and sex education were not the same as obscenity.

A TIMELESS TRUTH of the pornography wars is that those who promote censorship are necessarily just as obsessed with sex and pornography as those who are being censored. Whether in 1900 or 2000, critics have questioned both the motives and means of pornography's opponents. In 1900, Comstock sent three detectives to the Black Rabbit, an infamous nightclub in New York City. In his written testimony, one of the detectives described how a performer advertised as a hermaphrodite "lifted up her dress and skirts and exposed testicles and what she described as a penis . . . then made further display by lifting up the testicles and penis and said 'underneath was a vagina, the same as a woman's.'" This would have been more than sufficient to arrest the performer and the club's owner, but instead, the detectives went on to buy more drinks and accepted invitations for special shows, this time involving sexual performances among both men and women. Of course, whether the detectives experienced any pleasure as a result of their raid was not the legal question put before the court. Instead, following their arrests and guilty verdicts, the proprietors of the club were convicted of sodomy and sentenced to seven years in prison and fourteen years' hard labor, respectively.

In her suicide note, Ida Craddock called Comstock a "sex pervert" who prosecuted sex crimes for his own pleasure. Historians offer varying interpretations of Comstock's motives, some more aligned with Craddock's accusation than others. Yet obscenity battles of the late nineteenth and early twentieth century teach us that more is at stake than pornography itself. As the case of Mary Dennett illustrates, Comstock's efforts to criminalize obscene material were also a way to codify into law his own Protestant beliefs that young people should not be taught anything about sex other than that they should avoid it.

Sociologists have described efforts like Comstock's as "symbolic crusades." Whether social panics over sex, drugs, crime, or immigration, they reveal an effort to promote a particular political or cultural agenda. In his now-classic study of the Temperance Movement, sociologist Joseph Gusfield argued that temperance was championed by white, middle-class Protestants not because they cared so deeply about drunkenness, but because they saw themselves as what Gusfield describes as a "doomed class." Their attitudes about and efforts related to abstinence from alcohol symbolized their deeper opposition to immigrant, urban, and Catholic groups who were growing in size and power in the late nineteenth and early twentieth centuries. Not coincidentally, this is the same era of Comstock's reign, when support for his anti-obscenity laws was marshaled by a similar agenda to preserve the status quo. This was a time when women advocated for voting rights and access to birth control; when artists, writers, and playwrights critiqued censorship and suppression; and when the public put its faith in science in addition to religion. Naming obscenity as a large-scale social problem symbolically justified a broader set of social and political values perceived to be under threat.

CHAPTER 2

Obscene Files

For nearly fifty years, J. Edgar Hoover took on the mission that Anthony Comstock had begun: to rid America of obscenity. While Hoover shared Comstock's moral sentiments, unlike Comstock, who technically worked for the U.S. Postal Service, Hoover had unprecedented power in law enforcement. He served as director of the Federal Bureau of Investigation from 1924 until his death in 1972, and in that time, he used his position to bully political adversaries, celebrities, and activists and to use law enforcement to punish those with social and sexual values different from his own. For most of his tenure, the courts, offering only vague definitions of obscenity, enabled a broad range of citizens to become Hoover's targets.

When Hoover was named director of the bureau, the FBI had established its reputation as the nation's law enforcement arm. He would spend the next decade transforming it from an organization whose main job was to reduce crime to one that was responsible for protecting national security. For Hoover, this meant protecting the country from threats of all kinds: not just ordinary criminals, but also Communists, civil rights activists, homosexuals, and pornographers, categories he believed often overlapped.

Hoover expressed the strong moral conviction that was typical of many white upper-middle-class Protestants of his era: a fear that "immorality" was taking the nation down a dangerous path. He personally opposed pornography, but more important, he believed it was his duty to eliminate what he called "merchants of filth." Near the end of World War II, he directed the FBI to create its "Obscene File," thus making pornography and obscenity a significant priority for the bureau for decades to come. By the 1990s, the file contained more than a hundred thousand cases that were investigated, often at the personal instruction of Hoover. The amount of smut confiscated is unknown, as it was periodically destroyed throughout Hoover's reign, but the numbers are startling. In one of its first major raids in New York City, the FBI reportedly confiscated eight million items, ranging from playing cards to novels.

Though there is much speculation about Hoover's personal life, he was protective of his public image, and we therefore have few certainties when it comes to his sexuality. Some have claimed that for all his opposition to what he dubbed "sexual deviancy," he had some queer habits of his own, including cross-dressing. Others have accused him of having a secret gay identity, pointing to his long-term relationship with Clyde Tolson, the FBI's associate director, who worked alongside Hoover for forty years. The two ate lunch together nearly every day and traveled as a pair for both work and leisure, and upon Hoover's death, Tolson inherited most of his estate. Still, Hoover mostly avoided any large-scale public scandal over the contradictions between his personal life and his political position, likely because of his vast power for retribution and retaliation against his critics.

Hoover used the Obscene File to do more than just crack down on the distribution of stag films and dirty pictures. He also used the file for a kind of "social regulation," as described by historian Douglas Charles. Hoover investigated Black R&B musicians for obscenity, purportedly due to the music's sexual innuendos, but really to prevent "race music" (as it was called at the time) from rising in popularity and spreading into white homes. And although Hoover kept a separate "Sex Deviants" file, the names in the Obscene File helped him during the Lavender Scare to weed out gay government officials, employees, and political figures. Hoover promoted the belief that homosexuality would corrupt the nation, and he provided evidence to the Senate in its hearings and in a subsequent report on the *Employment of Homosexuals and Other Sex Perverts in Government.*

Long before the development of the Obscene File, J. Edgar Hoover kept a file on Samuel Roth, a writer, editor, and publisher. A Jewish immigrant who moved to New York City at age seven in 1900, Roth had been entangled in obscenity cases since the 1920s. He was well known in the literary community, and his magazines included the work of D. H. Lawrence and Ernest Hemingway. He lost his good standing in these circles, however, after he published excerpts from the novel *Ulysses* without the permission of James Joyce. One hundred and sixty-seven writers and intellectuals, including Hemingway and Albert Einstein, signed a letter in protest of Roth's publication. Having lost his respectable literary reputation, Roth turned to the less respectable world of illicit literature.

Anthony Comstock's successor, and president of the New York Society for the Suppression of Vice, John Saxton Sumner was bent on Roth's prosecution and drew the FBI's attention to him in the 1930s. Roth published and sold illustrated copies of *Fanny Hill*, *Lady Chatterley's Lover*, *Studies in the Sexual Life of African Savages*, *Girl on City Streets: A Study of 1400 Cases of Rape*, *Cities of Sin*, and *The Body's Rapture*, among many others. The level of explicitness varied across titles. For some, the titles themselves constituted the raciest content of the books. These books challenged social conventions of the time because they removed sex from its silent, private sphere and placed it out into the public.

Roth faced many trials on account of obscenity charges. Some he won, and many he didn't. He spent some time in prison and more time on probation. All the while, he continued writing and publishing texts that pushed against social standards of decency. Beginning in the 1940s and into the early '50s, he began winning more cases than he lost. Courts were beginning to side more often with the censored rather than the censor. This meant Roth's legal battles were inconsistent and recurring, as the High Court did not provide guidance for clear rulings on what counted as obscene.

In 1951, Roth faced criminal charges for selling *Beautiful Sinners of New York*, an illustrated catalogue in which prostitutes described their services. Roth, now savvy with regard to obscenity laws and their loopholes, had purposely inserted a foreword written by a Louis Berg, M.D., who described the book as "a social document of the first order of importance." This case became different from all the rest when Roth's defense attorney, Nicholas Atlas, tried a new strategy, moving to dismiss the case on the grounds that the charges violated Roth's right to free speech, as protected by the First Amendment. The judge would not dismiss the case, but he did allow Atlas to use the First Amendment as the basis for his client's defense. Atlas therefore argued that *Beautiful Sinners* was no different from other best-selling books at the time, most notably the famous sexologist Alfred Kinsey's *Sexual Behavior in the Human Male*, published just three years earlier to much controversy, but with no successful attempts to make its distribution illegal. The jury found Roth not guilty.

In this decade, Roth's circulars would reach four hundred thousand readers, most of whom subscribed to his two most popular magazines, *American Aphrodite* (debuted in the late 1940s) and *Good Times: A Revue of the World of Pleasure* (debuted in 1953). Both centered on sex, with *American Aphrodite* offering literary stories and *Good Times* featuring nude photos and tabloid-like stories of sexual scandals and celebrities. In 1955, Roth appeared before a Senate committee hearing on the dangers of pornographers. Most of his peers refused to testify, pleading the Fifth Amendment, but Roth agreed, perhaps motivated by the same tenacity that had for decades kept him publishing while battling arrests. Though Roth attempted to defend himself and his profession as both legal and within the ethos of American values, the Senate pushed the clear message that pornographers were responsible for social decay throughout America.

One month after his testimony, Roth was arrested again, this time on twenty-six federal charges. He faced a lengthy prison sentence if convicted on all counts. His lawyer deployed scientific experts who claimed that Roth's publications were not obscene because social standards regarding offensive material had changed over time. Atlas's second argument, the one that would make Roth's case a landmark decision in constitutional law, was that these charges against Roth violated his First Amendment rights. After a day's deliberation, the jury acquitted Roth on most charges but found him guilty on four obscenity charges related to the mailing of *Good Times* and *American Aphrodite*. At Roth's sentencing hearing, Atlas insisted to the court that Roth wanted to leave the smut business. "He has other plans," Atlas said, "among them merchandising of razor blades, and is interested in the publication of religious classics." Whether this claim was intentionally flippant is unknown, but the judge issued the most severe sentence Roth had ever faced: five years in prison and a five-thousand-dollar fine.

Roth began working on his appeal. In the first appellate case, the judge upheld the lower court's ruling. The next logical step for Roth was to petition the Supreme Court of the United States to consider his case. By 1956, the Court was long overdue in taking a stand on obscenity charges. Conservative politicians, along with the FBI, claimed to have issued a purge of obscene materials, but no federal body since the previous century had successfully defined "obscenity." The Roth appeal was grander than his previous cases, in that it both challenged the federal Comstock laws and extended the interpretation of the First Amendment. The Supreme Court agreed to hear the case.

Roth v. United States was argued on April 22, 1957, and two months later, the Court released its opinion. In a 6–3 decision, with Chief Justice Earl Warren on the side of the majority, the Court ruled that obscenity was not protected under the First Amendment. This had been the de facto law of the land since the time of the Bill of Rights, so this part of the ruling merely upheld existing law. What the Court did, however, for the first time since the Comstock laws, was create a precedent-setting federal definition of obscenity. The author of the majority opinion, Associate Justice William J. Brennan, wrote that the test to determine obscenity was "whether to the average person, applying contemporary community standards, the dominant theme of the material taken as a whole appeals to prurient interest." By this standard, Roth's publications were, without a doubt, according to these six justices, obscene.

Though he was never convicted of a violent crime, Roth was sent to Lewisburg Federal Penitentiary, one of four federal prisons at the time that housed some of the country's most violent criminals. Meanwhile, many of those formerly arrested on obscenity charges were able to successfully appeal. Publishers of a pair of nudist magazines, for example, saw their charges of obscenity successfully dismissed after a district court determined that magazines did not meet the Supreme Court's new definition of obscenity.

Still, the *Roth* decision left more questions unanswered than resolved. Historian Whitney Strub writes of the dissatisfaction felt by all sides. The case "both opened the cultural gates to a 'flood tide of filth' and deserves credit or blame each time another citizen stands behind bars for publishing pornography." In other words, it both empowered magazines and books, art, and film to depict sexuality so long as it wasn't "obscene," and it maintained obscenity as a criminal charge to justify the continued arrest, and sometimes imprisonment, of anyone charged with distributing obscene material. Anyone whose work intersected with sex continued to tread very carefully in those years between 1957 and the next landmark and transformative case, which wouldn't arrive on the Court's docket for over a decade.

BETWEEN 1958 AND 1972, the Supreme Court considered thirty-one cases pertaining to obscene material. In twenty of those cases, its ruling either reversed obscenity convictions or provided opportunities for a more liberal interpretation of sexual material to fall outside the "obscene definition." In an 8–1 decision in 1963, *Bantam Books, Inc. v. Sullivan*, the Court ruled a Rhode Island commission to be unconstitutional. The commission investigated books it determined to be "obscene" and then sent lists of those books to booksellers, warning them of the content. The effect was that booksellers, fearful of obscenity charges, took those books off their shelves—in essence, enforcing obscenity laws without due process. One publisher included on the list sued the state. While it lost in the lower courts, it brought its appeal to the Supreme Court, which agreed with the publisher that the commission was unconstitutional in violating the First Amendment and suppressing free speech (given that there had been no trial to determine whether the material in question was in fact obscene) and violating the Fourteenth Amendment (in having a state law that contradicted a federal one).

Still, the Court upheld the illegality of obscenity. In 1966, for instance, the Court sided with the state in *Mishkin v. New York*. Police had seized fifty pulp paperbacks published by Edward Mishkin and subsequently charged him with obscenity. The Court noted that nineteen of the books had covers depicting women as victims of torture and abuse. Mishkin was convicted and sentenced to a three-year prison term and a twelve-thousand-dollar fine. On appeal, the Supreme Court upheld his conviction in a 6–3 decision using the Roth standard to determine that the content of his books was only for the prurient interests of a "sexually deviant group" and that the New York State law met all federal standards, including the one requiring a "scienter element" (legalese for intent of wrongdoing). Two years later, the Supreme Court sided with New York State again in *Ginsberg v. New York*, agreeing with its law that "material concerned with sex" cannot legally be sold to minors, even if that material was not deemed "obscene" and thus could be sold to adults.

The Court also ruled, for the first time, that privately owning obscene material was not a crime. The 1969 case centered on whether Robert Stanley, a bookmaker, or bookie, could be arrested on obscenity charges when police officers were carrying out a warrant in his house. The court determined that the seizure of books kept in Stanley's nightstand were not admissible as evidence. As Justice Thurgood Marshall wrote in the majority opinion, "a State has no business telling a man, sitting alone in his own house, what books he may read or what films he may watch." This ruling, steeped in a sense of American individualism and right to privacy, protected subscribers to pornographic magazines at the time and previewed changes to the pornography industry decades later, when porn films were produced not for public screening but for home consumption on televisions and, eventually, personal computers.

In 1973, the Supreme Court announced its decision in *Miller v. California*, effectively creating a bookend to the rise in obscenity cases started by the *Roth* decision over fifteen years earlier. The case got its start in 1971, when Marvin Miller was arrested after his company sent out a brochure advertising pornographic books and films for sale. The brochure itself included graphic illustrations, a preview of what could be purchased for just a couple of dollars. Though the brochure was sent to many loyal customers on Miller's mailing list, it also mistakenly arrived at a restaurant in Newport Beach, California, whose owner opened it while beside his mother, a detail that Chief Justice Warren Burger's majority opinion made sure to describe. The restaurant owner called the police, who obtained a warrant for Miller's arrest. He was convicted of violating California's obscenity laws (a misdemeanor crime) and sentenced to two years in prison and a fine of $22,500 (what today would be almost $150,000).

The Supreme Court did not side with Miller in the appeal of his conviction. But the Court did offer him a chance at acquittal, sending his case back to California to be reconsidered alongside new national standards for defining obscenity. What would come to be called the Miller test, or the Miller standard, was: (a) whether the average person, applying contemporary community standards, would find that the work, taken as a whole, appealed to the prurient interest; (b) whether the work depicted or described, in a patently offensive way, sexual conduct specifically defined by the applicable state law, as written or authoritatively construed; and (c) whether the work, taken as a whole, lacked serious literary, artistic, political, or scientific value. Gone were the vague and universal standards set forth in Roth. Instead, the Court applied a relativistic approach, one that would come to shape debates over pornography well into the next century.

The same year as *Miller v. California*, the Court ruled on eighteen other cases having to do with obscenity violations. In seventeen of them, the Court remanded the cases back to lower courts to be retried given the Miller standard. Miller's own case was remanded to the Ninth Circuit Court of Appeals, where the court upheld his initial conviction, noting in its opinion that "the materials in question are clearly obscene" according to the test that now bore Miller's name. Other cases had more success, given that the Supreme Court had expanded the space in which non-obscene pornography and other sexual materials could legally reside.

IN THE SIXTEEN years between Roth and Miller, there were eighteen justices, spanning six presidents' appointments, who diversified the Court. It saw three Jewish justices, two of whom served terms of less than five years, and in 1967, Thurgood Marshall was the first African American to join the bench. Though appointed by presidents ranging from Franklin D. Roosevelt to Richard Nixon, the justices boasted political affiliations and backgrounds that did not neatly map onto political ideologies of conservative or liberal. Thus it was, and is, the intent of the judicial branch to enforce laws without the political bias of the other branches of government. Hugo

Black, for example, who served the Court between 1937 and 1971, was appointed by Franklin D. Roosevelt and was a vocal supporter of FDR's New Deal. As a white senator born and raised in Alabama, he was also a former member of the Ku Klux Klan and a supporter of segregationist and racist policies, including the internment of Japanese Americans during World War II. Still, as a textualist in his interpretations of constitutional law, he believed that all speech (including that which was obscene) should be protected under the First Amendment. He, along with William O. Douglas, considered a more liberal justice, often joined in dissenting opinions to challenge obscenity convictions. They served an influential Court, much of it led by Chief Justice Earl Warren, now recognized for extending civil rights in landmark cases such as *Brown v. Board of Education* (1954), *Miranda v. Arizona* (1966), and *Loving v. Virginia* (1967). Still, even justices whose decisions favored individual civil liberties, separation of church and state, racial equality, and reproductive rights ruled in favor of obscenity regulations.

Opinions written throughout the influential 1960s, even those that seemingly liberalized obscenity laws, showed their hand in terms of the conservative sexual ethics informing the justices' decisions. By 1973, the year of the *Miller* decision, the Court was entirely Christian—with one Catholic among a sea of Protestants—and made up of almost all white men in their sixties. The youngest on the Court was William Rehnquist, forty-eight at the time, who joined the bench just a year before and who would go on to serve the Court, eventually as chief justice, until his death in 2005. William Douglas, born the previous century, was the oldest. Seventy-four at the time of the *Miller* decision, he was appointed by Franklin D. Roosevelt and would leave the Court two years later. Most justices came of age during tumultuous political and cultural changes in the United States: the Great Depression and World War II, the Cold War and McCarthyism, Jim Crow racism and its pushback with the civil rights movement. On a micro level, though, these justices lived as highly educated, married upper-class men. Smut was assuredly beneath them, at least in terms of their public presentations to the world.

Four of the five justices siding with the majority in the *Miller* decision were appointed by President Nixon who, alongside J. Edgar Hoover, made it a part of his presidential campaign to wage a war against pornography. Nixon and Hoover found common ground, in part, in their shared interest in obscenity convictions. The two brainstormed ways to introduce cases that would make their way to the Supreme Court and overturn the increasingly liberal obscenity laws. They never succeeded, in part because the justices appointed by Nixon created the biggest loophole to date for pornographers to legally produce their trade without calling it "obscene." Pornographers successfully demonstrated that sexual content is not automatically "patently offensive," given a specific community standard, and that it *can* have literary, artistic, political, or scientific value.

President Nixon had to reckon with not only the *Miller* decision's ambivalent effects, but also the aftermath of his predecessor's Commission on Obscenity and Pornography. President Lyndon B. Johnson formed the commission in 1967, but its report was not scheduled to be released until after Nixon took office. Despite the inconsistent effort of courts to regulate obscenity, Johnson, like many Americans, saw pornography as largely inevitable and growing in its popularity and accessibility. He sought an impartial, nonpartisan research group to get to the bottom of whether opening the "floodgates of filth" really would ruin generations to come, as the Senate hearing two decades before had concluded. The great problem for Nixon, however, was that Johnson's commission found that pornography was *not* a significant social problem, far less significant than other social conflicts at the time, including race relations, crime, growing income inequality, and reproductive rights. This directly challenged Nixon's public claims and commitment that pornography was bad for society.

Nixon managed to appoint one member to the commission, Charles Keating, after sending another one to serve as ambassador to India. As a devout Catholic, Keating had established Citizens for Decent Literature in his hometown of Cincinnati in 1955. The organization mobilized to support censorship and anti-obscenity laws and also produced pamphlets and short films like *Printed Poison* and *Perversion for Profit* to blame pornography for a number of social problems, including communism, the decline of small-town industries, reduced children's literacy, and the rise of "homosexuality, lesbianism, and sexual sadists." By the time of Keating's appointment to the Commission on Obscenity and Pornography, Citizens for Decent Literature had grown to include three hundred chapters nationwide, with nearly seventy-five members of Congress serving on the group's various committees.

Formerly a champion collegiate swimmer, Keating brought vigor and resolve to his role in the commission. But he was alone in his positions over the course of commission hearings, proposing a number of outlandish strategies to prove pornography's widespread harm (including studying the case histories of convicted sex offenders), which the commission voted against. Before the commission's report was released to the public, Keating petitioned a court to halt its release in order to give him time to write a minority report that could be published alongside the main findings. The court agreed.

The whole affair was a publicity nightmare for Nixon. Because the report was authored by "The President's Commission," newspaper outlets made it seem like his administration endorsed its findings that pornography wasn't so bad. Nixon, thus, had to work diligently to counter that message by insisting that his administration was committed to the opposite. In order to control messaging surrounding the commission, the White House leaked Keating's minority report to the press, who covered it prior to the report's official release in late September 1970. Keating's report very clearly threw the original report under the bus, insinuating that it was a misguided attempt under the previous administration, one steeped in the rhetoric of "radical liberals."

Still, the *Report of the President's Commission on Obscenity and Pornography* came out two weeks later. At over six hundred pages, it detailed a number of findings suggesting that the social fear of and contempt for pornography were largely without merit. To the contrary, the commission found that the increase of available pornography in the past decade had not corresponded to an increase in sex-related crime and that there was no difference in response to pornography among juvenile delinquents and nondelinquents. Ultimately, the commission recommended decriminalizing pornography made by and for adults.

The head of the commission, William B. Lockart, dean of the Law School at the University of Minnesota, used a strategy that has since come to be a hallmark of many public figures defending the rights of pornographers: he noted that, personally, smut turned him off, but that he and most other members of the commission believed the science was clear and that the public should be able to read the findings and make decisions for themselves. The Senate voted to denounce the findings in a resolution passed the following month. In a written statement, Nixon called the commission "morally bankrupt" and repeated his antipornography stance: "So long as I am in the White House, there will be no relaxation of the national effort to control and eliminate smut from our national life." Less than four years after the commission's report was released, Nixon's presidential demise would come from his own questionable morals, as would Charles Keating's, who is notorious not for his antipornography activism but for his conviction on charges of fraud, racketeering, and conspiracy following the largest investment scandal of the 1980s.

SINCE THE 1970S, the courts have consistently distinguished pornography from obscenity; the former is protected under the First Amendment's right to free speech, while the latter is not. The ambivalent legacy of the *Roth* and *Miller* cases, along with those in between, paved the way for what is called pornography's "golden era," in the 1970s, with unprecedented legal freedoms for the first time in U.S. history. Still, the efforts of mid-twentieth-century anti-smut crusaders were not in vain. The courts set the stage for local battles over obscenity regulations, as it was now the task of "community standards" to determine the threshold for obscene material. These battles would come to represent the antipornography movement of the 1980s, as the Christian Right and feminists both attempted local ordinances to regulate pornography.

CHAPTER 3

Christian Right v. America

Over the course of the twentieth century, pornography came to represent social tensions that were much bigger than any single dirty magazine. At stake were both religion and sexuality within a changing American society. From Anthony Comstock's crusade for obscenity laws at the turn of the century, to Charles Keating and his Citizens for Decent Literature half a century later, to Jerry Falwell and the Moral Majority in the 1980s, white conservative Christian men developed their moral and political agendas from a broader stream of history. At times in America, their beliefs appeared to align with widespread social values. At other times, they appeared to be swimming against the current.

The French philosopher Michel Foucault divides his history of sexuality into two eras. The premodern era, prior to the nineteenth century, was marked by an obsession with *not* speaking about sex. Secrecy and repression, enforced by religious authorities, dominated sexual life. A shift occurred in Europe and the United States when medical and scientific authorities became keepers of sexual knowledge and so-called truth. This shift meant that respectable society could speak more openly about sex and sexuality, but only under the guise of medical and scientific objectivity. Important for Foucault, this out-in-the-open sexuality was not a freer, more autonomous type but, rather, a sneakier form of social control.

The end of the nineteenth century marks the transition from premodern to modern, according to Foucault, but never was there a neat and tidy exchange of power from religion to science. A popular liberal Christian theology that emerged at the time in America, called the New School Theology, embraced scientific discoveries. Congregationalists, whose tradition led "the Great Awakening" a century earlier, believed that God granted humankind the power to think with reason and logic. All scientific advancements, therefore, were in fact emulating Jesus Christ, the most divine human. Their theology also taught the Bible as a kind of literature, rich in metaphor and imagination, but not the literal word of God.

Then there were the Protestants who disagreed. Touting themselves antimodernists, they opposed the social changes of the time: immigration, industrialization, women's rights, and scientific advancements. Collectively, their voices made up a new sect that came to be known as fundamentalism after a series of 1910–15 publications titled *The Fundamentals*, which outlined their beliefs. Fundamentalists grounded their theology on two central tenets, biblical inerrancy (the Bible being the literal word of God) and premillennial dispensationalism (the idea that the world was getting progressively worse, as God intended it to, as human history moved through seven biblically inspired dispensations that ended with Christ's return).

Historians cite the *State of Tennessee v. John Thomas Scopes*, commonly referred to as the Scopes Monkey Trial, of 1925 as a turning point for fundamentalists in America. The case was argued in a courtroom in Dayton, Ohio, and it centered on whether a public school teacher should be permitted to teach Darwin's theories of evolution. Although the teacher, John Scopes, lost the trial, social commentators at the time ridiculed the leading prosecutor, William Jennings Bryan, for his views on creationism. Science was pitted against religion, and public sentiment was clear: Americans chose evolution and reason over irrationality and creationism. This is not to say that the public rejected Christianity, but rather, that they rejected a fundamentalist interpretation of it. Fundamentalists began putting energy into creating their own separate institutions (churches, schools, and social organizations) rather than integrating into existing ones, such as public schools and denominational churches.

In the 1920s, the rest of America, by and large, was becoming more progressive and less religious. This was the decade when a new ethos surrounding sexuality emerged, what historians John D'Emilio and Estelle Freedman call "sexual liberalism," a widespread belief system that allowed, and even encouraged, the practice of sex beyond its practical purpose of reproduction. Sigmund Freud and the emergence of psychotherapy helped invent the idea that we have an "orientation" regarding our sexuality—that is, a meaningful and natural part of our identity development related to sex. The capitalist marketplace encouraged consumer rituals surrounding dating as a social practice. Though social norms maintained that the proper place for sex was within heterosexual marriage, a new generation of white middle-class young people was increasingly experimenting with sex before marriage. Sexual pleasure was becoming an American value and prerogative.

At the same time, Hollywood emerged in the 1920s, making cinema a major American pastime, along with reading about movie stars, whose lives appeared to be full of extravagance, sex, and scandal. Newspapers across the country covered the death of Virginia Rappe, for instance, whom the papers called "a young starlet" and who was allegedly raped by comedian Roscoe "Fatty" Arbuckle, whose excessive weight caused Rappe's bladder to rupture. She became severely ill and died days later in a hospital. Theaters banned Arbuckle's films, six of which were playing at the time. Even though he was eventually exonerated of all charges, his career was ruined.

Despite the adult themes when it came to media coverage of Hollywood stars, early Hollywood produced only movies by the major studio companies and rated for a general audience. In the 1930s, most states did not have laws to enforce film censorship and, instead, left it to the Hollywood industry itself and the Motion Picture Producers and Distributors of America (MPPDA), which would later become the Motion Picture Association of America (MPAA). Founded in 1922, the MPPDA created a new department, the Production Code Administration (PCA), to curb criticism over content in its films. National theater organizations committed to screening only PCA-approved films. Films produced without that label received a hefty fine. The approach of the PCA was to approve only those that were G-rated.

Whereas Protestants tended to be the ones advocating for federal legal reform when it came to obscenity (i.e., Comstock and his comrades), many Catholics spent their time organizing boycotts and protests of local theaters and bookstores. Historians have reasoned that Catholics focused their attention locally rather than nationally because of their pessimism about the U.S. government, which had a well-established reputation of animosity and discrimination toward immigrant Catholics. In 1934, the Catholic Church formed the Legion of Decency, an organization that rated motion pictures. The group gave an "A" grade to those movies it found to be acceptable; a "B" for films containing some parts that were "morally objectionable"; and a "C" (for "condemned") to those that were seen as wholly "morally objectionable." In theory, the group rated films on depictions of crime, violence, and sexuality, but sex was the clear focus of the legion's efforts. By one estimate, 95 percent of the ratings given were related to so-called sexual content in films.

BY THE 1950S, America had an identity crisis on its hands. A counterculture was emerging in postwar America that was increasingly popular among young people, such as the Beat poetry of Allen Ginsberg, who was eventually arrested on charges that *Howl*, his famed poem, was obscene. Nude films and photographs were produced by well-regarded, if controversial, artists. Feature-length films depicting nudity and simulated sex were beginning to be screened in public theaters—that is, if theater owners could manage to carry out a screening before being arrested on obscenity charges. Called "exploitation films," this genre was less explicit than stag films and made a greater attempt at narrative cohesion. These were also the films that were the subject of many of the legal battles over obscenity in the 1950s and '60s.

Pornography in the 1950s—including magazines, films, and cheap "pulp" paperbacks—both defied and catered to strict social norms. Lesbian pulp fiction enticed readers (both straight men and lesbians alike) by violating expectations regarding women's sexual behavior, only to idealize women's desire for men upon their conclusion. Typical of this genre was an ending that involved either heterosexual conversion or the death of the lesbian protagonist. Magazines like Hugh Hefner's *Playboy*, which premiered in 1953, portrayed women as "liberated but compliant," in the words of historian Elizabeth Fraterrigo. Unlike with the nameless faces on *cartes de visite* and in stag films, Hefner wanted his models to have personalities and identities. Playmates, as he would call them, were celebrities, secretaries, college students, flight attendants, or shop girls; they were not merely mothers or wives. Yet they were never men's equals, either, and many expressed a desire to settle down in marriage after their time as Playmates ran its course.

With the near-instant success of entomologist turned sexologist Alfred Kinsey's two books, *Sexual Behavior in the Human Male*, published in 1948, and *Sexual Behavior in the Human Female*, published in 1953, alongside numerous other "marriage manuals," sex took on a new personality in American conversations. Kinsey's reports, based on in-depth sex history interviews with more than 18,000 participants, suggested that Americans' sex lives were diverse and active. And rather than tout this as a reason for concern, Kinsey instead wrote of his findings in a matter-of-fact tone that normalized and naturalized sexual desires and behaviors not neatly contained within heterosexual matrimony. Talking openly about sex meant that sex also took on the broader American ethos of the postwar 1950s: hard work, commitment, and abundance. One marriage manual published at the time told readers that sexual "success comes to those who consciously and deliberately have the will to achieve it." The message was that good sex, like the American dream, required hard work and was deserved by all Americans.

But like any claim about *all* Americans, this rhetorical device of marriage manuals left out Americans who were not white or middle class. While African Americans, Latinos, Native Americans, and Asian Americans coming of age in the 1950s, like white Americans, consumed these increasingly liberal messages about sexuality, these groups also had the historical and contemporary reality of racism with which to reckon. Black men and women were not afforded similar freedoms when it came to sexuality as white Americans, given that racist stereotypes already assumed sexual deviance: sexual aggression for Black men and sexual finesse for Black women. Social class and gender played an important role, too, in policing sexual norms. Even as the sexual world was expanding around them, middle-class women were typically pressured to remain chaste. Middle-class men, however, were able to indulge in sex not through sex workers, as would have been the case in decades past, but by dating working-class girls, often referred to as "pickups."

MANY CHRISTIAN MEN and women made clear that they would be opting out of any progressive changes to sexual norms in the second half of the twentieth century. In a 1953 radio sermon, evangelist Billy Graham warned that "we have become so accustomed to immorality that it no longer seems to us to be immorality!" "From the very beginning God has given us moral laws governing the subject of sex that are absolute and unchangeable," Graham cried through the radio waves. "Nowhere does the Bible teach that sex in itself is a sin, but the Bible condemns the wrong use of sex from Genesis to Revelation." Sex in America, according to Graham, had gotten "cheap and filthy," a far cry from the Bible's description of "the most glorious act of love between two people." Though many Jewish and liberal Protestant leaders actually responded favorably to Kinsey's findings, conservative Protestants and Catholics marked Kinsey as the face of America's moral decay. Graham insisted that progressives like Kinsey should not be the face of a changing America.

While peddling a strictly conservative theology that supported traditional messages about sex, marriage, and family life, Graham critiqued American culture not as an outsider, like the fundamentalists before him, but as an insider attempting to enact change from within. Just like Anthony Comstock nearly a century earlier, Graham believed that America should be a Christian nation, respecting Christian rules and traditions. But unlike Comstock, who set his sights on changing American society by enforcing strict and punitive laws, Graham put his energies into transforming society from the ground up, beginning with the beliefs and everyday practices of ordinary Americans. Described by the *New York Times* as the "affable crusader" and "the antithesis of the stock picture of a dour and strait-laced evangelist," Graham represented a turning point for conservative evangelicals in America.

Though virtually all religious leaders at the time preached about social problems, the 1960s and '70s saw a divide among Protestants. For religious leaders on the left, the most salient social problems were racism, poverty, and the militant state. These religious groups supported the progressive social movements of the 1960s and '70s. The civil rights movement created a lasting division among evangelicals, where Graham, though more liberal than many other Baptists on the issue of desegregation, still urged both Black and white Southerners to "follow the law" at a time when Martin Luther King Jr. was urging them to break it with sit-ins and marches. Graham's evangelicalism, along with that of other conservatives, saw personal conversion as the solution to social problems. A nation committed to Christ, Graham believed, would extinguish Communist threats and bolster sexual morality, thereby reducing what he saw as widespread social ills, including pregnancy out of wedlock, homosexuality, and pornography.

Though Graham was a Southern Baptist, he attracted followers from a wide range of Protestant denominations, and he aspired to create a coalition of interdenominational evangelical leaders. Graham's evangelicalism blended religion with national identity and is credited as the start of the modern evangelicalism we know today. By the 1970s, the word *evangelical* became shorthand for this broad mix of conservative, mostly white Protestant denominations and nondenominational Christian churches.

IN 1979, THE Rev. Jerry Falwell had a mission that was virtually identical to the one Billy Graham had started two decades earlier: to convince Americans to become born again, to get baptized, and to register to vote. While both preachers emphasized the importance of personal salvation and involvement in politics to save the nation from its pressing social problems, they differed in their understanding of those problems. Evangelicals like Graham saw macro-level problems (economic decline and communism) as the cause of micro-level ones (instability in family life and the decline in marriage). Evangelicals like Falwell in the 1980s reversed this order to suggest that the moral decay in individuals was what was causing the nation to decay. Falwell thus empowered ordinary Christians—who may have otherwise felt relatively powerless when it came to the impersonal threat of communism or national security—to feel that their individual actions mattered. By making the right choices and judging the choices of their neighbors, Falwell insisted, conservative evangelicals could shape the fate of the nation.

Falwell and other evangelicals like him mobilized their followers to oppose pornography using a wide range of tactics: letter-writing campaigns, public protest, litigation, and political lobbying both of city ordinances and of federal policy. In addition to his Sunday morning church services in Virginia, Falwell reached his followers on a national radio broadcast, *The Old-Time Gospel Hour*. He toured the country in events like his "I Love America" series, where he preached about resisting what he believed to be the radical social change of the 1970s, including racial integration, feminism, and sexual liberalism. In 1979, he founded the Moral Majority, a nonprofit organization intended to encourage conservative Protestants to participate directly with conservative politics, and urged them to vote for presidential candidate Ronald Reagan.

Ronald Reagan was a self-professed born-again Christian and a member of Moral Majority director Tim LaHaye's Council for National Policy, a secretive network of powerful conservative activists and government officials that still exists today. In the first year of his second term, Reagan appointed attorney general and fellow born-again Christian Edwin Meese to lead the Attorney General's Commission on Pornography, the second of its kind following the one started by Lyndon B. Johnson. With a budget of nearly half a million dollars, Meese recruited commission members who were mostly fellow religious conservatives, despite his claim that the commission was a "balanced group." Commission chair Henry Hudson had previously prosecuted pornographers in the suburbs of Washington, D.C., and he boasted that Arlington, the county where he served as chief prosecutor, was one of the few counties near the city with no adult bookstores. The executive director, Alan Sears, would go on to represent the antipornography lobbying group Citizens for Decency Through Law (CDL), and James Dobson, another commission member, was founder of the evangelical group Focus on the Family, along with a more explicitly right-wing political organization, the Family Research Council.

The Attorney General's Commission on Pornography called dozens of witnesses, most of whom were conservatives but some of whom were feminist scholars and activists. In its final report, known as the Meese Report, an incredible 1,960 pages, the commission declared definitively that pornography was harming individuals, families, and overall society.

In 1986, the same year the Meese Report was published, the Moral Majority numbered over six million members. The Old-Time Gospel Hour Inc., the corporate wing of the Moral Majority, bought the National Christian Network, one of the first Christian TV stations in the United States, whose reputation and finances had plummeted when the public learned that it had once leased its signal to the Playboy channel. A representative from Falwell's company told the media that "of course we couldn't and wouldn't" continue its agreement with Playboy upon taking over the network. Falwell moved the company to his hometown in Lynchburg, Virginia, and set up twenty-four-hour religious programming on the station.

The network promised not to air explicitly political content, but it did explicitly promote a position on political issues. This was indeed the heart of the Christian Right in the 1980s, and it marked a shift from earlier decades. In 1965, Falwell preached that Christians should not become involved in political protest and, instead, should focus on witnessing to nonbelievers and spreading the good word of Jesus Christ. A decade later, however, he insisted the opposite: that Christians must become involved in politics, for the future of the nation was at stake. "If I only preached the gospel of Jesus Christ," Falwell told a news conference, "there would be no problem. But because I say there is a standard of right and wrong, that upsets the abortionists, that upsets the pornographer." The rise of the "New Right" in the 1980s, of which the Moral Majority and its sympathizers made up a significant part, was a political philosophy that warned against the rise of liberalism and its impact on the nation state. But this philosophy was always intimately tied to conservative gender and sexual politics.

AS THE CHRISTIAN Right admonished pornography in the 1980s, industry moguls pushed back. *Penthouse* magazine published an interview with Jerry

Falwell alongside his picture, placed in between a photo spread of two naked women. Falwell unsuccessfully sued *Penthouse* in 1981 for publishing his image without his consent. In its November 1983 issue, Larry Flynt's *Hustler* magazine published a satirical advertisement for Campari liquor, which was well known for its ads in which celebrities evocatively shared "their first time"—their first time tasting Campari liquor, that is. In the spoof, which was called in the table of contents "Fiction. Ad & Personality Parody," Falwell was the celebrity, and the advertisement insinuated that he had had a sexual relationship with his mother in an outhouse and that he got drunk before preaching. At the bottom of the page, following a small asterisk, was the disclaimer AD PARODY—NOT TO BE TAKEN SERIOUSLY.

Falwell did, however, take it quite seriously. He sued Flynt for libel, invasion of privacy, and intentional infliction of emotional distress. Falwell's chosen lawyer was none other than Norman Roy Grutman, who happened to have represented Penthouse CEO Bob Guccione when Falwell sued his magazine just two years before. The Moral Majority sent out mailers to a million of its supporters asking for monetary donations to support Falwell's legal effort to "defend his mother's memory" and to put a stop to what the mailer called a "filthy plague" of pornography that was spreading across the country.

For all their obvious differences, Flynt and Falwell had much in common. Born in Appalachia (Flynt in Kentucky, Falwell in Virginia), both had bootlegger fathers during Prohibition. They both told similar bootstrap narratives about their impoverished roots and their hard work and dedication to their respective causes: Jesus Christ for Falwell and, for Flynt, in his words, to become "the King of Sleaze." Each displayed a masterful public persona that commanded media attention throughout the 1980s. Each also became very rich, with an expansive media empire. First Amendment scholar Rodney Smolla calls these men "hustlers" who were "passionately seeking converts to their worldviews, propagating their versions of truth through multimillion-dollar empires."

Flynt said the Campari advertisement was "meant as a chuckle," and he called Falwell "more of a politician than preacher." Flynt's intention with the ad was to call into question what he described as the hypocritical relationship between conservative politics and sex. Later, he told reporters he expected to lose the case and said to the jury that the case was being set up as "good versus evil, the preacher against the pornographer." The Virginia jury ruled against Falwell's libel claim but did support the charges of intentional infliction of emotional distress. The judge awarded Falwell two hundred thousand dollars in damages.

After losing his first appeal, Flynt's lawyer appealed to the Supreme Court, which agreed to hear the case. In 1988, in a unanimous decision—rare for First Amendment cases—the Court ruled against Falwell, determining that public figures cannot sue for emotional distress caused by speech protected under the First Amendment. Judge William Rehnquist, a notable conservative who had served on the Court since 1972 and who had been chief justice since 1986, wrote the majority opinion. While noting that the *Hustler* parody ad was "offensive" to Falwell, "and doubtless gross and repugnant in the eyes of most," the state must prioritize protecting freedom of speech over the emotional distress of a public figure. That the speech did not count as libel was no longer contested. In order to count as libel, the Court must find that the advertisement was attempting to present as fact false information that would malign Falwell's reputation. The jury in the lower court had agreed in the first trial that the advertisement was so extreme that there was no disputing it was satire. Falwell insisted that this particular satire was more outrageous than other political cartoons, but the Court disagreed. "There is no doubt that the caricature of the respondent and his mother is at best a distant cousin of political cartoons," like one portraying George Washington as an ass, Rehnquist wrote, but "'outrageousness' in the area of political and social discourse has an inherent subjectiveness about it which would allow a jury to impose liability on the basis of the jurors' tastes or views." In other words, just because something embarrasses or offends someone, that doesn't mean that person is entitled to damages.

THE PROBLEM WITH pornography for Falwell and his allies was never pornography alone. Rather, pornography was intertwined with what the Moral Majority named as the "sins of America." "The four-billion-dollar-per-year pornography industry is probably the most devastating moral influence of all upon our young people," Falwell once wrote. For the Moral Majority and other members of the Christian Right, this influence taught all the wrong messages and required a challenge at every turn. Curbing the production and dissemination of pornography would help the Moral Majority movement combat two other pressing social problems they had identified: abortion and homosexuality.

Protestants were, in fact, a relatively recent addition to antiabortion efforts, or "the pro-life" movement. In the late 1960s, Ronald Reagan, then governor of California, supported the legality of abortion. The Southern Baptist Convention in 1971, two years before *Roe v. Wade*, supported abortion as a legal right in cases of rape, incest, fetal deformity, and "damage to the emotional, mental and physical health of the mother." Beginning in 1980, though, Southern Baptists began to pass a series of resolutions dubbed "pro-life." In that same year, Falwell compared abortion to the Nazi genocide of the Jews, describing it as the murder of millions of unborn babies each year. At the start of the decade, evangelicals nationally had more liberal views on abortion than Catholics, the religious group that had most stridently opposed abortion rights prior to the 1980s. By 1984, however, white evangelicals held more antiabortion views than any other religious group in the United States, including Catholics. This trend has continued to the present day.

On homosexuality, Falwell called it a "disease that will spread if not condemned." "Because God will judge the nation given over to homosexuality," he insisted, "I believe the United States will be destroyed if we permit homosexuality as an alternate lifestyle." Falwell supported Anita Bryant's campaign in Dade County, Florida, to oppose a local ordinance that would have protected gays and lesbians from employment discrimination. Bryant, a Catholic and former beauty pageant winner, began a newsletter asking for donations to support her cause, writing emphatically, "I don't hate the homosexuals! But as a mother, I must protect my children from their evil influence." According to Falwell, "The worst thing about homosexuals is that they draw others into their net. They proselyte after the worst order—they prey on children. Little children are exploited and their bodies are ravaged by human animals." Opponents to gay rights like Falwell and Bryant used the threat of children's victimization to advance their cause.

The trio of perceived threats of abortion, homosexuality, and pornography, and the accompanying conservative activism surrounding them, shaped white evangelical identity for decades to come. The Christian Right of the 1980s cemented conservative positions on gender and sexuality as a defining feature of its particular version of Christianity. Yet its beliefs were not, in fact, outliers compared to those of nonevangelicals. Abortion support among all Americans declined over the course of the 1980s. Relatively few Americans supported abortion without restrictions, and opinions were divided over abortion for social or economic reasons. Throughout the 1970s and '80s, Americans' attitudes about homosexuality stayed largely the same, beginning to liberalize only in the 1990s. For most of the 1980s, around 40 percent of Americans believed pornography should be illegal to everyone. What distinguished white evangelicals from other Americans at the time who held similarly conservative beliefs was the former's ability to mobilize belief into action. Their war against pornography was also a war against a version of America marked by progressive gender and sexual values that were perceived as a threat to their children, families, and way of life.

CHAPTER 4

Porno Chic

A s the Christian Right waged its war against pornography in the 1970s and '80s, a majority of Americans shared its perspective that pornography was immoral. Yet, at the same time, the country saw an unprecedented boom in pornographic magazines and films. The golden era in porn (when pornography was first popularized in mainstream public theaters in the early 1970s) and the silver (when it transitioned to the at-home VHS rental market in the early 1980s) were both made possible by changes to the entertainment industry that happened decades earlier. And the impact of these eras would last for decades to come.

Right in time for Christmas 1953, Hugh Hefner published the first issue of *Playboy* magazine with Marilyn Monroe on the cover as "Miss December." The photographs of Monroe came from four years prior, before her fame, when she agreed to the photoshoot in order to pay her bills. As Monroe later told close friend and eventual biographer George Barris, she never consented to Hefner's publishing the photos; nor was she ever paid by *Playboy*. This controversy did not stop *Playboy* from becoming an instant success and also an instant target for anti-obscenity crusaders. Yet, unlike Samuel Roth, Hefner did not engage with congressional efforts to investigate obscene materials in the 1950s. A more cautious advocate of reforming obscenity laws and eventually promoting free speech, he nonetheless faced many legal battles of his own. In 1955, amid the turmoil of inconsistent obscenity rulings, a court ruled in *Playboy*'s favor after Hefner was charged with violating the Comstock laws in distributing the magazine through the mail. The case was ultimately dismissed for lack of evidence, and thus the court permitted mailing privileges for *Playboy*.

Perhaps emboldened by wildly popular publications like *Playboy* and tabloid-style magazines featuring sex scandals, film directors and producers in the 1950s and '60s began to produce a steady stream of films without the approval of Hollywood's MPPDA. Some of these films went on to become box-office hits, no doubt a result, in part, of the scandal stirred by avoiding the rating systems. The industry welcomed the new popularity, a change in direction since the steady decline in profits before World War II. A film's success meant that producers could easily afford the $25,000 fine that resulted from releasing it without submitting it first to the Production Code Administration. In 1967, the PCA declined to approve forty-four films, dubbing them "for mature audiences only." In comparison, a year earlier, only three were so labeled. One of those was *Who's Afraid of Virginia Woolf?*, in which Warner Bros. allowed the phrase "hump the hostess" but required cutting the use of "screw you." The film won five Oscars, including for Best Actress. The times they were a-changing, and the ratings system, in order to ensure maximum profits for Hollywood studios, needed to keep up.

In 1968, the MPAA created the rating system still in use today. The possible ratings that the Classification and Rating Administration (CARA) could give a film at the time were: G (general audiences), M (mature, i.e., parental discretion advised), or R (restricted; a parent or guardian is required to accompany a moviegoer under age sixteen). Eventually M would morph into PG and PG-13 ratings. Since its establishment, the MPAA did not support a rating beyond R, because the organization's president, Jack Valenti, advocated parental involvement in children's exposure to movies, rather than having the industry itself police the audience.

The MPAA never owned a trademark for the X rating, and so it, along with its hard-core counterpart, XXX, were both largely self-imposed, often arbitrarily and not always in response to sexual content. Producers of the 1969 Academy Award winner for Best Picture, *Midnight Cowboy*, chose to rate the film X, though it was far from pornographic. Starring Jon Voight and Dustin Hoffman, the film centers on the life of a male prostitute and does include brief flashes of nudity and also violence and recreational drug use. The strategy to indicate it as a film "for adults only" proved successful, as it was a box-office hit, spurring large audiences who wondered what might warrant such a rating. It was the first unrated film to win an Oscar for Best Picture. Though no Hollywood studio attempted to take on hard-core pornographic films as part of its label, after *Midnight Cowboy*, studios did begin to produce feature films with more nudity and sexuality than ever before.

The same year the MPAA established its new rating system, Dave Friedman founded the Adult Film Association of America (AFAA). Though he declined to call himself a "pornographer," Friedman would go on to own adult theaters and produce X-rated films, along with blood-and-guts horror films. As he describes it, he invited Hollywood's outcasts, who were producing "the nudie cuties, the roughies, the kinkies and the ghoulies," to a second-rate hotel in Kansas City, Missouri. At their meeting, they planned to establish the AFAA as a nonprofit organization, hire lawyers, and start a public relations campaign. One of their first tasks was to push to replace the word *hard-core* with *sexually explicit* in media coverage of the porn industry. Public advertisements for "hard-core" pornos were popularized for a brief period in the years leading up to the Supreme Court's 1973 decision in *Miller v. California*. The *Miller* decision, along with its new guidelines for defining obscenity, would once again force the industry into using euphemisms, for fear of facing obscenity charges.

Still, the sexual revolution was well on its way, and pornography both reflected and contributed to the broader social trends. Dubbed "porno chic" by journalists at the time, pornography in the 1970s was trendy and profitable. *Deep Throat*, which premiered in 1972, was the first feature-length porno film containing a plot, albeit a terrible one. The FBI sent agents to attend screenings so the bureau could determine if the film was obscene. Eighteen field offices in cities throughout the country were involved in soliciting arrests of theater owners who chose to screen it. Eleven people involved in the production of the film were also arrested. Herbert Streicher, the lead male actor in the film, known as Harry Reems, was among them. He was convicted but later managed to have the conviction overturned. Linda Boreman, the instant star known as Linda Lovelace, was immune from prosecution because of a deal she had made to help police investigate possible Mob ties to the film's distribution. These legal scandals merely enticed a massive audience, who couldn't wait to see the film. Major newspapers reviewed it and covered the public reaction. Late-night TV hosts invited its stars for interviews. Within six months of the film's release, it had grossed more than three million dollars in more than seventy theaters across the United States. One Midtown theater in New York City averaged five thousand patrons weekly, who paid the five-dollar admission (more than twenty-six dollars by today's standards) to see the movie. As the *New York Times* reported, this audience included "celebrities, diplomats, critics, businessmen, women alone and dating couples."

The film is full of sex (close-up genital and ejaculation scenes, what the industry calls "meat" and "money" shots), but it is also a parody of American cultural trends, including feminism and the therapy industry. It epitomizes the emerging sexual ethos of the 1970s when Linda's friend says to her, "Different strokes for different folks." On the surface, the film centers on Linda's quest to achieve orgasm and her entitlement to mind-blowing pleasure, rather than the "little tingles" she reported when having sex with men. Any feminist motive, however, is quickly overshadowed by the misogynist plot, which locates Linda's missing clitoris deep within her throat, thus setting the audience up for numerous scenes of fellatio, supposedly all in the service of Linda's pleasure. Linda is diagnosed and "treated" by a sexologist doctor, played by Harry Reems, who helps her perfect a "deep throat" technique. The final money shot, his ejaculation, occurs simultaneously with Linda's orgasm, marked in the film with fireworks exploding, large bells ringing, and rockets firing. In the end, Lovelace herself becomes a sex therapist alongside Reems, a nod to famous sex researchers and therapists William Masters and Virginia Johnson.

Along with *Deep Throat*, two other feature-length pornos released between 1972 and 1973, respectively, *Behind the Green Door* and *The Devil in Miss Jones*, earned more in total revenue than all but a few of the major studios' new releases. All three films received serious reviews in mainstream newspapers. Roger Ebert reviewed *The Devil in Miss Jones* in the *Chicago Sun-Times*, giving it three stars and calling it "the best hard-core porn film I've seen." "Though I'm not a member of the raincoat brigade," Ebert muses, referring to the stereotype of men who watched porn in theaters, "I have seen the highly touted productions like *Deep Throat* and *It Happened in Hollywood.*" *The Devil in Miss Jones*, a sixty-seven-minute film, stars Georgina Spelvin, whom Ebert calls "the Linda Lovelace of the literate," commenting as an aside that "she never seems exploited." The film centers on Spelvin's Miss Jones, who commits suicide and ends up in hell. After living a demure and proper life and condemned only for the final act that ended it, she asks the gatekeeper for a do-over. If she's headed to hell anyway, she may as well indulge in the vices she once avoided—thus, the setup for several explicit scenes of Jones indulging in her vast sexual desires. But she never manages complete satisfaction and finds herself perpetually frustrated and unfulfilled. The final porno plot twist is that she's been in hell the whole time.

BY THE LATE 1970s, public theaters were mostly rejecting hard-core features, and the pornos whose titles had once graced marquees were relegated to small screens in private booths in seedy adult stores and bars. The industry appeared to be headed for decline . . . until a Japanese invention was introduced in the United States in 1977. The Video Home System, or VHS, was bad for cable television but very good for pornography and the film industry more generally. The companies that produced video disks, also known as LaserDiscs, the VHS tape's main competitor, refused to produce X-rated films, which led one investment analyst to observe in 1981 that "these manufacturers are making a big mistake. For a lot of people, X-rated product is one of the inducements to buy a machine, and so they're buying the video-cassette recorder instead of the videodisk player." Video disks never managed to secure much of a market in the United States. Instead, by 1985, nearly 30 percent of all American homes had at least one videocassette recorder, or VCR. By 1992, that number had more than doubled, to 74 percent of American homes, and by 2005, the number was at its highest, with 92 percent of American households owning a VCR.

The manager of the Video Shack, one of the first VHS rental stores in New York City, reported that the store was propped up by X-rated VHS rentals in its early years in business. Gradually, Hollywood studios began to put their blockbusters on video, thus providing additional revenue. For pornographers, it was a Hail Mary pass to save the industry. By releasing films on VHS tapes, producers could sell directly to consumers or to rental stores. To purchase a single X-rated VHS tape cost between seventy and eighty dollars. Their high price meant rentals were a popular lower-cost option, with rental stores offering deals for annual membership. Throughout the 1980s, the porn industry released hundreds of thousands of new titles on VHS for at-home consumption.

Along with the VHS market, porno magazines proliferated in the 1970s and '80s, cementing pornography as an at-home entertainment. *Playboy* was the most popular, with a peak readership of 5.6 million subscribers. By the 1980s, *Penthouse* magazine, one of *Playboy*'s oldest competitors, had a readership of nearly 5 million, making its founder, Bob Guccione, alongside Hugh Hefner, one of the richest men in America.

A New Jersey native who had considered the Roman Catholic priesthood at one point in his life, Guccione started the magazine after taking out a loan for just over a thousand dollars while living in London in 1965. His hope was to win over *Playboy* fans in the United Kingdom and usurp *Playboy*'s reign as king of the pornographic magazine. He did not know at the time that the mailing list he used for a brochure advertising the first issue was outdated. Instead of the bachelors he anticipated would be on the receiving end, a number of clergy, children, and wives of members of the British Parliament received the flyer, which contained photographs of ten nude women. A media and legal frenzy ensued. Guccione was fined $280 and $88.20 for having sent "indecent articles" in the mail, a cost well worth the publicity, given that all 150,000 copies of the first issue of *Penthouse* sold out almost immediately.

Penthouse succeeded by upping the ante of the adult magazine market. *Playboy* may have been the most popular, but it was also the most conservative. Hefner had tempered his magazine's content in order to successfully navigate legal challenges in a manner that did not get in the way of his growing wealth or the success of the magazine. Guccione and *Penthouse*, for their part, constantly pushed the boundaries of explicit content. The magazine featured its first full-frontal nude model in 1970, two years before *Playboy* and three years before obscenity laws had liberalized.

Playboy's competitors attempted to gain an edge by segmenting the market—for example, *Players* magazine catered to an explicitly Black readership—or by positioning their magazines as racier and raunchier than

Playboy, as was *Penthouse*'s strategy. Magazines in the latter category often faced legal consequences as a result, but even court battles added to the publicity. All press is good press, as they say. Larry Flynt, founder and owner of *Hustler* magazine, for example, had been charged with sodomy, obscenity, and contempt, and had been sued hundreds of times before his case against Jerry Falwell appeared before the Supreme Court. In 1984, Flynt ran for president as a Republican, challenging the incumbent, Ronald Reagan. "I am running as a Republican rather than as a Democrat, because I am wealthy, white, pornographic," Flynt declared in a press release. "If elected, my primary goal will be to eliminate ignorance and venereal disease."

WITH THE INVENTION of porn stardom in the 1970s, pornography became a public-facing industry for the first time in American history. Moving aboveground meant it was forced to reckon with broader social upheavals happening at the time. Some pornographers used their platform to connect sex and sex work to social justice issues. In interviews following the release of *Deep Throat*, Linda Lovelace, for instance, emphasized that her film was less obscene than the scenes from the Vietnam War that Americans were witnessing on TV. Even before the golden age of porn, street-based sex workers had been mobilizing social protests. The iconic 1969 Stonewall Riots, which are often remembered as sparking the gay rights movement, were in fact led by African American and Latino transgender sex workers. These protests, and the social movements of which they were a part (including the women's movement, the sexual liberation and gay rights movement, and the civil rights movement), all made their mark on the porn industry for decades to come.

For the first half of the twentieth century, gay porn—that is, depictions of sex between men, since sex between women was often a feature of main-stream porn—was the underground of an already underground industry. Aboveground and sold at newspaper stands and bookstores, "physique magazines," supposedly for the fitness conscious, presumably straight American men, experienced a rise in readership in the 1950s. But it was an open secret that these magazines—with titles like *Trim*, *Physique Pictorial*, and *MANual*—were intended for gay men. Their covers typically depicted a muscular young white man in minimal clothing; inside were images of men, sometimes completely nude. In 1962, Herman Womack, the publisher of many of these magazines, appeared before the Supreme Court, having been arrested on obscenity charges. The Court declared his magazines "dismally unpleasant, uncouth, and tawdry," but not obscene.

In that same year, a young gay man from Pittsburgh who grew up as Andrew Warhola Jr. had his first solo art exhibition at the Stable Gallery in New York City. The show featured what became two of his most famous works, *100 Soup Cans* and *Marilyn Diptych*. By 1968, the prolific artist known as Andy Warhol was a household name. When word spread of his latest project, a film called *Lonesome Cowboys*, the FBI sent agents to the first screening. Their report—which some critics have noted could be considered obscener than the film itself—described the film in vivid detail: "The next scene shows a man wearing only an unbuttoned silk cowboy shirt getting up from the ground. His privates were exposed and another cowboy was lying on the ground in a position with his head facing the genitals of the cowboy who had just stood up." J. Edgar Hoover pursued prosecution of Warhol, arguing that because the film had been produced in Arizona and then screened in New York and Atlanta, it had crossed state lines and thus had violated federal obscenity laws. The U.S. Attorney in Arizona did not pursue the case, and Warhol was never charged.

Gay icons like Warhol placed the pornographic within the broader movement pushing gay and queer visibility. Warhol befriended some of the directors and actors of gay pornos produced in New York City, a place where theaters, bathhouses, clubs, and bars intersected to build a community among gay men in the 1970s, described by one documentary filmmaker as the "most libertine period that the Western world has ever seen since Rome." In the decade between the Stonewall Riots of 1969 and the emergence of the HIV/AIDS epidemic in 1981, gay pornographic films openly rejected a primary tactic of the early gay rights movement to *avoid* overt acknowledgment of sex and, instead, to emphasize respectability and decency. Gay porn stars and directors have described the genre as the pinnacle of gay pride and acceptance. With the HIV/AIDS crisis, gay pornography changed: condoms became an industry norm, and a genre of sexually explicit sex education films emerged to teach safe sex practices through erotic film. Yet, in gay porn and beyond, AIDS activists rejected the shame associated with sexuality and, instead, directed their anger and blame at the government for its lack of response to the crisis.

Though gay hard-core porn titles would never get their place on commercial theater marquees like those of mainstream straight porn of the early 1970s, what did make its mark on the big screen was a genre dubbed by Mireille Miller-Young as "soul porn"—porn depicting Black bodies and what white directors believed to be "Black culture" (aesthetics, music, art) for largely white audiences. Only two Black performers in the 1970s achieved large-scale name recognition, though: Johnnie Keyes and Desiree West. Other Black performers were largely nameless on the credits reels, did not have notable director or producer roles, and were paid less than their white counterparts. Keyes, a former boxer, gained fame for the first interracial sex scene in a feature-length porno, *Behind the Green Door*. Bare-chested and wearing tribal face paint, an African-looking bone necklace, and tight white shorts with a hole for his erect penis, Keyes has sex with the film's white star, Marilyn Chambers, the former Ivory Snow laundry detergent model. Chambers's character is kidnapped and taken to a bizarre sex stage show, where she becomes the feature act. Unwilling at first, she eventually gives in to her sexual desires. The Black man who "ravages" her, to use film historian Linda Williams's description, confirms the racist idea of Black men as sexual threats to innocent and naïve white women, but it also challenged the taboo of interracial sex.

Desiree West began her career in the adult industry when she posed for *Players* magazine in 1973, its first year of publication. Like *Playboy*, it was more than just a porno magazine; it also had articles about culture: music, movies, and technology. It was the first of its kind intended for a Black male readership, featuring predominantly Black models. Both Keyes and Desiree West appeared in the 1978 film *SexWorld*, a spoof on the *Westworld* franchise depicting a Wild West theme park populated with androids.

SexWorld is a theme park for visitors to carry out their desires with human-looking sex robots. Unlike *Behind the Green Door*, the film incorporates racism directly as a plot device. One of SexWorld's visitors, an explicitly racist white character named Roger, finds himself in a room with a Black woman named Jill, played by Desiree West. Roger first assumes she is a robot maid before realizing that she, too, is a paying guest at the resort. Jill dismisses Roger's racist claims about "you people" and not wanting to have sex with her because she is Black. She teases him, calling him a "first-class honkey bigot," speaking in a dialect stereotypical of Black enslavement—"I's provides the entertainment, suh"—and says in a now-famous line, "I'll prove your spigot ain't no bigot." Roger loses control of his desires, and eventually the pair has sex. After they part, Roger becomes obsessed with finding Jill again, telling a SexWorld attendant desperately, "See, there's this girl . . . it might turn out to be serious!" Are Roger's racist attitudes cured? Maybe or maybe not, but the character of Jill, rather than embarking on a quest to fulfill her own sexual desires as a customer at SexWorld, instead is used for Roger to access his unrealized racialized desire. As Miller-Young writes, "Sex World rehearses a scenario that dates back to the plantation sexual economy in which black women's sexuality was made available to white patriarchy, objectified and imaged as desirous."

Yet, to understand soul porn of the 1970s as simply, or only, racist is merely part of the story. It was rumored, for example, that Desiree West was a member of the Black Panther Party, the militant Black activist group targeted by the FBI. Whether or not this was true, West's celebrity status was marked not by victimization and oppression, but by her reputation as being strong and powerful. According to Miller-Young, West herself, and soul porn as a genre more generally, was "located in a social context where radical antisexist, antiracist, and anticapitalist black nationalist and black feminist politics were very much in the air."

The story of Desiree West shows how changing cultural norms and messages surrounding both race and gender intersected in the porn industry. Pornography has long epitomized men's dominance over women and the sexualization and objectification of women's bodies. But with the growing women's movement in the 1960s and '70s, pornography became a heightened target of second-wave feminist scrutiny. The common stag trope of "no means yes" rape scenes, in which a woman begins by resisting but ultimately becomes an enthusiastic sexual participant, remained a frequently used plot device, especially in early 1970s porn. But as the decade progressed, porno directors who included rape scenes did so to signal "bad sex," sex that violated women, as opposed to "good sex," sex that appeared to empower women. At the same time, porn directors began to recognize a largely untapped market of women consumers who were newly "sexually liberated." These were the audiences who happily attended screenings of *Deep Throat* and similar films at the time.

Some of the most famous white female porn stars from the 1970s formed a support group for women in the industry in New York City that they called Club 90. Candida Royalle, a founding member who starred in films such as *Kinky Tricks* and *Hot and Saucy Pizza Girls* in the 1970s, went on to start the first woman-run porn company, Femme Productions, and an activist organization, Feminists for Free Expression, with the goal of transforming the porn industry to value women as both performers and consumers. Porn stars like Royalle used their leverage as rich celebrities to demand a place at the table of porn production, from start to finish. They advocated change within the industry to disrupt the patriarchal norms so common in porn plots and behind the scenes. A genre called "couple's porn" emerged in the 1980s to tend to these feminist sensibilities and to acknowledge women as a different kind of porn audience from straight men. Women performers, almost exclusively white, demanded roles as writers and directors so that films could showcase women's pleasure in the service of women themselves, rather than their male partners or the presumably male audience. The feminist porn movement was born before it was ever branded as such.

As feminist organizing made its way into the porn industry, porn also made its way into feminist organizing. Throughout the women's movement, feminist activists produced sexually explicit material for magazines and art exhibits and staged protests. The pornographic lesbian feminist magazine *On Our Backs*, whose tagline was "Entertainment for the adventurous lesbian," poked fun at the more serious and antiporn feminist publication *Off Our Backs*. One of *On Our Backs*'s founders, Susie Bright, would go on to review porn films for *Penthouse* and became the first woman to join the X-Rated Critics Organization. *On Our Backs* represented one arm of feminist activism that found itself in opposition to the broader mainstream women's movement that opposed pornography. These were the infamous sex wars: antipornography feminists, many of whom called themselves "radical feminists," versus anticensorship or pro-sex feminists. Each claimed to be the "true" keeper of feminism and called out the other for collaborating with the enemy.

CHAPTER 5

Women Against Pornography

N ine members of the women's liberation movement were arrested yesterday after they invaded the offices of Grove Press, a pioneer publisher of erotic literature," wrote the *New York Times* on April 14, 1970. "Grove's sadomasochistic literature and pornographic films dehumanize and degrade women," the demonstrators told the press. The women, about thirty in total, marched to the sixth floor of the Greenwich Village office building to sit outside Grove's executive suites. They remained there in silent protest for five hours, until the police came to arrest them for trespassing.

The impetus for the event was not pornography per se, but the company's firing of six female employees after they participated in union organizing. "Grove Press won't let women be anything but secretaries, scrub women, and sex symbols," one of the women's liberationists said, as union organizers held a rally across the street. Eventually, representatives of Grove Press said "in the interest of peace," they did not support prosecution, and all arrested were acquitted. The company later agreed to rehire four of the women it had fired.

Looking back on the protest decades later, feminist writer and poet Robin Morgan, who was among the protestors that day, noted that it was "the first time feminists openly declared pornography as the enemy." In the decades that followed, feminists and conservative women alike would take on pornography as a shared target for their opposition. Grove Press had long been on the radar of anti-obscenity conservatives, having gained notoriety in the 1950s and '60s for producing and publishing censored books and films. On the heels of success in several courtroom battles, the owner of the press, Barney Rosset, decided to publish *Story of O*, an English translation of the 1954 French book *Histoire d'O*, written under the pseudonym "Pauline Reage," which had been sent to Grove Press six years earlier at the behest of its French editor. *Histoire d'O* resembles *Fifty Shades of Grey*, which would become a bestseller fifty years later: a beautiful, modern woman with a successful career as a photographer willingly becomes a sexual slave for her lover, René, a rich and powerful man who is a member of a secret society. She is subjected to bondage with chains and ropes, whipping, piercing, branding, and violent sex with multiple men who are members of the same clandestine club. In 1975, Gerard Damiano, the director of *Deep Throat* and *The Devil in Miss Jones*, would produce *The Story of Joanna*, based on the book. In 1970, *Story of O* was but one of many Grove Press titles that outraged feminists.

As the women's movement grew, radical feminists coalesced around what they thought was a series of commonsense truths. First, these feminists opposed pornography because of its literal harm to women. Women were forced into performances to which they did not consent. Women's bodies were abused. Even for women who were supposedly willing porn performers, scripted scenes of forced or coerced sexual encounters glorified rape and contributed to what feminists were beginning to call "rape culture." This harm to women overlapped with a second key feminist concern: that pornography symbolically harms women by reinforcing the notion that women are sexual objects used in the service of men. Scenes like those depicted in *Story of O* and *Behind the Green Door* suggest that women *want* to be abused by men. Porn stars who appear on-screen to please and satisfy men, both performers and audience, were not having sex for their own pleasure, but rather, for a flawed system that provided economic reward for women who participated in the patriarchy. Finally, pornography harmed women by reducing them to their sex appeal and, thus, further cementing sexism and gender inequality in broader society. The image of women in porn, the thinking went, carried over into other aspects of social life. If women only had value as sexual objects, then it was all the more likely that they would face discrimination and harassment as they attempted to excel in jobs and education.

Radical feminists were particularly critical of talk of "sexual liberation" that sometimes appeared under the guise of feminism. "Sexual freedom," from the point of view of white feminist activist Dana Densmore, did not include the "freedom to decline sex, to decline to be defined at every turn by sex." Densmore, a software engineer for MIT in the 1960s, who supervised the navigation system that would be used for the Apollo missions to land on the moon, was also a member of a radical feminist group based in Boston that called itself Cell 16. The group encouraged women to remain unmarried and celibate and was an early advocate of a separatist-feminist philosophy. The excess of the "free love" movement cannot make up for past oppression, Densmore and her peers insisted, and the notion that sexual freedom was a "right" was actually, for women, more akin to a "duty." Black and Chicana feminists had already made this point, recognizing the complex social mechanisms (including racism, sexism, and capitalism) that made "sexual freedom" difficult to achieve.

THE IRONY IS that opponents of feminism had long championed a similar argument. Women on the right had been saying for years that "sexual freedom" harmed women. But instead of blaming the patriarchy, as feminists did, conservative women blamed beatniks, hippies, and homosexuals, along with feminists themselves. Women's sexuality, as it appeared on-screen—whether through Marilyn Monroe in *Niagara* or Linda Lovelace in *Deep Throat*—was counterfeit. Real and authentic sexual expression was found only where God intended it to be: in heterosexual monogamous matrimony.

Some conservative religious women, like their activist feminist counterparts, insisted that they opposed pornography not because they were antisex, but because they wanted to reclaim women's sexuality. Beverly LaHaye, born Beverly Ratcliffe, met her husband, Tim, in the 1940s while attending Bob Jones University, the conservative evangelical South Carolina college. Two decades later, Beverly had raised four children and supported her husband as a Baptist pastor and writer of Christian self-help and nonfiction. Christian sex advice was an emerging genre, taking advantage of the broader market of bestsellers like *The Joy of Sex*, published in 1972. Together, in 1976, Tim and Beverly LaHaye authored one of the first widely popular sex advice books geared toward a Christian audience. When it came to both women's and men's sexual pleasure, it was, they insisted, their opportunity to set the record straight.

Though the title itself is a euphemism, *The Act of Marriage* blends anatomical drawings and step-by-step advice to serve as a practical companion for Christians who married presumably as virgins. The book is part sex education, part marital counseling, part Bible study. The authors outline in great detail what a couple's first sexual encounter may be like, providing instructions on how to engage in foreplay and have sexual intercourse. This includes tips for communicating ("the husband should proceed . . . with verbal expressions of love") and practical advice ("it is a rare bride who will be able to provide sufficient natural vaginal lubricant on her honeymoon").

The book is full of gender stereotypes, and the LaHayes promote gender complementarianism, or the dominant ideology of conservative Protestantism, which presupposes that God created men and women to be distinct from one another in order to come together in marriage. This belief assumes that men are naturally assertive and dominant and that women are natural caretakers and helpers. Yet, in their book, the LaHayes also break the silence surrounding women's sexuality within conservative Christian communities, insisting that women have the right to sexual pleasure just as much as men. They cite the Bible (a verse in First Corinthians, specifically) as justification: "[B]oth men and women have sexual needs that a partner is obliged to fulfill." The LaHayes were riding a wave started by Marabel Morgan's *The Total Woman*, published two years earlier, which overlapped in its messaging that women should be pleased to please their husbands, but the LaHayes pushed this idea one step further, by offering plain advice on how women can achieve pleasure of their own.

On pornography, the LaHayes wrote unequivocally of their condemnation, but they couched their concerns in the context of marital satisfaction rather than moral opposition. Those who have the best sex lives, they insist, "don't have an obsession with sex nor read pornographic literature to be stimulated properly." Instead, these Christian couples "just go on year after year enjoying it—just as our heavenly Father intended," the LaHayes write. Their advice to couples was to avoid any "suggestive material," including pornography, and also "most movies" and "questionable TV programs," because this kind of media can draw attention away from one's spouse as the right and true object of one's sexual desire. In the years following the publication of *The Act of Marriage*, Tim LaHaye would become a full-time conservative political activist. Now best known for his apocalyptic fiction bestsellers, the *Left Behind* series, he wasn't much for predicting the future: in 1982, he wrote of his confidence that "we will succeed in putting pornographers out of business."

In 1978, Beverly LaHaye became a political activist like her husband when she saw a television interview with the feminist activist Betty Friedan, who spoke of her 1966 founding of the National Organization for Women (NOW). LaHaye recalled that it was in that moment that she recognized the need for an alternative organization for women who disagreed with Friedan's views but who cared about politics and the future of the country. That same year, she founded Concerned Women for America (CWA). Later, in her own media interviews, LaHaye liked to boast that CWA, which had chapters in nearly all fifty states, had twice the national membership of NOW.

The concerns of these concerned women were many: pornography, for one, along with homosexuality, abortion, big government, sex education in schools, the feminist movement, and the Equal Rights Amendment. Amid the growing visibility and popularity of the women's rights movement, "not all women are feminists," as one Associated Press journalist put it. LaHaye's CWA collaborated with Phyllis Schlafly's campaign to oppose ratification of the ERA. As a devout Catholic and conservative Republican, Schlafly became a household name for her efforts to mobilize conservative Christian housewives who opposed progressive social change, what the media at the time called "kitchen table advocates." They wrote letters to politicians and newspapers and organized rallies and other events to voice their concerns. For all her defense of traditional gender roles within marriage, Schlafly herself had more formal education than more than 90 percent of

American women at the time. Boasting a master's degree in government from Radcliffe, Harvard's college for women, and a law degree from Washington University, she traveled the country giving speeches at rallies, wrote a newspaper column, and edited a newsletter. Still, she told the press that motherhood was her occupation and that she took responsibility for her children and her home alongside her activism through careful time management and a full-time housekeeper.

Schlafly, LaHaye, and the other conservative women who opposed the Equal Rights Amendment in the late 1970s insisted that they did not oppose women's equality. Schlafly's campaign, STOP ERA, was an acronym for "Stop Taking Our Privileges," signaling her claim that the ERA would take rights *away* from women, not the opposite. Of course, Schlafly believed that women held equal worth and value within society, she quipped to reporters. Rather, anti-ERA activists claimed that the law, as written, would not in fact support women's equality because it erased gender differences. The ERA, according to LaHaye, "would eliminate the common-sense distinction between the two sexes and make up for a genderless, unisex society." Similar arguments are echoed today in debates over transgender rights, one of the concerns of the CWA in 2021. Then and now, LaHaye and her peers were focused on protecting their vision of womanhood.

HARM TO WOMEN did not become a key frame for the conservative anti-pornography movement until feminists championed the message. Since the time of Anthony Comstock, conservatives have lamented that pornography contributes to the deterioration of the family, citing women and children as innocent victims of men's vices. But it wasn't until feminism took cultural hold in the 1970s that conservatives began to take up the argument that pornography's distinct harm to women was reason to oppose it. Prior to feminist advocacy on behalf of women victims of rape and sexual assault, the prevailing cultural narrative often blamed women for making themselves available to men. For women deemed true victims, the threat was not misogyny but individual male predators, often men of color pathologized as threats to white female innocence. Though these narratives never went away, feminist activism insisted on alternative ones, and eventually, this insistence went mainstream, as evidenced by the hugely visible MeToo movement and its expansion into even such spaces as U.S. sports and conservative TV news networks.

Rape and sexual violence were among the earliest concerns of the women's movement that emerged in the 1960s. Gradually, activists began targeting the media as perpetrators of the idea that men were entitled to women as sexual objects. Pornography was booming and increasingly mainstream in the 1970s, and thus was an obvious target. Feminist discussions surrounding sex and sexuality in the 1970s presented multiple positions, all under the broad banner of feminism. Yet, by the early 1980s, two feminist positions regarding pornography were cemented within the movement. Anticensorship feminists, like FACT (the Feminist Anti-Censorship Taskforce), accused antiporn feminists like Women Against Pornography (WAP) of collaborating with the Christian Right, which fundamentally opposed women's liberation. Antiporn feminists called the anticensorship contingent "a small group of lesbians into sadomasochism" who hypocritically collaborated with liberal men, such as members of the American Civil Liberties Union (ACLU).

Though critics named antipornography feminists as the strange bedfellows of religious conservatives, who also organized in opposition to pornography in the 1980s, sociologist Nancy Whittier effectively demonstrates through in-depth archival research that, beyond the fact that they both opposed the same thing, these groups were not actually collaborators. They opposed pornography for different reasons, using different tactics and with different legal goals. Though, at times, feminists spoke in support of legal initiatives that were championed by conservatives, they never co-organized or cosponsored events. Religious conservatives advocated for widespread prohibition by using and expanding the criminal code related to obscenity. Feminists advocated for pornography to be considered a form of sex discrimination and, thus, a civil offense that women could use to challenge pornography producers and distributors and force them out of business. Neither antiporn feminists nor conservatives were very concerned with differences among women, such as along racial or class lines, and thus were uniformly critiqued by many nonwhite feminists.

In the fall of 1983, Catharine MacKinnon, a law professor at the University of Minnesota and an outspoken feminist opponent of pornography, invited Andrea Dworkin, fellow antiporn feminist, for a visiting appointment at the university. The two co-taught an interdisciplinary course called Pornography, and upon the semester's end, they submitted an ordinance they had drafted to the Minneapolis City Council that would amend the city's civil rights code to include pornography as a form of sex discrimination. It outlined a cause of action for women who believed they had been harmed by pornography and defined it broadly as any representation of women as "sexual objects, things, or commodities." Any woman could bring suit against a pornographer if she felt they had contributed to her subordination. On December 30 of that year, the city council passed the ordinance. The mayor, however, vetoed it, citing First Amendment concerns.

Meanwhile, a city council member in Indianapolis, Beulah Coughenour, a conservative Christian who opposed the ERA, invited MacKinnon to help draft an ordinance for her city. This was as far as a collaboration between feminists and conservatives opposing porn in the 1980s would go. The ordinance, like the one in Minneapolis, defined pornography as portrayals of women as sexual objects who enjoyed pain or humiliation. Thus, pornography constituted discrimination against women. The ordinance this time was signed into law by the mayor after it passed in the city council. Opponents, including the ACLU and the American Booksellers Association, took the city to court. MacKinnon, Dworkin, and the organization Morality in Media (which would eventually become the influential National Center on Sexual Exploitation, or NCOSE) filed briefs defending the ordinance. Eventually, the Supreme Court would consider the case, and it upheld the lower courts' rulings that the Indianapolis ordinance was unconstitutional in that it violated the First Amendment right to free speech.

But before the High Court weighed in on Indianapolis, MacKinnon and Dworkin drafted a revised proposal for the Minneapolis City Council in July 1984. This time, they presented a narrower definition of pornography, hoping to curtail the mayor's concerns about free speech. When the ordinance was being considered by the Minneapolis City Council, anti-pornography feminists organized rallies in support. One woman who attended, twenty-three-year-old Ruth Christenson, spoke out in favor of the ordnance during the city council debate and also wrote letters to city council members explaining that "sexism has shattered my life." On July 10, a Sunday, she walked into a Shinder's bookstore, a small local chain that specialized in sports trading cards, magazines, and comics and that also included a back row of pornographic magazines and books. Christenson did not bother making her way to the back of the store, instead stopping near the front counter, where she poured gasoline over her head and set herself on fire. When she fell to the floor, leaflets titled STOP PORN NOW tumbled out of her backpack.

The store clerk and another customer quickly extinguished the flames, and Christenson was admitted to a hospital with third-degree burns. Eventually, she was released, but tragically, six years later, on a December day that had Minneapolis firefighters rushing to extinguish eight fires throughout the city, Christenson was found in her locked apartment, amid flames, fatally burned. The medical examiner ruled her death a suicide. "It's tricky to say anything about an individual," a feminist activist and coordinator of the city's Sexual Violence Center said to reporters who were covering the story, "but it is certainly true for large numbers of women who have experienced violence in their lives that they feel there's nowhere they can go and be safe."

Newspapers across the country printed stories on the self-immolation of Ruth Christenson at Shinder's bookstore, though few covered her eventual suicide. Any story about pornography and harm to women was, and still is, easy fodder for media sensationalism. In 1980, newspapers and television stations across the country covered a press conference held by the feminist organization Women Against Pornography, with Linda Marchiano, née Boreman, the former porn superstar Linda Lovelace. Standing beside feminism's own celebrities, Gloria Steinem, Catharine MacKinnon, and Andrea Dworkin, Marchiano used the stage to speak out against pornography and to promote her new book, an autobiography titled *Ordeal.* In it, she explains how she was forced into the porn business by her abusive husband, Chuck Traynor. WAP used Marchiano's story to decry pornography for its harm to women (performers and the rest) by normalizing coercion and sexual abuse perpetrated by men. Later, Marchiano would appear before the Meese Commission to testify that viewers of *Deep Throat* were watching a recording of her repeated rape.

Four years after the WAP press conference in 1984, Colleen Applegate, a twenty-year-old white woman from Minnesota, committed suicide in Palm Springs, California. The story made all the major papers in the country because Applegate, better known as Shauna Grant, was a porn star. Grant had left her parents' home in the cold Midwest at the age of eighteen and moved to sunny California with a boyfriend. Within weeks of the move, she began modeling for magazines like *Hustler* and *Penthouse* to make money. Eventually, she and her boyfriend split up, and Applegate began appearing in pornographic films. Though she didn't have much enthusiasm on camera, she had, according to the people who worked with her, a "girl next door" look that was key to her success. Within two years, she had earned more than a hundred thousand dollars (over a quarter million dollars by today's standards) and had appeared in more than thirty films. Over the course of Applegate's short career, as all the newspaper stories made sure to describe, she was infected with herpes, had an abortion, and became addicted to cocaine.

In the years following her death, three films examined Applegate's tragic story. One made-for-TV movie provided a fictionalized account of Applegate's dramatic life and death. One documentary, a serious affair produced by the PBS series *Frontline*, featured photographs of Applegate as a child and as a high school cheerleader and included the tearful voices of her family members wondering aloud what went wrong. Their stories helped construct a classic morality tale message: that innocent young women should not wander into risky spaces. The other film, calling itself an "X-rated documentary," was released by adult filmmaker Robert Findlay just one year after Applegate's death. *Shauna: Every Man's Fantasy* weaves together explicit sex scenes of Shauna Grant, outtakes of Applegate while on set, and interviews with those in the industry who knew her. The film goes for maximum titillation, using both sex and death without any pretense of moralism. But all these films were exploitative in their own way: capitalizing on a young woman's long struggle with mental health and the porn industry that exacerbated her problems.

THROUGHOUT THE 1980s, feminists and conservative women overlapped in their rhetoric of pornography's harm to women, but they diverged in their assessment of the problem. Days after the self-immolation of Ruth Christenson in Shinder's bookstore in Minneapolis, and just a few months after Applegate's death, *Penthouse*'s September 1984 issue made media headlines across the country when Vanessa Williams, then the reigning Miss America, appeared in its pages. The magazine sold out nearly instantly. *Penthouse* editor Bob Guccione had paid fifty thousand dollars for the photos, which had been taken two years earlier. The scandal was so great that, at the end of July, Williams somberly announced that she would be resigning as Miss America. She was the first African American to win the title and also the first woman in sixty-three years to give it up. "I've let other women down and I've let the whole black community down. I made a terrible error in judgment and I know I'll have to pay for it as long as I live," she said regretfully to *People* magazine.

Feminists largely came to the defense of Williams and, instead, targeted both *Penthouse* magazine and the Miss America Pageant organization. Williams had been exploited by both, they insisted. Feminists had long critiqued the national pageant for equating a woman's worth with how well she looked in a bikini. In 1968, a group of feminists gained national attention when they protested the pageant by burning bras and girdles and parading around a sheep that had been donned in bows and a yellow victory sash. In 1984, Women Against Pornography released a statement to the press criticizing *Penthouse* directly: "By degrading this outspoken and talented woman at a time when women are achieving national recognition for their intelligence and political abilities, *Penthouse* is telling women that any attempt to achieve equality will be in vain."

Conservative activist Phyllis Schlafly managed to critique Guccione and Williams in one fell swoop. Reflecting a broader ethos of conservative women's activism at the time, Schlafly saw danger in both the pornographer and the Black woman who defied traditional white gender norms. "What Penthouse did was exploit [Williams] and ruin her," Schlafly told a newspaper in 1984. "I do think she's a victim and I also think she violated civilized standards and I think that the Miss America Pageant did the only thing they could to keep their integrity—to uncrown her." The pageant is "quite a competition," Schlafly went on. "It's moral and decent and I think it inspires young women to look their best and compete with some kind of talent." For conservatives like Schlafly, both Williams and *Penthouse* had tainted what they saw as a core American institution, the Miss America pageant.

In the aftermath of the Vanessa Williams scandal, pageant officials named Suzette Charles, Miss New Jersey, formerly the runner-up, Miss America. Charles, also African American, held her title for two months before the following year's pageant announced its winner, Sharlene Wells, a white, blond Miss Utah who was a devout member of the Church of Jesus Christ of Latter-day Saints and who opposed abortion, premarital sex, the ERA, and of course pornography. In the end, though, the American public mostly forgot Charles and Wells, even if they successfully held the Miss America crown. Vanessa Williams, for her part, went on to have a successful and award-winning career as a singer and actor. Meanwhile, ratings for the televised Miss America pageant plummeted, and Guccione's empire slowly crumbled. He lost investments on projects that never materialized and was forced to pay over one hundred million dollars in back taxes to the IRS. Eventually, internet pornography in the 1990s drove down readership of his magazine. He resigned as CEO of the *Penthouse* enterprise and foreclosed on his mansion four years before his death in 2010.

NEITHER ANTIPORNOGRAPHY FEMINISTS nor conservative women won their battles in the porn wars. By the 1990s, there was no pushing sex back into the private sphere or public underbelly. It had come out victorious in the courts and was making its mark in virtually all sectors of society: politics, health care, education, consumerism, and media. Playboy Enterprises Inc. had a TV and film division, clubs and casinos, a clothing line, a limousine service, and a modeling agency. Larry Flynt of *Hustler* magazine opened a Hollywood latte bar that also sold sex toys. Music videos that played on MTV featured actual porn stars, or female musicians who looked like them. Prestigious art galleries displayed artistically rendered photographs of an adult film shoot. Jerry Springer slid down a stripper pole to greet the audience for his daytime TV talk show, which often featured sex workers and LGBTQ guests. Oral sex, along with a semen-stained dress, became the obsession of Congress during what the media called the Clinton-Lewinsky Affair. Even though the golden and silver eras of pornography were relics of the past, pornography and its impact on American culture was here to stay.

CHAPTER 6

The Internet Is for Porn

I n the fictional world of the Broadway musical *Avenue Q*, Kate Monster is a puppet with a sweet demeanor, a lavender-colored turtleneck, and a bob hairstyle. She works as an assistant kindergarten teacher, and when she finally gets to teach a kindergarten lesson all by herself, she chooses to teach children about the wonders of the World Wide Web. But when she describes her lesson to a reclusive, shaggy-haired neighbor named Trekkie Monster, he interrupts every line with what he says is the *real* reason for the Internet: porn.

When *Avenue Q* premiered in 2003 with its song "The Internet is for Porn," it became the first Broadway cast album to be released with a PARENTAL ADVISORY label. At the time, a majority of American households, 62 million of them, owned a computer that connected to the internet. And when it came to its emergence, Trekkie Monster captured a widespread fear. "All-pornography, all-the-time," is how Pamela Paul, the author of the 2005 book *Pornified*, put it. According to her analysis, based on a number of internet polls not generalizable to the American population, virtually everyone had come across internet porn by the early aughts.

But neither Trekkie Monster nor Paul quite captured the reality. The pornography industry's profits at the turn of the century, with accurate estimates ranging from $2.6 billion to $10 billion annually, were far below those of other lucrative vices, such as the tobacco industry, with profits of around $45 billion, and gambling earning $50 billion. Most of the earliest online porn sites made money through paid subscriptions, in which users could tour for free but were forced to enter their credit card number to be charged for either a one-time pass or for various tiers of monthly memberships. As early as 2000, owners of these sites were lamenting the decline in online profits, as those that were once able to charge $30 for a monthly membership were now charging $10 thanks to growing competition.

Between 2000 and 2005, the Pew Research Center asked a national sample of American adults, "Do you ever visit an adult website?" and only 13 to 15 percent of respondents said yes. This estimate is similar to data reported by the *New York Times* from the Juniper Media Metrix survey in 2001, which estimated 28 million users of pornographic websites that year. This number sounds big, but comparing it to the total number Americans ages eighteen to sixty-four (just over 174 million in 2000) or the number of Americans with basic cable at the time (nearly 73 million households) suggests that internet porn was not quite the national epidemic that some assumed.

Porn viewership has steadily increased since the 1970s, especially among porn's most loyal consumers, young adult men. Between 1973 and 1980, 45 percent of men ages eighteen to twenty-six reported they had viewed porn in the past year, compared to 61 percent between 1999 and 2007. The internet did cause a jump in porn consumption, but for most Americans that increase was relatively small. In 1973, 31 percent of men across all ages reported that they had viewed porn, compared to 33 percent in 2000. These data come from the General Social Survey that tracks Americans' *reported* consumption of porn, which may be different from their *actual* consumption. Still, the authors of one study controlled for attitudes regarding pornography (that it should be illegal) and found that these attitudes remained relatively stable between the 1970s and early aughts, suggesting that people now are no more or less likely to report porn viewership honestly. The internet did not cause a generation to suddenly become porn crazy. We were already porn crazy, and men especially had long been exposed to dirty pictures through a variety of media prior to the World Wide Web.

Still, pornography by the turn of the twenty-first century had infiltrated virtually all forms of contemporary media: television, movies, magazines, and music. Commentators came up with various names to describe its impact; most agreed our society was "sexualized," even "hypersexualized." We lived in a "raunch culture," said journalist Ariel Levy; in a "strip-tease culture," according to journalism professor Brian McNair; and a "pornified culture," a term bestowed by Pamela Paul.

The growth of the pornography industry between 1998 and 2001 surpassed online shopping and other arts and entertainment industries. Porn stars who were lucky enough to sign contracts with the two largest production companies, Vivid and Wicked Pictures, could make $10,000 a week by shooting two scenes. Then they could go on to make even larger paydays from public appearances, like dancing at nightclubs. Jenna Jameson, whom the *New York Times* called the "Julia Roberts of Straight Porn," worked an exclusive contract with Wicked Pictures. By 2001, she was earning around $60,000 per film. She also appeared in mainstream Hollywood films and on television, was a regular on Howard Stern's radio program, and wrote a bestselling memoir.

One porn industry mogul, John Stagliano, who produced the series *Adventures of Buttman*, reported to the *New York Times* that his production schedule had doubled between 1990 and 1993, along with his profits, which grew dramatically, from $34,000 to over $1 million. Not only was there the robust home video market, but there were also cable networks dedicated exclusively to adult entertainment, and the internet, which offered a new opportunity for paid home consumption. As David Marshlack, the founder of Entertainment Network, a company that owned thousands of pornographic websites, said at the end of the decade, "It's as if I owned a bank and printed my own money."

IN 1995, WHEN only about one in four households had a computer and far fewer had an internet connection, the media was full of scary stories about the World Wide Web. It was the year of the movie *The Net*, starring Sandra Bullock, a thriller whose villain was a contract killer hired by cyberterrorists. That July, the same month *The Net* premiered in theaters, *Time* magazine published an exclusive cover story featuring a "new study" by Marty Rimm on the startling dangers of internet pornography. In reality, the study was an eighty-five-page undergraduate research paper, possibly partly plagiarized, that managed to get published in a law journal without undergoing any peer review. With these delegitimizing details obscured at the time, the *Time* story prompted coverage in news outlets around the country, including national television programs like *Dateline*. All discussed the so-called findings that 85 percent of images on the internet were pornographic, and many of those images would most certainly be judged obscene in the courts—images of children; of "deviant" behavior such as bestiality, urination, and defecation; and torture scenes.

In the weeks that followed, the internet fought back against its critic Mr. Rimm. Journalists, academics, and interested laypeople took to online message boards to tear apart the study's findings, analysis, and conclusions and to ruin the reputation of Rimm, who was no social scientist but, rather, a scrappy entrepreneur who used his sensational writings for his own success. The proverbial final nail in the coffin came when the public learned that Rimm had, the year before, published *The Pornographer's Handbook: How to Exploit Women, Dupe Men, and Make Lots of Money*. Rimm, it seemed, was trying on a variety of viewpoints when it came to porn, not based on conviction or science, but rather, to see what would most effectively lead to his fame and fortune. Now antipornography activists could hardly come to his defense.

Still, the dust that the Rimm study stirred was in the air. Most politicians agreed that online content, especially pornography, needed regulations, but they faced a challenging puzzle over how to impose them. The internet was like the Wild West, a place where normal rules and expectations did not apply. The same year the Rimm study was debunked, Senator James Exon introduced his solution in the form of a Senate amendment, the Communications Decency Act (CDA). The CDA was proposed as an amendment to the broader Telecommunications Act passed in 1996, which overhauled federal laws regulating telephone, television, and computer broadcast services for the first time in over sixty years. Senator Exon, a conservative Democrat and former governor of Nebraska who never lost an election, made it his mission to ensure that, in his words, "the information superhighway should not become a red light district." He proposed that the CDA explicitly prohibit using a telecommunications device to make or transmit obscene material. Existing laws dating back to Comstock dealt only with transmission via the U.S. Postal Service.

Another of the CDA's explicit aims was to protect children as potential consumers of pornography. Throughout the 1980s, the relationship between kids and porn reflected a broader cultural panic over child sexual assault and abduction. In 1987, the FBI boasted 249 child pornography prosecutions, compared to only 3 in 1983. Prohibiting minors from consuming pornography had already been established through court precedent in 1968, when the Supreme Court ruled in *Ginsberg v. New York* that even if "material concerned with sex" could be legally sold to adults (i.e., was not deemed obscene), that material could not legally be sold to minors. The CDA articulated this precedent and applied it to the internet, criminalizing the use of "any interactive computer service to display in a manner available to a person under 18 years of age, any comment, request, suggestion, proposal, image, or other communication that, in context, depicts or describes, in terms patently offensive as measured by contemporary community standards."

Exon himself admitted that he had virtually no internet experience. A friend who was more technologically savvy than he downloaded and printed a series of pornography images, which Exon filed in a blue folder. Calling this the "blue book," he stored it on his desk in Congress so that anyone could see the "filth" available online. In Exon's personal testimony, he implored Congress to pass the CDA. "In my eight years as governor of Nebraska and my seventeen years of having the great opportunity to serve my state in the Senate, there is nothing that I feel more strongly about than this piece of legislation," he said. The CDA, as part of the Telecommunications Act, was passed by Congress with widespread support and signed into law by President Clinton.

One small provision of the Communications Decency Act that received little fanfare at the time was Section 230, which states that "no provider or user of an interactive computer service shall be treated as the publisher or speaker of any information provided by another information content provider." In other words, website owners themselves were not to be held accountable for the content that others might post to their site. Thanks in part to the legal protection offered by this provision, three former PayPal employees started the video-sharing site YouTube in 2005. It was the first major online platform that made it easy for those with only basic computer skills to upload personal videos or recordings to share with other users. The site, depicted with a computer whose screen was a mirror, was dubbed *Time* magazine's "Person of the Year" in 2006 and, by that time, had more than twenty-five million user-uploaded videos.

FABIAN THYLMANN WAS a teenager living in Düsseldorf when the internet, and online porn along with it, was gaining momentum in the 1990s. He wasn't old enough to have a credit card, and so he found chat rooms where users traded passwords to get access to subscription sites. With the benefit of hindsight, journalist Jon Ronson, who has written extensively about adult entertainment, names Thylmann's early encounters bypassing porn sites' paywalls as the beginning of a butterfly effect: the small and mundane choices made by a teenager that dramatically shaped internet pornography as we know it today. "The porn world was there for the taking," Ronson reflects, "not by some gangster or some porn devotee, but by somebody *techy*." Thylmann, whom *New York* magazine later referred to as among THE GEEK-KINGS OF SMUT (adding a technological adjective to a title adopted decades earlier by Larry Flynt), fit the bill. He became familiar with website production when he wrote code to track the traffic for a few online porn sites. By 2006, a handful of sites had emerged that followed the YouTube model. Thylmann managed to buy a small company called Mansef, which operated one of them. It was called Pornhub.

Thylmann changed the company name to Manwin and set out to convince investors to support his business, which he insisted was a *technology* company first and foremost. Its formal purpose, as agreed upon in a meeting of shareholders, was boring and nondescript: "the provision of technical services in the field of IT and website development as well as the associated administrative and organizational services of all kinds for affiliated companies as well as for other clients and third-party companies." Yet what this translated into in practice was buying up and overseeing the operation of porn sites. "I figured out that it seems to be an awfully good thing to buy adult websites in the current climate," Thylmann told one reporter in 2011, "because you can get things cheap, and there are obvious ways to improve what they're doing." He secured a $362 million investment from venture capitalists and, as he explained to Ronson, "I bought pretty much everything there was to buy." Along with Pornhub, he bought other free streaming sites, including YouPorn, ExtremeTube, Tube8, and Spankwire. He would eventually also buy the leading pay subscription sites, including Playboy TV, Brazzers, Twistys, Digital Playground, Wicked Pictures, and Reality Kings.

On porn-sharing sites like Pornhub, users uploaded either illegally pirated pornos or ones they had made themselves for others to watch for free, without entering credit card information or registering as members. The sites made money through advertisers, who paid to have their banners seen by the millions of daily users. Free streaming sites also complied with requests to remove illegal content—for example, if a user uploaded a recording of a DVD sold by a commercial porn studio—but the user uploads far outpaced the digital paperwork required by the Digital Millennium Copyright Act (DMCA) for removal requests. Today, some commercial porn studios hire out firms who make full-time work out of tracking down pirated content for removal, but still, they cannot keep up.

Most of Manwin's early earnings came from advertisements on free streaming sites, but the media conglomerate was also beginning to use its free sites to advertise the pay sites that Thylmann's company was purchasing. This bridging of revenue created the façade of distinct porn markets (amateur vs. professional), but in reality, Thylmann had created a monopoly. In 2013, he sold his shares of the company under allegations of tax evasion, and the company changed its name to MindGeek. In 2015, MindGeek's total assets had nearly doubled since 2011, when the company was called Manwin. That year, the company reported an annual revenue of $460 million. Today, on its website, MindGeek remains nondescript, calling itself "A Leader in Web Design, IT, Web Development." Despite the site's vague tech-speak, it's no secret that MindGeek's operations are in porn. By some estimates, the company owns 90 percent of all pornographic content on the internet.

Until recently, the Communications Decency Act protected MindGeek from accountability for illegal content posted by users on sites like Pornhub. Before the CDA and its Section 230, obscenity laws focused on distribution, rather than production or possession of obscene materials. Throughout the twentieth century, bookshops, publishers, and theater owners, even if they had nothing to do with creating porn, were on the receiving end of criminal charges. With the passage of the CDA over a century after the Comstock laws were enacted, the opposite came to be true. Section 230 protected website owners as the distributors of their users' content. It also allowed websites that contracted with independent performers (like OnlyFans and other sites used for what has come to be known as camming) to flourish. The provision has come to be credited with what pornography's sympathizers say is pornography at its best and what opponents say is pornography at its worst.

In the current century, amid new internet technology, pornography debates may appear to have altered course from decades and centuries past. And yet, as the pornography wars have evolved, the battlefields have stayed the same: the law is one front, and American culture is another. From the 1880s to the 1980s and into the present day, the pornography wars have been fought over the hearts and minds of a broader public to convince them of what each side insists to be right and true.

PART II

The Battle over Making Porn

O bserving turmoil in France in the middle of the nineteenth century, when Napoléon III staged a coup to ensure his continued reign, French writer Jean-Baptiste Alphonse Karr remarked, "Plus ça change, plus c'est la même chose," or "The more things change, the more they stay the same." The phrase has broad resonance, also becoming the title of a song by the American rock band Cinderella, for their 1990 album, *Heartbreak Station*. And it more or less captures the pornography wars as they shifted to target an online industry.

The internet changed everything and nothing. The industry itself transformed with the MindGeek takeover of the vast majority of porn websites. Performers were forced to adjust to a new reality that they couldn't make a living from commercial porn shoots alone, as there were fewer and fewer of them after the emergence of free streaming sites. Yet they continued to face similar challenges as in decades past: an industry where white men largely controlled the production of commercial porn, content that capitalized on negative stereotypes of women and people of color, and the social stigma associated with sex work.

For the antiporn movement, new tactics emerged in the twenty-first century to advocate for sex-trafficking laws as a way to shut down pornographic websites and to support health regulations to make commercial porn more difficult to produce. Although these efforts were relatively new, the motivation behind them was not. When it comes to the porn industry, concerns of the antiporn movement are largely unchanged from forty years ago. For feminists, pornography exploits and harms women. Conservatives have taken up this rallying cry alongside claims that pornography violates obscenity laws. Together, their goal is largely the same: to shut down the porn industry writ large.

CHAPTER 7

Trafficking Hub

Pornographers are committing some of the biggest crimes of the century," a woman wearing a badge reading LAURIE announced to a crowd of about forty people, most of whom were white women like Laurie and me. The room was clearly set up for a smaller audience, with two dozen or so chairs forming a large circle at the center. Those of us who couldn't find a seat in the circle pulled down chairs from the stacks in the corners to form clusters wherever there was floor space. We sat with takeout boxes atop our laps from the food trucks in the parking lot of the conference hotel. Laurie, like me, had chosen the taco truck.

I almost did not attend this lunch session because I was tired of the hotel's windowless rooms and the heaviness of the conference message: that pornography is ruining us all. I wondered if the next day would include more hope and optimism because this day was all doom and gloom. I received permission from organizers to attend the Freedom from Sexual Slavery (a pseudonym, or FFSS) national conference in 2019 as a researcher. On this particular day, I had been in conference sessions all morning and had even joined the Continental breakfast, where I sat with three white women, all friends, who had flown to the East Coast from Portland, Oregon, where one roasts her own coffee beans. They all were "passionate about sex trafficking," as one described it, and were members of the same church.

The conference was held in an industrial plaza that was not quite the suburbs and not quite the city. It was conveniently close to the airport, and all I could see from my hotel room window were parking lots and another hotel. With conference programming running from seven in the morning until ten at night, and catering provided by the conference for breakfast, lunch, and dinner, there was no reason to leave the building. Within the mid-tier hotel chain there were large banners advertising the conference and a single entry point guarded by security. All who entered had to show their name badges as proof that they were registered for the conference. We were reminded to wear our badges at all times. In previous years, unregistered protesters had attended and "tried to cause trouble," as one conference speaker described it. I would come to learn that this was more or less the same arrangement for events on the other side of the porn debate, hosted by sex workers' advocacy organizations and adult industry workers, where security was just as tight.

After waiting in line at the taco truck, I was planning to take my Styrofoam box up to my room for a lunch break, but on impulse, I decided to walk into the room with the electronic sign on the door, flashing the name of the session, PORNOGRAPHY AND THE LAW. Whispering excuses as I stepped over handbags, I made my way as unobtrusively as I could to the stack of chairs in the far corner of the room. Two others had followed me to make this whispering waltz, so Laurie paused her introduction to let us settle in and welcomed those of us who had just arrived. She began again with this line, which she had clearly prepared to rally us into passionate discussion:

"Pornographers are committing the biggest crimes of the century."

Laurie believes there are two main crimes committed by pornographic websites: the crime of obscenity and the crime of facilitating illegal activities, including sexual assault, rape, and human trafficking. "Obscenity is not now, nor has it ever been, legal in this country," she explained. "Obscenity in 2019 is as illegal as it was in 1919 and 1819, but nobody is enforcing these laws. Who could deny that the scenes that are readily available on Pornhub are not obscene?" she asked us incredulously. "Internet pornography is a complete cesspool full of rapists and pedophiles who are documenting their crimes," she explained to nodding heads. "If the laws were enforced, pornographers would be off the streets and where they deserve to be: in jail."

In 1973, the year of the landmark *Miller v. California* decision, over 40 percent of Americans believed that all pornography should be illegal. In 2018, only about one in three (or 32 percent) held this view. For religious conservatives like Laurie, though, the direction of this change from the twentieth to the twenty-first century has been the opposite: a greater percentage of conservative Protestants and other biblical literalists support outlawing pornography today than in decades past.

Upon leaving the conference session, I heard one participant mutter to another, "I just had no idea about any of this." At that point in my research, I could relate. I was confused by Laurie's claims that pornography was illegal and did not understand that she was conflating obscenity and pornography, which, according to the law, are not one and the same. Laurie was correct that the two primary legal concerns for pornographic websites in the twenty-first century are obscenity laws and laws that hold websites accountable for the content of their users. Obscenity laws, though, are notoriously difficult to prosecute, given the Miller test's subjective definition distinguishing obscenity from other forms of speech that are protected under the First Amendment. Many of the antipornography organizations I encountered made a point to emphasize their support for free speech and their opposition to censorship. Yet most, like Laurie's organization, also stipulated that existing laws should be used to prosecute and shut down the porn industry.

The primary strategy of the antiporn movement in recent years has been to advocate for the shutdown of pornographic websites using laws against sex trafficking. Both sides in the pornography debate agree that fear over the enforcement of such laws (and their vague definition of what actually constitutes "sex trafficking") has irreparably changed the pornography industry. Pornography's opponents insist that, thanks to their efforts, crimes of trafficking and sexual violence are reduced. Pornography's sympathizers say it's the opposite: that the push to crack down on sex trafficking makes sex work *more* dangerous. There is one point upon which both sides agree: that sex-trafficking laws situate all internet pornography on tenuous ground.

IN 2014, THREE women whom the courts call Jane Doe Nos. 1, 2, and 3 filed a civil suit against Backpage, a website similar to Craigslist that hosted classified ads for a variety of services and became a frequent destination for those looking to sell or buy sex using its "Adult" section. The plaintiffs were attempting to carry out one provision of the Trafficking Victims Protection Act (TVPA), passed by Congress in 2000, which allows victims to file suit against their traffickers.

In court, all three women told harrowing stories. Jane Doe No. 1 ran away from home when she was fifteen and, soon after, was "trafficked by pimps" who used Backpage. As a result of three hundred Backpage ads, Jane Doe 1 reported that she was raped over a thousand times. As a minor, she was unable to legally consent to sex with an adult. Any sexual encounter between her and an adult customer would constitute rape rather than the crime of prostitution. Jane Doe No. 2 was also fifteen when she first appeared on Backpage, in advertisements placed by her pimp; she estimated that she engaged in up to fifteen sexual transactions per day, resulting in over nine hundred incidents of rape. Jane Doe No. 3, whom the court records also described as a minor but whose age it did not specify, was trafficked by a pimp using Backpage; he placed an ad with her photograph and described her as "new," "sweet," and "playful."

Backpage did little to screen its users or verify their identities. The site required users who posted under the "Escort" page to verify that their age was eighteen or older, but this was little more than cursory. If a user entered an age of seventeen or younger, they would be denied an account but could immediately refresh their browser to enter their age again. If they entered eighteen or above, an account was successfully created. Backpage also removed "metadata" (such as time stamps and geolocation) from photographs posted to the site, which made it harder for law enforcement to track down its users.

Though the court described the practices of Backpage as "sordid," it determined that the site was not breaking the law. Sex trafficking—which the TVPA defines broadly as "the recruitment, harboring, provision, obtaining, patronizing, or soliciting of a person for the purpose of a commercial sex act"—is illegal across the United States, as is prostitution in every state but Nevada. Yet in merely *advertising* these illegal activities, Backpage had not violated the law; nor did it violate the law for its lack of content regulation. The TVPA contains a provision within its final five paragraphs at the end of eighty-six pages: "Nothing in this section may be construed to authorize any injunction against an interactive computer service used by another person to engage in any activity that is subject to this Act." *Doe v. Backpage.com* was dismissed because of the CDA's Section 230, which protected Backpage from civil liability. On appeal, courts affirmed this initial decision, and the Supreme Court refused to hear the case.

News of the *Doe v. Backpage.com* decision sparked outrage among activists and politicians over the lack of accountability of internet providers when it came to sex trafficking. In 2017, two Republican members of Congress proposed nearly identical bills in the House and Senate. In the Senate, Senator Rob Portman from Ohio presented the Stop Enabling Sex Traffickers Act (SESTA), and in the House, Representative Ann Wagner of Missouri presented the Allow States and Victims to Fight Online Sex Trafficking Act (FOSTA). Ivanka Trump championed these initiatives as part of her campaign against human trafficking, as did a diverse array of celebrities (including Amy Schumer, Seth Meyers, D'Brickashaw Ferguson, Tony Shalhoub, and Malaak Compton Rock—who appeared together in a somber public service announcement supporting the bills).

SESTA-FOSTA, as the laws would come to be called, amended the Communications Decency Act of 1996 to remove the protection granted to websites for the content of their users if that content was found to "promote or facilitate the prostitution of another person." In other words, under SESTA-FOSTA, websites like Backpage could be held legally liable for sex trafficking, and the plaintiffs Jane Doe Nos. 1, 2, and 3 would have the grounds to sue the website for civil recovery and restitution. This strategy mirrors antipornography efforts of the 1980s, when first feminists and eventually conservatives attempted to enact laws that would provide a means by which individuals could sue pornographers. But their efforts were never successful. SESTA-FOSTA, though, passed with overwhelming bipartisan support in the House and Senate and was signed into law by President Trump in the spring of 2018.

The same month that SESTA-FOSTA became law, federal law enforcement shut down Backpage and indicted its founders on ninety-three charges, including facilitating prostitution. While few defended the corporate practices (or lack thereof) of Backpage's owners, sex workers who used the site lost one of the means by which they had communicated online with potential clients. Pornographers worried, too, that online porn sites would become the next SESTA-FOSTA target.

THOUGH THE TERM *sex trafficking* is a relatively new one—it was first used in the 1970s, according to one anthropologist—fear surrounding sexual slavery of innocent victims, especially young white women, has been around for centuries. The FBI became a successful government agency in large part as a result of such social panic. In 1910, the White Slave Traffic Act (commonly referred to as the Mann Act, after the bill's sponsor, James Robert Mann) made it illegal to transport women across state lines for "immoral purposes." The nation's earliest sex-trafficking laws grew out of a fear both of increased immigration and, not so different from today's political rhetoric, of immigrants as the source of crime and prostitution. The FBI's first director, Stanley Finch, had a personal obsession with what was called at the time "white slavery." The groups opposing so-called white slavery, including Christian and progressive women's organizations, eventually shifted focus to the broader and more tangible problem of prostitution, whether it was forced or consensual. Early twentieth-century feminists opposed prostitution long before they opposed pornography, and conservative groups have, for over a century, opposed both. Antiporn and antitrafficking activists today on both the left and the right call themselves "abolitionists," believing their mission is to free victims of sexual slavery.

In the twenty-first century, the antipornography movement has been rebranded as a broader antitrafficking movement. Every group and organization I studied that mobilized opposition to pornography also included explicit language about sex trafficking and its connection to porn. The Freedom from Sexual Slavery conference, for example, got its start as an event to oppose pornography but gradually morphed into one dedicated to combating "all forms of sexual slavery." At the FFSS conference I attended, speakers repeatedly applauded the event and, indeed, the overall movement to end sexual slavery as "incredibly diverse" and involving people "of all political persuasions and religious backgrounds." By all scholarly investigations of the antipornography and anti-sex-trafficking movements, this is an overstatement. But it is true that these movements attract two groups that are normally in opposition: feminists and conservative Christians.

Still, this is a movement led by conservative Christians. Though FFSS highlighted one notable antipornography feminist activist, none of the conference sponsors was a feminist group or organization, and the vast majority of sponsors and speakers was affiliated with conservative Christianity. And yet, this event (and the broader antiporn movement) downplayed the role of religion. "Anything religious or political just shuts people down," Laurie, the FFSS speaker, explained. That's why the National Center on Sexual Exploitation (its initials pronounced "nuh-CO-see" by insiders) changed its name from Morality in Media, because it "just didn't have enough traction," Laurie said. Morality in Media was founded by a group of ecumenical clergy in the 1960s to support censorship of sexually explicit media. Today, NCOSE is a nonprofit, nonpartisan, and technically nonreligious organization. "They just stick to the truth," Laurie said of the group, "without putting Jesus on everything." The truth of which Laurie speaks is her belief that pornography and sex trafficking are one and the same.

NCOSE uses *prostitution* and *trafficking*—what it calls the "proper terminology"—instead of *sex work*, given that, according to its guiding values, "the commodification of sex acts is inherently exploitative." Another organization, Exodus Cry, considers itself an antitrafficking group but similarly opposes all forms of sex work, including prostitution, stripping, and pornography, seeing each as "one facet of a much larger system of exploitation." It was founded by conservative evangelicals as a prayer group, but like NCOSE, has since distanced itself from its religious origins. Exodus Cry created the "Traffickinghub campaign" in an attempt to shut down MindGeek's largest website, Pornhub. On Exodus Cry's site, visitors can buy T-shirts, hoodies, and face masks bearing the phrase SHUT. IT. DOWN., in letters that mimic Pornhub's font. Over two million people signed the group's petition to shut down Pornhub and pursue criminal charges against MindGeek executives.

For pornography's opponents, MindGeek and Pornhub represent a long list of all that is wrong with internet pornography, including that the sites do little to regulate content and, thus, are complicit in sexual crimes. In a lengthy exposé titled THE CHILDREN OF PORNHUB, *New York Times* columnist Nicholas Kristof quotes a MindGeek employee who says the company makes use of around eighty moderators, compared to Facebook's reported fifteen thousand. The job is called "content formatter," and according to one reviewer on the employment website Glassdoor, "[B]e aware you're basically a glorified child porn screener, and you will be watching disgusting videos all day." "The issue is not pornography but rape," Kristof writes. "Let's agree that promoting assaults on children or on anyone without consent is unconscionable." In his investigation, Kristof says, videos of sexual assault of both adults and children are easy to find, and MindGeek "profits from sex videos starring young people." Other journalists have corroborated Kristof's claims about Pornhub and have discovered similar incriminating material on other adult websites. While Kristof insists he is anti-Pornhub, which is not necessarily the same as antiporn, his stories repeatedly emphasize victimization rather than consenting performers, tipping the scale of the sex industry toward a single, albeit important, story. Thus, he is aligned with the broader antiporn movement, which largely perceives consensual sex work as an impossibility.

To consumers who believe they are watching consenting porn performers, one sex-trafficking survivor turned antiporn activist, Elizabeth Frazier, says, "I'm calling your bluff because stuff that I was in looked consensual and I'm here to tell you right now, it never was. So every time you go to get porn, you think of that. You think of how I was forced to do that. Even though it looks innocent, it is not innocent." Frazier recalls how she was sexually abused as a child and young adult and forced to make pornographic videos. "Ninety-nine percent of the time it was important that I looked happy and that I was enjoying it and that I wanted to be there." But in fact, that image was masking crimes being committed against her.

Antiporn activists, both feminist and conservative, leave little room for the stories of consenting porn performers because, as they describe it, the stakes are simply too high. The risk of sexual violence and trafficking is too great and their consequences too serious. Phrases like "humanitarian crisis," "epidemic of violence against women," and "public health threat" surround their messages about pornography and its harm to women.

ANTITRAFFICKING EFFORTS APPEAR universal, as they appeal to basic human rights and the premise that no person should be forced into labor or servitude, sexual or otherwise. But in practice, antitrafficking organizations have been accused of exaggerating statistics in order to help the aims of their organizations rather than helping sex workers themselves, many of whom reject the label "trafficking victim." In 2014, *Newsweek* published an investigation about Somaly Mam, a Cambodian trafficking "survivor and activist," as she calls herself, who has given testimony to the United Nations about her experience, written a bestselling autobiography, and also founded a nonprofit organization, AFESIP (Agir pour les femmes en situation précaire, or "Action for Women in Danger"), which "rescued" sex workers in Cambodia and helped law enforcement in brothel raids. The *Newsweek* story drew from interviews with members of Mam's family, community, and schools to claim that much of her personal story was made up, as was the story of one other alleged trafficking victim, who admitted that one of her injuries previously attributed to violent traffickers was in fact a result of a surgery to remove a tumor. Mam was previously featured in the reporting of Nicholas Kristof to highlight the dangers of sex trafficking.

What anthropologist Laura Agustin calls the "rescue industry" has grown in numbers and influence in many places around the world. In 2020, the Trump administration announced committing one hundred million in grant dollars to antitrafficking organizations. Groups like International Justice Mission and Not for Sale claim to "rescue" sex workers from developing countries, but they often channel them into low-paying jobs, where their task is to make products for Americans to buy. Sociologist Elizabeth Bernstein calls these sex workers "brokered subjects," not because they are being trafficked, but because they are being leveraged by the amalgam of governments, nongovernmental organizations, religious groups, and feminist activists to further stigmatize and criminalize sex work.

AFTER THE *NEW York Times* published Kristof's THE CHILDREN OF PORNHUB in December 2020, a number of things happened very quickly. Antiporn activists applauded each subsequent event as a sign of momentum behind their movement. Pornhub released a series of new policies effective days after Kristof's op-ed, though the company insisted the timing was coincidental. They described a new model for the site that would allow only verified users to upload videos and that would prohibit all downloads. Prior to this point, virtually anyone could upload anything. If it was eventually flagged by a moderator and removed from the site, it could already have been downloaded thousands or millions of times to be stored on personal devices. Kristof, for one, is skeptical of the implementation of these changes, and he urged the government to ensure that the company followed through.

For Kristof and antiporn activists, the most effective way to shut down Pornhub is to shut down its revenue stream. This worries porn performers and sex worker advocates, who fear that such changes will make legal sex work (like pornography and camming) more difficult. At the time of the Kristof op-ed and the surge in the Traffickinghub campaign, PayPal had already cut ties with porn and camming sites, including Pornhub, eliminating PayPal as a secure form of payment for internet sex workers. In the days following Kristof's op-ed, both Visa and Mastercard announced that they would cut ties with Pornhub and most of the other websites owned by MindGeek. Critics of the move immediately pointed out that credit card companies pulling out of Pornhub would not actually reduce sex trafficking or the number of nonconsensual videos posted to the site; nor would it significantly affect Pornhub's profits, which are largely driven by ad revenue. But removing these credit cards from Pornhub's payment structure does affect porn performers directly. On the affiliate site, Modelhub, performers can upload videos that users pay to see, and as the largest porn website, Pornhub helps generate traffic to independent performers' other sites. Without Visa or Mastercard, Modelhub performers feared their revenue from the site would be nearly eliminated. One performer who used Modelhub, Mary Moody, put it this way: "Everything I do is legal. I really do love my job. I'm not a victim. Well, now I'm a Visa victim. I'm a Mastercard victim."

A day before the Visa and Mastercard announcements, Republican senator Josh Hawley, who has since blamed feminists for driving men to online pornography and video games, introduced a bill that would allow individuals to sue Pornhub or other websites posting videos of them without their consent. This bill fit neatly alongside other pieces of legislation pushed by antitrafficking activists who have regularly turned to the state for laws to advance their cause. Critics have pointed out that these efforts of anti-traffickers have the unintended consequence of making sex work more dangerous. SESTA-FOSTA, for instance, does not distinguish consensual sex work from trafficking, and in fact, it uses the words *prostitution* and *sex trafficking* interchangeably, without adequately defining either term. Critics also say that SESTA-FOSTA is chipping away at the legality of internet pornography, as pornographic websites could reasonably be found to "promote" or "facilitate" prostitution.

The unintended consequence of laws meant to help trafficking victims is that these laws strengthen the penal system regulating sex work, making it more dangerous. Sex workers' rights organizations have expressed concern that SESTA-FOSTA will actually harm the people it is intending to help: sex workers who have turned to the internet in order to make their work safer. This was a talking point in nearly every session I attended at the Sex Workers United (a pseudonym, or SWU) conference in 2019. In one SWU session, the speaker taught the audience how to engage in what they called "guerrilla marketing" in order to generate business without using the internet. "You've got to get creative and change everything you used to do with clients," they said. For example, they have made stickers and buttons with discreet signaling of their services as a sex worker and have also created an LLC company selling legal services as a way to connect with potential clients as an escort. "You have to be an onion. In the center, you have sex work, but you've got to make sure the outer layers are okay to be seen," they suggested.

Like the Freedom from Sexual Slavery conference, SWU took place in a hotel in the middle of nowhere, in rooms that were windowless, bright, and freezing cold at the start of the day and that slowly warmed as bodies populated the space. As a participant at SWU and FFSS, I was struck by the surprising similarity in aesthetics in both spaces. The majority of participants were white. Black women were the majority of people of color, and I observed very few men of color. For the young people present (folks who appeared to be in their twenties), dyed hair, torn jeans, and tattoos were common. SWU participants were prone to reveal more skin than those at FFSS, but if one judged by looks alone, many of those in the young, white, hipster-looking crowd could have found a place for themselves at either conference. The same goes for the slightly older and professional-looking crowd, like me in my mid-thirties. The only notable demographic difference between the two conferences was that white men, from their fifties to their seventies, made up a notable presence at FFSS. At SWU, almost all the bodies I assumed were male were visibly queer in some way, some wearing dresses and makeup and others donning leather jackets and pants.

Like the Freedom from Sexual Slavery conference, Sex Workers United gives participants a swag bag upon registration. Unlike at FFSS, the swag bag for SWU included an anal plug, small—"good for beginners," the instructions describe—but mighty in its symbolism. "Radically sex positive" was the phrase one speaker used to describe the conference. SWU, like FFSS, sees pornography as but a tree within a larger forest of other forms of commercial sex work and sexual politics. Though people in both spaces talked about the importance of freedom and justice when it came to sex and sexuality, freedom and justice meant very different things.

The most common concerns voiced at SWU were not sex trafficking but, rather, the formal and informal policies making life outside sex work hard for sex workers. One conference session discussed, for instance, the fact that employers in most states can legally fire employees who also work part time in the legal sex industry, due to laws related to off-duty conduct. Banks can refuse to open accounts for sex workers or can close accounts with little notice, claiming that sex work, even if legal, is a high-risk industry or a violation of a morality clause. But as sex workers have pointed out, banks no longer take on the risks of customers who are unable to finance transactions, as most of the internet sex industry relies on third-party websites like OnlyFans or Pornhub's Modelhub. These sites take on financial risks, and indeed, this is how they justify taking a percentage of all performers' transactions.

At SWU, many speakers lamented, in the aftermath of SESTA-FOSTA, the shutdown of websites that had allowed them to post client reviews and "bad-date lists." Without the ability to use websites to screen and interact with potential clients or to discuss clients and work environments with other sex workers, their work becomes riskier. In 2020, Senator Elizabeth Warren, Democrat from Massachusetts, proposed a bill to direct the U.S. secretary of health and human services to study the unintended impacts of SESTA-FOSTA for people "engaged in transactional sex" and the impact of "the loss of interactive computer services that host information related to sexual exchange." At the time of this writing, the bill has been sent to committee for further consideration.

The problem with bills like SESTA-FOSTA and the one proposed by Senator Hawley is that they are unlikely to reduce incidents of actual trafficking, instead, pushing traffickers farther underground. It is true that SESTA-FOSTA may reduce ads for underage victims and video uploads that document sexual violence, but this is very different from reducing actual incidents of trafficking and sexual violence. And, ironically, shutting down websites used by sex traffickers, such as Backpage, has actually made investigations into sex trafficking more difficult without this evidence from web content. No one in the porn wars has advocated that illegal content should remain on websites like Pornhub, but porn-positive activists insist that laws like SESTA-FOSTA are a part of the problem rather than the solution. Instead of targeting traffickers, police departments in many cities reported turning their focus to massage parlors and strip clubs to investigate prostitution cases.

Sex worker advocacy groups, unlike most antitrafficking organizations, insist that decriminalizing sex work is the most effective strategy to protect people who choose to work in the industry *and* to help victims of trafficking. Decriminalization (distinct from legalization, which would require further government regulation and control) would allow sex workers autonomy and control over their work without fear of monitoring, arrest, or prosecution. Amnesty International, the World Health Organization, the Global Alliance Against Traffic in Women, Human Rights Watch, and the ACLU all support a decriminalization model.

As the following chapters describe, both sides of the porn wars share concerns over safety and consent, risks of violence, and sexual health. Yet this common ground is lost in efforts to crack down on sex trafficking within the porn industry, given that the activists leading the charge conflate trafficking with all forms of sex work. Their perspective leaves little room for nuance within the pornography industry because, as they explain it, women's lives are at stake. Yet many women sex workers, the very group intended for "rescue" within the antipornography and antitrafficking movements, insist their lives are no better off in the wake of sex-trafficking laws. In fact, it's the opposite.

CHAPTER 8

Safer Sex (Work)

As the antipornography movement morphed into what insiders now call the "antitrafficking" movement, objective and measurable harm to performers became a key rallying cry. Language of harm has propelled the movement since its nineteenth-century origins: harm to men who succumb to temptation, harm to society's moral foundation, and eventually harm to women who were exploited or objectified through pornography's production and popularity. The integration of health-related and medical language—from Kinsey's use of scientific terms to the Meese Commission's reference to research studies on pornography's harms—emerged in the latter half of the twentieth century either to confirm or to refute these claims. Yet the twenty-first century marks a shift from science, medicine, and health being at the periphery of antiporn arguments to being their very core.

Since 1975, the World Health Organization, the premier global health agency run by the United Nations, has included "sexual health" as one of its domains. The WHO definition includes the absence of physical health risks and what the agency describes as "disorders, diseases, and deficiencies" as well as "the right to sexual information and the right to pleasure." Today, the term *sexual health* is thrown around all the time: by companies selling condoms and vibrators, self-help books, and school districts. It can mean anything from safe sex practices to sexual liberation. Sociologists Steve Epstein and Laura Mamo trace the proliferation of the term to the 1990s, some twenty years after the WHO's initial report on the topic, when it began making regular appearances in both scientific studies and news media. The term has come to legitimize talk about sexuality within the public sphere. Sex itself may still represent what is private, dirty, or deviant, but "sexual health" is an altogether different thing: a moral obligation and necessary component of the broader social good.

What better way, then, to convince others that pornography is bad for them than from the angle of sexual health? An initiative in California in 2016 became exactly the fodder the antipornography movement needed to claim both the moral and scientific high ground compared to the porn industry and many outspoken performers. The initiative, Proposition 60, would have required performers to wear condoms during porn shoots involving sexual intercourse. The antiporn activists, clinicians, and educators I interviewed referenced the condom requirement as a basic, commonsense strategy to protect the health and safety of performers. It seemed a no-brainer and a win-win for citizens as well as porn stars: condom use would reduce the risk of sexually transmitted diseases (STIs) for performers, and it would set an example of safe sex practices for consumers. The industry's rejection of such efforts signaled one more piece of evidence of its disregard for the well-being of performers and the public. But the reality was more complicated.

LONG BEFORE PROPOSITION 60 was on the ballot in California, its creator, Michael Weinstein, and his organization, the AIDS Healthcare Foundation (AHF), had been targeting the porn industry with a condom crusade. Weinstein had filed complaints with the Occupational Safety and Health Administration (OSHA) claiming that the work environment of porn companies was a health hazard. Specifically, he alleged that porn producers violated the state's requirement that employers protect employees who are exposed to blood or bodily fluids as part of their work. Weinstein mailed fifty-eight porn DVDs to OSHA as evidence.

In 2012, Weinstein funded a ballot initiative in Los Angeles County to require the use of condoms in all porn shoots. Taking the issue to the voters was a change of tack from Weinstein's previous efforts, which had led to fines for some pornographers but did not ultimately change industry practices. The Los Angeles County ballot initiative that followed, Measure B, or the Safer Sex in the Adult Film Industry Act, included San Fernando Valley, the so-called porn capital of the world. Weinstein called Measure B a "public health resolution," one that would require an expensive permit for all adult film shoots, a contract signaling that these shoots would follow all health and safety laws, and specifically, that a condom would be immediately visible in any scene of sexual intercourse.

Other than gay porn since the AIDS epidemic in the 1980s, the industry had not adopted condom use as a widespread practice. As an HIV/AIDS activist, Weinstein said his concerns became heightened after one performer contracted HIV while off set and transmitted it on set to three other performers in 2004. The outbreak forced porn producers to stop all shoots for about a month. Since then, many companies halt production when one of their talent tests positive for HIV or other STIs, until contact tracing can be completed. Most companies outsourced this task to a company called AIM (for "Adult Industry Medical") Health Care, which provided testing and treatment for the porn industry, until the company declared bankruptcy in 2011, in part as a result of a legal battle with Weinstein's AHF. Though AIM did not release its data publicly, the media have sensationalized stories of a handful of porn performers testing positive for HIV since the 2004 outbreak. The Los Angeles County Department of Public Health released data suggesting that rates of STIs for porn performers were higher than for the general public, and the Measure B initiative pointed to "widespread transmission of sexually transmitted infections associated with the activities of the adult film industry within Los Angeles County."

Many industry executives and performers insisted that these claims misrepresented the stakes of the ballot initiative. Yes, porn performers, who often do other forms of sex work in addition to pornography, are at greater risk of exposure to STIs due to the nature of their work. Still, positive cases do not automatically indicate transmission on porn sets. Though some performers have tested positive for HIV since 2004, one industry executive pointed to over 340,000 scenes shot between 2004 and 2012 and zero cases of HIV transmission.

In California, porn companies still require STI testing within two weeks of a shoot, and performers are required to bring their test results with them to a set. After AIM Health Care closed in 2011, the Free Speech Coalition, an advocacy organization for the adult industry, established PASS, or Performer Availability Screening Services. Some public officials pointed to the system as a model for contact tracing during the Covid-19 pandemic. "If you do not have a recent test that is all clear, then you will not be allowed to shoot pornography," Andre Shakti, a sex worker who has worked in porn for over a decade, explained to me. "The vast majority of the porn industry abides by strict, strict testing guidelines," she said. "And that's why out of the thousands of performers out there, we only see like one or two STDs in the industry across a year. When compared to the general public, it's so statistically insignificant."

Andre Shakti once shot a scene with a partner who had clear test results for the shoot but who disclosed that she had a skin rash on her stomach. Still, she downplayed the rash and insisted it wasn't contagious. "And I was like, cool, I believe you," Andre Shakti explained to me. "I looked at her tests, and she was telling me it wasn't an STD, it wasn't transferrable." About a week after the shoot, however, Andre Shakti and her girlfriend both broke out in a rash that looked exactly like her scene partner's. "Well, it turns out this woman had something called *Molluscum contagiosum*, which is a physically and sexually transmitted skin rash, and it doesn't have other symptoms, but it is highly communicable," Andre Shakti said. "So, I called her up and was like, 'Hi, I'm having these symptoms, and so it looks like your thing is in fact contagious, and I just wanted to give you a heads-up,' and she blew up and was like, 'How dare you accuse me of this?' and had this huge reaction." The phone call gave Andre Shakti the impression that her scene partner and the director of the scene had intentionally deceived her. She decided to call the porn company, "not expecting them to really do anything for me," she explained, given that it was the first time she had worked for them and given that the other performer was someone Andre Shakti described as "very prominent in the industry." "And you know what they did? They fired the performer and director and said they would never hire them again. They tore out the set and disinfected it and everything, and they started including *Molluscum* in their testing panel after that. I was just so impressed, and I think it goes to show that the porn industry is really actually committed to sexual health, in a way that most people wouldn't even know."

In the lead-up to the 2012 election, when Los Angeles County voters would decide on Measure B, proponents drew from what they deemed commonsense logic about safety and health. Even negative STI/STD tests are not foolproof, Weinstein would often tell reporters: it can take nine to eleven days after exposure for a positive HIV case to appear on tests. Condoms, however, are 90 to 95 percent effective against the spread of HIV. Shelley Lubben, a former porn performer and founder of the anti-pornography group Pink Cross Foundation, endorsed Measure B, giving public testimony about how if the measure had been enacted while she was on porn sets, she would never have contracted STIs. Another member of the Pink Cross Foundation, Jan Merritt, said she didn't trust the industry testing system. "I've done a scene with twenty-five men and even though I was assured that all of the STD testing had been taken care of by the producers, in my heart I realize now that this was probably a lie because I never saw the tests for myself."

Some current porn stars, including Jenna Jameson and Aurora Snow, supported Measure B, but most performers speaking out were speaking out against it. Nina Hartley, a longtime performer, used her background as a registered nurse to explain the dangers of required condoms for porn shoots. When scenes can last for hours, friction caused by the condom could be painful and physically harmful, she insisted. The Free Speech Coalition, the lobbying group that represents the porn industry, pointed to the existing rigorous testing standards and the rights of individuals to make choices for themselves.

Although heralded as an effort to protect porn performers, Measure B, its opponents insisted, was in fact an effort to put the industry out of business. In a public letter to Los Angeles County voters, Steven Hirsch, a second-generation pornographer and the founder of one of the largest porn companies of the San Fernando Valley, Vivid Entertainment, emphasized a loss of jobs and revenue that the county would experience if the measure passed. Andre Shakti, who paid attention to the debate even though she was not living in Los Angeles at the time, put it this way: "It's being sold as trying to protect these poor porn performers who don't know how to take care of themselves, and they are all disease ridden, and we need to help them. But what it was actually doing was setting up a system to put these new laws in place that would make it very difficult and expensive for porn companies to abide by and then setting up an elaborate fining system. So, it would actually make it very difficult to shoot legit porn in California."

In the 2012 election, 57 percent of Los Angeles County voters supported Measure B, and one month later, the Safer Sex in the Adult Film Industry Act became law. Steven Hirsch and Vivid Entertainment, which uses a "condoms optional" policy, almost immediately took the county to court. Vivid was one of the most powerful porn companies in the country. It was the first to release porn on DVDs and the first to hire contract stars. Today, it competes with MindGeek's empire by specializing in parody films of popular movies (*Star Wars*, *Batman*, *Cruel Intentions*) and celebrity sex tapes, like that of Kim Kardashian. For a brief spell in the early 2000s, Vivid required condoms for its shoots. But since then, according to Hirsch, testing effectiveness increased dramatically, and so, the company changed its policy to allow performers themselves to choose whether they used condoms during their shoot. Vivid, along with Wicked Pictures, stopped all production for a short time in 2010 when one of its performers tested positive for HIV. There was no indication of subsequent HIV transmission on set, and the companies resumed production.

In its lawsuit against the Los Angeles County Department of Public Health, Vivid Entertainment argued that Measure B burdened the company's right to free expression and violated performers' First Amendment rights. The court disagreed and ruled that the condom mandate did not significantly violate constitutional rights, given that its purpose was to achieve the "substantial government interest" of reducing rates of STIs and because there were alternative avenues of free expression. In 2017, five years after Measure B passed, a County Board of Supervisors finally passed a law detailing regulations for adult film video permits in conjunction with the ordinance. For $1,671, producers could apply for a permit to make adult films in Los Angeles County for two years, provided they agreed to all the terms detailed in Measure B. Regulation. Enforcement of the permit, however, remains uncommon.

As the Measure B legal battles unfolded, Weinstein and the AHF broadened their efforts to the entire state of California, funding Proposition 60 for the 2016 election. Like Measure B, Prop 60 would have required all adult film performers to use condoms during sexual intercourse and all producers to purchase a permit and pay for performer testing. The initiative went one step farther than Measure B, in providing language that would allow any California resident to sue an adult performer they observed in a sex scene that didn't make a condom "immediately visible." The ten largest California newspapers all opposed Prop 60, as did both the California Republican Party and the California Democratic Party, and most AIDS advocacy and health organizations, LGBTQ organizations, and organizations for the adult industry. Opponents of virtually all political persuasions saw flaws in the ordinance: it would cost the state over a million dollars each year to enforce, and that cost could be made up only partially through permits; California would lose revenue and jobs as porn producers left the state; and it would encourage porn performers to shoot underground, increasing their risks rather than reducing them. Yet, despite widespread outcry, polls in the months preceding the election suggested that a majority of California residents was in favor of the measure. As the election drew nearer, support diminished, and Prop 60 narrowly failed on Election Day.

Antipornography organizations used the Prop 60 debate to side with Weinstein and claim concern for the health and well-being of porn performers. Weinstein, though, has never described himself as antiporn. The *New York Times* has called him the "CEO of HIV," because he wields significant power and resources in the world of HIV/AIDS treatment and health care. The AHF has a huge budget of around $1.4 billion a year, comparable to that for Planned Parenthood and about half the size of the annual budget of the World Health Organization. It generates revenue from pharmacies and clinics that provide primary care and uses that revenue to provide free care to more than seven hundred thousand HIV/AIDS patients around the world. Criticisms of Weinstein in the twenty-first century parallel those of Anthony Comstock in the late nineteenth century: both white men of significant influence who, to their detriment, avoided collaboration even with organizations with which they shared goals.

One of Weinstein's critics, a fellow AIDS activist, called him "the Koch brothers of public health," meaning that his ideology drove the organization and its efforts, and that ideology did not always align with that of other activists and health workers. Weinstein is virtually alone among major AIDS activists in his outspoken opposition to drug therapies used to prevent HIV, for example. He has called PrEP (for "pre-exposure prophylaxis"), a daily pill that has proved highly effective at preventing HIV transmission, a "party drug" that will encourage young people to engage in risky sex practices. In this way, Weinstein again parallels religious conservatives who argue against allowing minors to access contraception because it will encourage them to have sex.

Weinstein's logic that adding condoms to porn shoots will reduce the spread of HIV and STIs is true on the surface, but it misses the bigger picture that the law, along with its pricey permits, would be obeyed by only a few of the biggest and most profitable companies, leaving fewer opportunities for legitimate work for performers. Production companies that moved underground would be even less accountable to testing procedures. Further still, the risk of STIs and HIV to performers actually lies outside the porn industry, as performers increasingly turn to riskier forms of sex work in order to make a living.

PORNOGRAPHY IS IN fact one of the safest forms of sex work, a point brought up repeatedly by my interview respondents, compared to street-based sex work, which is the riskiest. Macro-level factors, including social class, race and ethnicity, gender identity, and citizenship, all correlate with whether individuals get involved in riskier forms of sex work. In one interview study of sex workers in New York City, conducted by the advocacy group the Sex Workers Project, researchers found that the vast majority of street-based sex workers reported unstable housing, drug or alcohol dependency, and near-daily confrontations with police, many of which resulted in arrest.

Capria, one of the activists I met at a sex workers' rights conference, insisted that if the antipornography movement were truly interested in the health and safety of sex workers, it was targeting the wrong sector of the industry. At first glance, Capria, a fifty-six-year-old Black woman who identifies as a Christian and lives in the suburbs, doesn't seem like a sex worker advocate. Yet she spends her days helping transgender women working in street-based sex work find HIV testing, providing them with condoms and lubricants and collecting clothing and food to give to them. She compares these women to a friend of hers who works in porn. "She's making good money just doing stuff with her toes. She's got a website, and she does foot jobs, where she just masturbates dudes with her feet. She's certainly not being trafficked," she told me with a short laugh. The women Capria works with, for their part, are doing what she called "survival sex work." "The reason they're doing survival sex work is because society is very slow about accepting them for who they are, and they are not allowed to be able to work in regular society as the person they choose to be," she said.

On the side, Capria started selling sex toys through a company that facilitates at-home parties (an adult version of Mary Kay or Tupperware) and used the proceeds to fund her activist work. "It's really just me and a couple of friends, and it's just the little bit we can do. I'm working on becoming an official nonprofit, but right now it's just us concerned citizens trying to make somebody else's life a little bit better." Her group also served LGBTQ homeless youth. "That's just where my heart is. I'm a momma who jumped out there and started helping everybody's baby."

Activism found Capria relatively late in life. Nearly twenty years ago, when she was in her thirties, a close friend was nearly killed by her abusive husband. "Her husband was a truck driver, and he was away from home more than he was home," she shared with me. "One day," Capria said of her friend, "she found out that she was pregnant with their fifth kid. She goes to a doctor, and one of the routine tests that they did was for HIV, and she tested positive. And of course, that's a shock to her, because the only person she'd been having sex with was her husband. She confronted him, and he beat her within an inch of her life. She almost lost the baby." The event was a catalyst for Capria. "I was just feeling so angry and helpless, like there wasn't a whole lot I could do for her other than to just be a shoulder to cry on. So, I decided to volunteer my time at a HIV nonprofit organization, and even then, I felt like I wasn't doing enough. So, I just decided to volunteer some more," she recalled.

For one of her volunteer gigs, she ended up at a local prison, where she led a support group for transgender women. Across the country, transgender women of color are disproportionately much more likely to live in poverty, experience homelessness, and be unemployed compared to the general population—all of which leads to the greater likelihood of incarceration. Capria saw her work helping sex workers as having "a ripple effect," as she described it. "You know, if I'm teaching a person who is selling their body how to protect themselves sexually from getting a disease or contracting an STI, then I've kept them from spreading something [with which] they could endanger three, four, five, twelve families down the line."

The real public health crisis, according to activists like Capria, is not a lack of condoms within the porn industry, but a lack of physical and mental health care and social support services for sex workers who are most at risk. With higher rates of workplace and housing discrimination and unemployment and homelessness, transgender women of color are much more likely to turn to sex work than any other group. A 2015 national survey of transgender respondents found that nearly 20 percent reported having engaged in some form of sex work in exchange for money, food, or a place to sleep. Black, Native American, multiracial, Latina, and Asian trans women were more likely to report this experience than white trans women. Regardless of sex worker status, more than 20 percent of Black transgender Americans reported a positive HIV status, compared to 0.6 percent for the general population. Black transgender women may face harassment from police regardless of whether they are sex workers, because police are likely to assume they are. For those who have worked in sex work in the past year, 41 percent reported that they had been physically attacked, and 36 percent reported being sexually assaulted.

"Indoor" sex workers generally have more autonomy and greater protections from these risks. Those who work in porn, from home or in a public establishment like a strip club or massage parlor, are less likely to have unstable housing, substance abuse problems, or run-ins with or arrests by police than those who are street-based. The former can more effectively navigate dangerous clients because they can screen them in advance, using telephone or online correspondence. If sex workers work under an employer, that employer can serve as a buffer, with rules and regulations to help manage clientele. Yet a third party, whether an employer, pimp, or trafficker, can also pressure or force women to engage in sex acts without their consent. Still, rates of reported violence are lower for this group than for those working on the streets.

In the New York City study, the majority of indoor sex workers, like those who were street-based, cited finances as motivation for their work. Indoor sex workers typically enter into sex work when they cannot find other work or when other work does not offer sufficient pay. Many indoor sex workers interviewed by the Sex Workers Project were immigrants (some undocumented) who had trouble finding jobs that paid even minimum wage. Many used their income from sex work to support their families and to save to eventually leave the sex industry. All sex workers in the industry face stigma associated with their work and often lack support services and resources, including adequate health care, banking and loans, and legal assistance. The health and safety concerns of the porn performers and industry advocates I interviewed were not the policies of porn sets, but rather, the formal and informal policies making life outside sex work hard for sex workers.

Sex workers struggle to find mental and physical health care providers who are empathetic and informed about their work. Performers typically pay out of pocket for their health care. Without adequate physical mental health support, the result can be deadly. In a period of less than three months in 2017 and 2018, five women who worked in porn died unexpectedly. Olivia Nova, age twenty, died of sepsis as a result of a urinary tract infection. Olivia Lua, age twenty-three; Yuri Luv, age thirty-one; and Shyla Stylez, age thirty-five, died of drug overdose. August Ames, age twenty-three, died of suicide.

Leya Tanit, a ten-year veteran in the porn industry, founded the organization Pineapple Support in 2018, after the deaths of these young performers. Named after a commonly used safe word, Pineapple Support aims to help people working in the adult industry find free or subsidized therapists who are "sex-worker friendly and kink-aware." "The reason this resource is so important for people working in the industry is stigma," Tanit explained to an interviewer. Sex workers must navigate the social stigma they face alongside the stress of working in the industry. It's not that pornography performers are more likely to need therapy than the rest of the population, Tanit insisted, but rather that they cannot count on supportive providers. "People are people, and they struggle with mental health no matter what walk of life they are from or what career they have."

Shortly after Pineapple Support was established, Pornhub announced it would partner with it. The director of Modelhub said in a press release, "Here at Pornhub, we stand in solidarity alongside sex workers, their advocates, friends, families and allies to help call attention to the violence committed against sex workers. We won't stand for it, and neither should you." Critics accused the move as a PR stunt to detract attention from MindGeek's complicity in sexual crimes and other illegal activities.

BOTH SIDES IN the pornography debate articulate as their goal the health and safety of sex workers. Yet when laws and policies affecting the pornography industry are involved, a chasm emerges. The porn-positive movement insists that laws should help ensure that the industry is safe and legitimate. Antipornography activists seek regulation of the industry, in the hope of extinguishing it entirely. In debates over whether condoms should be required on porn sets, pornography's opponents use the language of health and safety to insist that their perspective is objective concern over the health risks associated with contracting HIV and other STIs. Yet, as the next chapter will describe, arguments over harm within the porn industry are never value-neutral and, in fact, can reveal conflicting beliefs when it comes to choice, consent, sex, and exploitation.

CHAPTER 9

Hot Girls Wanted

Jade, a porn performer and former women's studies major, told me that Gloria Steinem, the famous second-wave feminist who opposed porn, inspired her entry into the industry. For one of her college classes, Jade was assigned Steinem's "A Bunny's Tale," published in *SHOW* magazine in 1963. The essay, written as a diary exposé, was based on Steinem's experience working for eleven days undercover as a "Bunny" at the Playboy Club. Far from the glamorous world portrayed in *Playboy* magazine, Steinem detailed low pay, constricting uniforms, blistered feet, and taunting and harassment from male customers and staff alike. The topic of porn and women's sexuality came up all the time in Jade's classes some forty years after Steinem's undercover experiment. The questions were the same as those that had sparked feminist division over porn in the first place: Is porn always bad for women? Can it ever be empowering? What should be done to reduce harm? Is the solution to get rid of the porn industry or to try to make it better?

These are questions without easy answers. As sociologist Bernadette Barton has described, feminist division over porn stemmed not so much from opposite beliefs, but from differing vantage points. The antiporn side narrowed in on the broad problem of a patriarchal society and its constraints, what sociologists call "structure," while the porn-positive side emphasized individual choice and autonomy within that structure, what sociologists call "agency." The result was antiporn feminists, like Steinem, who emphasized exclusively how pornography reflected and contributed to a misogynist society. While sex-radical, or anticensorship, feminists resisted any effort to shame, blame, or censor women who participated in sex work, their perspective insisted that antiporn feminists perpetuated stigma against women who made the choices available to them within the structural constraints of the misogynist world in which they lived. For Barton, neither side is more or less feminist than the other. But those fighting in the porn wars don't see it that way.

As Jade read "A Bunny's Tale," an idea popped into her head, an idea that Steinem herself anticipated with fear after publishing her piece. Jade wondered if she could write a similar essay about auditioning for a porn shoot. She wondered if such an essay could launch her own career as a writer and journalist, as it had done for Steinem. Jade was in a better position than most to embark on such a task, having grown up in the San Fernando Valley, what she had known since grade school was considered the porn capital of the world. She was also naturally thin, conventionally attractive, and white. After she graduated from college without a job lined up, she returned home to live with her parents to save money and figure out what she wanted to do with her life.

She kept thinking about "A Bunny's Tale" and decided to google "how to be a porn star." The first step, according to all the advice offered on the internet, was to get an agent. And so, she searched for "Adult XXX agencies" and found one run by two men who touted twenty years of experience in the industry, both having been award-winning performers and directors before becoming agents. Without giving herself a chance to reconsider, she snapped some selfies with her cell phone and submitted them. She got a fast reply and agreed to meet the men at a nearby diner.

After looking her over, the agents said they would sign her and asked if they could all drive to one of the agent's apartments to talk about next steps. When Jade arrived, the agents asked her to undress. They commented on her body, telling her she should do more squats and grow her hair longer. One of them kissed her. Startled, she told them she needed more time to think about their contract, got dressed, and left. Over the following days, the agent who kissed her started texting with come-ons, asking her if she wanted to watch porn with him so he could see her turned on. She decided to text the other agent that she wasn't ready to commit to a contract.

Jade returned to her life working low-paying jobs and living with her parents. A year passed, and she was feeling hopeless about beginning a career. After applying unsuccessfully for jobs even tangentially related to her field, she decided to contact a few other porn agencies, but found them to be even more unappealing than the first. So, she returned to the two men she had met a year earlier, who, it turned out, were still interested in representing her. She signed a contract and quit her job at a coffee shop, because her agents said she had to be available at any time for the shoots they would book for her. At twenty-nine, she was considered too old to play "teeny-bopper," but she was also too petite and small-chested to play a MILF (the typically voluptuous role of "Mom I'd Like to Fuck"), so her agents warned her she might have trouble getting booked.

That warning proved to be true, and Jade managed to book only about one scene a month. Her entry into the porn world was not the lucrative experience she had hoped for, but in fact put her even deeper in debt. She had to pay for her own wardrobe (lingerie, countless pairs of lacy underwear, and high heels) and beauty regimens (body hair removal, hair extensions and blowouts, manicures and pedicures). She had to pay for STI testing every two weeks and was told by her agents that she must attend the *Adult Video News* (*AVN*) Awards, the so-called Oscars of porn, so she could meet potential directors and producers. For this, she had to cover the cost of a hotel room and food.

She was beginning to think that her agents were in fact sabotaging her work by refusing to book shoots as she continued to deflect the one agent's advances. Jade has since come to learn that this kind of behavior is common practice in the industry, while also acknowledging that "it's absolutely sexual harassment." Agents will "text you something inappropriate or flirt with you and then that automatically puts you in a position where you already feel like your ability to work is dependent on that." She, like many of her peers in the industry, began working as a stripper for extra money.

Then she received an offer from her agents for a three-scene shoot that would pay for her to fly to a European city in addition to a ten-thousand-dollar payout. The production company was known for its rough scenes, but Jade knew performers who booked with them regularly. The offer was for three anal scenes, and as part of her contract, Jade had to try double anal. She had never had anal sex, personally or professionally, and certainly not with two penises at the same time. But her agent insisted she would never get that kind of money for a single booking in the United States, and that the shoot would increase her visibility as a porn star. Ultimately, Jade accepted the offer, feeling she was too broke to refuse.

After turning down her agent's offer to help her "practice" for the scene, Jade took off for Europe. It wasn't her first shoot involving rough sex, and she stressed to me that her experiences with other production companies specializing in BDSM (bondage, discipline, sadomasochism) were overall positive ones. This trip, which she called "a complete nightmare," was very different. Jade managed to get through the first two scenes, and while she described them as painful, she was also glad to have them finished and looked forward to her compensation. The final day of shooting, however, which was supposed to involve a forty-five-minute scene recorded without pausing, ended up lasting the entire day, over five hours of intense and painful penetration. "It went on and on. If I grimaced in pain, then [the director] would stop shooting and tell me to smile. 'Ten more minutes,' he kept saying. I couldn't feel anything. I texted my agents that the shoot had no end in sight, but received no reply until the next day."

It wasn't until her return flight home that she began to realize the extent of her physical and emotional injuries. During the shoot, the director had applied a numbing cream to her anus, so she could better tolerate the rough sex. The consequence of this was that Jade was unable to recognize when the penetration was damaging her body. She ended up in urgent care, where she was told she had an infected rectum. To make matters worse, she had an allergic reaction to the antibiotic prescribed to treat it. Porn stars have to pay for their own health care, as it is not included in their work contracts. Exacerbating the financial strain of her medical bills, Jade lost months of work because she couldn't book shoots until she was fully healed.

When a check finally arrived in the mail, the payout was less than half of what she'd been promised. Angry and shocked, Jade called her agent, who insisted that he had never promised her ten thousand dollars. When she reminded him how difficult and traumatizing the experience had been, he blamed her for the extended shoot time. "He insisted it was 'just business' and [that] I wasn't even qualified for the 'kiddy pool,' since I was being a 'baby,' and that I 'lacked drive' to thrive in the industry. I wanted to tell him to take two dicks up his ass." Jade left the agency and stopped working for commercial porn shoots. She shared her ordeal with friends in the industry, and eventually, a lawyer from the group the Adult Performer Advocacy Committee (APAC) offered to take her case pro bono to sue the agency and the porn production company for the compensation owed to her. "Hopefully they'll settle, because I really don't want to go to court," she told me with a nervous laugh.

The tragedy of her story, Jade believes, is that it is a common one for women in the porn industry. "Not necessarily the European trip part, but how I was treated by my agents is extremely typical of how women enter the industry," she said. "They go to an agent who is operating a sketchy business from his apartment in the Valley. He doesn't even have an office, you know, and he signs you. And then there's a lot of stories like mine, where if you don't sleep with your agent, he ices you out and you don't work." She mentioned Derek Hay, owner of the agency LA Direct Models, who is currently being charged with twelve felony counts, including pimping and pandering. Multiple women have accused Hay of coercing them into prostitution, telling similar stories that they signed a contract with him; moved into model housing, often leaving their homes thousands of miles away; and then couldn't get booked for porn shoots. Instead, Hay offered them escorting opportunities, essentially forcing them into this kind of sex work because they lacked other options. Hay has denied the allegations against him.

Jade's departure from commercial porn seems, at this point in her story, like that told by antiporn activists for decades—for example, Linda Marchiano, aka Linda Lovelace, who left the porn industry and joined feminist rallies to speak out about the sexual, physical, and emotional abuse she encountered at the hands of her husband, who also worked as her agent; or Shelley Lubben, who worked as a sex worker in the 1990s and contracted HPV, which led to cervical cancer. Lubben quit making porn, became a born-again Christian, and founded the Pink Cross Foundation to help other women get out of the industry. Elizabeth Smart, who was kidnapped from her Utah home in 2002, at the age of fifteen, and held captive and raped daily for nine months before being rescued by police, has become an outspoken opponent of pornography, saying that her captor looked at hard-core magazines, which made her "living hell" even worse.

Jade's story, however, has a different arc from those of these survivors turned antiporn activists. "I'm not antiporn," she told me, "I'm pro-woman." "That's the biggest thing women feel in the industry, that no one cares about their stories. There's the narrative 'What do you expect? You know, you should expect to get raped.'" Jade is eager for this narrative to change, because she has hope for women who want to stay in the industry. "We're trying to work in a professional environment and industry just like any other." For her, the singular perspective that women should leave porn because it's bad for them leaves no alternative for women who actually want to continue making it, but to do so free from abuse and exploitation.

For a time, Jade signed with a woman-owned agency that she hoped would offer more support and professionalism than the harrowing ordeal with her former agency, but she was ultimately disappointed. "There was one time where a guy who worked for the agency decided to book himself as one of the talent for one of my shoots." Jade found this both uncomfortable and unprofessional. "Agents just shouldn't book talent with themselves," she said. The reason, she explained, is that an agent cannot prioritize their client, the performer, if they themselves are also involved in the performance. When the roles of performer and agent are entwined, the agent no longer is in a position to represent what's best for you, Jade explained, but rather, what's best for the shoot or the agent's personal interests.

Jade ultimately decided to become an independent performer, free from agencies and, most of the time, from directors and production companies, preferring instead to create porn entirely on her own terms. She uses sites like OnlyFans to maintain contact with her followers and earn money. She does mostly solo work, but will occasionally work with other performers she knows and trusts. She told me that on commercial porn shoots, "the content was always cringeworthy, like 'Now I fuck my adopted daughter and my adopted son.' Ew." (Commentators and industry insiders have noted a rise in the genre "fauxcest," or family role play porn, since it was first listed on Pornhub's most popular searches in 2014.) Now that Jade has left commercial porn, she sets the terms of her scenes. "I feel good and empowered," she said, "and I only want to be an independent content creator. I just want to do sexy art that actually inspires me."

————

IN 2017, RASHIDA Jones of *Parks and Recreation* and *The Office* fame hosted a panel based on the documentary she'd produced, *Hot Girls Wanted*, which premiered two years earlier at the Sundance film festival before being released on Netflix. The panel was set up to appear like a debate stage, giving people with multiple perspectives a chance at air time. On one couch sat the two directors of the film, Jill Bauer and Ronna Gradus; a prominent antipornography feminist activist, Gail Dines; and Kourtney Mitchell, the only person of color on the panel, who was a member of Veterans for Peace and an outspoken opponent of men's porn consumption. On the other couch, presumably the "pro-porn side," was Mark Kernes, a lawyer who had worked for *Adult Video News* for thirty years; and Nadine Strossen, a constitutional law professor and former ACLU president. Despite Kernes's and Strossen's impressive résumés, they were cast as villains, repeatedly challenged by every other person onstage, including Rachel, a young white woman, who also sat on the "porn side," perhaps because of her six months in the industry, though her perspective now was clearly one of anger and opposition.

The directors of the film said they did not seek to make a film focused on victimization in the porn industry, but that this was what they had found when they followed the lives of several young women who had signed up with Florida-based porn agent Riley Reynolds. A twenty-three-year-old white man with a criminal record, Reynolds is a leading character in the documentary film as owner of Hussie Models LLC. He specializes in women new to porn, who are typically eighteen to twenty-one years old, and who respond to his advertisements on sites like Craigslist for "Free Flight to Miami" to launch their careers as porn stars. In the trailer for *Hot Girls Wanted*, the first words spoken after a clip from a porn video are from Reynolds: "Every day, a new girl turns eighteen."

The website for Hussie Models features photos of dozens of current models, all smiling and topless. Most are petite and white—a type Reynolds calls in the documentary "teeny-boppers." The "Apply" link on his website contains a lengthy questionnaire, including a place to upload photos. There is also an FAQ page, where the answers repeatedly emphasize a model's control and freedom. "Your body—your choice. You are in complete control of what you do or don't do on camera" and "Communicate if your [*sic*] uncomfortable—your safety is our number one concern." The film *Hot Girls Wanted* tells a different story, one where women may not be physically forced into sexual encounters, but where they end up doing things they don't want to do.

One of the film's most powerful stories is about Tressa, aka Stella May, who leaves her small town and working-class family to join Hussie Models in the hope of making a better life than her parents and peers back home. After just a few months in the industry, though, Tressa struggles to get booked for shoots and instead remains in sweatpants on the couch as her roommates put on heavy makeup and platform heels to prep for their shoots of the day. We hear from Tressa's boyfriend and her parents about how disappointed they are that she has chosen this path, and we watch as Tressa tells her boyfriend casually, while taking a bite of pizza, that she has managed to book a high-paying shoot but that it involves bondage. Hussie Models's Reynolds has already explained to the audience that Tressa is going to have to do more "niche shoots" and that she'll have to "tone up" to remain competitive in the industry. Tressa recounts the bondage scene she agreed to with a tone of resigned indifference. "I was strapped together and just force fucked, hard core. No vomiting today," she says numbly, implying that in days past, her scenes had caused her to vomit. "I didn't eat breakfast, so nothing really came out." She shrugs dismissively as somber music plays in the background. The message conveyed throughout Tressa's story is that, although she willingly flew to Miami to work for Hussie Models, pornography, at best, degraded and humiliated her and, at worst, assaulted and abused her. At the end of the film, she returns to her hometown, where she expresses regret about her time in the industry.

When Kernes, the *AVN* lawyer on the panel, pointed out from the stage that Reynolds was not a typical porn agent—he is based in Florida rather than California, where most porn is shot, and it appears he is not a licensed and bonded entertainment agent—other panelists pushed back. "I've met 'licensed and bonded' agents, and the agent who was 'licensed and bonded' was the worst agent I've ever met," Rachel, the six-month porn veteran, said with anger and impatience in her voice. That agent was from LA Direct, the company accused of forcing women into escorting and what Rachel called "bachelor parties," where women are expected to have sex with men after stripping for them. Being licensed and bonded "almost makes them worse," Rachel said, "because it makes them feel like they have more power than the girl walking in there." Though Rachel has attempted to get out of her contract with LA Direct, the agency told her she must pay three thousand dollars to do so, and so, her nude picture remains on its site.

Nadine Strossen, the constitutional lawyer and former ACLU president, jumped in to say that Rachel absolutely had a strong case for legal action against LA Direct, but insisted that her story did not mean that the entire porn industry was exploitative. Rather, the industry should be forced to follow practices that protect the rights of their workers. The Adult Performer Advocacy Committee (APAC), which connected a lawyer with Jade to support her case, is one organization leading this mission. It published a "Performer Bill of Rights" to explain the basic rights to which all performers should be entitled, including knowing in advance the content of a shoot, fellow performers, and pay; declining any requested act or stopping a scene if feeling uncomfortable or unsafe; and avoiding pressured negotiations or unexpected changes during a shoot. APAC also provides performers with a list of businesses (ranging from therapists and doctors to insurance agencies) that provide sex worker–positive services, and it offers a mentoring program so that veteran performers can model and offer advice to new performers on how to successfully navigate the industry.

The problem is that while organizations like APAC can advocate for performers' rights, they cannot implement sanctions when companies or agencies violate those rights. "The porn industry's not going into collective bargaining! What kind of world do you live in, Nadine?" Gail Dines shrieked in exasperation when Strossen emphasized workers' rights. Dines, who has spent her career as a feminist sociologist speaking out against pornography, frequently pointed out from the stage that the porn industry is largely controlled by business*men*, whom she described as more interested in their profit margin than supporting women. For Dines, pornography is like patriarchy on steroids. Widespread misogyny is bigger than pornography alone, but pornography feeds off and into patriarchal culture.

DOCUMENTARIES, MAGAZINES, AND newspapers are quick to report on tragedies and abuse affecting women in the porn industry. The five performers who died unexpectedly in 2017 and 2018 attracted headlines for a time before the media moved on. The most sustained interest was to the life and death of August Ames, who grew up as Mercedes Grabowski in Ontario, Canada, before beginning her career in porn in 2013. She would eventually star in nearly three hundred movies. The media were quick to report on events taking place days prior to her death: a storm of Twitter criticism against Ames that her husband, a porn producer named Kevin Moore, believed led to her death. The criticism surrounded Ames's declaration on social media that she would not do a scene with a cross-over performer—that is, a man who performs in both straight and gay porn. The backlash was swift and intense, with criticisms ranging from accusations of homophobia to one tweet that said Ames should "swallow a cyanide pill." Ames's final tweet before her death was "Fuck all y'all."

The media used Ames's story to talk about cyberbullying, internet trolls, and toxic social media culture alongside the dysfunction of both the pornography industry and the people who work in it. A *Rolling Stone* feature article declared that Ames's death "revealed a schism between the gay and straight communities in the porn industry." That article, titled DEATH OF A PORN STAR, is reminiscent of the 1987 PBS *Frontline* piece about Colleen Applegate, "Death of a Porn Queen."

Journalist Jon Ronson, who had already produced a successful podcast about the porn industry, decided to investigate Ames's death at the urging of her husband. Yet what he discovered for his series, *The Last Days of August*, was that Ames's suicide was likely spurred by far more than social media hostility. That tweet about the cyanide pill was in fact posted after her death. What Ronson found, echoing the talking points of feminists from decades earlier, was that Ames had been victim to aggressive men throughout her short life. As a child, she was sexually abused by her grandfather. As an adult, she was married to a man who some described as controlling and emotionally distant. As a performer, less than two months prior to her death, she performed with a male actor, Markus Dupree, who violated her boundaries and consent. "It felt like rape," she texted a friend, "but I was in a 'fuck it' mood and I was just pissed and wanted to get paid for the bullshit I went through." She finished the scene, but it was never released.

In the wake of the MeToo movement, the media has increased its coverage of male porn performers accused of assault. For decades, both performers and journalists have alleged that iconic porn star Ron Jeremy groped them without their consent. It took years of these allegations piling up to result in an industry response against Jeremy, who has appeared in more than two thousand films since 1979. Finally, in 2017, the EXXXOTICA Expo banned Jeremy from attendance, and in 2018, the *AVN* Awards followed suit. In 2020, he was arrested and charged with twenty counts of rape and sexual assault dating back to 2004. Jeremy has pled not guilty, but if convicted, he could face up to 250 years in prison. Another porn star much younger than Jeremy, James Deen, has been accused by nearly a dozen women of sexual assault. He has denied wrongdoing and continues to work as a performer and win *AVN* Awards, though some companies refused to hire him after allegations first surfaced in 2015. Since Ronson's podcast *The Last Days of August* aired and named Markus Dupree as the male performer who allegedly assaulted Ames on set, many other women came forward to share similar stories. The industry did nothing. Dupree later became an "Exclusive Contract Star" by Brazzers, a MindGeek-owned company that is one of the largest and most popular of the twenty-first century.

Abuse and violence against female porn stars may make the news, but rarely do they lead to significant changes in the industry. Many women who have accused men in the industry of violence insist that the problem is sexual harassment and assault in the workplace; the problem is not pornography itself. Yet their stories are used by antiporn activists to insist that pornography overwhelmingly mistreats women and pressures them into out-of-control lifestyles where they depend on men for economic security, drugs, and self-esteem. Gail Dines and other feminist activists present consent in the porn industry as an extremely rare commodity. "The majority of women are young and up against predators who use you and know how to manipulate you," Dines has pointed out. "This idea that you're actually consenting is ludicrous."

Manipulation includes that "free trip to Miami" advertised by Riley Reynolds in the *Hot Girls Wanted* documentary, which was in fact not free at all. Reynolds will cover upfront travel costs to Florida or California, provide "model houses" for girls to live in, and even pay for wardrobe, makeup, and required STI testing. But he runs a tab for all these costs and then charges his models for expenses after they book a shoot. According to performer Lenna Lux of Hussie Models, she worked for four months and never saw a paycheck, because all her earnings went to paying Reynolds back for her expenses. In fact, she eventually received a bill from him for $891.64. An industry lawyer agreed to work with Lux to take Reynolds to court.

Despite the critical and moralizing tone of *Hot Girls Wanted*, Reynolds says that applications to work with him only went up since the documentary was released on Netflix. And here is a sticking point for a feminist position against pornography. Antipornography feminists must assume that they know what is best for women collectively, and that individual women who indicate otherwise—by flying to Miami to work with Reynolds even *after* seeing *Hot Girls Wanted*—are little more than dupes. "False consciousness," in the words of Marxist philosopher György Lukács, who coined the phrase based on Karl Marx's discussion of why factory workers throughout Europe put up with dismal working conditions and did not instead revolt. Certainly, they far outnumbered those who ran the factories, yet the minority bourgeoisie managed to control the proletariat workforce, convincing them that it was in their best interest to continue their work without organizing unions or making a fuss. Similarly, antipornography activists suggest that the reason women participate in pornography is that they think it is good for them when actually it is not.

THE SINGLE NARRATIVE of pornography's exploitation of women falls short in explaining women from middle- and upper-class backgrounds who graduate from college and decide to work in porn even when they have other, so-called legitimate choices to become successful outside the X-rated marketplace. Lola Davina, a sex worker who also writes self-help books for sex workers, describes writing in her diary at the age of ten, "I want to grow up to be a prostitute." As a white middle-class woman who would eventually obtain advanced degrees, she had multiple career paths she could follow. She chose a career in sex work spanning decades when, in San Francisco in the early 1990s, she auditioned for a live peepshow theater, which she describes as "not your typical strip joint," full of Riot grrrl punks, feminist and queer activists, and sex positivity.

Duke University freshman Miriam Weeks, aka porn performer Belle Knox, also insisted that she chose to work in porn over alternatives. She told *Rolling Stone* in 2014 that she thought waitressing was more demeaning than performing in porn and that she preferred the latter as a more feasible and effective way to pay her hefty tuition bill. Weeks repeatedly told journalists that she was not exploited and that she loved performing in porn. And still, many did not believe her. Media commentary was swift in the aftermath of Weeks's doxing, or being publicly outed as a porn star. Sherri Shepherd on *The View* said about learning of Weeks's story, "My heart just breaks. It really, really does." In a CNN interview, Piers Morgan insisted, "I've got no moral hang-ups about what you do or the industry you're in," but he then went on to describe his imagined reaction if Weeks were his own daughter. "If I'm honest, I've got a young daughter, and if she were your age and she decided to do this, I would be pretty upset. I would be pretty angry." Weeks ultimately didn't pursue a career in porn. The *New York Post* reported in 2018 that she had been accepted to New York University Law School and enrolled under an alias. Even though she gave no reason to believe she was exploited or abused during her time in the industry, her story has been used to confirm a key message of the antiporn movement: that "hot young girls," once they know better, leave the industry.

ON THE OTHER side of the porn debate, the question sex workers have asked rhetorically in my interviews with them is: Leave the industry *for what?* Historian and porn studies scholar Mireille Miller-Young argues that in the early twentieth century, Black women—who, as this book later describes, are often the subjects of disturbing racist content in pornography—found sex work to be less exploitative than the alternatives available to them. Working as "the help" within white households typically involved hard physical labor, long hours, little pay, and likely sexual assault and rape. Black women who performed in stag films and worked as prostitutes were undoubtedly victimized by racist ideology, but abuse and exploitation of Black women was true in virtually any work that would have them, including domestic labor and the broader Hollywood industry.

Today's reality is that women continue to face misogyny, objectification, and violence in many facets of social life, well beyond pornography. Approximately 44 percent of adult women in the United States have experienced rape or other forms of sexual assault. Most teenage girls and young women report experiencing pressure, coercion, or outright violence when it comes to men's entitlement to their sexuality, and this is an even more likely reality for African Americans, Latinos, and Native Americans. As Andrea Dworkin, the prominent antipornography activist in the 1970s and '80s, has observed, sexual violence happens everywhere, "in homes, in cars, on beaches, in alleys, in classrooms."

Antiporn feminists like Dworkin and Dines insist that pornography both draws from and contributes to this larger system of patriarchy and misogyny. But in turning virtually all their efforts toward pornography as an exceptional source of the problem, they may undermine feminist efforts to improve the lives of women more broadly. The gender pay gap and many women's continued economic dependence on men, the low rates of satisfaction among women in heterosexual marriages, and the high rates of gendered violence especially against poor women and women of color are all examples of how patriarchy is insidious and damaging. If mainstream commercial pornography sets the standard for feminist outrage, does this leave more "ordinary" forms of patriarchy off the hook?

The exploitation of women within the pornography industry is a problem bigger than porn, many sex workers insisted to me. Feminist pornographer Tristan Taormino put it this way: "Would you rather pick fruit in ninety-five-degree weather for nine hours or get fucked hard and choked for one hour? Are people having the best time of their lives right now in a warehouse packing our stupid shit in packages for Amazon? People who are on their feet for too long, who are not being offered enough breaks, who are being given these minimums that they have to meet in an hour, that if they don't pack this many fucking boxes they are going to get in trouble? Just because it involves sex doesn't mean it's automatically worse. Porn is operating under capitalism, not outside of it. It's just smack dab in the middle of it. Like people who are picking our food, people who are working in the banking industry, people who are working in the service industry. It's all the same system." As the next chapter goes on to describe, the capitalist system provides constraints and opportunities for the internet sex industry and for pornography debates.

CHAPTER 10

Hustlers

Carol Leigh coined the term *sex worker* in the early 1980s to describe what was formerly named through derisive euphemisms: *prostitute, hooker, working girl*. She first used the term at a feminist conference where she was asked to speak on the "Sex Use Industry." She found that the term *sex use* diminished her role within said industry, focusing only on presumably male consumers, so she suggested the alternative. The press picked up the label when covering the one-woman play Leigh wrote and performed. When her character, the Scarlot Harlot, calls herself a "sex worker" to try to explain herself, her mother, upon hearing what seems the unimaginable pairing of "sex" with "worker," conjures up an absurd scenario: "What, you work in a dildo factory?" Today, sex work is a broad category. Over the course of my research, I met many people whose jobs involved sexuality and the internet but who weren't working in pornography.

When I interviewed Beth, a thirty-four-year-old Black woman living in the South, she described herself as a "body worker." She manages three different websites to advertise the various dimensions of her work. First, boasting a degree in health and wellness and years of experience, she works as a fitness coach and created a program integrating dance and hip-hop. Her individual training sessions can be virtual or in person and she tends to work with clients who are mothers and caretakers and people who are LGTBTQ.

In addition to working as a personal trainer, Beth also works as a kink coach, offering virtual consultations to either one-time or recurring clients. It's "a lot of heterosexual women," she said with a laugh, referring to her clients, women who want to be exposed to different kinks they enjoy and learn how to perform them safely. On her kink coach site, Beth advertises her experience as a sex worker, dominatrix, speaker, and performer. She's working on more official credentials, like becoming a certified sex coach. Even without this training, she said she "has a natural gift for this sort of thing," and all too often she encounters "folks who've got the paperwork but have no experience and have no idea what they're talking about." Beth credited her success to her real-world experience.

Beth uses a third website to advertise her services as a kinky fitness coach, for which she blends her work and knowledge in BDSM and fitness. "I think anybody who gets a personal trainer is engaging in an erotic power situation. You know we hear all the time, like, 'My trainer killed me today,' with all smiles and satisfaction. So, essentially, I am just playing off of that existing power dynamic. I see that as very much a part of an erotic dynamic even for people who are not conscious of it." Kinky fitness classes are "just a regular workout class," Beth explained, but they make this erotic power dynamic explicit. "I'm telling you to do the push-ups or do the crunches, but I may be using some BDSM toys—I may have a paddle or frock or things like that."

When Beth was in her early twenties, with the optimism and spontaneity typical of young adulthood, she decided to quit her job in the Midwest and move to Las Vegas. "I ended up meeting a guy who was like, 'Yo, let's go to Vegas and make some money.'" Life didn't unfold exactly as she had planned: she had a child, split up with her boyfriend, and became a sex worker and activist—but she wasn't complaining. Reflecting on how Las Vegas shaped not only her future career pursuits but also the values that guide her work, she told me, "Looking back now, I can see I always had a very activist lens. I was in jail once, and I organized the women to show their breasts at a certain time, so that the guards would give us soap and menstrual pads." She laughed as if the story were a fond memory. But she also shared the heaviness of activism, the toll she observed its taking on herself and other Black women, and how victories were few and far between. "We were organizing on behalf of sex workers, drugheads, women who had former charges on their records, and it was very easy to dismiss them." Her work involved protesting, following court cases, and launching informational campaigns to support incarcerated women and women who are victims of domestic violence and police brutality.

As part of her self-care practice, she started performing spoken-word poetry. She left sex work and became active in her local BDSM community. She started working as a dance fitness instructor, eventually organizing dance parties that were "liberation parties," what she described as "events for women rooted in healing justice to just come in and celebrate their autonomy and their bodies." When these women learned of Beth's involvement in BDSM, they wanted to know more about both the physical varieties of BDSM (spanking, bondage, etc.) and also the emotional (punishment and role play). "So, I started hosting workshops and performances, just spaces where people could be kinky." "I just kept building," she told me. Eventually, Beth blended her interests, experience, and passions into the career she has today.

Feelings about sex work aside, Beth is an example of both the constraints and possibilities within the internet economy and what is often described as "late-stage capitalism." This term was first circulated among Marxist scholars in the 1960s and '70s to describe a type of capitalism distinct from its earlier forms with regard to the extent of what can be commodified—which is virtually anything. In the words of American Marxist theorist Fredric Jameson, this new economy became "catastrophe and progress all together." It represented progress as technological innovations allowed for workers to increasingly set their own terms for their work and avoid the nine-to-five toil. Work was no longer constrained geographically; industries transcended the globe; progress became a winner-take-all economy, where the winnings were greater than ever before, like the billions in profits seen by leaders at MindGeek. But the new economy represented catastrophe, too. As wealth for the top 1 percent has skyrocketed since the 1970s, the median earner's income has stagnated. The employment rate for people aged twenty-five to thirty-four was lower in 2019 than in 2000, even for those with college degrees. The catastrophe lies in the fact that the new "gig economy" has created jobs where employers do not commit to the future or well-being of their employees, who are considered largely replaceable.

Beth avoided many of the pitfalls of the gig economy by creating her own businesses. Coaches are everywhere across both sides of the porn wars—life coaches, sex coaches, marriage coaches, kink coaches, porn addiction recovery coaches. Like the authors of marriage manuals in the 1950s and sex advice books in the 1970s, coaching in today's porn wars operates as an industry that profits from the idea that our sexual experiences are a core part of our overall happiness and life satisfaction. Entrepreneurs like Beth become successful if and when they can convince consumers (no longer bound by geography) that they need and want their services in a competitive market.

ONE IRONY OF internet porn is that as online videos proliferate, the industry simultaneously plummets. Most antipornography activists and organizations claim it is the opposite. Some reference annual earnings of $97 billion, which can be traced back to a 2007 "study" conducted by a Utah-based company that "compiled statistics from more than 10,000 sources, including the pornography industry, media reports, and anti-pornography organizations." No additional details were offered by the company, and the estimate was circulated among antiporn groups and in the national news. Others estimate annual earnings at $10 billion but credit a source, Forrester Research, which *Forbes* magazine has found never to have published such a statistic—instead, estimating in 1998 that earnings in the porn industry ranged between $750 million and $1 billion. According to the research firm IBIS World, adult and pornographic websites earned nearly $300 million in the U.S. market in 2005. In 2020, that number had grown to about $800 million. These earnings, though, are driven largely by ad revenue and benefit primarily website owners and their tech employees, rather than performers themselves.

Described to me as the Amazon of porn, MindGeek has either bought out or forced out of business nearly all its competition. Now that users can watch porn for free online, magazine and DVD sales have dropped. The number of commercial porn shoots have declined. Tristan Taormino, who worked in commercial and independent porn in the 1990s and early 2000s and who today makes a living through public speaking, writing, and facilitating workshops and trainings, told me that she stopped making porn because "there's just simply no money." Production companies have asked her to make additional films, but as she describes it, "they're like, 'We're hanging in there and trying to figure out how to make this work, so can you make, like, three of the same movies as that one movie you made before, but for half the price of that one movie, and can you shoot it all in one day?' And my answer to that is, 'No, I can't.'" With the rise of free streaming sites thanks to MindGeek, producers can no longer offer performers what Taormino considers fair pay.

MindGeek is not only a lead villain in the antiporn movement. For the porn-positive activists, educators, and performers I interviewed, it represents the corporate takeover of an industry to the detriment of most people working within it. The vast majority of performers cannot book enough shoots to make a living through porn alone, and they certainly can't assume they will become rich and famous. They can also expect that any content they create on their own, including live-streaming cam sessions, will show up on sites like Pornhub. Many performers have taken an "if you can't beat 'em, join 'em" mentality and have started producing clips specifically for Pornhub, as a way to entice viewers to other sites with better payouts.

The result is that, in the words of Taormino, "Most porn stars I know today have like eight hustles. They're doing OnlyFans and clips, and they're doing feature dancing and appearances, and then they're making porn, and many of them are also escorting. People have all sorts of gigs. It's not like in the 2000s where you could basically be the contract girl, and all you had to do was make a few movies a month and make some public appearances, and you were good. And now it's like every sex worker I know is on the hustle, and no one is rolling in money anymore. I mean there was so, so much money, but it's just not there anymore, unless you own one of these Tube sites."

The hustle that Taormino explained was true for every sex worker I interviewed. They worked multiple jobs, in and out of sex work. Jade, introduced in the previous chapter, worked full time in the industry, serving as her own agent and marketer to get booked on porn shoots and also to maintain an OnlyFans page and social media presence to advertise her content. Jessie Sage worked as a phone sex operator, cam model, and porn performer and also wrote a regular magazine column, hosted a podcast, and taught college classes in women's and gender studies. Rayne, a cam model and amateur pornographer, made a little money on the side by reviewing sex toys and also worked full time in retail. They planned to go to graduate school eventually, to become a sex therapist. Melissa Harris, who used the stage name "Mz. Berlin" and once worked full time as a director for a porn company, reported various part-time sex work gigs, including writing scenes for porn shoots, escorting, doing phone sex, and producing her own and others' content. Since the industry's decline, she made an exit strategy to leave sex work entirely and dreams of someday opening a chain of med spas.

IN 1996, WHEN Americans were beginning to adjust to life with computers and dial-up internet at home, Jennifer Ringley, a junior at Dickinson College in Carlisle, Pennsylvania, decided to set up a webcam in her dorm room. *The Real World*, the hugely popular MTV series that premiered in 1992, had just seen more than ten thousand young adults audition for the latest season. Unlike its approach of editing endless tapes into twenty-two minutes of high drama, Ringley's webcam was on air all the time. When Ira Glass of NPR's *This American Life* asked Ringley what people saw on the website she created, Jennicam, she responded, "Oh nothing, really. I write email, I sleep. I have friends over. Pretty much just regular college life, as far as I know. It's just a camera that sits in my room and takes a picture every three minutes and uploads it." What Jenni broadcasted—now called "lifecasting"—was the mundane but also the explicit (nudity, masturbation, and sex), which is what enticed many of the half a million people who visited her site each day. "I sleep naked, and I get changed. And when I get out of the shower, I'm all wet. There's no hurry to put on clothes," Ringley remarked casually. The first time she was beginning to have sex with a partner on camera, the site crashed because of the number of people suddenly logging on.

Ringley insisted that her intention was never to get rich off the site, nor to become an amateur pornographer, but rather, to embark on a kind of experiment in taking technological innovations to an extreme. "It's not about exhibitionism," she said. "It's an experiment in letting people view a person's entire life without editing." In 1998, she decided to start charging a membership fee to help cover what she described as fifteen thousand dollars in annual costs to keep the site up and running. On December 31, 2003, when she was twenty-seven, she shut the site down after PayPal closed her account for depictions of nudity that violated company policy. By this time, there were porn parodies of her and other sites that offered similarly voyeuristic live streaming of solo and partnered sex acts.

Because porn consumers today can watch what seems like a limitless stream of free porn, online sex workers must cultivate specific services that are different from the endless queue of Pornhub clips. They must sell something that customers can't get elsewhere and are, thus, willing to pay for. Sociologist Angela Jones, who studies the camming industry, calls this "embodied authenticity," or the emotional labor of online sex work that proves performers' "realness" to their clients. One of her interview respondents, Amelia, described it like this: "Guys don't spend all that money because they want something fake. I mean, they come because they want to believe that it's a real woman they're talking to and it's a real person. And that they can tell you what to do; they can get exactly what they want." The key here is Amelia's phrase "they want to believe that it's a real woman." Less important is that it *is* a real woman, expressing her actual desires and personality, which may in fact get in the way of male clients who anticipate that they, in Amelia's words, "can get exactly what they want." The interaction between performer and client offers the client the kind of control he does not have when passively watching porn.

Reality TV is not so different. On some level, the audience understands that the famous opening lines of *The Real World*—"find out what happens when people stop being polite and start getting real"—is setting up not "reality" but, rather, edited entertainment. What one TV critic, comparing *The Real World* to *The Monkees* (the real band that began as a fictional one for a TV sitcom), also captures is how the world of sex on the internet blurs reality and fiction. Is the pleasure of the cam model or porn performer real or fake? Andre Shakti, who has worked in both porn and camming, tells me that's the wrong question to ask. "Sure. Encouraging performers to use whatever they want, like choosing sex toys—that is going to help them get off, which of course could lead to more authentic experiences and usually lead to more genuine pleasure. But," she goes on, "it's still work. Like a job. There are days when I'm more into it than others, but that doesn't affect my performance."

As early as 1993, adult entertainment was attempting to integrate new technologies to make porn interactive. A disk inserted into a CD-ROM drive could respond to keyboard commands, for example, allowing the user to direct a *Penthouse* model to "Take Bra Off," among other preprogrammed instructions. The model, licking her lips, begins the show with a seductive "Let's get interactive." Another program, *The Interactive Adventures of Seymore Butts*, advertised as an "adventure game," involved helping Butts on a quest to hook up with his beautiful neighbor, Brianna. Computer expo events and technology magazines mostly banned the advertising of such technology, for fear of ruining the home computer's reputation.

Nearly three decades later, camming as a genre thrives on a sense of realness through interactive performances that happen in real time, live-streamed to either a group or a private audience. Cam models typically require clients to buy tokens (or payments) before the models advance their performance. Users on the lowest tier may get a model to remove her shirt, while those on the highest may get a model to masturbate to the point of orgasm. Teledildonics (computer-controlled sex toys) were described in the 1990s as the sex of the future. In 2006, OhMiBod was among the first companies to actually produce and sell them. Its vibrator, which sold for sixty-nine dollars, plugged into an iPod and vibrated to the beat of the music played. Today, the latest versions connect to the OhMiBod Remote App and offer an assortment of shapes and sizes. For cam models, using an OhMiBod vibrator means that clients can pay to control the sexual experience: the greater the tips, the greater the vibrations. In 2020, teledildonics were described as a tool for safe sex amid a pandemic.

CAMMING AND PORNOGRAPHY are two distinct but overlapping genres of adult entertainment. All the porn performers I interviewed also worked as cam models as a way to make additional money. In sociologist Angela Jones's study of more than one hundred cam models, the vast majority purposely sold recorded content in order to market their brand and compete in the online sex marketplace. Many reported that sharing some content for free was how they dealt with "capping," the illegal practice of recording and sharing videos without a performer's permission.

In Jones's study, the most common motivators for camming were the good pay with a flexible schedule and limited time commitment. Jessie Sage, the cam model and phone sex operator I interviewed, put it this way: "A lot of people who are doing online sex work are parents who have to work around kids' schedules, a lot of them have disabled kids, a lot of them are caregivers. A lot of them have their own disabilities that prevent them from having nine-to-five jobs." Sage, a white woman in her forties and a mother of three, has a graduate degree in philosophy and is a certified birth doula and a freelance writer. She never imagined that her most reliable income would come from sex work, but she chose her career path over alternatives. "There's flexibility and autonomy that I just haven't had with other sorts of jobs," she told me.

Since its start in 2016, the website OnlyFans has been popular among cam models and independent pornographers. On its "How It Works" webpage, the company notes, "As far as we're concerned, if you use social media and produce your own content, you should be using OnlyFans. Whether you're uploading tutorials, tips, behind the scenes footage or just endless selfies, a lot of your followers would be willing to pay for them!" Though the company markets itself as a way for virtually any entrepreneur using the internet to promote their business, its reputation is for porn. In compliance with the law, its terms of use require that all people using the site are over eighteen and that they do not display obscenity. This means the site has a long list of words that are banned, ranging from *abduct* to *zoophilia*. But it also permits pornographic content: explicit sex scenes and nudity.

The London-based company began in 2016, and by 2020, it was reporting eight hundred new creators every day. One cam model who has been with the site since the beginning, Dannii Harwood, reported earning $257 in her first month. In November 2018, just two years later, she reported monthly earnings of just over $50,000. The company's model is fairly straightforward. "Content creators" who use the site charge a monthly subscription for followers to be able to see their content. They can also charge a "pay-per-view" (PPV) rate for single images or videos, which is how cam models create custom products for their clients. OnlyFans takes 20 percent of all these fees, while creators keep the rest.

In 2021, OnlyFans made national headlines when the company suddenly announced its plan to ban sexually explicit videos from the site. One of the groups that took credit for the company's announcement was the National Center on Sexual Exploitation, the organization that lobbies for the criminalization of porn and a crackdown on sex work. Since 2013, NCOSE has published an annual "Dirty Dozen" list of companies it targets as "major contributors" to the sex-trafficking industry (companies that repeatedly make the list include Google, Amazon, and Twitter). In 2021, NCOSE added OnlyFans for the first time, declaring that the site "is the latest iteration of the online sexual exploitation marketplace." NCOSE referenced the Covid-19 pandemic as contributing to the growth in OnlyFans popularity for content creators and consumers. Both sides suffer, NCOSE insists, as the site "normalizes prostitution among young persons," fuels pornography addiction, and causes "psychological, emotional, and physical harm."

The OnlyFans announcement about the change to its content came shortly after Republican representative Ann Wagner of Missouri—who also authored FOSTA, the 2018 Fight Online Sex Trafficking Act—gathered more than one hundred signatures to support a letter to the Department of Justice urging a criminal investigation of OnlyFans. The letter was endorsed by NCOSE and referenced an independent investigation conducted by the BBC that did uncover evidence that OnlyFans, like sites owned by the MindGeek empire, had problems in its age-verification system and that users could find illegal content depicting minors.

OnlyFans said publicly that scrutiny from banks is what prompted its decision to remove pornographic content. The company feared that it would become the next Pornhub, with major credit card companies, like

Visa and Mastercard, refusing to work with the site. Yet, as many sex workers made clear in the aftermath of the announcement, OnlyFans executives would be relatively unaffected by the site's new policy. Instead, sex workers using the site—for whom it was often a major or primary source of income—would instantly lose access to that platform. After an outpouring of criticism on behalf of sex workers and their allies, OnlyFans walked back its decision less than a week after its original announcement, saying the company's intention was never to harm legal sex workers and that executives had negotiated a deal with financial institutions to continue their partnership.

This wasn't the first time OnlyFans was criticized by sex workers for its reactive policies. One year prior to the back-and-forth over permitting sexually explicit videos, in August 2020, Bella Thorne, of Disney kid show stardom, reportedly made two million dollars in less than one week after starting an OnlyFans account and advertising a nude photo costing two hundred dollars for followers to view. The problem was that the photo disappointed many, given that her bare breasts were covered with her arms. They demanded a refund, and OnlyFans complied. Soon after, though, the site announced a new policy that capped pay-per-view rates at fifty dollars and tips at one hundred. A company statement insisted the new policy had nothing to do with Thorne but, instead, was meant to protect users from overspending. The problem was that many cam models depended on the site's PPV and tip functions to take custom orders and interact directly with clients.

Thorne apologized on social media for any harm she may have caused to the sex worker community, insisting that she was their ally and advocate. Many sex workers responded skeptically, insisting that Thorne could never understand the work required. "It's not a get-rich-quick scheme," Jade, who maintained an OnlyFans account, told me. After leaving commercial porn, Jade had relied on OnlyFans to independently produce and distribute content. "People all over Twitter be like, 'Do you know you can make eight thousand dollars a month selling pictures of your feet on OnlyFans and you don't even have to show your vagina?!' It's like, no, that's not it at all. You have to work hard to build relationships with your fans. You have to provide quality content. Like people who, you know, shoot a video on their cell phones and then upload it, and they're like, 'How do I get a fan? This is harder than it seems,' and yeah it is. It's a business. You have to approach it as a business."

Rayne, a nonbinary performer, told me they ultimately quit camming because it was just too hard to get a foothold in the industry. "I love taking nudes. I love filming myself. It's a really good time, and I knew a bunch of cam performers and a bunch of people who made amateur pornography, and I thought, 'Wow, that looks like a lot of fun. I just wanted to give it a try and see what I could make of it.'" Rayne set up an account for camming, but then didn't know what category to advertise in. "I didn't know if I should market myself as trans masculine, because so many people who are trans masculine are very thin. So, I wasn't fitting in with what they call 'Twinks.' But I also wasn't technically a BBW [big beautiful woman], and so it was really hard to figure out. Like, is there even a market for my body? And how do I tap into that market? And how do I not tie everything to my own personal self-esteem? If I put up a video and no one buys it, that's not necessarily a reflection on me." Though camming allows sex workers independence and autonomy, cam artists are also forced to work within the structure of websites themselves and, thus, are dependent on predetermined categories and algorithms to be visible, or invisible, to potential clients.

Different cam sites have different structures, and models choose some sites over others based on their preferences. Some sites get a lot of traffic but pay less per minute, whereas other sites may get fewer visitors but have a better payout structure. The participants in Jones's study reported huge pay disparities. Only 11 percent of her sample (12 of out 105 models) had ever earned more than $10,000 in a month. Most of the top 12 earners reported monthly incomes of between $2,000 and $5,000. Alisha, the top earner in Jones's sample, had been a cam model for seven years and reported her highest monthly income of $54,000. Jones found that cam models who were the most likely to be successful were cisgender women who performed femininity in socially desirable ways, playing up qualities of youthfulness, singleness, and bisexuality.

This is also true in mainstream commercial porn, where performers, especially women, are fit, thin, mostly white, and gender normative—in short, women who look like the stereotype of a porn star. But independent porn creators as well as cam models use individualism and personalization as marketing tools. Since most porn performers can no longer make a living exclusively performing in commercial porn, many make money by creating custom videos for their clients. Some make money from selling personal clothing, like panties; others, by selling subscription services so that clients will receive a regular stream of exclusive new content and, depending on the pay tier, may exchange texts or phone calls.

While mainstream commercial porn shoots have declined in the twenty-first century, independent and amateur markets have grown to reflect a wide range of performer genders, skin colors, and sizes and a wide range of clients' sexual interests. In turn, content that was once considered too niche or marginalized for commercial studios has become a part of their purview as companies seek to expand profits. For instance, porn studies scholars Sophie Pezzutto and Lynn Comella describe how commercial companies like those owned by MindGeek are taking an interest in trans-gender porn, "transforming it from a niche genre into a staple of commer-cial pornography production." Driven by both increased visibility and acceptance of transgender people in broader society as well as market opportunity, trans-identified men and women and nonbinary sex workers have greater opportunities in porn than ever before. This means greater safety within the sex industry for a population most vulnerable to violence. Reports of homicide suggest that transgender victims who have been killed while engaging in sex work, mostly trans women of color, were working as escorts or prostitutes, not in pornography.

For decades, the pornography industry has named distinct markets (gay porn, interracial porn, Asian porn, anal sex, group sex, and so on), but the internet has taken this market segmentation to a new extreme. All porn websites place videos into at least one category. Algorithms determine which categories, and which videos within categories, users see. To maxi-mize user interest and exposure, commercial studios produce films that fall under as many categories as possible. For independent performers, though, their identities may either maximize or limit their market. Appealing across genres, and thus amassing multiple audiences to increase potential income, is easiest for performers whose identities place them on multiple axes of privilege: those who are conventionally attractive, straight or bisexual, white, and cisgender.

WHEN I ASKED Andre Shakti, a white, queer thirty-year-old woman, how she would describe what she does for a living, she called herself a "professional slut." In recent years, she had stopped working with commercial porn studios, though she still occasionally performs for the independent queer-owned CrashPadSeries. At the time of our interview, most of her income came from work as a professional dominatrix and stripper. The day before our interview was the grand opening for her dungeon, which she had created in her home's garage. "I'm so stoked about it," she told me. "Definitely a milestone in my sex worker career so far. It just means more clients, more money per client. I don't have to pay to rent spaces anymore. I don't have to travel anywhere, which cut into my unpaid labor time. I can take same-day appointments if I want to, because it's my space. And I get to rent it out to other people and make passive income off of it, so that's pretty great." For the variety of work she performed, in addition to some income from freelance writing and sex coaching, Andre Shakti reported typical earnings of forty to fifty thousand dollars annually before 2020. She helped cover living expenses for her aging father and was still paying off student loan debt, so she hoped the dungeon would increase her earnings.

But then the coronavirus pandemic eliminated her in-person sex work almost overnight. The onset of the pandemic sent both sides of the porn wars into panic. With people stuck at home, the world's largest porn site, Pornhub, was boasting a record number of daily visitors by March 2020 and began to offer complementary membership to its premium-access program. Antipornography groups doubled down on their messages about the harm of internet porn. But sex workers were not celebrating: Porn shoots were canceled. Those who offered in-person services, like Andre Shakti, lost their clientele. Some strip clubs successfully sued the government over withholding relief funds from the Paycheck Protection Program, which had excluded businesses that profited "through the sale of products or services, or the presentation of any depiction or display, of a prurient sexual nature." But independent sex workers had few options to recuperate lost income. Turning exclusively to camming and solo content online meant increased competition and, for many, a struggle for reliable and adequate income. Still, many made their way in the hustle of online sex work. In transitioning more of her work online, Andre Shakti decided to create her own website, a virtual strip club, where users could buy tickets and tip the night's performers, who were fellow strippers from across the country.

Pandemic aside, porn work in the digital age is precarious. And yet, in the words of feminist studies scholar Heather Berg, "precarity brings insecurity, but it also nurtures the nimble creativity workers need in order to navigate uncertainty in life and work." In her interview-based study of porn performers, Berg finds that many describe parallels with other forms of work, including drudgery, anxiety, and exploitation, and at the same time name the pleasure of porn work as a distinguishing feature. This, she insists, is what makes sex work uniquely poised to undermine and resist capitalism's overwhelming and stifling hold in the twenty-first century.

CHAPTER II

Shades of Grey

In a 2010 study often mentioned by antipornography activists, psychologist Ana Bridges and her coauthors analyzed the fifty highest-selling porn movies from 2005 and found that nearly 90 percent of them included scenes of physical aggression. In 94 percent of those scenes, women were the targets of the aggression, and they responded with either neutrality or pleasure. Critics of the study have pointed out that the majority of instances coded as aggression were spanking, not exactly the kind of sexual violence we most fear. Bridges coded for frequency of aggression—Was it there? Was it not?—rather than for qualitative differences, such as if aggression stemmed from a consensual BDSM scene. Some research suggests that the prevalence of violence in mainstream porn has gone down since the Bridges study of 2005 films, theorizing that there was an uptick with the advent of internet porn, but that violence became less common between 2008 and 2016. Still, twenty-first-century porn is more violent than pornography in decades past. And that violence is directed unevenly, with members of marginalized groups (including both cisgender and transgender women of color) most likely to be depicted as victims.

IN 1985, THE Dark Bros., two of the most notorious porn producers of the decade, released *Let Me Tell Ya 'Bout White Chicks*, which they advertised as "the controversial scorcher that made the Dark Bros. notorious!" Riding on its success, they released that same year a sequel of sorts: *Let Me Tell Ya 'Bout Black Chicks*. In *White Chicks*, Black men performing as pimps and criminals convince white women to become enthusiastic participants in a variety of sex acts. In *Black Chicks*, the race and gender roles are reversed, and it is *Black women*, appearing on-screen as maids and nannies, who banter to one another about their desire for *white men*.

In the most controversial scene from the film, and arguably the most controversial porno scene of the decade, one maid tells the others about a time when, as she puts it, "I let these two whiteys do me at the same time." The flashback shows her character masturbating on a bed when, all of a sudden, two white men in KKK hoods and robes appear from behind the headboard. In thick Southern accents, they talk about their plans to rape the maid. Rather than responding with fear, she taunts them, "You guys can go ahead and try if you want to, but I don't think you can do anything down there." "Shut her fucking mouth with your dick," one of the Klansmen, whom the other calls "Grand Master," orders the other. The maid again casts doubt on their masculine aggression: "You're going to have to prove it to me. I ain't afraid of no ghosts!" The sex scene that follows, scripted and directed by white men for a white male audience, shows the maid expressing pleasure not pain, enthusiasm not trepidation. Yet the cultural reference to a Klansman, the epitome of racist terrorizer of Black communities, having sex with a Black domestic worker, one of the few occupations available to Black women and that often made them victims of sexual assault, makes the maid's seemingly willing participation all the more disturbing. The woman playing the maid, a performer calling herself Sahara, began appearing in fewer movies after the film's release, though it's left to speculation whether her experience with that particular film was a direct cause.

I first learned about the Dark Bros. and their films at the Freedom from Sexual Slavery (FFSS) conference I attended in 2019. In a session on Black women and pornography, the presenter, a Black woman named Pamela who boasted a Ph.D. in clinical psychology and identified herself as a feminist, used *Let Me Tell Ya 'Bout Black Chicks* as an example of how racism saturates the broader pornography industry. Both the films that preceded and the ones that followed *Black Chicks* profit from racist violence, Pamela told us. Yet, in the decades since the Dark Bros. released *Black Chicks*, the conference audience learned, racism in pornography had gotten worse thanks to the internet. Before beginning her presentation, Pamela warned us about the disturbing content we were about to see. She added that in order to "combat hypersexualized images," we must know what they are. "It's important that we not look away." Not everyone in the audience was convinced, it seemed, and as Pamela began her talk, pausing intermittently to play censored clips from hard-core films, I watched a steady stream of people head for the exits.

Pamela was careful to point out that the abuse and sexualization of Black women and girls stem from the broader culture, not pornography alone. "Images in porn are not new. They are deeply rooted in our nation's history. Although pornography profits from these images and stereotypes, pornography didn't really create them." Pamela referenced the legacy of slavery and the racial stereotypes that persisted long after emancipation: that Black women were sexually deviant and permissive, and that white audiences believed they had a right to see Black women's bodies on display. She told the tragic and disturbing story of Sarah Baartman, a Black woman from South Africa whose body was made a spectacle across nineteenth-century Europe. *Let Me Tell Ya 'Bout Black Chicks* is a natural progression of the racist history Pamela described, where the rape and assault of Black women were woven into the social order.

Pamela used porno titles from the 1980s to illustrate her point: *Ghetto Gaggers, Nappy Headed Hos, Juicy Black Butt*. She also shared a still shot from the 1939 stag film *KKK Night Riders*, which may have served as inspiration for the Dark Bros. some forty-five years later. The plots in both films are similar. Both rely on the typical porno plot device, where women who say no really mean yes, but with the disturbing element that white men are masked in KKK hoods and, in the 1939 version, brandishing weapons. The Black women in both films are at first resistant, but eventually they become enthusiastic participants in the ensuing sexual encounters.

Pamela's argument was that as a result of racism, sexism, and classism, Black women have been "dehumanized [in pornography] in ways different than other ethnic groups." They tend to portray strippers, hookers, and other stereotypes associated with poor "inner-city" communities—in other words "ghetto porn," as Pamela named it. Because of what she described as "economic, structural and social factors," Black girls are more likely than other girls to fall victim to both pornography and sex trafficking. Even porn performers who consented to work in the industry were "not really able to make a choice," Pamela insisted. If pornography or "survival sex," as she called it, is "the only way out of the inner city, the only way out of poverty, then that's not really a choice at all." Still, Pamela ended her talk on a message of hope: "I believe in the strength and resiliency of black girls."

In the Q-and-A that followed the screening of the film, the audience moved away from the speaker's emphasis on structural racism as the problem that Black women and girls face and, instead, focused on the power of individual experience and choices. Several women, both Black and white, disclosed their own experiences of sexual assault and abuse. Yet Pamela's portrayal of historic and modern-day racism as the context for racist porn appeared to be overlooked as members of the audience repeated a series of conservative talking points.

A Black woman referred tearfully to her community: "We don't want to own the mess. Poverty and drugs are the real problem, and we've become the perpetrator." Another complained about Beyoncé: "The problem with her platform is that it mistakes power for empowerment. She has a huge platform, but she just confuses the conversation." Pamela countered that her aim was not to stigmatize Black women—just as a white woman jumped in to blame a generation of teenage girls: "You just cheapen yourself by wearing those clothes. Those shorts with your butt hanging out." Again, Pamela patiently repeated her message: "But the issue is systemic. It's not just Beyoncé twerking." A white man in his sixties—the only remaining white man in the crowd at that point in the session—chimed in with: "There's a lot worse porn out there. Oriental women, white women, who are being trafficked." It's unclear if he was questioning Pamela's focus on Black women or suggesting that she had overlooked some disturbing content by focusing only on Black women. Pamela repeated her history lesson: that Black women had been and continued to be uniquely subject to violence and objectification. But to that, a Black woman responded with an affirmation of reverse racism: "You can google any race raping any race."

As a highly educated Black feminist, Pamela was trying to teach a socio-logical lesson that the audience of mostly white evangelical Christians was not all that interested in hearing. According to national surveys, this group (the distinct majority at FFSS and, indeed, the leaders of the antiporn move-ment), when compared to other religious groups and those who are religiously unaffiliated, represents the people least likely to believe in systemic racism. The vast majority, for example, says that Confederate monuments are symbols of southern pride, not racism. They see the killing of Black men by police as isolated incidents rather than a broader pattern of racist discrimination. And at the FFSS, they didn't want to complain about the causes and consequences of systemic racism; they wanted to complain about how awful pornography was, period. A white woman summed up the tone from many audience questions and comments: "We need to take a stand and say, 'I don't watch porn. I won't date somebody who watches porn. I won't have sex until I'm married.'" Pamela simply nodded politely. I wondered how many times she had reacted in that way to white women who didn't appear to be listening.

For conservatives who don't have much of an eye toward acknowledging structural racism or sexism, pornography is the problem. For feminists like Pamela, combating pornography is one necessary step in eradicating larger structural problems. Both groups have wielded racist pornography to fuel their arguments against the industry. For both the left and the right who oppose pornography in the twenty-first century, examples of the copious online supply of extreme, disturbing, and potentially illegal content (featuring racism, degradation and abuse, rape, and child sexual assault) make it clear to them that the pornography industry must be shut down. For instance, amid widespread protests over the police killing of George Floyd and increased media visibility of the Black Lives Matter movement, Gail Dines and Carolyn West, both antiporn feminist activists, wrote an op-ed criti-cizing Pornhub's BLM hashtag. The hashtag linked to videos revealing what Dines and West called a "classic marriage of racist themes," like one video that is described as "black lives matter thug choking out a white cop daughter." This video appeared around the same time that Pornhub released a statement promising to donate one hundred thousand dollars to antiracist causes.

––––––

PORN VIDEOS LIKE *Let Me Tell Ya 'Bout Black Chicks* and modern-day equivalents seem utterly indefensible. Yet some people within and beyond the pornography industry take a different view. They challenge antiporn narratives by focusing on performers' agency, the diversity of sexual fantasies and desires, and the artistic and political possibilities of pushing porn to its extreme.

"People imagine porn stars all dressed up and having sex by a pool. And that's not what I did," Melissa Harris, aka "Mz Berlin," told me. "I created pornography where people are sobbing and snot is coming out of their nose. It's not pretty." Harris, a white woman in her forties at the time of our interview, worked for years directing and starring in porn created by the largest porn producer in the world, Kink.com, which specialized in what Harris called, without any qualms, "torture porn." These are the scenes that the antipornography movement warns us about, scenes that disturb and disgust—yet also entice, according to Kink.com's 2020 year in review, which revealed more than 1.7 million searches per month and more than 56,000 searches per day on its website. There is humiliation and verbal abuse; hitting and spanking with hands and objects; burning and electric shocks with things like cattle prods; there are ropes and medieval devices to constrain and contort naked bodies. "I didn't like sit at home and watch torture porn and then decide to go make torture porn," Harris said. "I made torture porn, and then I edited torture porn, and that's the first time I watched torture porn."

Harris likes being pushed to her physical and emotional limit, she explained to me, and she likes pushing other people there as well. That's the appeal of BDSM, she said, "seeing where other people begin and I end. I like seeing those moments." For over twenty years, she worked in all different corners of sex work: stripping, phone sex, escorting, professional dominatrix. But she is best known for her work making and sometimes starring in extreme BDSM and fetish porn. The word *kink*, as a noun, simply means a sharp twist or curve in something that is otherwise straight. The genre of kinky porn reflects this broad definition and can signal unusual sexual interests, fetishes, and hard-core BDSM scenes. Despite the decline in the commercial porn industry, performers who cater to kinky customers can become successful within niche markets.

When Harris was eighteen, a fellow stripper told her she had a *look*. "You could go to L.A. and be in movies," her friend told her, like Dita Von Teese, the red-lipped, dark-haired, big-bosomed "queen of burlesque." This struck a chord. As a teenager living in Louisiana, Harris had loved Anne Rice's vampire novels and was enamored of their Southern Gothic setting, along with sex, violence, and corsets. After high school, she started working at a tattoo shop learning body piercing. "There's not a lot of belly buttons to pierce in Shreveport, as it were, so I took a job in the evening stripping to make extra cash." Even at eighteen, she was drawn to the work of directing sexual scenes. "I just loved it. I loved putting together the outfits. I loved constructing songs and little sets. I really enjoyed the theatrics of it all."

A year after she started stripping, she packed up her costumes and moved to Los Angeles. She started booking shoots as a fetish and bondage model and was also hired at a feminist-run sex toy shop. "I started meeting all these people, all these big names in the industry." One of those people was Chanta Rose, who was starting a new BDSM porn company, Twisted Factory, and who wanted Harris to join as a director. Harris quickly learned the enormous responsibility that comes with such a role. Not just making decisions about camera angles and capturing recorded content, directors are also often on camera themselves, as the "top," or "dom," in the scene. And most important, they keep the "bottom," or "sub" (the one being tied up or tortured), safe. "It's not for everyone," Harris told me, but she loved the work and was good at it. Kink.com noticed and eventually offered her a job to work there full time.

Kink.com, which specializes in extreme BDSM porn, was one of the last major porn production sites to stay in business without being scooped up by the MindGeek corporation. In 2006, its founder, Peter Acworth, placed a bid to purchase the San Francisco Armory, or "the castle," as it was called by insiders, which had sat vacant for thirty years due to its status as a historic landmark. It became the perfect venue for a BDSM empire. "It's the biggest machine I've ever seen," Harris recalled. "They had a wardrobe department. A makeup department. They had a team that would build us sets. There was a chef on site. We literally had everything that we needed as artists to execute our vision." It was the only time in Harris's career when she felt she had virtually limitless possibilities in terms of her resources and creative potential.

Still, "it was one of the most intense times I've ever had in my life as a pornographer," she told me. She worked at the castle forty hours a week. The work was relentless and exhausting. "I have friends in the industry who direct and edit maybe one shoot a week, but at Kink.com, every team was responsible for two to three full movies—that's an hour and a half of edited footage—every week."

I asked Harris to walk me through a typical week at work.

On Monday: "I'd riffle through maybe five hundred applications for people who wanted to work at Kink.com. I'd look for people who had some potential and some experience, which would be looking at photos and being able to understand explicitly what their desires were and what experience they had. That was difficult, because a lot of people had no experience or just didn't fit an on-camera aesthetic. Monday, I also finalized my plans for the shoot the next day."

On Tuesday: "I'd have a shoot. So, first I go through the paperwork that the talent has filled out. I would interview the bottom, who's the person being tied up or beaten. I would interview them about what their limits were and what their desires were. I'd then confirm all of those things for the person topping on the shoot. Sometimes that person would be myself, and sometimes that would be another person. It's a big day for everybody. It's a big day for me. A lot of weight and responsibility. You know, I don't want to kill anyone. I don't want to knock out anyone's teeth. I was always afraid of someone falling or being injured. So, we get through the shoot, and then I do an interview with the talent, talk about everything that has happened that day and how they felt going through it." After each shoot ended, directors interviewed performers about their experience. Kink.com has been heralded by those in the industry for setting the gold standard when it comes to consent and aftercare. "The official line is that the bottom holds the responsibility for what's happening. They're adults. They gave consent. And we make sure they continue to give consent," Harris explained.

By Wednesday: "Maybe I would have my own shoot, where I was being directed by another director. So, then I'm the person going into makeup. I'm the one being interviewed about my own consent and boundaries, and then I'm getting my ass kicked all day, going home, feeding my cats, going to bed, and then, you know, starting again on Thursday and Friday." Harris said "getting my ass kicked all day" casually, like it's just another day on the job. And that's what it was. She consented, and she was paid. Her team understood her boundaries and limits and the safe word protocol used on every shoot: *yellow* to slow down or ease up; *red* to stop immediately.

"Torture porn is really intense to create, produce, and participate in. I feel like I was able to do that as ethically as I could," Harris reflected. When I told her that many of the people I've interviewed for my research would say *ethical torture porn* is an oxymoron, she understood my point, but pushed back.

"Look, I got consent as clearly as I could. And I tried to work with people who I perceived as able to give me that consent. Like, if you show up on my set and I'm like, 'What do you want to do today?' And you're like, 'I don't know, I don't know.' I'm not going to want to work with you. But if you show up and you're like, 'I really like impact play and hard bondage, and I'm okay with a little electricity,' then I've got somebody I can work with."

Harris acknowledged that her motivations for doing the work were different from those of people doing "survival sex work," as she put it. "If somebody said yes to a shoot but didn't know what they were signing up for—like, all of a sudden, a girl is sent to a shoot by her agent, and now she's getting signed up to be electrocuted? That's heavy." The official protocol for Kink.com would allow that performer to decline any scene for which she didn't feel fully prepared or comfortable. But unofficially? "The girl doesn't want to disappoint their agent," Harris explained to me, "and I've got content requirements to meet. So, where's the line? How do you figure that out?" Harris let the question linger. "I've had to use my own judgment."

To be successful in the industry, performers may push past their comfort zone and shoot extreme hard-core scenes in order to book work. "There are two types of ways to be successful," Jade told me about the porn industry today. "An easy one is if you are eighteen to twenty-one and especially if you're blond and petite. They call you a 'teen,' and you can play one until you're twenty-four. And then there's MILF. And if you're like a blond

bombshell—voluptuous, curvy—then you're also good. If you don't fit
into those two stereotypes, which is 90 percent of the shoots that we are
booked for on set, then all you have going for you is what you're willing
to do." And "what you're willing to do" is not exactly the same as "what
you enthusiastically consent to," Jade and other industry workers pointed
out. Within the porn industry, choice and coercion operate on a
continuum.

Harris believed that she was able to successfully prioritize the care and
safety of those she was directing in intense scenes. But she acknowledged
that this was not always the case for other directors. When she started
working for Chanta Rose at Twisted Factory, Harris didn't realize how rare
it was for her to be a woman director working at a woman-owned company.
Later, she worked for a short period as a performer in mainstream commercial porn. "I hated it. *Hated it.* Nobody was asking me what I wanted to
do. These dudes were handsy and grabbing me, and I'm just not sexual in
that way. I look at it as creating content, not that I'm there to fuck. So, it
was a weird disconnect for me. I felt dirty after those shoots. I didn't enjoy
it. And I realized that working with Chanta, I was so lucky, and I hadn't
appreciated that it was unique."

As a director and performer for many different porn companies, Harris
observed persistent double standards and both covert and overt sexism. She
told me about a shoot she did for a Kink.com series, *The Training of O* (based
on the 1954 French book *Story of O*), where the talent worked for days on end
in extreme torture scenes. "The comments from some of the other producers
were really awful and just really hurt my feelings. Like, 'You didn't hit her
hard enough.' 'She didn't work hard enough.' That really bothered me."
Harris also explained that in bondage scenes with male directors serving
as "tops," they typically remain clothed throughout the scene. For female
directors serving as "tops," they are expected to be unclothed and sexualized, even though they perform largely nonsexual roles, such as securing
bondage.

Looking back on her work, Harris said she was proud of what she had
accomplished but also expressed ambivalence about how it may have been
received by viewers. She was regularly disturbed by comments made on
Kink.com's sites, like Public Disgrace, a website where a "bottom" would be

publicly humiliated and forced to have sex, often with bystanders who were actually plants from the production team but who created the impression that ordinary strangers (most often men) were forcing themselves on women's bodies. "The comments on that were intense. To me, it felt like rapists were watching this. It wasn't people watching this in a good-spirited way. It was people watching in a really negative way."

She told a therapist once that she felt that the content she had spent her career creating was made for rapists. Because the therapist had spent time counseling sex offenders, he was able to offer his informed perspective. "He was like, 'You're exactly right. The people who are watching this are choosing to watch this pornography as opposed to going and making their own memories, you know?' That has stuck with me. It was never my intention to make pornography for rapists and wannabe murderers. That wasn't how I thought about it. How I thought about it at the beginning was that I was pushing the boundaries of art. But it's sobering to think about and to look back and think about who's watching my content." She paused before continuing: "I don't feel bad about what I've done, but if you would've told me that, 'Oh, by the way, thirty percent of the people who are watching this are rapists or aspiring rapists,' I don't know if I would have participated as wholeheartedly in it."

When Kink.com could no longer compete with the MindGeek empire to make enough money to sustain its massive staff and production operation, Harris was laid off. The company's profits declined by 50 percent between 2013 and 2016, due to a drop in subscription memberships, and Harris's fate was the same as that of two thirds of the site's 150 employees. In 2018, Peter Acworth sold the castle and all its contents. At a sale on Mission Street, shoppers could find sex toys and props, including things like candlesticks and lamps as well as a human hamster wheel and torture racks. Today, Kink.com no longer produces any of its own content, but it distributes content for independent producers. Twenty seventeen was the first year that brought the company out of the red based on this new model.

IT WAS TWO decades after *Story of O* was first published in 1954, and just a few years after feminists protested the U.S. publisher of the book, that the public finally discovered the true identity of its author, who wrote under the pen name "Pauline Reage." Many had speculated that the author must be a man, given the book's obsession with men's dominance over women and women's complicity in what appears to be violent abuse. They were therefore shocked to discover that Pauline Reage, who more commonly used the pen name "Dominique Aury," was in fact Anne Desclos, a woman and a highly accomplished one at that. Desclos, a French journalist, said that she wrote *Histoire d'O* to prove to her lover, the writer and literary critic Jean Paulhan, that a woman could write an erotic novel as well as a man. Paulhan was an admirer of Marquis de Sade, the eighteenth-century French writer from whose name the word *sadism* is derived and who was imprisoned for much of his life for sexual crimes. A feminist pioneer in her own right, Desclos was the only woman to serve on the awards committee for Gallimard, France's largest publishing house. She was awarded the Légion d'honneur, France's most prestigious award, granted by the head of state. A fellow French writer and personal friend of hers described the book as "absolutely a feminist work, empowering to women. For the first time, a woman is revealing her sex life, and it is the woman who dominates the situation, her feelings, her responses, her trajectory."

The porn wars have long debated whether sex scenes that include violence and degradation are always and inevitably instances of victimization. For pornography's opponents, the answer is yes—that reasonable and fully empowered people would never readily consent to what they label as abuse. Instead, performers (mostly women and often women of color) are coerced or forced into scenes that harm them, mentally and physically. At the events I attended for pornography's sympathizers, however, I heard uttered over and over the expression "Don't yuck someone else's yum." At Sex Down South, an annual event for people who are "sex professionals" and/or "sex enthusiasts," the maxim was listed as one of the conference's core values, along with, in the words of the organizers, "There is no such thing as too kinky or not kinky enough."

Sexuality is always both "pleasure and danger," in the words of feminist activist and scholar Carole Vance, "simultaneously a domain of restriction, repression, and danger as well as a domain of exploration, pleasure, and agency." Vance was speaking to the 1970s and '80s feminist debates about whether women who had sex with men were inevitably reproducing patriarchy and the tension between the structural conditions of sexism and the choices that individuals made in order for their lives to be more bearable, even pleasurable. Sex is never fully removed from broader inequalities embedded in the social world, yet it is not completely determined by these inequalities, either. Culturally, we tend not to think of vanilla sex, or the normative man-woman/penis-vagina pairing, as dangerous in comparison to queer or kinky sex. Yet there's nothing inevitably or automatically *safer*, in porn or real life, if sex is vanilla than if it is not.

For some BDSM performers, submission to partners and consent to violence within the parameters of a sexual scene can be desired and can feel good. Researchers of BDSM communities have found that its practitioners, including those who take on the role of "bottom," or "sub," are no more likely to be victims of assault than the general population and that they tend to score higher on a variety of measures related to psychological health. This may be attributed to the community's emphasis on nuanced understandings of consent. The dungeon at the 2019 Sex Down South conference, available to paying participants for "sex, BDSM, exploration, education, conversation, and hot hook ups," required all practitioners to agree to the following characteristics of consent: Consent cannot justify serious injury; even if someone consents to pain play, all parties involved must commit to avoiding serious bodily harm. Consent means no one is manipulated or coerced into any activity. Consent is informed in that everyone knows the activities that are planned. Consent can be given only by adults of sound mind, who are not impaired by drugs or alcohol. And finally, consent is revocable and can be withdrawn at any point in a scene using plain speech, a safe word, or a safe sign.

Reflecting on the controversial KKK scene in *Let Me Tell Ya 'Bout Black Chicks*, historian and porn studies scholar Mireille Miller-Young writes, "This scene exposes the ways in which fantasies of interracial sex by white men . . . are necessarily informed by our collective history of racial and sexualized violence." And still, Miller-Young insists, "This is not a filmed rape." The performer playing the Black maid teases the Klansmen, exaggerates her own pleasure, and indeed, maintains an air of control in the scene. "Sahara's complicity does not condone white supremacy, and she does not take up a pure victim status either," Miller-Young writes.

Though stereotypes, cultural appropriation, and overt racism saturate porn featuring nonwhite actors, Miller-Young argues that these genres also allow performers of color to deploy "their own racialized eroticism into sexual media." This "racialized eroticism," Miller-Young believes, had both practical and political consequences. In the 1970s and '80s, the industry created jobs for Black performers and a market for Black consumers in a way that was previously unheard of. And the genre also provided opportunities for performers to resist and challenge racism and white supremacy, albeit in subtle ways.

There has been much speculation over Desiree West, the Black performer who appeared in more than fifty porn films between 1974 and 1981, after she left the industry. One Duke professor, Jennifer Nash, reached out to West while writing a book on race and pornography that included a chapter about *SexWorld*, the film that features West's character having sex with an explicitly racist white man. West asked Nash how it was that academics were telling her story without asking her to tell it. Though Nash never set out to write West's biography, she was eager to ask the former porn star what she thought about *SexWorld*. West responded, "I never saw it" and explained that she had forgotten the names and story lines from her many films. "The films that have preoccupied me, what I have always called 'West's work,'" writes Nash, "simply are not that important in how West narrates her life."

That coercion and exploitation are problems in the industry is a shared sentiment across the porn divide. Yet, for performers and their allies, eliminating porn in order to rid the industry of coercion and exploitation is like throwing the baby out with the bathwater. Porn performers navigate constraints and possibilities just as they do in the real world. And, they insist, eliminating porn would not actually eliminate racist and misogynist violence.

CHAPTER 12

Come as You Are

Inka Winter describes herself as an artist, activist, feminist, and porn director. I flew to Los Angeles in 2020 to observe her at work. She is the founder of ForPlay Films, an all-woman porn production company that creates what she describes as "erotic short films through a feminist gaze." Winter was just getting out of her old Hyundai when I arrived at the parking lot of a large, nondescript warehouse. "Kelsy?" She approached, perhaps because I looked clearly lost or perhaps because she had seen my picture online. I had not seen a picture of Winter and did not know what a feminist porn director would look like. Bright red lipstick maybe? No, that was wrong.

Winter is a petite white woman with brown shoulder-length hair and cropped bangs. That day, she was wearing a worn gray sweatshirt, black sweatpants, and lace-up leather ankle boots. I suddenly felt overdressed in the same clothes I wear to work as a college professor: dark jeans and a cardigan buttoned all the way up. We introduced ourselves, and I helped her unpack her car, which was full of equipment piled on the passenger seat, on the back seat, and in the trunk. We hauled lights, a foam mattress, and various other boxes and bags into the building, to the end of a long hallway, and into a studio room that Winter rented from noon until the evening.

As is true of virtually all media, the pornography industry is not only made up of profit-driven commercial studios with budgets, sets, and paid staff. Like indie movies or nonprofit journalism, some people like Winter make porn not primarily for money but for art and activism. Some people make porn because they want to make the world a better place.

Eventually, Winter's crew arrived—"Everyone is always late," she said, laughing. Barbara, a white woman in her twenties wearing leggings, a zip-up gray hoodie, and Converse sneakers, drove herself in a car slightly newer than Winter's. Susy, a Puerto Rican woman also in leggings, under a baggy white T-shirt and a flannel shirt tied around her waist, got out of an Uber. Both Barbara and Susy worked full time in television as producers and cinematographers, but they believed in the mission of ForPlay Films and so, worked with Winter on the side. Winter joked with me that the day I would spend with them wouldn't exactly be representative of most porn shoots. All the lights and props were rented, thanks to Winter's friends, who helped her secure good deals. Winter explained that to book studio spaces, she generally asked permission beforehand to shoot adult content, to which she received mixed results. Susy jumped in to tell the story of one studio they considered renting for this shoot, saying that it looked to be the perfect space, except for the fact that it was right next to an office where the studio's owner worked. Winter asked, "Are you okay with adult films?" "The look on the man's face," Susy said, laughing, "when he realized that we were wanting to shoot porn. It was so funny, because he *never* expected that from *us*." The answer the man eventually gave was no.

Winter started ForPlay Films for herself, she explained to me, not to become famous or start some lucrative career. "I was feeling broken in my own sexuality," she said, and she wanted something to help her feel more sexually alive. But she couldn't find it when she turned to porn. "Men watching porn—I have no judgment. They can do whatever they want and whatever turns them on. And I know there are some women who watch mainstream commercial stuff, and I'm like, 'Great for you,' but personally, I'm just not into it." She took control of the camera for her first shoot and said it felt like she was reclaiming her own sexuality. In her words, "I get to direct, and that is really empowering. I'm kind of rescuing that which was broken."

Winter got her start directing porn working with "real people and real relationships," as she described it. "In our films, people have sex for pleasure. I don't tell them what to do. Whatever they do to enjoy the sex, that's what they do." She maintained this philosophy as ForPlay Films expanded, but she now works primarily with industry performers. She doesn't typically have a budget to pay them and so creates content for trade that both ForPlay Films and its performers can access and monetize. For the past four years, she has also produced videos for people wanting to enter Dan Savage's amateur porn film festival, HUMP! Twice, she won the award for Best Sex. "People love what we do. There are people who are really appreciating our mission," she said.

After we carried in the props, Winter made one final trip to her car to bring in two overflowing grocery bags from Trader Joe's, full of snacks: bananas, apples, chips with salsa and guacamole, granola bars, packaged salads, and bottled water. Before the talent arrived, Winter, Barbara, and Susy prepared the set, hanging a long black drape from the ceiling down to the floor, testing the lighting, and preparing the "bed" (really just a foam mattress on the floor) with a silky black sheet.

On the shoot I observed, Winter had arranged to film commercial performers for trade. She was hoping to sell the film to an adult website that had taken an interest in her work, and the performers would use the film on their sites, such as OnlyFans. She met with Darius first for coffee and told him her idea. He agreed to the role of "male talent," as Winter described him to me, and Winter asked him to choose a female partner with whom he had chemistry and enjoyed working with. He invited Kristi, a young, thin white woman in her early twenties. She arrived to the set first. Winter had never met Kristi in person, and so they first sat in a small dressing room off to the side of the main room to discuss the scene Winter envisioned. Kristi confirmed that she had brought lingerie, and Winter asked if she could restyle her hair to bring out a natural and messy curl rather than the sleek, straight style with which she'd arrived. Kristi agreed but said she would need some sort of hair gel, and Barbara offered to run out and buy some at a nearby drugstore. Before Barbara returned, Darius arrived. He was a tall Black man maybe a few years older than Kristi. He said hello to each of us and presented his STI test results to Winter. Kristi followed suit. Then the two filled out more paperwork, standard forms giving consent for the filming.

The setup for the shoot took hours, but no one seemed in a hurry. "A lot of snacking and chatting," I wrote in my field notes. At one point, I entered the dressing room, where the snacks were located, before realizing that Kristi was in the room, topless and pulling a lacy bra from her bag to put on. She casually recommended the salsa to me, saying, "It's bomb," and as she adjusted her bra straps, we proceeded to talk about all the things we like to buy at Trader Joe's. "The Bolognese sauce, though," she warned, "don't be fooled. It tastes just like spaghetti." Meanwhile, there was a leaky sink in the studio bathroom, and the bucket catching the drips was overflowing. Winter found another bucket and mop in a utility closet, laughing about needing to mop a floor as part of the work of directing a porn shoot. As we waited, Kristi, in her lingerie, showed me pictures on her phone, one of her dog and one of landscape with deep snow, sent from a friend in Wisconsin.

As Susy made final adjustments to the lights, Kristi stretched her legs with a few yoga poses. Darius scrolled on his phone. And then the camera was ready. Winter reminded Kristi and Darius that the film was intended to be all about a woman's fantasy.

"In terms of sex, it would be nice if you would just think about it as your fantasy and to do the things that you or maybe that a lot of women want to do," Winter said to Krisi. "No legs behind the head, things like that," she joked.

Kristi responded that, as a matter of fact, she had just had sex the other day and, indeed, she did put her legs behind her head. "I think it's a habit," she said, laughing.

Winter nodded, but held firm: "You'll have to deprogram the porn star. Just think about regular women."

"I'll just take a back seat," Darius said, to acknowledge that he understood. With his warm smile and demure disposition, I had a hard time imagining him as the stereotypical aggressor in porn films.

Susy, behind the camera, spoke directly to Kristi and Darius before she started recording: "If you ever need to stop, take a break, get some water, just let us know. Or, if you want to keep going, even if we're adjusting the camera or lights or whatever, you can do that, too."

Darius and Kristi gave each other a gentle hug and a peck on the lips and then got into position for the first shot, where Darius is off camera at first and enters to stand behind Kristi to begin kissing her neck and stroking her shoulders. Winter intervened as soon as the camera started recording, and Kristi began to sway her hips and rub up against Darius. "Don't be concerned about pleasing him or pleasing the camera. This is all about pleasing you. Maybe think about it being more like a sex scene in a movie, not mainstream porn." Kristi nodded in understanding and said playfully, "I'm trying not to say, 'It's so big!'"—apparently, one of her usual lines for a commercial porn film.

The sex that followed was not so different from that in real life, I thought, for they struggled with buckles on pants, hair sticking to their faces, and awkward sex noises. Of course, none of this comes through in the final film, which Winter produced to be a sensual and sleek twenty minutes of a woman's fantasy. But at the time of the shoot, Darius and Kristi let their actions unfold slowly, performing in various positions, while the camera worked around them. After about an hour, I wrote in my field notes that porn sex could be "long and boring," as I started thinking about what I would eat for dinner and my to-do list for the week. Finally, it was time for Darius to finish. He ejaculated on Kristi's thigh; this was followed by a few minutes of filmed caressing and cuddling and holding hands. This was Darius's last scene, while Kristi moved on to film what would become the first and last scene of the film, her character in a large clawfoot tub, touching herself. All the women on the set giggled while rolling the tub into place—as a film prop, it was set atop wheels and was indeed the reason Winter had rented this particular studio space. She hauled in a five-gallon bucket of warm water, which Barbara used to sponge Kristi's neck and chest, to give the illusion that she was soaking in hot water. In the produced film, the sex scenes between her and Darius take place in her character's mind while she is in the tub.

WINTER CALLS HERSELF a "feminist pornographer" on the heels of feminist women in the porn industry who for decades have advocated for what she calls "a feminist gaze." Feminist pornography developed as a brand in the 1990s, and in 2006, a Toronto-based sex toy shop hosted the first Feminist

Porn Awards, recognizing leaders in the industry. For a film to be considered for this award, it must meet at least one of the following criteria: a woman helped create it, it depicts "genuine female pleasure," and it challenges stereotypes of mainstream porn. Though it is not as lucrative or popular as the sites owned by MindGeek, the "feminist" work created by independent producers and directors like Inka Winter has birthed a market alongside free streaming sites and for-pay subscription sites.

Food analogies were the most common way my interview respondents explained the meaning of feminist porn, or a related and overlapping genre that recently joined the vernacular, "ethical porn." Tristan Taormino called the genres "organic, fair trade." Elle, a sex educator, compared them to her motivations to eat a vegan diet. "When we're not critical about the ways in which our meat is processed, and we just go, 'Oh, our meat is fine. Oh, our porn is fine,' and we're blindly consuming them, then we are not talking about all of the unethical practices in these industries." Elle, like virtually all the porn-positive educators, activists, and sex workers I interviewed, blamed the commercial porn industry for causing harm. But unlike those in the antiporn movement who want to eliminate the industry altogether, these proponents of porn see the solution as advocating for better alternatives. Like paying more money for pasture-raised meat or organic produce, paying for porn is one way to support a more ethical industry. "You have to pay for it," Swedish director Erika Lust, one of the most successful and well-known feminist pornographers of the twenty-first century, told a reporter. "It's just logical reasoning—if you pay a pound for a hamburger, it's going to be a shitty hamburger. And when it comes to porn, how the hell can it be free?"

"What people think when they think 'porn' basically has nothing to do with me," Winter told me, acknowledging that her work is very different from commercial porn. And yet, directors like her are making and selling porn. They *are* the porn industry, at least one arm of it. Still, the genre is dismissed by antiporn feminists as an oxymoron. "Akin to climate change deniers," Gail Dines has accused, signaling that feminists making porn are in denial about pornography's harm to women. Other commentators take less of a hard line than Dines, but they still set feminist porn aside to focus on mainstream misogyny. "Watching natural-looking people engaging in sex that is consensual, mutually pleasurable, and realistic may not be harmful—heck, it might be a good idea," journalist Peggy Orenstein writes. Yet, in her investigations of pornography's impact on teenagers, she says that feminist porn is simply not what teens are watching. Sociologist Bernadette Barton puts it this way, "This content does not solve the problem of sexism in internet porn because feminist porn is a niche."

Winter and nearly every other porn-positive person I interviewed shared concerns over sexism in commercial porn. But they insist that feminist-created porn can serve as a remedy to the problem and is not simply an outlier to be cast aside. Dismissing feminist porn is like dismissing online shopping at small businesses making and selling their own products because they are overshadowed by places like Amazon and the websites of big-box stores. True, most consumers will find and buy products at the large chains rather than from the more expensive and harder-to-find small businesses online. And true, these big corporations are largely the cause of unethical labor and sourcing practices. Refusing to acknowledge the efforts of feminist pornographers in the service of critiquing the broader commercial industry is a bit like refusing to acknowledge the efforts of small businesses within the capitalist marketplace. Capitalism, like patriarchy, is the water in which we swim. It is largely unavoidable.

In her book *Barbie's Queer Accessories*, Erica Rand notes the dissonance between the messages Mattel sends about how girls should play with the iconic doll and how they actually play with Barbie. Mattel, like MindGeek, has an interest in sustaining its profits and does so by subtly controlling the choices available to consumers. Mattel makes Barbie play *seem* limitless: Barbie has no age, no location, comes in an assortment of skin tones, and can have virtually any career and hobby. Yet she is forever the thin, conventionally attractive, and presumably heterosexual representation of idealized and unrealistic female beauty. MindGeek also makes fantasy play appear limitless—indeed, there are categories on the site for both "feminist" and "ethical" porn along with every other niche category imaginable—but in practice, it reproduces the same reel of predictable gender stereotypes and violence. And yet these corporate behemoths do not have the last word when it comes to their products. As Rand describes, political activists along with ordinary children have "queered" Barbie, both in the sense that they have used her to represent something other than gender-normative hetero-sexuality and in the sense that she can push the boundaries of what is normal in a variety of ways. Pornographers, even within the mainstream commercial industry, can do the same.

GORDON B. KNOWS this lesson firsthand. "Grab your dick" was one of the first sex education lessons he recalled. The line was said by his father, as a solution to nearly every complaint of an eight-year-old boy. "Can't sleep? Struck out in Little League? Got shampoo in your eyes? Grab your dick." Today, Gordon B. is an artist and sex educator. He is also the son of a porn star. "Let me put your minds at ease," he says, addressing the audience directly in his one-man show, *Debbie Does My Dad*. "There aren't fake-breasted blondes fucking in every corner of my house. I don't have to dodge directors or boom mics over naked twins. I'm not woken up in the morning by shouts from the next room from some girl about how she's never seen a dick that big and 'Do me now, dammit,' no. We're normal Americans. Well, almost. In the home my dad made with my mother, we can talk about sex. I can ask and get real answers."

In hindsight, Gordon B. realized that his upbringing was unique not only because his dad was an adult film star in the late 1970s and early '80s, but also because of his parents' frank talk about sex and sexuality and their explicit encouragement of their children's sexual exploration. When Gordon B. was caught stealing his dad's copies of *Playboy* a few years after he was first encouraged to "grab his dick," he braced himself for being scolded by his parents. But instead, he came home from school one day to find a stack of his own *Playboy*s and a newly installed lock on his bedroom door.

Gordon B.'s upbringing was also unique because, despite his father's career in an industry that epitomized gender stereotypes, at home his father defied them. In my interview with him, Gordon B. was up front and critical about the many negative messages so prevalent in porn—what he called "a world of misogyny." He was not raised on those messages, but was instead taught to value open and honest communication between partners, to respect women's consent and desires, and to recognize and express his own emotions. His dad's flexible work schedule meant that he was actively involved in his children's lives. "My dad drove to every baseball practice and, to the annoyance of my sisters and I, never missed an opportunity to parent." Addressing his dad in his show, Gordon B. reflects, "This world thinks you're weird for being a porn star. But much more telling is how weird you were *for* a porn star. A heartfelt, sincere soul in the land of 'Grab my pole, bitch' and 'Make me cum, slut.'"

The antipornography movement uses this distinction between real people and porn stars to emphasize objectification and victimization, but Gordon B. is making an alternative point. Performers may follow a script that is very different from who they are in real life, but they can do so because their work permits them to live a life that aligns with their values and beliefs, such as having a flexible schedule in order to be an involved parent. Individuals themselves do not always, or even often, reflect or represent the broader industries in which they work.

Gordon B.'s parents raised him to become, as he puts it, a "sexual and sensitive" man. In high school, he found spoken-word poetry. "I wasn't being made fun of or considered the runt of the social litter because I could talk about my emotions; instead, I was being applauded for it. And that was the moment when art and expression really allowed me to access my humanity beyond the limits of my gender roles." Now in his thirties, he wants to help young men do the same. For a time, he worked for a university facilitating what he called "arts-based sex education theater," where he taught college students, who then brought the curriculum to local high schools. Like in his one-man show, in which he reflects on his earliest lessons about sex and gender, he asks students to devise their own autobiographical performances. "They can use poetry and dance and theater to be able to tell their own stories," Gordon B. described. He calls himself a "creative midwife" for students to "use art to figure out their own sexual lives, their own sexualities, their own gender roles."

Still, there were limits to what Gordon B. was allowed to talk about with his students, bureaucratic red tape enforced by school administrators. "I found myself really curious about exploring what would completely uncensored education look like," he said. "If there was absolutely no censorship, and the only things guiding what would be included were artistic and

pedagogical and ethical considerations, rather than censorship and bureaucratic policy. What would that look like?" He asked me rhetorically because
he knew the answer.

Unlike most sex educators, Gordon B. is personal friends with many a
porn star. "Nina Hartley is basically my unofficial aunt," he told me fondly.
Hartley, a famed performer with roles in more than six hundred films and
a career spanning decades, pioneered a genre of instructional pornography
through books and videos called *Nina Hartley's Guides*, including her *Guide
to Total Sex*, *Guide to Oral Sex*, and *Guide to Better Cunnilingus*. These
resources, which blend explicit sex scenes with Nina's instructions and
commentary, provided inspiration for Gordon B.

A few years ago, he was introduced to Erika Lust, the Swedish feminist
porn director who produces independent films that emphasize women's
pleasure, consent, and safe sex practices. She has, perhaps most successfully
in the twenty-first century, branded feminist and ethical pornography as a
distinct genre. "Her work has such incredible artistry," Gordon B. said.
"And I think it is also incredibly sex positive with sex education information. It might seem strange to describe porn as sex positive, but I think
actually a lot of porn is quite sex negative." Here, Gordon B. repeated a
theme he had wrestled with throughout our interview: the commercial
porn industry, with all its misogyny and gender stereotypes, gives porn a
bad name. Independent directors and performers are attempting to reclaim
pornography's potential to expand sexual knowledge, health, and pleasure
for their audience. Gordon B. told Lust about an erotic film he imagined
that decentered the heterosexual male orgasm and also dealt with sexual
health themes. She loved the idea and hired him to direct a film for her
website, XConfessions.

One of Lust's online platforms, XConfessions allows members to pay
$34.95 a month (or a discounted bundle price of $143 a year) to gain access.
Lust started the site in 2013, asking users to share secret desires or illicit
encounters, from which she would choose to create a catalogue of short
films. Today, she works with dozens of independent directors and
performers to create content for the site. "Together we are changing the
rules of pornography," Lust said in her 2014 TED Talk, "It's Time for Porn
to Change." "We don't just show what sex looks like; we tell stories about
what sex and desire feel like and how we communicate and interact

intimately with each other." XConfessions lists Lust's core values as a pornography director, which include women's pleasure, equal and respectful representation of diverse bodies, fair pay for performers and production staff, safe and consensual sex practices, and fair labor practices, including breaks, food, and a relaxed environment.

Gordon B. took a confession from one XConfessions user and cowrote a film that reversed the typical story line of commercial porn. "I was really curious as to what it would look like if the male orgasm happened at the beginning of the sex instead of the finish line. Almost like it was the Best Supporting Actor at the Oscars. It's just one moment, and then everything really centers on the female character's pleasure." Gordon B. also wanted themes of consent and communication to be showcased throughout. Rather than having "sexual health information sprinkled in," he saw it as "the idea at the core of the film." "I wanted to experiment with work that is sex affirming and humanity affirming, that is intelligent, that is *saying something*."

FOR ALL THE ethical motives behind feminist or ethical porn, proponents of these genres must contend with the fact that they can be labels to generate profits, too. Feminist pornography is "hot," according to industry magazine *XBIZ*, but it is not without controversy. In 2018, two directors who worked for Erika Lust were accused of abusive behavior on set. One accuser, Lina Bembe, who performed for several Lust films, told the website Jezebel that "the people who are really ethical, they're not like, 'We're ethical, *trademark*!'" As Mattel did when it came out with a gender-neutral doll in 2019 ("a doll line designed to keep labels out and invite everyone in"), virtue signaling is a way for corporations to express care and understanding for diverse consumers without significantly altering corporate practices or profits. The 2020 "Holiday Barbie" is as white, blond, and thin as ever. Melissa Harris, the former porn director and performer, pointedly responded to my questions about the genres of feminist and ethical porn: "Feminist porn is not real. Ethical porn is not real. These are marketing terms. I would say the only ethical and feminist content is from independent producers." Lust, for her part, has since published a set of guidelines for her directors to follow and has resolved conflicts between directors and performers through mediation.

Andre Shakti, the independent sex worker and porn performer, is also critical of the label "feminist" for porn, because it places value judgment on the content itself. She disagreed with one of the hallmarks of feminist porn, as described by the Feminist Porn Awards, that porn should depict "genuine pleasure." "I'm a performer. This is my job," she told me. "And I'm going to put on a great performance regardless of whether my orgasm is real or not." As Stoya, the famous porn performer and now advice columnist for *Slate* magazine, has described, "My politics and I are feminist . . . but my job is not." "I use my body to make gender-binary-heterosexual-oriented pornography for a production company that aims to have as much mass appeal as possible." Nothing about this is feminist, Stoya writes, but it is consensual—and the way she makes a living.

IN HER BOOK *Female Chauvinist Pigs*, journalist Ariel Levy insists that the problem with contemporary culture in the aftermath of sexual liberation and the women's movement is that it appears to liberate women's sexuality but, in fact, confines it to a limited narrative. Some women (namely, the pretty, young white ones) may feel entitled to express their sexual desires and showcase their bodies, but Levy insists that this has come at the expense of their actual and authentic sexual pleasure. Citing Olympic athletes appearing in *Playboy*, the *Victoria's Secret Fashion Show* airing on primetime TV, or the hugely popular *Girls Gone Wild* franchise that profits on drunk female college students willing to lift up their T-shirts, Levy blames "raunch culture" for limiting women by catering to straight men's desires and pockets.

Raunch culture may appear to empower or liberate women, but in fact, it does the opposite, as Levy and other feminists who share her view assert. Sure, in the wake of the feminist movement, young women grew up believing they could pursue educations and successful careers alongside men. Most American women, as well as men, believe that marriages should be egalitarian and that each partner should actively participate in both the domestic and the work sphere. They have pushed back against conservative values that forbid sex outside marriage and that shame women for having sexual desires. The contradiction is that for all the gains in the name of so-called sexual freedom, women's sex lives have not been radically trans-formed for the better. In one of the largest surveys of sexual experience since the work of Alfred Kinsey, sociologists Elizabeth A. Armstrong, Paula England, and Alison C. K. Fogarty found that nine out of ten female college students reported that they do not experience orgasm in a one-time "hookup." Studies find that, within heterosexual marriages, women are less sexually satisfied than men. Rates of self-reported rape and sexual assault against women appear to be on the rise.

Sociologists make sense of these data by describing a "stalled revolu-tion," as many goals of the women's movement (like equal pay for equal work) have been largely unmet. When it comes to women's sexual libera-tion, Levy calls it "the future that never happened." Instead, "we have determined that all empowered women must be overtly and publicly sexual," she writes, but "the only sign of sexuality we seem to be able to recognize is a direct allusion to red-light entertainment." In short, according to Levy, women are pressured "to be imitating strippers and porn stars" in the name of sexual liberation. There's nothing inherently wrong with strip-pers and porn stars, she is careful to repeat. The problem lies in the fact that women lose sexuality as something of their own and replace it with a superficial commodity that is all glitz and glam to please straight men. Left behind are women's actual needs, desires, and pleasures.

When the filming at the ForPlay Films porn shoot ended, I helped Winter, Barbara, and Susy pack up the props and was reminded of an exchange on the set that happened hours earlier. Before she agreed to wrap up the scene with Darius, Winter asked Kristi, "Did you come?" and Kristi responded casually, "Oh yeah. Like six times." I found myself automatically skeptical, and I asked Winter if she believed Kristi. "Yeah, sure. I think she was telling the truth." My skepticism of Kristi's perfor-mance and her assertion of multiple orgasms is the same as Levy's critique: the exaggerated moaning and the *Yes, don't stop*s, even as Darius used his hands and his mouth to pleasure her, seemed so performative, so quintessentially "porn star" that I doubted those six orgasms were real. They seemed to me not unlike the "orgasm" of Sally Albright, who simulates one in a deli while sitting across from Harry Burns in *When Harry Met Sally*.

In her 2010 book, *Pornland: How Porn Has Hijacked Our Sexuality*, Gail Dines asks, "[W]hat if you are a feminist who is pro-sex in the real sense of the word, pro that wonderful, fun, and deliciously creative force that bathes the body in delight and pleasure, and what you are actually against is porn sex? A kind of sex that is debased, dehumanized, formulaic, and generic, a kind of sex based not on individual fantasy, play, or imagination, but one that is the result of an industrial product created by those who get excited not by bodily contact but by market penetration and profits." She uses the analogy of someone who is critical of McDonald's for its labor practices and food sourcing who is then accused of being anti-eating. It's absurd to equate being antiporn with being antisex, Dines insists.

The antipornography position of Dines and other feminist activists rests on their distinction between good and bad sex. Good sex (that which Dines calls "wonderful, fun, and deliciously creative") is never truly found in porn, which by definition is, according to her, bad sex (debased, dehumanized, formulaic, and generic). To be ejaculated on, to be penetrated by more than one object, to be choked—all scenes that are common in mainstream commercial porn—is so obviously violent and degrading that there is no alternative reading of pornography's treatment of women. Even Levy, who is careful to insist that she is not antiporn, falls back on similar values judgment by assuming she knows what authentic sexuality for women should look like.

Queer feminist sociologist Jane Ward grapples candidly with the tension of her identity and politics and the fact that commercial porn turns her on. "Lucky are those whose arousal results from homegrown and independently produced feminist porn with gender-variant people of various races, body sizes, and abilities. But for some of us mainstream porn—for all its sexist and racist tropes and questionable labor practices—still casts its spell." For Ward, the problem with Levy's and Dines's arguments is that they regulate some sexual desires and pleasures as good (i.e., feminist) and others as bad. Instead of admonishing those "bad," or unfeminist, sexual interests, Ward says the better and more realistic solution would be to mindfully contemplate, for better or worse, where they come from.

What makes feminist antipornography positions problematic, along with my own reaction to the claim of a porn star's authentic orgasms, is that we end up taking on the authority of other people's desires and pleasures. We dare to assume that we can distinguish real from fake when virtually everything about sex is a little bit of both. Sex is a deeply social recipe, mixing together the ingredients of our childhood, the media, our values, and our peers. Sociologists John Gagnon and William Simon call the result "sexual scripts," in which not only what we think about sex but also *how* we think about it stems from the social world in which we live. In the 1970s, Gagnon and Simon pioneered the radical claim that our deepest physical and private sexual feelings and desires are in fact produced within a specific social context. They are never *pre*social (that is, mere biological drives), as was the focus of much early sexological research; nor are they *supra*social (repressed psychic desires), as was the focus of Freud and the psychoanalysts. Rather, according to Gagnon and Simon, the social world teaches us a series of sexual scripts that we learn and internalize over the course of our lives. Perhaps the efforts of feminist and ethical pornographers to literally change the script in porn films is one strategy to change our internal desires. But until then, given that we all experience sex with society at our side, any assertion about "authentic" sexuality is pretending that sex can ever leave its social baggage behind.

PART III

The Battle over Watching Porn

As antiporn activists, religious leaders, educators, and clinicians have come to terms with the fact that pornography is here to stay, many have directed their efforts not at the industry but instead at consumers. Theirs is an uphill battle, though, as Americans have become increasingly progressive in their attitudes about porn. In response, the antiporn movement has dovetailed two overlapping strategies. First, it has expanded its purview beyond morality to include harms of watching porn that are described as objectively true. Second, it has focused on children and teens as uniquely harmed by exposure to online porn.

Both these strategies, which are rooted in the language of science and health, have bubbled under the surface of the antiporn movement for over a century. Protecting children's exposure to smut has been used as the rationale for censorship and restriction on the production and distribution of pornographic materials. Antivice organizations in the nineteenth century warned that illicit literature was like a "deadly acid" akin to "strychnine, or arsenic." In the 1980s, activists and politicians made references to pornography's addictive potential. The internet became a geyser to force these perspectives into view and into the center of the antipornography movement.

Whereas fights over making porn have mostly to do with women, who make up the majority of the sex industry, fights over watching porn have mostly to do with men, who are the majority of pornography's consumers.

This empirical fact takes on symbolic weight as pornography use comes to represent ideas surrounding men, women, and their supposed innate differences. While religious conservatives are often behind the rhetoric surrounding pornography's harm to men, the Christian Right is not alone in sounding the alarm. Online communities, made up of many secular Millennial men, strategize about overcoming porn addiction by abstaining from what users call "fapping" (masturbation). Former *Playboy* model Pamela Anderson has warned of the harms of porn addiction by calling today's youth the "the crack babies of porn." Science and morality collide in debates over whether and how pornography consumption is harmful.

CHAPTER 13

To Your Health

N ot exactly the stereotype of the antiporn Holy Roller, Noah Church is not religious, has a degree in creative writing, lives on the West Coast, and is a vegan who's passionate about animal rights and promoting plant-based diets to curb global warming. As a sign of his progressive politics, he told me that for the 2016 presidential election, "I voted for Hillary but wanted to vote for Bernie." Church was just a kid when he first saw internet porn—nine years old when he first searched for pictures of naked women on Google. He described it as thrilling, and he quickly became obsessed with what seemed like the limitless supply available through a simple online search. By the time he was eleven, he was using peer-to-peer sharing sites to download porn videos. His family had switched their internet connection from dial-up to broadband, so he could set up a download overnight that wouldn't interfere with the phone line. Some of what he downloaded disgusted him and made him angry. He questioned whether it was legal. But eventually, as he told the story, he became desensitized to this "more extreme content" and "more fringe content" and began to seek it out. In middle school, he looked at porn almost daily. His parents were totally in the dark. "I was told nothing at all about pornography," he recalled. His parents just didn't understand what was available to Church online. And he was a good kid—did well in school, had a few friends. Still,

"I was lonely," Church said. "I was never happy going to bed after looking at pornography."

The first time he tried to have sex with his high school girlfriend, he couldn't maintain an erection. He described the "out-of-body experience," where he was shocked, ashamed, and confused that what he thought of as his extremely high sex drive and eagerness to have sex (as evidenced by all that porn he was watching) was not matching up with his body's physical response. This was in 2008, and at the time, he tried to search Google for answers. "Young man erection problems" didn't yield many helpful results, other than to tell him he could have some obscure disease or illness or that he had psychological problems that were getting in the way. After a series of unsuccessful relationships throughout college, he stopped dating altogether. Other than his nonexistent sex life, he was doing well. He ate healthy foods and exercised and got a good-paying, fulfilling job. Eventually, he felt ready to "face this demon again," as he described it. So, he tried once again to search the internet for answers, and this time he found a vibrant online community that appeared full of young men with problems just like his. But unlike him, they had managed to quit pornography and recover their sex lives. "They were pioneers, forged off into the unknown," he said. "They quit. They recovered. And they became sexually healthy again." And Church joined them, participating in online forums and blogging about his own journey. He quit porn for good and now works full time helping other men who want to do the same.

Church works as a recovery coach based on, as he put it, his own "path to sobriety." "It wasn't just a switch that flipped from 'I'm a recovering porn addict' to 'I'm gonna dedicate my life to this,'" he told me. "It happened incrementally, in stages. Seeing people's responses to my stories and realizing just how many people out there were struggling with similar issues without trustworthy information and a clear path toward recovery, I realized there was a big need, so I decided to write a book as a guide for people. I was also making YouTube videos, because people were sending me their questions, and I wanted to answer them in a public way so that other people could benefit from that information." The book he self-published, called *WACK: Addicted to Internet Porn*, is available as a free e-book on his website for people who sign up for his newsletter.

Church made it a priority to make his content free, he explained, but eventually he found he couldn't keep up with all the questions readers were sending him. So, he said, "I needed to find a way to make this my career and part of my living. That's when I started offering my services as a personal coach for those who wanted some one-on-one help." Like Beth, the kinky fitness coach, Church took advantage of the entrepreneurial possibilities in the coaching industry, which estimated a profit of nearly three billion dollars in 2019. Five years after he started coaching, he was able to quit his job as a firefighter and work as a recovery coach full time.

Church himself rejects the label "antipornography" when I asked him about it, preferring instead "pro-sex" for the label of the movement of which he is a part. I heard this often from respondents who, like Church, did not have moral opposition to sexually explicit material per se, but who believed that internet pornography caused physical and emotional harm to the men who watched it. "Sexual health" and "wholeness" are what motivate Church and his peers—the hundreds of thousands of members of online communities trying to recover from the harm they believe pornography has caused their bodies and minds.

IN 2016, THE same year California voters were considering Prop 60, the GOP declared in its platform that pornography itself was a "public health crisis" and was "destroying the lives of millions." Utah legislators followed suit, passing a resolution with a unanimous vote declaring pornography to be a "public health hazard leading to a broad spectrum of individual and public health impacts and societal harm." Senator Todd Weiler, a former lawyer and Republican in his fourth year serving in the Utah State Senate, sponsored the resolution. In an op-ed penned with Pamela Atkinson, an adviser to the governor, and Orrin Hatch, the Republican who holds the record for the longest time spent in Congress, they described the 1986 Meese Commission on pornography as motivation for the resolution. "Every issue it documented has grown worse, and every warning it contained has come true." Their concerns were many: pornography is biologically addictive and negatively impacts the brain; it contributes to the hypersexualization of teens and "prepubescent children"; hard-core porn has become mainstream porn; porn normalizes and leads to violence and abuse of women and children; it shapes "deviant sexual arousal." The goal of the resolution was for the state of Utah to "recognize the need for education, prevention, research, and policy change at the community and society level in order to address the pornography epidemic that is harming the people of our state and nation."

National media covered the story when Weiler introduced his resolution and when it was eventually passed in the Utah legislature. *Penthouse* referenced Utah governor Gary Herbert, who signed the resolution into law on April 19, 2016, on the cover of its August issue later that year. UTAH'S GOVERNOR WANTS TO HANDLE YOUR PENIS, the cover headline read, alongside a model wearing a red-and-white-striped bikini bottom in front of an American flag. The magazine mailed the issue to the governor's door and to the headquarters of the Church of Jesus Christ of Latter-day Saints. "Since the Mormon church brings its unsolicited moral, religious, and political values to our doorstep, we decided to return the favor," said *Penthouse* editor Ralphie Aronowitz. Larry Flynt also started sending complimentary copies of *Hustler* magazine to Utah lawmakers' offices. When comedian Chelsea Handler invited Senator Weiler on to her talk show for a serious segment on the harms of pornography, she also invited Noah Church and Gabe Deem, two self-proclaimed nonreligious men active in the online porn addiction recovery movement. Each of them insisted that morality was beside the point. Pornography was, in fact, a serious health concern.

The Utah resolution was based on a model drafted by leaders of NCOSE. Since 2016, twenty-nine states have considered nearly identical resolutions declaring pornography to be a public health crisis, and as of 2021, sixteen have written them into state law. Most resolutions have received bipartisan support. In Montana, for example, a university student who led an antitrafficking student group gathered signatures from Montana residents and then used draft language from NCOSE to approach a Democrat to sponsor the resolution. It passed in Montana's legislature in 2019. While these resolutions do not change laws regulating pornography, antiporn activists have heralded them as an important sign of support for their cause. "They aren't changing the laws, but they're an important step, because it's political officials who are making a declaration," one speaker at the Freedom from Sexual Slavery conference described. Gail Dines, the feminist sociologist and antipornography activist, also writes positively of these resolutions. "The science is there," she wrote in an op-ed in 2016. "By taking a health-focused view of porn and recognizing its radiating impact not only on consumers but also on society at large, Utah's resolution simply reflects the latest research."

Pornography's opponents have been using the language of science and health to justify their positions for a long time. As early as 1984, the conservative Catholic activist Phyllis Schlafly used the language of addiction to describe pornography: "My view of pornography is that it is an addiction like alcohol or drugs or tobacco," she told a journalist. "It moved from what is commonly known as calendar art, pinup girls, to awful, bizarre, exotic, lesbian, bondage." She noted that *Penthouse* had recently started publishing what she called "lesbian pictures." "They're catering to people who want more and more of the exotic and bizarre," she explained, using a common story of addiction and the mistaken belief that some drugs, like marijuana and alcohol, can serve as a gateway to more dangerous substances.

In the twenty-first century, the name of a Utah-based antiporn organization, Fight the New Drug, captures a similar sentiment: pornography is physically harmful and potentially addictive. The organization has given hundreds of presentations at schools, at churches, and for community groups across the country, promoting its message that the founders insist is not religious or political. Its message is simple: it is a scientific fact that pornography is bad for your health. The organization explains: "In the same way that a junkie eventually requires more and more of a drug to get a buzz or even feel normal, regular porn consumers will end up turning to porn more often or seeking out more extreme versions—or both—to feel excited again. And once the porn habit is established, quitting can even lead to withdrawal symptoms similar to drugs."

Opposing pornography for reasons having to do with health distances antiporn positions from those of religious zealots, who seem puritanical and unmodern. "We're not here to talk about if porn is evil or whether it should be banned," says the narrator of the Fight the New Drug documentary series, *Brain Heart World*. Though critics have accused the organization of its own religious agenda—the organization was founded and is mostly employed by Latter-day Saints living in Utah—the group emphasizes repeatedly that it is nonreligious and nonpartisan and that its goal is *not* to censor pornography. Fight the New Drug is run by a bunch of straight white Mormon guys, yes, but they are also hip Millennials, many of whom voted for Hillary Clinton and who support gay rights, interview respondents have told me. And they believe that the strongest case against pornography is not a religious one, but a scientific one. In *Brain Heart World*, they explain that there is "a massive effort in the porn industry today to teach you that porn is harmless." Fight the New Drug believes it is its job to set the record straight.

State resolutions declaring pornography to be a public health crisis base their evidence on the negative health consequences of pornography use. Twelve of the twenty-nine resolutions that have been proposed claim that pornography can "contribute to emotional and medical illnesses." Many resolutions refer to specific consequences, such as Georgia's resolution, which describes pornography use as "leading to low self-esteem and eating disorders." All mention that porn is biologically addictive, and most make the broad declaration that pornography use "shapes deviant sexual arousal." Pornography addiction "means the user requires more novelty, often in the form of more shocking material, in order to be satisfied," most resolutions claim. Hawaii's resolution refers to pornography depicting "extreme degradation and violence" that consumers desire as a consequence of their addictive cravings. Allusions to "deviant," "shocking," and "extreme" forms of sexual desire that develop *from* pornography use assume that pornography taints normal, expected, and demure forms of desire. This language also gives the impression that "normal" men would not choose or intentionally seek out "deviant" depictions of sex were it not for pornography's addictive qualities.

Nearly all these resolutions say that pornography use fuels criminal behavior—typically, acts of violence or participation in the illegal sex industry (i.e., prostitution or sex trafficking). Most imply that pornography increases the likelihood that men will commit violence against women. The Louisiana resolution includes the claim that the age of first exposure to violent pornography impacts the likelihood of the user committing acts of violence: "the younger a boy is exposed to images depicting rape, bondage, abuse of women, and other deviant behaviors, the more he is prone to commit violence and force nonconsensual sex with others."

Nearly all the state resolutions declare that pornography harms marriages and families, along with man-woman romantic relationships. Some include the claim that pornography "teaches girls to be used and teaches boys to use." Most suggest that widespread pornography use contributes to the declining marriage rate, specifically that pornography lessens the "desire in young men to marry." Emphasizing this harm to the family helps to establish the case that the harms of pornography go beyond the individual and threaten broader social norms. Framing these harms as a threat to the family and, by extension, public health situates pornography use within the purview of the state, facilitating increased regulation of both gender and sexuality.

THE NCOSE MODEL on which these resolutions were based includes a long list of academic articles the organization believes support its claims. Yet, despite the resolutions' confident language and the declaration that pornography is a public health crisis, few conclusions as to whether pornography is good or bad for you are universally supported by peer-reviewed academic research. Points of agreement are more descriptive than explanatory. We know, for example, that surveys consistently reveal a negative relationship between men watching porn and marital quality for heterosexual couples. But for most surveys that ask questions at a single point in time, it's impossible to tease out whether watching porn is bad for marriage, or if bad marriages prompt men to watch porn. The same goes for studies that find a correlation between porn consumption and mental health problems such as depression and anxiety. It's the classic chicken-versus-egg dilemma. What's more, sociologist Samuel Perry has found that at least some of these negative effects are the result of masturbation, not pornography itself. After publishing numerous articles on the negative relationship between marital quality and porn use, he decided to control for masturbation practices— meaning, he examined the effects of porn consumption among men who reported the same frequency of masturbation and found that the negative effects of porn on marital quality went away. In other words, men who masturbate more tend to report poorer-quality marriages, regardless of porn use. And, interestingly, some studies have found that married women who watch porn report higher levels of satisfaction in their marriages to men than women who don't. Findings like these suggest that it's not pornography that affects marital quality, but rather, the context in which the porn is viewed.

Researchers also agree that boys and men look at porn more frequently and at an earlier age than girls and women. But when it comes to explaining to what effect, results vary widely. Several studies have found evidence that pornography consumption is associated with men's likelihood to commit acts of violence toward women—a rallying cry for both conservatives and antiporn feminists in the 1980s. Yet these studies offer proof of correlation, not causation. One study found the relationship between aggression and pornography consumption to be true only for men who already exhibited antiwoman attitudes or for men who watched violent pornography. One national study finds, to the contrary, that men who watch porn have more feminist views than men who don't.

Why are these studies so contradictory? Because their findings depend on the types of questions researchers asked and whom they were asking. The wording of questions—asking if a user feels guilt while using porn, if they believe pornography is bad for society, or if they have tried to quit using porn but couldn't—implicitly suggest that pornography is wrong and undesirable. Surveys rarely ask if users believe pornography is morally *good* for society, or if respondents wish they could use *more* porn. Survey methodologists, drawing from lessons learned by psychologists, call this a problem of "acquiescence," where people's responses to a question are likely to go along with the values implied in that question. Researchers who have sought to discover potential benefits of porn use have found that it can be associated with body acceptance, sexual orientation acceptance, increased self-esteem, and increased awareness of sexual techniques.

Some of the best surveys available to social scientists (those with national samples and that are carried out repeatedly over time) seem to ask the worst questions about internet porn. Take the University of Chicago's General Social Survey, or GSS, one the longest-running surveys in the United

States. It's an omnibus questionnaire, meaning it asks questions about a variety of different topics. Some of these questions have remained the same since the survey began in the 1970s, and some were added by researchers at various points over time. Since 1973, the GSS has asked the same question about porn: "Have you seen an X-Rated Movie in the past year?" The answer choices are "yes" or "no." Most years, the survey asks no other questions about porn use. For a brief spell (2000–2004), it asked respondents if they had viewed a sexually explicit website in the past thirty days. Data from these years suggest that the vast majority of Americans were not looking at online porn. Between 86 and 92 percent of respondents reported that they had "never" looked at a porn site in the last month, which could be because online streaming sites were just getting started. After 2004, the GSS stopped asking that question.

Asking whether respondents have viewed an X-rated movie in the past year has a number of obvious problems when it comes to usefulness for researchers. First, if we want to understand how often people look at porn and how frequency matters, this question is woefully unhelpful, asking people to sum up twelve months of habits in a single question. Second, X ratings are clearly a thing of the past, from a bygone era, when theater marquees announced feature-length porno films like *Deep Throat*. People who answer "no" to this question may very well be VIP members of Pornhub. Still, researchers will continue to publish articles and draw conclusions about Americans' porn consumption based on this question because, when it comes to data collected over time, it's the best we've got.

JOSHUA GRUBBS, a clinical psychologist, has dedicated much of his career to accurately measuring the effects of pornography use on consumers. He graduated with a bachelor's degree from Liberty University, the ultraconservative fundamentalist college founded by Jerry Falwell in the foothills of the Blue Ridge Mountains in Lynchburg, Virginia. It was the late aughts, before the ubiquity of smartphones, and Grubbs and his friends accessed the internet through personal computers in their dorm rooms. Back then, as is true today, internet porn was understood to be a common vice of young evangelical men—exactly the demographic of Grubbs and his peers. "Pornography was labeled 'the demise of guys' and that it was going to destroy a whole generation of men, my generation specifically," he told me. "And I was just kind of struck by this, and it didn't make a ton of sense to me at the time. A lot of people felt they were addicted to pornography, and there was a part of me that did not think that it made sense."

As a twenty-year-old psychology major, Grubbs didn't think his peers' behavior matched the definitions of addiction he was reading about in his textbooks. Porn might not have become the focus of his studies had it not been for a professor at Liberty who invited him to work on a project to measure problematic internet pornography use. That work eventually became the first iteration of Grubbs's Cyber-Pornography Use Inventory (CPUI) scale, a lengthy thirty-one-question survey to understand and classify problematic pornography use. Grubbs went on to receive his Ph.D. and has since spent the last decade refining the scale, which today, in its newer, shorter version, is called the CPUI-9. The scale itself attests to Grubbs's conviction, based in empirical and clinical evidence, that some people use pornography compulsively and to negative consequence.

The bulk of Grubbs's work has found that people's beliefs about pornography influence the consequences they experience from viewing it. For example, in one study he led, a national survey, people who *perceived* themselves to be addicted to porn were more likely to show signs of psychological distress than people who used porn more often but who did not *identify* as addicted. Grubbs and his frequent collaborator, sociologist Samuel Perry, call this "moral incongruence," in which the most significant problems that come from porn use are associated with believing pornography is morally wrong but using it anyway. In another study, Perry found that respondents who believed viewing pornography was "always morally wrong" were more likely to experience depression associated with their porn use. Other respondents—again, even those who used porn more frequently—did not experience such consequences.

Grubbs's and Perry's findings don't sit well with many of the creators and users of porn addiction recovery websites. They see pornography, regardless of social context, as objectively and physically harmful. Gary Wilson, founder of the website YourBrainOnPorn, has accused Grubbs and Perry, for example, of being "porn science deniers" and a part of a "pro-porn alliance." Perry, a sociology professor and Christian who teaches Sunday school on the weekends, finds such accusations laughable. In an interview, he explained, "Sure, porn can have a lot of negative consequences, but research suggests that's not always the case."

Still, after founding his website in 2010, Wilson criticized anyone who challenged the idea that pornography was biologically addictive. I heard Wilson described, on both sides of the porn wars, as alternatively an "intense guy," a "genius," a "wacko nutcase," and a "hero." Over fourteen million people have watched his TEDx Talk, "The Great Porn Experiment." His website receives nearly four hundred thousand visitors each month, and more than forty thousand copies of his book, *Your Brain on Porn*, have been sold since 2014.

On his website and in interviews, Wilson insisted he was not antiporn on principle, and he frequently mentioned the fact that he was an atheist, so as to not be mistaken for a religious zealot. He believed the brain science was definitive: online pornography is uniquely addictive and conditions the brain to crave more and more. His website tracks academic research articles on pornography and other forms of addiction, piecing together findings of neurobiological studies to explain why the pornography addiction model is scientifically sound. YourBrainOnPorn contains a whopping 11,000 web pages describing these scientific studies and personal accounts of the harms of pornography addiction.

Wilson, who died in 2021, maintains a massive online following, and many antipornography groups cite him as a scientific expert, even though his online biography doesn't boast a college degree. Wilson authored two academic articles, despite a lack of academic affiliation or credentials. Both are reviews of prior literature, one that he coauthored in the academic journal *Behavioral Sciences*, the other, of which he is sole author, is featured in *Addicta: The Turkish Journal on Addictions*. The national antipornography organization Fight the New Drug calls Wilson an "educator in the neuro-chemistry of addiction, mating, and bonding." At the Freedom from Sexual Slavery conference I attended, one speaker called Wilson's site "the most encyclopedic place for the science of porn." Online forums on porn addiction recovery consistently recommend the site for anyone interested in the "science side" of porn addiction, as one user described it. In 2021, NCOSE awarded Wilson with its Founder Award for "working tirelessly behind the scenes to help those seeking freedom from pornography addiction." All proceeds from Wilson's book go to an antiporn nonprofit located in the United Kingdom. Wilson, who lived in Oregon, claimed he never profited monetarily from his site.

SOCIOLOGIST KARIN KNORR Cetina calls the United States a "knowledge society," one in which individuals use scientific claims to advance competing truths. Though we generally assume that scientific authority stems from verified training and credentials, the value that Americans place on free speech also means that individuals or groups on the fringe of established science can make scientific-sounding claims. The antivaccination movement in the United States, for example, relies on claims that have been widely discredited by medical authorities. Through in-depth interviews with parents who refuse to vaccinate their children according to pediatric guidelines, however, sociologist Jennifer Reich finds that these parents accept the science, such as the risks posed by vaccine side effects, that aligns with their existing perspectives, and disregard the evidence, such as the risk of communicable disease, that challenges those perspectives. According to feminist philosopher Donna Haraway, science is always *sciences*, "lumpy" conclusions that can be used as a means to achieve various ends.

Online, users with no scientific background have developed an explanation for pornography addiction and recovery that they insist is accurate because it aligns with their personal experiences. NoFap, for example, is a booming Reddit forum of a million followers and a stand-alone website with over three hundred thousand members (data published by NoFap indicates members are mostly men) who want to quit watching porn in order to improve their lives. The group (whose name originates from the term "fap," an onomatopoeia for the sound of masturbation) is the brainchild of Alexander Rhodes, a twentysomething who describes himself as politically liberal, nonreligious, and having no moral qualms about sexually explicit material. As Rhodes told the *New York Times*, at one point he was watching porn and masturbating fourteen times a day and experiencing what he self-diagnosed as erectile dysfunction, in which he was able to get an erection only if he thought about porn, even when he was sexually intimate with real-life partners. While in college, he decided to detail on Reddit a one-week experiment in abstaining from porn. The forum became a sensation and was covered on national news.

A measure of success on NoFap is going ninety days "No-PMO" (porn, masturbation, or orgasm). This "rebooting" is hard but worth it, according to "Fapstronauts," as adherents call themselves. Rewards include a host of "superpowers"—spikes in confidence, the ability to sexually attract others, waves of creative genius, and newfound savviness in social interactions. There is no scientific evidence supporting the existence of these superpowers, but users insist they are real.

One member of an online porn addiction recovery community, Tad, told me he takes all the scientific talk on the particular site "with a grain of salt." Still, he said he has personally experienced the positive effects of the "reboot." "I mean, it might be placebo, but I definitely can feel a change," he explained. A couple of years ago, Tad said, he "just knew" he had to quit porn. "It was bad for me. It was bad for my mental health, and I just felt bad physically, like it was draining my energy. It was just a shitty, shitty habit." He attempted a reboot three times unsuccessfully, but each time, as he grew closer to the ninety-day goal, he said his physical and mental health would improve. "It's kind of hard to classify, but I definitely believe I was losing energy by masturbating, and so I was gaining that back. Some people talk about how when you ejaculate you lose testosterone and stuff, and I'm not sure if it actually does or not, but I do think I've just got more energy, I've gotten stronger."

I asked Tad about his goals related to quitting porn. He told me he wasn't religious and that he didn't think watching porn was morally wrong. "For me, it's a health goal," he said. "Honestly I can't even imagine a moderate amount of watching it that would be healthy. I just don't see that. You know, there are studies that say it's just not good for you, from a health sense. You know, it changes your brain structure to wire toward addictive pathways, so, for those reasons, it's really a health goal that I don't do it." Tad used a "self-control app" on his computer to block pornographic websites and regularly contributed to online message boards to give support to, and get it from, others. He started meditating, exercising, and journaling regularly. On the first page of his journal, he jotted a list of all the reasons he didn't want to watch porn, as a reminder to himself. "To be my best self" is what he wrote at the top.

Tad exemplifies the many men who intentionally avoid pornography to maximize their overall health and well-being, just like the rest of us who, in large numbers, are avoiding carbs, quitting alcohol, joining exercise classes, or using meditation apps. At an individual level, many of us strive to make personal choices that minimize bad habits and make our minds and bodies feel good. But collectively, we are buying into a broader trend, what political economist Robert Crawford calls "healthism." No longer used simply to signal the absence of disease or a physically well body, healthism reflects the value that Americans today attach to health: that wellness represents goodness. To name porn as a health crisis may seem to distance an antiporn position from religious beliefs or feminist commitments, but the language of health can also be a tool wielded for broader goals.

CHAPTER 14

In Recovery

In the United States, what is colloquially referred to as the recovery movement is made up of laypeople and professionals, many of whom have struggled with addiction themselves. Studies of the effectiveness of twelve-step programs have seen mixed results. But the sheer magnitude of recovery culture is evidence that something is working. Alcoholics Anonymous (AA) began in the 1930s, and a few decades after that, groups that used the AA model began appearing to treat a number of problems other than alcohol abuse. Narcotics Anonymous (NA) was the earliest spinoff (in 1953), followed by Gamblers Anonymous (1957), Overeaters Anonymous (1960), Potsmokers Anonymous (1968), Debtors Anonymous (1968), Emotions Anonymous (1971), and Pills Anonymous (1975). These offshoots marked a shift in popular understanding both of addictions and, indeed, of what we can become addicted to. Founded in 1977 by a longtime AA member, Sex and Love Addicts Anonymous (SLAA) was the first established sex addiction support group.

For most of the country's history, American society understood both sex and addiction as issues of morality. The word *addiction* comes from the Latin *addictio*, meaning "to give over" or "surrender." Of course, people have been surrendering to sexual vices for centuries. Religious institutions, not medical or scientific ones, took the lead in regulation and treatment.

Gradually, over the course of the twentieth century, convinced by the popularity of AA and similar groups and other social changes, the American public came to understand addiction not as a moral failing but more akin to a physical disease.

One of the founding members of SLAA was Patrick Carnes, a graduate student in counseling education from Minneapolis, Minnesota; a husband; a father of four; and, as he came to understand it, a sex addict. After years of failed attempts at changing his behavior, Carnes finally discovered a twelve-step approach. It worked. With a newly minted Ph.D., Carnes made sex addiction recovery his life's work.

A small press published his first book on the subject, *The Sexual Addiction*. It didn't sell. Undeterred, Carnes convinced the press to rerelease the book with a different title: *Out of the Shadows: Understanding Sexual Addiction*. This small shift—the naming of shame and secrecy that accompanies sex addiction—opened up a vast market. Letters came from wives of sex-addicted husbands, men who could not come to terms with their destructive sexual behaviors, and recovering alcoholics who also engaged in compulsive sex and knew there was more to their addiction than alcohol alone.

Out of the Shadows placed Carnes in the national spotlight, and today he is credited as the founder of the sex addiction recovery movement. He made appearances on national television programs, including *Oprah* and *Phil Donahue*, and became an expert on the nation's sexual problems. The author of twelve books, Carnes described how destructive sexual behavior could be understood through an addiction lens. He used the "SAFE" formula to explain what counts as a sexual addiction: sexual behavior that is Secret, Abusive (harmful to oneself or others), avoidant of Feelings, and Empty (outside a committed relationship). The framework he proposed rested upon and reinforced normative notions of sex: that it should be within a committed monogamous relationship. Anything else could signal a problem and, possibly, an addiction.

In the early days of the sex addiction recovery movement, Carnes made reference to pornography as one of the many behaviors associated with sex addiction, but not as the core problem. By the 1990s, though, some Americans were beginning to perceive the home computer as particularly dangerous. A decade earlier, workers producing a game for the Japanese company Atari Inc. spoke jokingly about how "addictive the game was." Parents of children and teens confirmed. One teenage champion at a New York tournament for Atari's *Space Invaders* told journalists that he had played six hours a day to prepare.

A recovery movement dedicated to gaming addiction developed in earnest in the late 1990s. In 2002, a year after her son died of suicide in his apartment with his computer monitor still displaying *EverQuest*, the game he spent hours playing every day, Liz Woolley founded On-Line Gamers Anonymous, which applied the twelve steps to video game addiction. As with online gaming addiction, internet pornography addiction emerged as a problem related to but distinct from a broader umbrella of addiction, in its case, sex addiction.

Today, clinicians working within a sex addiction framework frequently reference what they call the "triple-A threat" of online pornography: accessibility, affordability, and anonymity. In nearly every antiporn event I attended, at least one speaker referenced Pornhub's own boastful statistics, which included the fact that in 2019, 1.36 million hours of new content had been added, which would take 169 years to watch. Pornhub and other free streaming porn sites offer virtually limitless content literally at users' fingertips, setting them up to binge-watch or to visit the sites much more frequently than they would have visited a VHS rental store in the 1980s and '90s. Thanks to algorithmic models, porn sites expose users to new clips and suggested search terms. This is the perfect storm for addictive behavior, as porn companies profit from users who seek more and more novel content.

I ARRIVED AT Prairie Christian Church on a warm and humid summer evening. My directions first took me to the south parking lot, which was full even though it wasn't Sunday; there must have been an event in the main sanctuary. When I drove around to the other side of the megachurch complex, I found the north parking lot mostly empty, but I could see lights on in the rooms in the north wing. I later learned that most rooms are occupied seven days a week, from six in the morning until late in the evening. There, church members and visitors can attend small groups and classes on a wide range of topics, from finance to Bible study. This wing of the church also contained a day care and preschool. My invitation to the church had come from Cheryl, a thin, petite white woman in her fifties with dyed black hair and matching eyeliner. For nearly a decade, Cheryl had been leading Redeemed! (a pseudonym), which uses the twelve-step model of addiction recovery with explicitly Christian language to treat and support people wishing to quit a wide range of behaviors, from drug abuse to pornography use to codependency. For a decade before leading the group, she was a regular and active participant in it, rarely missing a weekly meeting.

Every Friday, Redeemed! has its public meeting, and once a month the meeting is preceded by a potluck; on the night of my visit, the potluck featured grocery store deli fried chicken and a crock pot of enchiladas. Knowing I was researching pornography addiction, Cheryl invited me to come hear Phil give his testimony. Curious about my background, she asked me about my life: what kind of addictions I might be confronting and whether I wanted to join the weekly women's group, which met after the general meeting. She shared with me that her ex-husband had been an alcoholic, but that she attended Redeemed! herself because she struggled with an addiction to codependency.

"Don't we all?" I asked, half joking.

"Mmm," Cheryl said. "Codependency is just human nature without God," she said earnestly. According to her evangelical beliefs, we are all born as sinners who need Jesus Christ to save us. "There's messiness every-where," she continued. "Relationships, broken people with lots of scars from their childhood, a lot of behavioral issues. Addictions come from the hurt places. People do screwy things."

When conducting research observations, I answer questions posed to me as honestly as I can, but without giving away too many details about my personal life. This is as much for me as for my research subjects—I want both of us to remember my role as a researcher, not a fellow participant. Somehow on this night, though, I ended up telling Cheryl that my dad was a recovered alcoholic who had spent months at rehab when I was twelve and who hadn't had a drink since. He had "worked the steps" and attended AA meetings for years. Sometimes, he would agree to be somebody's sponsor, and I remember answering collect phone calls and being instructed to accept the charges and hand the phone over to my dad.

"Sober twenty years," I shared with her.

"Praise God," she said.

I suddenly and unexpectedly teared up. Cheryl hugged me, and I hugged her back. Then we walked together into a small sanctuary for praise and worship and to hear Phil's testimony.

A small band (drum set, electric guitar, and keyboard) led us in a few songs of praise and worship, with the lyrics projected onto a screen partially obscured by the guitarist's head. After singing, Cheryl gave her thanks to the band, made a few announcements about upcoming events, and then introduced the night's speaker.

"My name is Phil," he began, after making his way to the podium at the front of the room. "I'm a believer, and I struggle with an addiction to pornography and video games."

"Hi, Phil," the audience responded.

Phil looked down at a stack of notes, clutched in a somewhat shaky hand, and told his story: "I have struggled with pornography from the time I was in, like, seventh grade up through the first few years of my marriage. I always knew it was a problem, but I didn't know what to do about it. I talked to a pastor and other people, because I didn't know what to do. They told me to stop, but I couldn't stop. I was always functional, but it was poisoning me and my marriage and poisoning my relationship with God."

Phil continued, explaining how he took a leap of faith and trusted God, whom he felt was telling him to turn down what seemed at the time like a good job offer. In hindsight, Phil could see that this was the right decision, a turning point in his life and on his road to recovery. He found a different and better job, he was able to improve his physical health and eliminate his chronic back pain, and a friend introduced him to Redeemed!

"Up until that point, I wasn't really sure what sobriety meant." Redeemed! helped him, he said, commit to "no porn and no masturbation," as he put it.

Phil's recovery was not a straight path. After five years attending Redeemed!, and finally eliminating porn from his life for good, he started to fill the gap with computer games. "It took me a while to realize that was also a problem, that it was just an alternative addiction." But he was able to bring this issue to his Redeemed! "family," as he called them, and use the program to help make sense of how he was using both porn and video games to cope with outside stressors and internal shame and guilt. To end his testimony, he shared how he had channeled his compulsive porn use and gaming into an activity that he believed both healthy and godly: "I've memorized one new Bible verse a day for about two years."

This wasn't the first time Phil shared his story with the group, but it was the first time he weaved together the different elements having to do with both pornography and video games. Later, in an interview, I asked Phil what it was like when he shared his testimony for the first time. "I remember it going really well," he said, "but I remember reading it and, about halfway through, thinking, 'I can't believe I'm saying this out loud to a group of people.' But at that point, I was like, 'Let's just get this over with,' and I did. I had a lot of people come up to me afterward and say, 'That was really brave.' I just felt really honest, and that felt really good."

The reason Phil has stayed involved in Redeemed! for all these years is because he feels it is a place for him. It doesn't matter that his addictions are not the same as those for people struggling with drugs or alcoholism. The focus of the group is on the recovery process, which is the same regardless of the addictive behavior.

GOOGLING "HOW TO quit porn" will inevitably, and ironically, result in myriad pornographic images and video clips. But below these, one will find a variety of resources that offer advice and products. Consider one article from Covenant Eyes, titled "How to Quit Porn: 6 Essential Steps." First step: You must *want* to quit. Second step: You need to find a different way from the unsuccessful strategies of the past. Third step: You have to be honest with at least one other person. Fourth and fifth steps: You have to get rid of all your porn and stop new porn from coming in. Sixth and final step: You need a friend to help you stay on track. The subtext is, of course, "Have you tried Covenant Eyes?"

It's convincing marketing that reinforces the problem it claims to solve. And the problem, according to company messaging, is a serious one. Covenant Eyes stresses the neurochemical impact pornography has on your brain—at one antiporn conference, I picked up a brain-shaped stress ball with the company logo from a table of swag—and so, it makes the damage of porn seem physical and hard to reverse. All the more important to sign up for a subscription! It costs about as much as a monthly subscription to Netflix or Hulu, and it is pitched similarly: $15.99 per month for the family plan, which includes unlimited devices and up to twelve users. In 2019, the company reported annual earnings of over $26 million.

Covenant Eyes software doesn't just block pornographic content (though it does that, too, through a convenient "add-on" feature, for an additional fee); it also tracks websites that are used each day and then sends a report to an "ally" of your choosing. As the CEO of Covenant Eyes, Ron DeHaas, explains, "The best means of losing weight is to weigh yourself every day, and so the best means of fighting pornography is to have an accountability ally. That ally is the person that you depend on to monitor what you're doing on the computer." For most of the men I interviewed who used the software, they chose male friends whom they trusted and who were often themselves on the journey to quit porn. In one unusual example, one interview respondent, Brad, explained to me that after he was caught looking at porn at work, reports of his history went directly to his boss—which happened to be an evangelical church. Rather than firing him, his supervisors decided that he could continue his work so long as he installed the Covenant Eyes app on his work and home computers and attended weekly support groups at a neighboring church for men like him who struggled with pornography addiction.

DeHaas, a devout evangelical Christian himself, started Covenant Eyes in 2000 from his home office in a small Michigan town. As he describes it, a personal tragedy made him realize the importance of protecting the family. In 1992, his wife and two young children were killed when a tanker truck hit the family's vehicle with them in it. DeHaas received over two million dollars in a settlement from the trucking company, and he decided to use it to start a company he believed in and that he believed the world needed. "I made the decision to spend all of my money," he told one journalist, "I did not have anything left . . . I couldn't afford a cup of coffee at McDonald's." With the help of a seventeen-year-old computer programmer, DeHaas developed the Covenant Eyes accountability software and made a deal with Promise Keepers, at the time the largest and most well-known evangelical organization for men's fellowship. The company grew slowly but steadily, and since 2010, it has been recognized by *Inc.* magazine as one of the fastest-growing private companies in the United States. As of 2020, DeHaas has employed a staff of more than two hundred people who work in a forty-thousand-square-foot complex.

Beyond Covenant Eyes and Redeemed!, there are hundreds of products and resources (books, websites, support groups, apps, and software programs) to help young men avoid pornography. Fight the New Drug's porn addiction recovery program, Fortify, is free for anyone under eighteen who can explain why they want to quit using porn. The app, normally costing $9.99 per month for adult users or $6.95 for college students, resembles countless other health and wellness programs, where users document daily habits in order to track incremental progress. Upon reaching milestones, such as thirty days without porn, users get coins, badges, or level-ups that offer a sense of pride and accomplishment. There are guided meditations, journal prompts, and opportunities to connect to other Fortify users, along with "allies" of your choosing, people in your real life who agree to support you on your recovery journey.

Though some porn addiction recovery resources like Fortify are not explicitly religious, evangelical Protestants more than any other religious denomination have dominated the pornography addiction recovery industry. In 2002, Craig Gross and Mike Foster, two young, hip white evangelical pastors, founded what they dubbed XXXchurch. The website advertised "Porn, Sex, Girls, Guys" on its home page to invite visitors who had no qualms about porn to read on to learn why they should avoid it. The organization now offers a software program similar to Covenant Eyes, called X3watch. One of its tag lines is "Jesus loves porn stars," and today, a former performer, Brittni De La Mora, leads XXXchurch, along with her pastor husband. Together, they spearhead a project, Strip Church, that ministers to dancers in strip clubs. They also attend the *AVN* Awards each year to spread their Good News.

Between 2006 and 2019, Pastor Gross publicly debated porn performer Ron Jeremy at universities across the country—"Porn Pastor versus Porn Star," as the event was heralded. Typically, Jeremy mustered the louder applause from whooping college guys upon first entering the stage. Without similar celebrity status within the presumably liberal "hookup culture" of universities, "I'm by far the underdog," Gross has reflected. He was always the one to present his position first, something that Jeremy demanded, since, in his words, "I have no problem with his career; he has a problem with my career."

"I'm not about shutting down the porn industry," Gross insisted to his audience at one event. "You have the right to view it." Still, "the next time you're tempted, you have a thought, you're visiting a porn site, I would just ask yourself why. Take a beat and just think about it."

Evangelicals are "cultural innovators," in the words of sociologists Shayne Lee and Philip Luke Sinitiere, and thus have remained successful and salient in contemporary American culture, even when denominational church membership and attendance has declined. What emerged in the late twentieth century was a "spiritual marketplace," where religions competed to produce innovative forms of worship and convince individuals that religion had a place for them. Evangelicals are successful in this marketplace because they are "in the world, but not of the world," as a common saying goes, meaning that they participate in secular culture even while clinging to traditional and conservative beliefs. Some examples of successful evangelical enterprises include televangelism, Christian self-help books, Christian rock music and movies, and the emergence of gyms, day cares, and coffee shops within nondenominational megachurches. Yet evangelicals don't see this as cultural appropriation, but rather, as cultural transformation. Craig Gross, onstage next to Ron Jeremy (with his slick, dyed black hair and pierced ears), epitomized this trend. Today, he leads an organization, Christian Cannabis, that promotes recreational marijuana as a spiritual practice.

Sociologist Jeremy Thomas has traced how *Christianity Today*, the largest evangelical periodical in the United States, started by Billy Graham in 1956, changed its coverage of pornography so that since the 1990s, an addiction framework has come to dominate. Before the mid-1980s, most articles relied on what Thomas calls the "narrative of traditional values" to discuss porn, with the articles centered on how pornography contributes to an overall moral decline of society along with the disintegration of the nuclear family. In the mid-1980s, influenced by the feminist antipornography movement, the narrative of public/performer harm (which centers on how pornography harms women both as porn performers and within the broader society) emerged. Around the same time, Thomas names the narrative of personal viewer harm (which emphasizes the harm pornography causes to individual consumers), which outlasts the public/performer narrative and has, indeed, shaped the antipornography movement into the twenty-first century.

By the 1980s, evangelicals could no longer pretend that pornography was a problem only outside their communities. Sex scandals involving televangelists Jim Bakker (who covered up a rape accusation by his secretary by paying $279,000 to the alleged victim) and Jimmy Swaggart (found to have paid prostitutes for sex) seemed evidence for a bumper sticker sold at the time: THE MORAL MAJORITY IS NEITHER. But far from admitting defeat, evangelical leaders instead began acknowledging that pornography's consumers were also Bible-believing men (and sometimes even women). Evangelicals confronted what they saw as the mistaken values and market of sexual liberation making their way into evangelicals' lives and relationships. Some of the most prominent evangelical political activists—including Tim LaHaye, husband of Beverly LaHaye and founder of the secretive conservative networking group the Council for National Policy, and James Dobson, leader of Focus on the Family—were also authors of bestselling Christian self-help and advice books. Their writing focused on how pornography harmed marital relationships and personal well-being, but at the same time acknowledged how devout Christian men might be tempted by it.

Sociologist Samuel Perry describes this as a shift from offense to defense—to defend against pornography addiction, which was perceived to be a threat to evangelical men. And in some ways, these evangelical leaders were right. Protestant men are more likely than any other groups, including those with no religious affiliation, to perceive themselves to be addicted to pornography. And yet, evangelical men as a whole actually watch less porn than their nonevangelical counterparts. In one national survey, about 25 percent of born-again Christian men reported that they had looked at porn in the past week, compared to nearly 50 percent of men who were not born-again. But those who look at porn are more likely to consider themselves addicted to it or to be troubled by their porn use than men who are less religious. Several studies have found that religious commitment is a better predictor of perceived porn addiction than actual porn use.

———

FOR MANY SEX therapists, Patrick Carnes's idea that sexual problems can be treated using an addiction recovery model was not well received. As sociologist Janice Irvine observes, the rise of sexology in the mid-twentieth century provided a catalyst for a broader movement whose goal was sexual liberation and freedom, not abstinence and control. Sexologists' "assertion that sex is 'natural' was meant to contravene thousands of years of punishment, prohibitions, and mysticism," Irvine writes.

The field of sex therapy emerged in the 1960s as a direct offshoot of sexology research. William Masters and Virginia Johnson, the pioneers of American sexology, for example, replaced their research laboratory with a therapeutic practice in 1964. Using clinical language, sex therapists named, diagnosed, and treated a multitude of "sexual dysfunctions," but just like sexology, the field was careful to distance itself from language that objectively described sexual excess as wrong or harmful.

Because the existing sex therapy network was antagonistic to an addiction model, Carnes decided to start a new profession. He created the first certificate program in sex addiction therapy (the CSAT, or certified sex addiction therapist) and a companion organization, the International Institute for Trauma and Addiction Professionals (IITAP). Today there are more than two thousand certified CSATs nationwide. It's a lengthy and expensive process for counselors to receive and maintain the certification. And it's often expensive for patients to receive care, though the CSAT professionals I spoke with blamed diagnostic red tape for the cost of treatment.

"Hypersexuality" is classified in the first edition of the American Psychiatric Association's *Diagnostic and Statistical Manual of Mental Disorders (DSM)* from 1952, but it was later removed. The latest edition, the *DSM-5*, recognizes gambling as the only classified behavioral addiction. Because sex addiction is not a diagnosable condition, the costs of treating it are not covered by insurance. The five-acre in-patient treatment facility specializing in sex addiction recovery founded by Carnes, Gentle Path at the Meadows, near Phoenix, Arizona, costs about sixty thousand dollars for a forty-five-day treatment. In an interview, Carnes described treatment as a "boot camp," where patients are expected to meditate, journal, and attend group and individual therapy sessions. They are also expected to commit to celibacy. It's rumored that producer Harvey Weinstein and actor Kevin Spacey both received treatment there.

Critics of IITAP and Carnes's model say that sex addiction therapists prioritize profit by stigmatizing nonnormative sexual behavior, including porn. David Ley, a clinical psychologist, has been one leader of this charge. For perspective, he shared with me that he has published three books, including one called *The Myth of Sex Addiction*, and in the past decade, he earned less than fifty thousand dollars for his writing. "Compare that to sex and porn addiction treatment facilities, who charge a thousand dollars *a day*. If I was financially motivated, I can tell you what industry I'd be in." According to Ley, he has been threatened with lawsuits from IITAP ever since he started writing critically of the CSAT model and sex and porn addiction. When I asked him if his attitudes had changed since *The Myth of Sex Addiction* was published in 2012, Ley paused to reflect. "I think I didn't really understand, when I wrote the book, that people who identify as sex or porn addicts experience my criticisms or challenges as personal attacks. I didn't realize the degree to which they had really made that identity a foundational kind of concept of who they were and the belief that they can exert control and manage their lives."

Ley insisted that his writing, along with his clinical approach, is not dismissive of people who believe they suffer from sex addiction. But it's easy for one to have this impression upon reading his quotes in articles with click-bait titles like ANTHONY WEINER IS NOT A SEX ADDICT AND NEITHER IS ANYONE ELSE. One blogger who writes about his sex addiction recovery journey published a blog post, WHY DR. DAVID J. LEY, PH.D. IS AN ASSHOLE, that ends with a "Fuck you, David Ley," for Ley's having discounted the blogger's personal experience. This was typical, according to Ley, of the most common attacks against him: "They are based on a very shallow response to the surface of my ideas and concerns. The typical attack is, 'Well, you say sex addiction is not real, but I'm a sex addict, so there.'"

One former certified sex addiction therapist I interviewed, Bernie, says his problem with sex addiction therapy is that the focus is on addiction rather than sex. He explains, "In the Patrick Carnes model, there's no training around sex. You learn nothing about sex, zero. So, you learn a lot about trauma, and you learn a lot about addiction, but you learn nothing about helping sexuality of any kind." After spending twenty-five years as a sex addiction therapist, Bernie moved away from an addiction model to one called OCSB, for "out-of-control sexual behaviors." This approach reframes unwanted sexual behavior as an action or practice that appears to go against an individual's values, rather than as an addiction.

Bernie shared the story of a client who was a "deeply religious, deeply monogamous man, married to a woman." He came to Bernie's private practice calling himself a "sex addict" because he was engaged in extramarital affairs with men. The client's perspective was that his affairs were a result of a disease that was beyond his control. From Bernie's perspective, "This is actually about not wanting to make a decision to let go of one of these three identities: to be monogamous, religious, a man who has sex with men." For this client and others, Bernie's therapeutic approach is to "help clients feel the tension" inherent in their complicated sexual lives, rather than labeling some sex as good and some as bad. "I'm not saying leave your religion, and I'm not saying you should go against what you believe. I am asking what's it like to hold both in place and what are you gonna do about that?" For Bernie, the CSAT model doesn't leave room for this nuance.

Stefanie Carnes, who has followed in her father, Patrick's, footsteps and is now president of IITAP, the organization he started, said that she would not consider many religious men to meet what she believes are the clinical criteria for pornography addiction. "I've certainly had people contact the center and say, 'I have an addiction,' and then you learn they've looked at porn twice in the last month. And they just don't meet the criteria of what we would classify as an addiction. It might be helpful for them to look at their behavior as problematic and seek treatment. If you only work outpatient, or if you don't specialize in sex addiction, you might see a lot of people who say they are struggling with pornography addiction, but really, it's just a question of 'Does my behavior match my values?'" But, Carnes insisted to me, there are also many people for whom pornography addiction constitutes a much more serious problem. "There are a lot of people that are more acute than that," she said.

Under her leadership, the CSAT training has been updated and today includes material that Carnes insisted is both sex positive and sensitive to a wide range of sexual identities, interests, and complexities. As she explained, "We teach that each client's sexual health plan is individualized, and you work with the client to help them determine what is right for them." As a clinical sexologist, she described herself as liberal in her attitudes about sexuality, but she said that fellow sexologists and sex therapists must recognize that "not all sexual behavior is benign. Some people hurt themselves and cross lines that are dangerous and get them in trouble."

Carnes told me the story of one man who recently signed up for the in-patient treatment facility she directs. "We had a guy that came in a couple weeks ago that masturbated in the car on the way to the airport, masturbated in the airport bathroom, masturbated in the plane on the flight to treatment, masturbated in the van on the way to treatment. You know, it's not like this guy can just say, 'Oh, I just need to let go of my shame or my religious quandaries and get over this.' That's not how it works. By the time people come to us, they're destroyed. Their families have been destroyed. And it's extremely painful. But the thing is: this is a very treatable problem, and people get better."

Having spent decades working in sex addiction recovery and treatment, Carnes believes that sex and pornography addiction are much more than religious guilt. She says that people for whom this is a struggle can get better only by recognizing their behavior as an addiction and treating it accordingly.

THE MAN WHO murdered eight people at two massage parlors in the Atlanta area in March 2021 told authorities that he was a sex and porn addict. According to police accounts, he targeted the victims, including six women of Asian descent, whom he perceived as sex workers, to remove "temptation" and was headed to Florida next because "they make porn there." The shooter was also a member of a local Baptist church and had sought treatment for his sex and porn addictions at a Christian facility, HopeQuest. Offering inpatient and outpatient addiction recovery services, HopeQuest is staffed by counselors boasting CSAT certification. That certification, along with IITAP's pastoral sex addiction therapist (PSAT) certification, was the credential I found most often associated with Christian sex and porn addiction treatment.

In the aftermath of the Atlanta shootings, IITAP released a statement explicitly denouncing them and to explain that sex addiction is never an excuse or explanation for violence. Antiporn organizations, including NCOSE, also released statements condemning these crimes and emphasizing their commitment to protect sex workers from exactly this kind of violence. And yet, the sex addiction treatment industry is embedded within the larger effort led by religious conservatives to criminalize pornography and crack down on sex work. Antipornography activists' core beliefs that all sex work is "inherently exploitative," a phrase used by NCOSE, alongside sex addiction rhetoric, is dangerous to both sex workers and their customers. The message is that men like the Atlanta shooter are consumers in the sex industry because they are addicted to sex. Sex workers are seen as victims but also as suppliers who fuel dangerous addictions.

The pressure on men to remove such temptation and to abstain from masturbation is centuries old, and some of its history is sinister. Drawing from medical discourse in the late nineteenth and early twentieth centuries, white nationalist groups, including the Ku Klux Klan, pushed the message that men needed to abstain from sexual release to demonstrate their strength over powerful urges and, thus, prove themselves capable soldiers of the white supremacist project. This movement also identified nonwhite men and women as sexual threats attempting to "taint" white purity. The Atlanta shooter claimed that his crimes were not racially motivated, and yet, as many commentators pointed out in the aftermath of the shooting, it is not coincidental that he targeted Asian women. An intersection of racism and sexism created the conditions for these particular victims to become the targets of his violence.

The Atlanta shootings are evidence of how messages surrounding porn and sex addiction can align with the ideology of the alt-right, the contemporary white nationalist movement that blends racist and sexist ideologies with ultraconservative politics. Gavin McInnes, cofounder of Proud Boys, an extremist organization of self-described chauvinists who believe straight men are society's underdogs, has publicly promoted abstinence from porn and masturbation. The bylaws of the group prohibit members from masturbating more than once a month and from using porn. The Proud Boys was an instigator of the riots at the U.S. Capitol on January 6, 2021, and is classified by the Southern Poverty Law Center as a hate group.

Explicitly racist and misogynist website users are a visible segment of the online porn addiction recovery movement. Many members of the alt-right and so-called incels (short for "involuntary celibates," or men who fail to achieve sexual relationships with women) promote porn addiction rhetoric online. One analysis of Twitter in 2019 for all tweets containing the term "nofap" found that alt-right accounts make up a meaningful segment of 211 nofap-supportive Twitter influencer accounts. "Pornography is blamed on almost interchangeable villains, with liberals and feminists, socialists and Jews," explains communications scholar Scott Burnett. In one survey of more than a thousand Reddit users, researchers found that the highest motivation to abstain from masturbation was correlated with religiosity and political conservatism. Though many members of these online communities frame porn addiction as an individual problem distinct from the broader social world, the subject of pornography addiction is in fact highly politically charged.

Though the sex addiction movement has robust secular roots and limbs, its model aligns with conservative Christian beliefs about sexuality because those beliefs provide justification for pathologizing certain kinds of sexual behavior. Even setting aside the extreme right wing of the online community, the subject of pornography addiction is an example of how the larger recovery movement, even those spaces characterized as secular, collides with conservative Christianity. This is because white Protestant beliefs about sex are synonymous, more or less, with good old American values. Protestant Christianity operates as an ideology as well as a religion—meaning it shapes what we think of as our "common sense." It works to exalt heterosexuality, marriage, monogamy, and a gender binary as normal. Even those who don't adhere to strict religious beliefs are affected by conservative Christianity's message. This is how ideology works. Religion has been there all along in American history, constructing ideas about what is normal, what is perverse, and indeed, what is obscene.

CHAPTER 15

Brain Battles

I n my interviews with scientists, clinicians, and activists who believe that internet pornography is biologically addictive, I heard one name over and over again. Nicole Prause is a neuroscientist who uses her public platform to assert that pornography addiction is based on "junk science." Her critics have called her "a nutcase," "corrupt," "cozy with the pornography industry," and "criminal." In June 2019, Donald Hilton, a neurosurgeon and antiporn activist, filed a ten-million-dollar lawsuit against Prause, accusing her of defamation (that is, intentionally making false claims to damage his professional and personal reputation). The suit included affidavits from nine others who similarly claimed Prause had harassed them because of their views on porn science.

Prause, who holds a Ph.D. in clinical science and specializes in sexual psychophysiology, never set out to be a pornography researcher. As she explained it to me, she thought porn to be "quite boring," as far as research topics went. At the time of our interview, she ran a private biotech laboratory out of Los Angeles, where she used brain scans and genital probes to study sexual arousal and response. She collaborated with universities across the country and has also been supported by nonprofit organizations and private funders—one of them, a company that sells vibrators. She says publishing on the effects of visual sexual stimuli (VSS)—in other words, the effects of watching porn—was "low-hanging fruit," as she had already collected the data as part of other studies. Never did she imagine that these publications would be the ones to place her at the center of lawsuits. "I'm not sure it's worth it," she said with a little laugh.

Prause and her defenders have come to consider pornography addiction as a label used by people with ulterior motives: religious conservatives, like Hilton, who believe pornography is morally wrong; clinicians who profit from the porn addiction recovery industry; and Millennial men, who, at best, don't know any better and, at worst, are part of the violent and misogynistic alt-right. I asked Prause why she opposes the labels "addict" and "addiction" when many people use them to describe themselves and their own behavior. "I have no problem with the general public saying things like 'Oh my god, I'm so addicted to chocolate,'" she said. "The popular use of words doesn't worry or distress me." Still, she explained that for clinical psychology, "the addiction model makes some very specific predictions, and the pornography addiction model just doesn't fit."

In his suit against Prause, Hilton argued the opposite: that there is a broad body of research supporting pornography addiction. "Over the past two decades, . . . the concept of sexuality having an addictive potential has been advocated by many," his petition states. Though neither sex addiction nor pornography addiction is a classifiable disorder in the *DSM* or the World Health Organization's diagnostics manual, the *International Classification of Diseases* (*ICD*), Hilton explained how compulsive sexual behavior (CSB) had recently been classified as a brain disease by the American Society of Addiction Medicine and had been added to the *ICD*-11 as an impulse-control disorder. Hilton also referenced the numerous states that have declared pornography to be a "public health hazard."

At the heart of Hilton's and Prause's opposing positions are claims about what counts as fact. Hilton's defamation lawsuit and Prause's follow-up motion to dismiss used lengthy academic résumés and publications full of scientific jargon as evidence that each had the upper hand. It's a he said/she said situation, with both claiming the other side is maligning their research and character and attempting to silence them. The stakes are higher than professional reputations, though. These debates have resulted in threats of physical harm, questioned people's moral truths, and challenged assumptions about scientific authority.

Hilton's lawsuit was filed in response to accusations levied against him by Prause. In April 2019, she wrote to the University of Texas Health Science Center at San Antonio, where Hilton holds an honorary title, to accuse him of sexual harassment. She requested that the university pursue an official investigation and remove Hilton's title and his affiliation with the university. According to an expert on sexual harassment laws, Prause's claims were unusual: Prause had accused Hilton of sexual harassment because—in her words—"As a female scientist, he is uniquely attacking my gender with false claims about my sexuality."

Prause complained Hilton had publicly criticized her character, describing her as "very pro-pornography." It is true that Prause has used social media to champion scientific studies that find that pornography and masturbation can improve one's sexual health. However, Prause alleged that Hilton had claimed that she had appeared in pornographic films herself and that she sexually molested children at her workplace, claims which in his lawsuit Hilton explicitly denies having ever made. Hilton has made critical remarks about Prause's alma mater, Indiana University, and about the Kinsey Institute, referring to Alfred Kinsey as having collaborated with pedophiles in his research and publications. Though Kinsey did record information about children's sexual behavior and victimization, these data came from adult respondents' memories. He also exaggerated his findings about pedophilia, claiming multiple respondents when, in fact, his data came from a single source, a man named Rex King, who admitted in interviews and correspondence with Kinsey to sexually assaulting infants and children. No substantial evidence suggests that Kinsey or his team engaged in sexual assault of minors. Nonetheless, Kinsey remains a vilified figured among religious conservatives. Hilton has also hinted that Prause's research was funded by the pornography industry, in part because he claimed she had attended the *AVN* Awards. Prause maintains that she has never attended the event and that to suggest as much constitutes sexual harassment.

Prause's accusation of sexual harassment is central to Hilton's defamation case against her. Hilton has claimed that he has never, and would never, sexually harass Prause or anyone else and that her accusations were "specifically designed to destroy [his] reputation and career." According to Hilton's lawsuit, "The real reason Defendant Prause lodged the complaint is because

Dr. Hilton is an internationally recognized expert on the subject of how pornography adversely impacts the brain." Hilton claimed that Prause's complaint was part of an effort to "silence her critics by falsely accusing them."

In his petition, Hilton explained that there had been no personal interaction between him and Prause other than a brief, public encounter a decade before. In 2009, Hilton gave one of his signature presentations on the neurological harms of viewing pornography. Prause approached him after the talk with some questions about his findings. Questions and even disagreements are typical and mostly innocuous in these settings. Yet, in the decade that followed, the two became the faces of the polarized factions in the scientific debate over pornography consumption and, specifically, the issue of whether pornography is physically addictive.

TO GET TO the bottom of the *Hilton v. Prause* feud, I set out to find and read every academic article that mentioned the phrase "pornography addiction." Spoiler: I don't have a definitive answer to many questions surrounding porn addiction; nor does anybody else, despite their bold claims. I read more than one hundred articles stored in PubMed, a database for medical and health-related research, and found that the majority of studies that mentioned pornography addiction were supportive of the concept. Yet, like porn research generally, most studies come out of psychology and the social sciences (I call these "psychosocial studies"), rather than biology or neuroscience (I call these "neurobiological studies"). Psychosocial articles are better positioned to support an addiction framework by using self-reports of perceived addiction or addiction-like behavior. For neurobiological studies, nearly half (45 percent) of the articles I read explicitly challenged a pornography addiction framework.

I kept hearing about one research study in particular from the proponents of the porn addiction model. I never came across it in my search of academic literature, though, because it wasn't about pornography or addiction. The story goes something like this: Back in the 1950s, a team of entomologists designed an experiment to study the mating habits of butterflies. To find out which markings were most attractive to male butterflies, the researchers made cardboard cutouts that were larger and brighter than the wings of real butterflies. As one storyteller explained, these were "the world's first butterfly supermodels." The researchers observed that male butterflies consistently flew to the better-than-real-life cardboard versions to try to mate. Their preference was fake over real every time.

When I first heard the story, I thought that this was the final lesson: that men who watch porn (full of airbrushing and editing and with thinness and plumpness in all the right places) will develop a preference for unrealistic standards of beauty rather than ordinary women. But this is a tale with a plot twist. As the storytellers eagerly go on to describe, after exposing male butterflies to shiny counterfeits, researchers then placed them back in an environment with only real butterflies and were shocked by what they observed: the males would not mate with the real female butterflies. The butterflies eventually died failing to fulfill this fundamental evolutionary instinct.

If the analogy holds, online pornography compels men away from real intimacy and relationships to what the butterfly researchers called "supranormal stimulus." Researchers theorize that the internet, unlike porn of the past, is uniquely positioned to do this. Hilton writes that "the enhanced novelty (internet porn) provides, metaphorically speaking, a pheromone-like effect in human males, like moths, which is 'inhibiting orientation' and 'disrupting pre-mating communication between the sexes by permeating the atmosphere.'" In other words, pornography has the power to disrupt human evolution.

By comparing men to butterflies, Hilton and others are able to set the stage for why men are inclined to want to look at porn, but in order to establish internet pornography as uniquely addictive, they must add to the story—and this is where brain science is key. The dopamine system is central to understanding behavioral addictions. Studies of shopping, gambling, eating, having sex, and even of listening to our favorite music—all reveal that it's the dopamine system that "lights up" when we anticipate and experience pleasure.

Hilton and his coauthors describe how orgasm is "a dopaminergic reward on par with morphine." In and of itself, orgasm is not addictive in the same way as chemical opioids, but the internet has changed that. The internet, like a morphine tap, sends endless stimuli that trigger men to crave that sexual release. In Hilton's words, pornography addiction is "a powerful neuroplastic response given its limitless novelty combined with the competitive edge it delivers as a supranormal stimulus, especially when fused with aggressive content." Aggressive content matters because it also fuels dopamine release, and so, when orgasm and aggression are combined (as in violent porn), "the reward is compounded."

The latest advancements in neurological research on drug and alcohol addiction suggest a distinct "addiction cycle," composed of binge/intoxication, withdrawal, preoccupation, and anticipation. Several studies have applied this addiction cycle to compulsive sexual behavior and pornography consumption. Many of these use brain scans to compare respondents who fulfill diagnostic criteria for CSB (typically, a self-report inventory test; more on these later) with those who do not. One study finds, for example, that CSB respondents react more strongly to novelty. Another finds evidence of habituation: men who report watching more porn appear desensitized to pornography when exposed to it in a laboratory. Other studies have examined withdrawal and negative effects and have found that individuals with CSB experience emotional and mental symptoms, including depression, anxiety, and irritability. These findings mirror studies of substance and other behavioral addictions.

THOUGH BOTH HILTON and Prause hold scientific credentials, the feud between them is as much about values as it is about science. Hilton has been practicing medicine for three decades and is trained in neurosurgery. He is also a member of the Church of Jesus Christ of Latter-day Saints (the Mormon Church) and therefore believes that viewing pornography is sinful and goes against God's design for sexuality. In his book *He Restoreth My Soul*, Hilton weaves together the scientific and spiritual, spending the first half providing an account of addiction and how pornography affects the brain. He spends the second half detailing how spiritual beliefs are necessary for addiction recovery and how, in turn, addiction recovery is necessary for salvation. Hilton quotes Mormon elder Bruce Hafen: "We can have eternal life if we want it, but only if there is nothing we want more."

Hilton has been accused by critics of pushing a religious agenda that is purposely disguised as science. But he and other religious conservatives leading the antipornography movement in the twenty-first century believe their opposition to pornography is common sense and that science is on their side. In a talk titled "A Population of Slaves: How the Pornography Industry

Is Capturing Our Brains, Hearts, and Humanity," Hilton references the dystopian novel *Brave New World*. In it, Aldous Huxley writes, "A really efficient totalitarian state would be one in which the all-powerful executive of political bosses and their army of managers control a population of slaves who do not have to be coerced, because they love their servitude." The "slaves," in this case, are both the consumers of porn (who are enslaved by their addiction) and porn performers (enslaved through exploitation and coercion). The porn user and performer may believe that they love their servitude, but in both cases, they are wrong. Hilton presents this moral claim, the wrongness of pornography, as objectively true.

Prause disagrees. She first met porn performers while being interviewed for a documentary, *After Porn Ends 2*, a film focusing on the lives of porn performers after they left the industry. I asked Prause if she had strong personal feelings about pornography, to which she responded, "I think more than anything my only concern that I have personally is that I now know some performers who are in the industry, and I think their jobs get misrepresented. Porn performers are thrown under the bus." To people who believe watching porn is wrong or bad for them, she replied succinctly, "then they shouldn't watch it." Prause, who is not religious, believes that science is on her side when she says there is no evidence that pornography is physically addictive or objectively harmful.

Indeed, Prause has argued that it's pornography addiction *therapy*, not pornography itself, that is harmful and unethical. On Facebook and Twitter, Prause and David Ley have criticized virtually all public groups that promote a porn addiction framework. In response to the SexAddictionIsReal hashtag, used by those sharing stories of addiction and recovery, Prause tweeted: "#SexAddictionIsReal for therapists who value #ProfitOverPatients like @IITAPLLC," criticizing the professional organization started by Patrick Carnes. She has even gone so far as to write state licensing boards to report sex addiction therapists as violating their professional standards of care. She has written to the health departments in Oregon and Pennsylvania to report leaders of online porn addiction recovery communities for practicing therapy without a license. And she has written to Washington and Arizona to register complaints against licensed therapists, including Stefanie Carnes, who works within a sex addiction framework. For her public, persistent, and targeted opposition to the concept of pornography addiction, Prause has developed a long list of public critics.

BEFORE THE 1960S, addiction science was a marginal field. But then America went to war. As protestors of the Vietnam invasion rose in numbers and public attention, American media incited panic over a radicalized youth for whom drugs were used freely and to excess. Exaggerated stories plastered newspapers and the nightly news about the harms of marijuana and psychedelics like LSD (the latter of which we now know isn't addictive at all). Veterans returning home from the war—many of whom were from middle-class white families—found themselves unable to adapt to daily life and abused drugs and alcohol. Richard Nixon declared a war on drugs in 1971 and began funding laboratories to help the nation cope. A psychiatry professor, Jerome Jaffe, became the first director of Nixon's newly created Special Action Office for Drug Abuse Prevention. Jaffe was an early supporter of methadone clinics because he took the opinion (unpopular at the time but fortuitous) that drug addiction was largely biophysical and thus required medical interventions in addition to therapeutic ones.

It's now a matter of common sense that our personal identities (what we think of as our "selves") stem from the neurological mechanisms that make such thinking possible. But discovering what British sociologist Nikolas Rose coined the "neurochemical self" came only after the rise in therapeutic drugs to treat it. In other words, therapeutic drugs appeared successful in treating some chemical addictions and other mental illnesses, like depression. We then needed an explanation for why such treatments were successful.

About those early neuroscientists, science writer Eric Vance describes them as modern-day Copernicuses who revealed the brain as the center of our reality. Today, it's hard to overstate the explanatory power of the gray lump inside our head. The brain is credited for our habits, decisions, and memories, our capacity to love and empathize. It's also largely responsible for regulating and relieving pain. In fact, modern medicine is based on its capacity to outperform the brain. Before pharmaceutical drugs can go on the market, they must outperform a placebo. And most fail. As Vance explains in an interview, "When you give someone a sugar pill, and you say, 'This is going to take away your pain,' it's not a circus trick. This is getting down to the very fundamental role that your brain has. And when you take that pill—this doesn't happen to everyone—but if your pain goes away, it's partly because your brain has an expectation that when you take a pill, your pain goes away." Placebos have a bad reputation and are often dismissed as not real, or made up. But Vance insists that this is not a lesson on effective medicines but, rather, on the command of our own bodies to heal us. Placebo effects occur when our beliefs and expectations have the power to make us feel better, often more effectively than medical intervention.

With the discovery of "brain plasticity" (the fact that the brain changes over the course of a lifetime and adapts in response to our environment), brain science has remained premier while acknowledging the role of society and socialization on shaping behavior. In other words, our brain is not some road map that predetermines who we will become, but rather, is more akin to virtual GPS software that automatically reroutes if we make an unexpected turn. We now understand that it's not nature *versus* nurture, but nature *and* nurture—and, indeed, not only that the two work together, collaborating side by side to make us into who we are, but also that the boundaries between nature and nurture are far from tidy. We know that what we do from day to day has the power to *literally* change our brains. Watching porn, just as with other habits, affects the brain. If someone regularly masturbates and orgasms to internet porn, even just the thought of watching it will become a cue that activates the brain's dopamine system to seek out pleasure. But does this mean pornography is addictive?

Most advances in our neuroscientific understanding of addiction are thanks to a single small furry creature: the *Rattus norvegicus*. In other words, the brown rat, or lab rat. Rats have been used in scientific experiments since the nineteenth century, when breeders, long before scientists, noticed similarities between rats and humans. Today, rats and mice make up 95 percent of animal experiments. Conveniently, rats are highly trainable and also omnivorous, so they'll eat just about anything. Given their undesirability in homes and on city streets, there is no public outcry over the estimated one hundred million rats that are killed each year in the service of science.

In a series of now-famous experiments beginning in the 1970s, researchers tested the effects of cocaine on rats. These experiments found that rats escalate their intake of cocaine over time as their brains become desensitized to its effects, and then a certain percentage of rats choose cocaine over other "rewards," such as food or exercise wheels. These are the rats we consider physically addicted: those who, just like an estimated 22 million adult Americans, continue to use drugs and alcohol despite the negative consequences in their lives.

For all the scientific and medical advancements credited to the rat, there's only so much it can tell us about human behavior. Studies of addiction work best when they consider not just biological factors of addiction but social factors as well. Even when therapeutic drugs accompany the recovery process (like the use of buprenorphine for opioid addiction), research suggests that that process is most likely to be successful when taking place in positive social environments. One interview study emphasized employment and housing assistance as equal to mental health care in its importance for recovery. This is because, as most interview respondents explained, their addictions happened alongside other personal challenges, of which drug abuse was just one. This has been observed to some effect in rat studies, such as in a series called Rat Park, where rates of cocaine addiction were significantly diminished for rats in stimulating and highly interactive environments. Scientists have criticized other rat studies that do not account for environmental factors as being skewed by a "couch potato effect," due to rats spending the majority of their lives in shoeboxes.

People don't live in shoeboxes, and the Disney movie *Ratatouille* notwithstanding, rats don't respond to the *je ne sais quoi* of human life: love and art and music. And when it comes to neurological studies of addiction, they don't respond to those addictions that are rooted entirely in human culture: shopping, gambling, and indeed, pornography. In addition to chemical dependencies such as alcohol and drugs, the scientific study of addictions that has emerged in the last half century incorporates various pleasures. For most of us, we can enjoy pleasurable activities in moderation. But for others, these behaviors (eating, shopping, sex) become compulsive, excessive, and disruptive to everyday life. Pleasurable behaviors stimulate the dopamine system, and we have a strong urge to repeat these behaviors and reactivate this pleasure center in our brains. When it comes to neurological studies of these kinds of addictions, we can't use rats. We rely instead on a *theory* of behavioral addictions—not decisively proved given that, in the words of medical sociologist Jules Netherland, "we haven't sliced open [any living person's] brain yet."

Brain science has tackled all kinds of human feelings and behaviors, from love and empathy, to art and aesthetic perception, to leadership and persuasion. On the topic of addiction, there were a mere 18 neuroscientific articles published in peer-reviewed medical or health journals in the 1980s. The following decade, that number jumped to 129. Between 2000 and 2009, there was an increase of over 800 percent, to 1,117 studies. Sociologist Gabriel Abend, in an article titled, "What Are Neural Correlates Neural Correlates Of?," questions how such studies relying on objective measures like brain scans are able to interpret subjective topics like behavioral addictions. Abend argues that "there is no neutral, noncommittal position" for neuroscience of human behavior. Researchers, in the words of Abend, "have to tell morality from non-morality, religion from non-religion, art from non-art, and love from non-love. What marks them off? And where should these demarcation criteria come from?" As researchers answer these questions, their ability to work under the guise of complete objectivity becomes all but impossible. Neuroscience begins to resemble sociology as researchers in both fields must come up with ways to measure variables that, by definition, are subjectively experienced.

FOR ALL THE studies that posit a parallel between pornography and chemical addictions, there are also studies (using similar neurobiological measures like fMRI scans) that find no evidence that pornography follows the same cycle as substance or chemical addictions. One study finds that variations in sexual desire cause people's brains to react differently to pornographic material (that light bulb of the dopamine system). In other words, people have differing sex drives, and those with a high libido aren't sex addicts; they are just people with a high libido. Other studies agree that viewing pornography triggers the pleasure/reward systems of the brain, but to good, rather than ill, effect. Further, some survey-based research finds that problematic pornography use, or perceived pornography addiction, may be caused by underlying conditions such as depression, rather than the other way around.

One of the biggest limitations to neurophysiological studies of pornography consumption is that robust experiments are all but impossible for researchers to design. Take one significant finding in the neurological study of chemical addictions: adolescents are particularly sensitive to the effects of drugs and alcohol because their brains are still developing. Logic suggests that the same, then, would be true for internet pornography: when young people are first exposed to pornography, they are also most at risk for getting hooked on it. Yet, to confirm this assumption empirically, researchers would need to design an experiment with test and control groups in which they exposed some children and teens to porn while others abstained. This would allow researchers to know if and to what extent viewing pornography did in fact impact the adolescent brain. Yet, for good reason, such a project would never pass a research ethics review board.

A second problem is that when studying addiction, researchers assume that the brain responds to cue and reward differently, but within experimental settings, they treat pornography itself as both the cue *and* the reward. Picture a typical scenario: a college freshman sees a flyer in his residence hall about a study on visual sexual stimuli that is recruiting male participants. If he successfully completes the study procedures, he'll get twenty dollars. Twenty bucks for watching porn? He signs up immediately. He enters a laboratory in the same building where he took Chemistry 101 last semester. Research assistants, who are undergrads like him, read aloud a consent form, which he signs. He then places his backpack and jacket into a locker and enters a private room, where another research assistant helps him put on a strange helmet that he is told contains a magnet that will be able to detect changes in brain activity. His only instruction is to sit still and watch the computer screen on the table in front of him. A stock image of a man and woman, a couple walking down a promenade hand in hand, appears on the screen. After several seconds, a pornographic still shot of a naked woman sitting atop a naked man appears. And on and on it goes, back and forth between banal and sexual. In this scenario, the research participant is never instructed to masturbate; nor would he spontaneously do so, given the less-than-private circumstances.

Most laboratory experiments test what happens to the brain when a person sits and watches porn, and that's it. Of course, this is not how it goes in real life, when pornography is most often a cue for some other reward, like masturbation or partnered sex. It's unclear, then, if we would observe the same findings outside these artificial laboratory conditions.

Another limitation to, and reason for inconsistent findings in, neurological porn studies is that they almost always rely on subjective measures about viewing habits to delineate the addict from the nonaddict. Self-reports (through surveys or interviews) are what make the results of brain scans meaningful. For example, one article measuring "neural correlates" of pornography consumption describes a series of negative outcomes associated with compulsive pornography consumption: lost jobs, damaged romantic relationships, diminished erectile function, financial irresponsibility, and depression. These outcomes were not evident in brain scans but, instead, were described in interviews with participants.

Psychologists have been refining the screening tests used to classify sex and porn addiction since Patrick Carnes's first iteration in 1983. In a 2018 paper based on a national survey, researchers found that approximately 8 percent of adult women and 10 percent of adult men met the threshold for compulsive sexual behavior. These findings suggest that the prevalence of sex addiction in the United States is comparable to chemical addictions. The thirteen-question index used for this study includes questions like: How often have you had trouble controlling your sexual urges? How often have you used sex to deal with problems? How often have you felt guilty or shameful about sexual behavior? How often have you made pledges or promises to change or alter your sexual behavior? How often have you had sex or masturbated more than you wanted to?

The problem with interpreting these screening tests is that they attempt to objectively and universally assess sexual behavior as healthy or problematic without taking into account different backgrounds or social contexts. This 2018 study, for example, finds that individuals who identify as lesbian, gay, or bisexual are statistically more likely to have experienced CSB than non-LGB people. Does this mean gay people are more likely to be addicted to sex? Maybe, but this question does not measure the heteronormative culture in which we live, making it more likely for queer people to hide, control, or feel shame about their sexual behavior.

Psychologist Joshua Grubbs, who is critical of the porn addiction framework, insists he does not think people who say they struggle with compulsive porn use are making it up. To the contrary, Grubbs told me, "At the end of the day, there is certainly evidence from clinical settings that some people become dysregulated or excessive in their sexual behaviors or even in their use of pornography. The general way that I approached it as a clinician is 'Hey, if you think that you have a behavior that's out of control,

it's our job to help you. And all that my research is trying to do is understand why you feel out of control. We just want to understand why so that
we can get you the help that you need.'" According to Grubbs, clinicians
and researchers must prioritize *the meaning* of pornography in people's lives,
rather than pornography itself. Because people are not rats or butterflies,
we must rely on individuals' perceptions and reports of their behavior in
addition to, or rather than, brain scans to make sense of porn.

LIKE DONALD HILTON, Gary Wilson, the author of *Your Brain on Porn*,
and Alexander Rhodes, the founder of NoFap, are among the set of characters who have been entangled in legal battles with Nicole Prause. Wilson's
dispute was the longest lasting. Prause's name has appeared thousands of
times on the YourBrainOnPorn website, most often alongside that of clinical psychologist David Ley. In 2013, Ley published an entry on *Psychology
Today*'s *Sex* blog titled, "Your Brain on Porn: It's Not Addictive." In it, he
discussed the results of a study directed by Prause that concluded that a high
sex drive—not hypersexuality or porn addiction—explained neurological
differences in response to pornography. Wilson has since reviewed and
critiqued every one of Prause's and Ley's publications related to pornography addiction. He has also described, in excruciating and lengthy detail,
Prause's supposed harassment and lies about him. Prause in turn has
claimed that Wilson cyberstalked and harassed her and led a letter-writing
campaign to UCLA, her former employer, with the intent to have her fired.
Wilson maintained that he never stalked Prause and that his letters to
UCLA were to detail Prause's egregious and unethical behavior.

In 2019, Wilson filed a complaint against Prause with the World Intellectual
Property Organization, the international body in charge of regulating internet
domains, after she and a colleague founded a website, RealYourBrainOnPorn.
The site name intentionally mirrored that for Wilson's YourBrainOnPorn and
claimed to be the source of *real* scientific information on porn consumption,
listing more than twenty scientists and clinicians as experts along with the
tagline "Science not shame." Wilson claimed the site infringed on his common
law trademarks on the basis that he had been using the YourBrainOnPorn
domain name and mark since 2010. Prause had also filed an application to

register YourBrainOnPorn and YourBrainOnPorn.com as trademarks, a move which Wilson considered was designed to prevent him from continuing to operate his site. Wilson filed an opposition to the application with the US Patent and Trademark Office and trial dates were set. WIPO concluded that the website RealYourBrainOnPorn was a genuine criticism site and use of the domain name was therefore justified as fair use. However, Prause ultimately abandoned her trademark application before the trial which had been set to hear Wilson's opposition, and Wilson obtained ownership of the YourBrainOnPorn and YourBrainOnPorn.com trademarks in 2020. To avoid trademark infringement proceedings, the team running RealYourBrainOnPorn forfeited the domain name. The URL now redirects to Wilson's site and a webpage containing a lengthy diatribe against Prause.

In 2019, responding to social media's annual NoNutNovember (a challenge to go the entire month without masturbating), the porn website xHamster tweeted, "#YesFap" and linked to an article critiquing porn addiction science. The violent, anti-Semitic response on Twitter was swift, with messages like "pornographers must die" and suggestions that the pornography industry was part of a Jewish conspiracy. A spokesperson for xHamster said that the site had never seen such hateful responses to a tweet. These are the seeds of alt-right misogyny and anti-Semitism within the porn addiction recovery movement that, according to Prause, sparked online harassment and threats directed against her. Prause shared with me a message she received in the spring of 2019: "Nicole you are a terrible human being and a filthy whore for money. You don't care how many people porn harms or how many kids grow up watching it and get addicted. No one is that stupid, we all know the truth. But you don't care what goys [non-Jews] you hurt as long as you get some sick Jewish revenge on them. The day of the rope is coming for you and your group of cosmopolitans."

"The day of the rope" references a day of mass violence described in a white supremacist manifesto that has inspired acts of violent extremism, including the 1995 bombing of the federal building in Oklahoma City. Prause told me this is typical of the messages she receives, especially after antiporn websites post something about her. Ley, who has collaborated with Prause on scientific articles criticizing the porn addiction framework, has also been on the receiving end of such threats. "It's a rare month when I don't get death threats of some kind or another," he told me.

Prause has publicly blamed NoFap for supporting misogyny and racism and promoting threats against her. A few months after Hilton filed his defamation case against Prause, the founder of NoFap, Alexander Rhodes, filed a similar lawsuit against her, denying Prause's accusations and seeking compensation of at least $75,000 from her in damages for her online attacks. Rhodes claimed that Prause had targeted him "because he runs one of the most popular websites for those who have suffered from the effects of excessive pornography consumption" and that her allegations were an attempt to "harass, embarrass and discredit" him personally and professionally. And he insisted that the stakes of his lawsuit were much bigger than he and Prause. As one NoFap tweet described, "There has been an escalating campaign by the porn industry and its friends to defame & de-platform NoFap and its founder. This is like the alcohol industry trying to take down Alcoholics Anonymous. We've filed a federal lawsuit to end the harassment."

To cover legal expenses, Rhodes and NoFap set up a crowdsourced fundraiser on the website. Sex addiction therapist and author Staci Sprout narrated a video that appeared on NoFap's homepage. In a soothing cadence, Sprout explained how Rhodes "has been forced to file a federal lawsuit." She asked supporters of NoFap, especially those whose lives had been positively impacted by the organization, to give what they could. A year after beginning the fund-raising, the site had raised nearly $170,000 toward its $200,000 goal.

IN FEBRUARY 2021, the lawsuits filed by Donald Hilton and Alexander Rhodes against Nicole Prause were settled by the parties on confidential terms outside of court. Still, scientific debates over pornography and its addictive potential continue to rage. As philosopher of science Bruno Latour writes, "The world is not a solid continent of facts sprinkled by a few lakes of uncertainties, but a vast ocean of uncertainties speckled by a few islands of calibrated and stabilized forms." The islands of certainty when it comes to the science of pornography are few. Instead, certainties are shaped by the values of those who make scientific claims.

CHAPTER 16

Opposite Sexes

T his mess we're in," Mary Ann whispered into her microphone as she leaned over the stage toward the crowd as if letting us in on a juicy secret. "It started in the garden." Mary Ann is the first speaker on the first night of the True Intimacy (a pseudonym) weekend retreat for women, a gathering in an airport hotel conference suite for five hundred Christian women whose lives had been affected by pornography and sex addiction. Before Mary Ann began, all five conference speakers—a mix of women who were white and Black, young and old—introduced themselves, and each one mentioned struggles in her marriage. Then we sang. It was Mary Ann's daughter, a white woman in her twenties with long, perfectly styled blond hair, who led us in praise and worship, playing chords on a keyboard, her beautiful voice projecting through speakers. Many women started to cry, while others hugged them or rubbed their backs. They held one another through the last refrain and the start of the next song. They gained their composure only to revert back to crying and hugging and patting as the next song crescendoed in an emotional chorus.

By the time Mary Ann began her talk for the evening, the audience had gained its composure and sat straight backed with Bibles and notebooks atop their laps. The Garden of Eden, as Mary Ann read from the Book of Genesis, began as a place of perfection, designed by a loving, almighty, and all-knowing God. Adam and Eve had but one rule: to avoid the fruit of the Tree of Knowledge that would reveal to them that the world contained forces of both good and evil. Satan chose the serpent as his mouthpiece to tempt Eve to eat the forbidden fruit. According to Mary Ann and others in her evangelical tradition, Eve's first bite marked the first sin of human-kind and the inevitability that the rest of us would also be sinners.

"We've been running from God ever since," Mary Ann told us sadly. She continued, weaving together personal stories and biblical scripture in a talk that can only be described as a sermon as captivating as that from the best born-again preacher. The theme was the toll of our human condition and our innate sinfulness. We must learn to constantly pivot back toward God rather than toward Satan, which was a difficult task given that, according to Mary Ann, "Satan is attempting to get in the way for each and every one of us." She ended her talk with a story from her own marriage. Her husband, an evangelical pastor, was "unfaithful"—we never learned what exactly this meant; if it was an affair, an addiction to pornography, or both—and decided to confess to Mary Ann by bringing her to a meeting at their church with a group of church leaders. She stormed out of the building, feeling furious, embarrassed, and ashamed. These feelings over-shadowed any others for a long time. But, in hindsight, she said, she now understood that when she allowed those emotions to take over, she was in fact running away from God rather than turning toward Him. "We cannot repay evil with evil. Forgiveness can feel like the hardest thing in the world, but we must do it," she said to the roomful of women for whom the Adam and Eve script had mostly been flipped: it was their male partners who had betrayed them by succumbing to temptation.

EVANGELICAL BELIEFS TODAY are relics of centuries worth of commit-ment to gender difference. In the seventeenth century, Puritan theology centered on sin: avoiding it, revealing it in others, and repenting. Historian Margaret Thickstun argues that Puritan men influenced a dominant belief about femininity in order to cope with their own anxieties around sin. Following a theological model dating back to the Apostle Paul, Puritans began to emphasize a proper femininity that was always dependent upon, in reference to, and less than a male Christian ideal. Women, like Eve, were by their nature impure and lustful, representations of the Original Sin. Masculinity became associated with God and with the presumption that men could and should control and lead women, both spiritually and sexually. Morality became associated not only with men, but also with whiteness, as stereotypes about indigenous people and Africans presented them as animalistic, unable to control their sexual urges. This was reflected both in popular theology at the time and in the application of the law: white women and people of color were subject to harsher penalties for deviating from sexual norms than were white men.

The Puritan-inspired idea that women were innately sexual and lustful remained prominent until the turn of the nineteenth century. Then a shift occurred, what historian Nancy Cott calls the period of "passionlessness," when women became known for *lacking* sexual desire and, in turn, being associated with spiritual morality. In order for women to be transformed metaphorically from Eve to Mary, they were taught to remain pure by avoiding contact with the outside world and by staying home and tending to the domestic sphere. Because men were expected to be hard at work amid a secular workforce, Protestant churches, in order to retain their members, began to emphasize a Christianity that elevated women from sin to a place of moral superiority.

At the turn of the twentieth century, though, fundamentalist Protestant men sought to reframe Christianity as a masculine and heroic pursuit. They faced a challenge, given that women held claim to the Church, both in terms of higher attendance and perceived morality. One group, the Men and Religion Forward Movement, explicitly excluded women and attempted to masculinize religious work by comparing the church to sports and corporate business and promoting the image of a strong, rational Christian man. This fundamentalist project resulted in the shutting down of some women's organizations and the loss of authority for women church leaders. It also had significant consequences for the gendered nature of conservative evangelicalism, in which women no longer had moral authority over men. What persisted and, indeed, what has become a key to evangelical Christianity is the belief in fundamental differences between men and women.

Beliefs in gender differences, of course, are rooted not only in religion. Best known for his Stanford Prison Experiment, a study that today is included in nearly every *Introduction to Psychology* textbook, Phillip Zimbardo has long been interested in what he depicts as the innate psychology of men. In 1971, his research team randomly assigned twenty-four young men, deemed "normal, average, and healthy," to be either prisoners or guards and then to carry out that role for a period of two weeks. Zimbardo observed that the men assigned to be guards, whose job it was to maintain order among the prisoners, quickly turned to tactics of coercion, degradation, and humiliation, which Zimbardo would later describe as psychological torture similar to what took place during the early stages of the Iraq War, at Abu Ghraib prison. After the fifth day of the experiment, Christina Maslach, a psychology professor at Berkeley who would marry Zimbardo a year later, convinced him to call off the experiment.

Zimbardo's research suggests that when ordinary men face extraordinary conditions, such as in prisons or war zones, they can come to accept or even celebrate behavior that most of us would consider atrocious and immoral. More than four decades after his prison experiment, Zimbardo turned his attention to a different extraordinary condition: the internet. "These guys aren't interested in maintaining long-term romantic relationships, marriage, fatherhood, and being the head of their own family," Zimbardo says. Instead, "these guys" are spending a lot of time on the internet, playing video games and watching porn, and that is holding back an entire generation of boys and young men from "what it means to be male," an idea included in the subtitle of Zimbardo's book *Man (Dis)connected*. Zimbardo captures the popular porn addiction narrative that online pornography is getting in the way of men's attraction to real-life women and, thus, their propensity to date and settle down in marriage. (Cue the butterfly experiment.)

But what exactly does it mean to be male? To be male is to want sex, according to sociologist Mark Regnerus in his book *Cheap Sex*. To be female, according to him, is to want commitment, which in the modern world is also known as marriage. As a sociologist, Regnerus became more famous than most when, in 2012, he published an article that purported to find that children of straight married parents were better off than children of gay and lesbian parents. He used the study as the basis for a brief to oppose the legalization of same-sex marriage for the 2015 Supreme Court case *Obergefell v. Hodges*. In the aftermath, the American Sociological Association and the American Psychological Association submitted amicus briefs of their own, supporting same-sex marriage and citing flaws in the Regnerus study. The problem was that Regnerus defined a gay or lesbian parent as anyone who had ever had a same-sex sexual encounter. In actuality, the study does not find differences between gay and lesbian parents and straight parents; it finds differences between stable households (parents who are heterosexual and married) and unstable households (parents who have had multiple partners). Yet Regnerus used these differences to argue for the inferiority of gay parents and to support his mission to save heterosexual matrimony.

In *Cheap Sex*, published five years after his now-infamous study, Regnerus insists that pornography—what he calls "the cheapest sex"—has disrupted the basic qualities of maleness and femaleness to the detriment of American families. Whereas women once exchanged sex for marriage, men now find sex outside real relationships with women and, thus, have less motivation to marry. This model of sexual exchange, Regnerus writes, "is rooted in stable realities about male-female differences that are not socially constructed and will not disappear." Zimbardo agrees, writing that "Male brains separate sex and romance, neural systems that are united in female brains, while female brains separate mental arousal from physical arousal, which are united in male brains."

Psychologist Cordelia Fine coined the term *neurosexism* to describe claims like those of Zimbardo and Regnerus, which have been championed by male doctors and scientists for centuries. Their studies supposedly uncovered evidence of male and female brain differences, but the studies' methods and results were in fact due to the scientists' own gender biases and belief in stereotypes. In one example, Fine debunks the research conducted by a biologist in the 1940s on fruit flies' mating patterns. Bateman's principle, named after English biologist Angus Bateman, suggests that variability in sexual mating is a part of the male's design (the ease with which the male releases millions of sperm cells); whereas selectivity is a part of the female's natural design (the fewer number of eggs released by the female over the course of a reproductive life stage). These findings were used to substantiate a widely accepted evolutionary account of men's sexual proclivities. The problem, according to Fine, was that Bateman excluded data that did not support his conclusions. When the study was replicated, researchers found that there were greater offspring when both male and female fruit flies had a greater number of mates. So, in fact, the species benefited when males and females were equally promiscuous.

Another example, seventy years later, comes from a 2014 study that purported to show how men's and women's brains are wired differently. Researchers published a series of images that made it look as though men's and women's brains were nearly opposites. Images of women's brains displayed a series of lines connecting the left and right hemispheres, whereas images of men's brains showed connecting lines *within* hemispheres. The media's distillation of the findings heralded evidence that men are wired for focus and productivity, whereas women are wired to multitask. Yet, as cognitive neuroscientist Gina Rippon has pointed out, these diagrams left out the majority of connections, which showed no difference across men and women. "Every brain is actually a mosaic of different patterns," Rippon writes, "some more commonly found in men's brains and some in women's. But none could be described as fully male or female."

Neuroscientists are beginning to acknowledge that Zimbardo's and Regnerus's insistence on "opposite sexes" may have gotten the causal explanation for gendered behavior backward. "Brains reflect the lives that they have lived, not just the sex of their owners," Rippon insists. And when we live in a world that saturates us from birth into adulthood with messages about gender difference, our brains will change to reflect this gendered world. Thus, when we observe real differences in so-called male and female brains, these differences stem from society, not biology. Fine puts it this way: even when a study finds evidence of a differing "male and female brain," "social realities mean that women and men in these studies are simply not participating in the same experiment."

Sociologists do not reject the influence of biology or genetics, but we have a keen eye on how *claims* about biology and genetics are disseminated in the social world, and to what end. Regnerus, for example, insists that his critique of porn is based strictly on what the scientific data reveal. It is true that the marriage rate is lower today than ever before, whereas pornography consumption is at its highest. Yet, as fellow sociologist Paula England points out, Regnerus blames internet porn for the declining marriage rate when much more plausible explanations are other modern inventions, such as birth control and legal protections for women pursuing education and a career. In other words, Regnerus's exchange theory could be used to predict the opposite of his argument: that men should want to commit to women because of women's higher economic status today than in the past. Instead, Regnerus's use of exchange theory is to advance the century-old conservative agenda to recuperate the "traditional" family from the threat of pornography.

In her review of *Cheap Sex*, anthropologist Barbara King points out that "there's no convincing evidence to suggest" that monogamy and pair bonding "characterized the mating of our hominin ancestors." Sure, if we managed to zap the culture out of all of us, humans would continue to procreate from some primal impulse. But in order for that activity to count as *sex*, a word that connotes far more meaning beyond the act itself, we must include the broader culture from which that word is derived.

IF THE FIRST day of the True Intimacy retreat felt like going to church, the second day felt more like going to school. We started in a session called "Love, Sex, and the Brain," learning about the limbic system through anatomical drawings projected on a large screen. In the audience, heads nodded vigorously as hands took notes. "You might be wondering what all of this has to do with sex?" Rachel asked, after spending nearly ten minutes talking about the anatomy of the brain and studies on attachment styles. Introduced to the audience as "the scientist," Rachel holds a bachelor's degree in psychology and a master's in criminal justice. "All of this science stuff is to give us an accurate depiction of why we are the way we are." According to Rachel, God designed the brain "on purpose," but Satan and sin, she said, have messed it up. Back to the mess of the Garden.

Rachel told us that God created men's and women's bodies differently. When men orgasm, they release more of the hormone vasopressin, which sends their brains the message "I have to protect," she explained. When women have sex, they release more oxytocin than vasopressin, sending their brains the message "I am content and want to nest." This mirrors evangelical-led abstinence campaigns that blend science with religion to insist that premarital sex is physically damaging. According to conservative evangelical Dr. Eric Keroack, who was appointed to oversee federal funding for abstinence-only programs under President George W. Bush, these hormones are "God's superglue," intending to attach husband and wife to each other in lifelong monogamous matrimony. Never mind that most scientists agree that neither premarital sex nor masturbation to porn will prohibit attachments later in life. Hormones like oxytocin surge in a wide range of relational contexts, from breastfeeding to dog petting. Rachel's explanation, though, makes science neatly align with evangelical beliefs about sex that uphold gender complementarianism (or the belief prescribed to by a majority of evangelicals that God created men to lead and women to nurture).

Every porn addiction recovery resource I have encountered (whether a book, app, small group, or online forum) makes reference to the brain and the claim that pornography is physically addictive. A common metaphor among the people I interviewed—regardless of whether they were evangelical Protestants, Catholics, Latter-day Saints, Jewish, or not religious—was that men's brains are "wired" in a way that makes them biologically preconditioned to become sexually aroused by visual stimuli.

Since high school, Elliot had struggled through tumultuous periods of "sobriety and relapse," as he put it, in his attempts to quit porn. When he was in college, a friend gave him a Christian book that explained how pornography was physically addictive. This knowledge is what prompted change. "It completely changed my mind-set," he told me. "I'm a believer, and I'm stuck in this sin," he said, "but, yeah, I feel like there is a physical component. Your mind is, like, rewired. You have pathways in your mind that are deeply entrenched, and even if you are a believer in Christ, it is just hard to get out of that."

For many Christian men like Elliot, admitting they had a problem with porn (even if they continued to occasionally watch it) garnered sympathy and understanding from both women partners and their broader Christian community. Heather, a participant in a women's group for dealing with men's porn addiction, said she once thought pornography was only a "moral issue," but later she changed her point of view: "When I started to realize what pornography really did to the brain—I mean, it really caused changes in the brain—that's when I started to get it, and why it is so hard to quit," she said. "Once I learned that, grace was much easier to show."

Similarly, Gina described her ex-fiancé, David, as a porn addict who was "really sick." David watched porn several times a day. As Gina described it, "That's so much dopamine getting released that your brain shuts down, and then, the only way to feel normal is by looking at porn." Gina eventually ended her relationship with David, but not because he watched porn. She didn't want to continue a relationship with someone who wouldn't admit to his "sickness" and work to change his behavior.

Pornography addiction support groups, both secular and religious, offer space for young men to discuss sex openly and seriously with one another rather than discussing it under the guise of masculine teasing and competition. My interview respondents often compared the emotional tenor of these groups to the churches and youth groups they grew up participating in that facilitated gender-specific programs for boys and girls. "They would pretty much always have one night where they would split up guys and girls," Jason recalled of his teenage experience with a church youth group, "and so the girls would have their talk about, quote unquote, 'girl things,' and us guys would have our 'man talk,' so to speak. And so, when it's a bunch of dudes talking about deeper struggles and those kinds of things, it's like the number one thing that was always talked about: sexuality and especially pornography." Mark, a Christian who joined a secular recovery program, called it "the popular sin to talk about" among his friends in high school, since "you just knew that it was something that every guy was struggling with."

THE PORN ADDICTION recovery movement parallels the hugely popular American self-help and wellness industry geared toward men that places its faith not in a Christian God but in evolutionary psychology. Entrepreneurs turned motivators like Tim Ferriss (author of *The 4-Hour Workweek*), Joe Rogan (Ultimate Fighting champion and *Fear Factor* host), and Lewis Howes (former NFL player) are among a group that historian Molly Worthen calls "podcast bros," who strive to win this game of life where evolution has set the rules. "The evolutionary hangover is pretty real," podcast host Cory Allen told Worthen in an interview. "We're not ready for the nuances of modern society. Shedding light on why we react and respond in certain ways and certain situations will help alleviate those reactions over time." This genre, a religion unto itself, spins self-improvement as the ultimate masculine pursuit: strength over weakness, victory over defeat.

Of course, these self-help and wellness books and podcasts have an audience beyond straight cis men, yet their messages, rooted so often in evolutionary psychology, reify the idea of "maleness" as something distinct from other categories. In the preface to *The Mask of Masculinity*, Lewis Howes's second book after his first bestseller, *The School of Greatness*, he writes of his friendship with Glennon Doyle, the blogger and author who blends memoir with self-help for her huge following of mostly women. "Of course, I also learned a lot in these conversations about the masks that women struggle with and the pressures and the unfair standards society forces on them (the same goes for the gay men I spoke to, as well as people of different races and different identities). But recounting these observations are [*sic*] for different books by writers much wiser than me." Howes makes explicit what is most often implicit among those of his ilk: women and queer people can turn to their own problem solvers, writers and podcasters like Doyle. Howes's advice, like that from other writers in this "self-help bro" genre, comes from a cisgender straight white man who is speaking to an audience of the same.

All these podcast hosts (Howes, Rogan, and Ferriss) have talked about pornography in the context of an addiction. In 2019, Lewis Howes interviewed Terry Crews, the actor and former NFL player, who explained how, when he was nine years old, to cope with his abusive home, he turned to pornography instead of using drugs or drinking alcohol. Finally, in 2010, at the age of forty-two, he went to rehab for his addiction. In a video he posted to Facebook, called "Dirty Little Secret," Crews says that he struggled with pornography for years. "Some people denied it. They'd say, 'Hey, man, you can't be addicted to pornography.' But let me tell you something:

If days turns into night and you're still watching, you've probably got a problem. And that was me." Crews blames what he calls "the cult of masculinity" for his entitlement to watch porn and the subconscious belief he held that men were better than women. "We have to rise above that mind-set," he says adamantly.

Men watching porn may be part of the normal gender order, but men like Crews make narratives of quitting porn also fall in line with the gender status quo. In recovery, men who struggle with what they call "porn addiction" are able to maintain their masculinity by conforming to the expectation that they do, in fact, want to watch porn. And for Christians in particular, they can avoid feeling shame about committing the sin of watching porn, as it's explained by factors beyond their control. The story that both secular and Christian recovery groups tell is that men must have the power to fight their biological urges. This sets up only men who are the strongest and most committed to win the battle. Instead of seeing pornography addiction as a weakness, the ability to recognize and overcome it is seen as a hard-won accomplishment. Indeed, it leads to what members of the NoFap community call "superpowers"—newfound confidence, attractiveness, energy, and focus.

"I was tired of being held down by the chains of pornography," Jonathan recalled when I asked him why he decided to join an online forum dedicated to porn addiction recovery. "I was tired of not being who I am meant to be and not being the person that God made me to be, more importantly." As a Catholic, Jonathan hoped that one day he would see "complete freedom" from porn. But at the time of our interview, he said he had had occasional "setbacks," or times when he succumbed to temptation and watched it. Still, he saw himself as a man on a quest to, as he described it, "win the war and be ready to keep on fighting."

MOST OFTEN, THE women who participate in the porn addiction recovery movement do so because they are partnered with men whom they perceive to have a porn problem. For these women, there are books, support groups, online message boards, conferences, and workshops. A much smaller group of women within this industry is there because they themselves struggle

with pornography addiction. Nearly everyone I interviewed who participated in a porn addiction recovery group made a point to mention the
fact that "some" women, though imagined as outliers, struggle with porn.
Still, pornography addiction is described as a "man's problem," according
to both the porn addiction industry and the people I interviewed. Sociologist
Samuel Perry has detailed a gendered double standard within Protestant
churches, where women's porn use is treated as a deviation from the
norm. Women who watch porn, in the words of Perry, are "sinning against
their gender."

"I know that for men and women, it's very different," Joe, a leader of a
Christian men's group, Clean Life (a pseudonym), explained to me. "Often,
for women, it's hard to understand the nature of a man's brain and where
it goes with these things and how much more difficult it can be for men.
I don't think it's more difficult for a man or a woman, but in my experience,
the numbers seem to be quite a bit higher with men. I think that's just the
way, you know, we're wired sexually." Joe acknowledged that some women
also struggle with pornography addiction, but then insisted that it's the
biological makeup of men's bodies in particular that make pornography
addiction more likely for them. The reason most women don't look at
porn, as described by the people I interviewed, is that women are "seeking
romance," "more relational," "not visually stimulated," or "looking for
emotional not physical connection."

Still, women who consider themselves to be porn addicts can find
resources geared toward them, like the memoir and self-help book *Dirty
Girls Come Clean*. "I thought I was the only one" is the book's first line.
Crystal Renaud, the author, tells her own story and the stories of several
other Christian women who found themselves stuck in what their church
and culture were calling "a guy thing." Renaud recalls her first exposure
to pornography, when she was home alone and found a brother's poorly
hidden porno magazine. "In that one moment, in less than a second's time,
I not only exposed my eyes to a concept I had never seen before, but I
exposed my heart, my mind, and my body to a world that no ten-year-old
should ever have entered," Renaud writes.

The stories of pornography use for men and women that I heard over
and over again normalized men's addictions and isolated and stigmatized

women. Renaud, for all her efforts to do the opposite for her women audience, reinforces the belief that women seek out porn as a result of something gone wrong, typically in childhood. She compares the "emotional trauma" of her first glimpse of pornography to the emotional trauma of being a rape victim. I never heard a similar parallel for men. Renaud explains how her childhood home was peaceful, but only because her mother suffered from depression and her father was often away on business trips. Renaud worked to maintain peace by defending her older brothers when her mother threatened to ground them or kick them out. "We always find that these women had something happen to them when they were little," Jesse, a Christian counselor who oversees pornography addiction support groups at an evangelical church, explained to me.

I interviewed Amber, a self-identified pornography addict, who told me she's struggled to find real-life community with other women to whom she can relate. Instead, she tends to stick to an online forum, an in-person Christian therapist, and a lot of Christian self-help books. About the books, she said, "It's so frustrating—most of the stuff is geared toward men. I just read this one book, and there was like one mention of women in the whole book." Still, when I asked her if she thought pornography addiction was mostly a "man's issue," Amber affirmed the gender stereotype. "I think, as a generalization, that's true," she said, "but for me, the visual stimulation thing is there. But, I mean, there's also more of an emotional thing. You know, I probably am attracted to more romantic porn videos, where there's more foreplay or more of what you perceive as connection. And that attracts me to it."

Similarly, Renaud writes in *Dirty Girls Come Clean* that pornography filled her need for emotional intimacy. "I can't speak for every woman, but what I found in my research surveys and what was definitely true in my own life is that, unlike for men, the addiction to pornography in women is not as much about how it makes her feel physically, but how it meets her emotional needs." Conservative Christianity supposes that God created men and women to be distinct from each other in order for them to come together in marriage. This idea rests upon the belief that God created men to have stronger physical needs, and women, emotional ones. In turn, women are described as largely dependent on men for sexual attention and pleasure to meet emotional and relationship fulfillment rather than as autonomous sexual actors with their own strong sexual drives and desires. For women who look at porn, the message is that some catalyst causes them to deviate from "normal" expressions of women's sexuality.

The True Intimacy retreat must strike a difficult balance among its audience of women, given that the event markets itself as for women who struggle with sex and porn addiction themselves and for women whose partners struggle with sex and porn addiction. I asked Lizzy, a conference organizer, why the event catered to these distinct groups. "That's such a good question, and it's one of the challenges we've been working on over the past few years," she recalled. For one thing, there's the practical reality that a conference designed exclusively for women who struggle with sex and porn addiction simply wouldn't attract enough participants," she explained. Though True Intimacy offers curricula for women who struggle with sex and porn addiction, many churches "just don't have the numbers," she said, to offer those groups. But because Lizzy is someone who herself has struggled with what she calls "an addiction to masturbation," there's a deeper philosophical reason that she wanted to include both types of women in the conference. Before she joined the staff at True Intimacy, the curriculum relied heavily on gender stereotypes—for example, referring to addicts as "he" and to those who were betrayed as "she." Lizzy, along with her team at True Intimacy, is working on revamping the curricula to be more gender neutral.

"It's true that we've had women who have joined the conference and then worried, for instance, 'Well, how can I be in the hot tub with her when she's cheated on her husband, and I'm here because my husband cheated.' So, we work really hard on our women's team to try to make it something that any woman can relate to, even if there are pieces that are, like, 'Yeah, that's not really me,' but that nobody is being put into a box. We try to make it so women can see each other on the same field rather than 'she's betrayed, she's addicted, she's a this, and she's a that,'" Lizzy explained.

The True Intimacy participants shared a conservative evangelical frame-work that told them that, as women, they were more similar than different. No matter if some were sex addicts and some were being betrayed by sex addicts, their common identity as (mostly white and middle-class) Christian women had brought them together. For them, this was both biblical and commonsense. The messaging at the conference explicitly supported a belief in gender complementarity as designed by God. But beyond religious beliefs, these women's daily lives continually reinforced beliefs about gender differences and what it meant to be a (white, middle-class) woman, which is different from what it means to be a (white, middle-class) man. Race and class, though never named explicitly in the conference, are far from inconsequential. Like many conservative evangelical spaces, True Intimacy is an example of what sociologist Howard Winant calls a "white racial project," whereby whiteness is associated with moral, appropriate, and good behavior. I observed women in the conference who were formerly strangers, regardless of how they related to pornography and sex, befriend one another because they could talk with ease about the joys and challenges of being wives and mothers. Over a lunch break, I found myself participating in a lively conversation about the sleep habits of babies and toddlers. Everyone at my table had a story to tell in the spirit of commiseration and camaraderie, and as a white, middle-class mother myself, I was welcomed into the conversation.

While True Intimacy works to acknowledge the diversity of women's experiences when it came to sex and porn, it still doesn't offer curricula for men betrayed by partners. Nor do any of the other groups I studied. For men, the assumption is that, even if their female partners struggle with sex or porn addiction, they struggle with it, too. The claim that "guys watch porn" is indeed both a stereotype and an empirical reality. But beyond the fact that men watch porn more often than women, ideas about masculinity and femininity also fuel this notion of pornography's gendered audience. Is it so different to say men are naturally inclined to look at porn because of their innate sinfulness, or because of their innate desire to procreate and protect our species? In the world of Christian pornography addiction recovery, these arguments become one and the same.

BOTH MEN AND women who participate in the pornography addiction recovery industry are on a path toward self-improvement. Religious or secular, they share the goal of avoiding pornography in order to better their lives. Yet men and women on this path have different starting points. The porn addiction recovery industry, which is predominantly geared toward men, teaches those men that they are not bad or broken for wanting to look at porn. Instead, it is completely normal and natural that they should want to look at porn. Women are on the sidelines of the porn addiction recovery rhetoric, either as the wives or partners of porn-addicted men or as the "exception" to the general rule that porn addiction affects men more often than women.

Some programs, like True Intimacy, are beginning to use gender-neutral language or to offer curricula for both men and women, but this does not eliminate the gendered patterns of "recovery." Men receive the repeated message that porn is bad, but that it is understandable and even natural that they are interested in looking at it. Their intervention is a validating one: *There's nothing fundamentally wrong with you.* But for women, it's nearly the opposite: *Porn is bad, and it's unusual for women to want to look at it. Therefore, there* is *something fundamentally wrong with you.*

Gender inequality is a constant theme in the porn wars. But usually when this phrase is invoked, both sides focus on men's entitlement to sex with women and women's objectification and victimization. Under the surface, though, there is another thread in these debates about gender inequality and difference. When blending religious beliefs about gender complementarity with scientific beliefs about biological differences between men and women, the pornography addiction recovery industry presents normal men as those with strong sex drives and normal women as those who lack strong sex drives. It presents men as powerful victors over natural urges and women as victims of sexual trauma. In these ways, porn addiction commentary about men and women inadvertently re-creates some of the most damaging gender stereotypes of pornography itself.

CHAPTER 17

Protect the Children

Nearly a century after the Second Circuit Court of Appeals defended Mrs. Mary Ware Dennett's right to distribute a sex education pamphlet and, thus, distinguished sex education from obscenity, the field of sex education remains contested. Dennett was part of an early twentieth-century movement of people who called themselves "social hygienists." "Hygiene" meant health, broadly defined to include the physical body and also the wellness and cohesion of families and communities. *Social hygiene* was most often a euphemism for *sex*. The American Social Hygiene Association insisted that solving society's sexual problems (venereal disease, prostitution, and double standards for men and women's sexuality) would solve other problems in America—namely, poverty and destitution, especially for unwed mothers.

This early sex education movement distinguished itself from religious teachings about sex, whose lessons revolved around abstinence for the unmarried and reproduction for married couples. Social hygienists emphasized the potential pleasures of sex, while also raising awareness about the dangers they associated with sexual excess. Though certainly more progressive than their religious counterparts, early sex educators presented a faithful marriage as the ultimate goal for which adolescents should strive. It was not until well into the latter half of the twentieth century that mainstream sex educators began placing healthy sex outside marriage. This shift was reflective of broader trends. Between the 1960s and '80s, premarital sex became more common across all racial groups and for both men and women.

The wide dissemination of the birth control pill in the 1960s and '70s meant that women's sex lives could more closely resemble men's than ever before. Efforts to normalize *birth control*, a term coined by Margaret Sanger in 1914, had long emphasized condom and diaphragm use. But in 1960, the FDA approved "the Pill," Enovid, a mixture of progesterone and estrogen hormones that prevented women's ovulation. In 1965, the Supreme Court ruled that married couples had the right to use the drug, and seven years later, it ruled that all people, married or unmarried, had the right to contraception.

Even as sex became disentangled from marriage among a growing segment of Americans, sex educators continued to stress a sexual ideal that persists to the present day: that sex should be "caring" and "nonexploitative." Today, there are two broad branches of sex education in the United States: abstinence-focused versus comprehensive. Abstinence-focused programs are often but not always "faith-based" and emphasize themes of self-respect, self-control, risk, responsibility, commitment, and marriage. Though the more comprehensive sex-ed programs overlap somewhat with abstinence curricula, when it comes to teaching about the consequences of sexual behavior, the former's curricula emphasize alternative themes of medical accuracy, informed decision making, safety, contraception, honesty, and communication. Both approaches have taken credit for positive changes in Americans' sexual lives over the past few decades: teenage pregnancy and abortion rates have both dropped. Teenagers are less likely to have sex today than in the immediate aftermath of the sexual revolution of the 1970s, and when they do have sex, they are more likely to use contraception.

Today in America, it's no longer up for debate whether schools will teach sex education, but rather, what kind of sex education will be taught. Thirty-five states have passed laws requiring that sex education include "abstinence," or the health and emotional benefits of choosing *not* to have sex. In comparison, only fifteen states have passed laws requiring that sex education be medically accurate, and only sixteen require teaching about contraception, aligning with a comprehensive model. Federally funded abstinence-only programs date back to 1981, under the Reagan presidency, when the Adolescent Family Life Act supported organizations that promoted "chastity and self-discipline." President George W. Bush created the Community-Based Abstinence Education (CBAE) program in 2000, which increased funding for organizations teaching abstinence until marriage. The program expired early in Obama's presidency, but conservative members of Congress had it reinstated as part of negotiations for the Affordable Care Act in 2010. As of 2018, the "abstinence-only" label was replaced with "sexual risk avoidance" (SRA) education, in an attempted rebranding for government-supported sex ed.

Unlike other subjects in school, where teachers obtain degree specializations, sex education is far less systematized than the teaching of math or social studies. Local school districts largely determine their own curricula and standards for teachers. Gordon B., who worked as an arts-based sex educator and contracted with local high schools, explained to me that "there are huge gaps between what students are hungry to learn about and what parents are comfortable with the idea of their kids learning about." This was echoed in my interview with Lindsey, a sex educator who worked with area high schools. Instead of receiving a list of requested topics from schools who hired them, these sex educators most often received a list of what they should *not* talk about. "Usually, the school point person will tell me, 'This list is a collaborative effort from the PTA and administration,' so it's coming from parents and the administration of things I cannot talk about." Even for schools that tout comprehensive sex education programs, this does not mean that educators can talk about an unlimited number of topics regarding sex. "Usually, it's very consent focused," Lindsey explained, making language and topics that schools deem explicit off limits for discussion. "It can be hard finding work-arounds to talk about consent but not to talk explicitly about sex."

Most secondary school health teachers are trained in some sexual health topics (usually, the prevention of STIs and HIV and how to teach the basics of reproduction), and they are often tasked with teaching sex education in schools. Alternatively, some school districts choose to contract with outside educators and organizations, like the just-mentioned Gordon B. and

Lindsey. Because no state requires specific credentials, educators can tout training from a wide number of organizations, ranging from the ultraconservative Christian Pure Life Academy to the ultraprogressive feminist pornographer Tristan Taormino's Sex Educator Boot Camp. Very few universities offer specialization in sexuality education for degree programs. The most rigorous and widely respected certification program for sex educators and counselors comes from the American Association of Sexuality Educators, Counselors, and Therapists (AASECT). This program requires those who enroll to have at least a bachelor's degree, along with core academic course work; a number of hours of professional experience; and fieldwork under supervision in sexuality education. Across the country, about 1,100 professionals have completed the certification program.

NO MATTER IF it is abstinence-focused or comprehensive, sex education in the twenty-first century faces a dilemma that is some parts old and some parts new. The old dilemma is teaching children, presumed innocent and free from sexual baggage, about sexual content. The new dilemma is the internet, where children's exposure to sexual material is imagined to be almost inevitable. Pornography is challenging because it is both a curricular quandary and a competitor in the arena of sex education. Kids are learning about sex from porn, but how should educators address it? Many public school programs simply avoid the topic altogether. Yet this is dissatisfying for both sides of the porn wars, whose advocates, regardless of their beliefs, shared the perspective that when it comes to sex education, porn should be a required topic.

Pornography's harm to children has arguably been the longest and largest concern among its opponents. In a Boston periodical from 1836, a concerned parent wrote about illicit literature: "it will teach them things they never thought of." Over a century later, in a 1955 Senate hearing on pornography, a major concern was if and how children might be exposed to it. From historian Whitney Strub's account, the chief counsel at the hearings, "albeit without much evidence," "brought sensationalistic detail to this aspect, being sure to spell out 'dildoes' for the record as he noted that such items were 'going out in the mail to youngsters as young as 12 and 13." Concern for children spans antiporn conservatives and feminists. In the 1980s, Women Against Pornography (WAP) conflated pornography's harm to both women and children, often citing exaggerated statistics about the billions of dollars of revenue from child pornography and the millions of preteen children who were abused in the porn and prostitution industries. Newspaper and magazine article titles asked fearfully, PORNOGRAPHY: WHAT CAN WE DO TO PROTECT OUR KIDS? and CAN WE PROTECT CHILDREN FROM PORNOGRAPHY? In 2016, Judith Shulevitz wrote in the *New York Times*, IT'S O.K., LIBERAL PARENTS, YOU CAN FREAK OUT ABOUT PORN.

Children are evoked in century-old debates because of what they symbolically represent within broader society. In the words of cultural theorist Gabrielle Owen, the idea of the child "describes someone who is naïve, unknowing, innocent, who is without agency or desire." In other words, "the child is emptied," Owen writes, so as to fulfill adult desires and projections of "the narrative inevitability of a normative adulthood"—that is, unless something goes wrong. Though children are presumed innocent, conservative movements have long emphasized the simultaneous fact that children are also constantly at risk, especially as they enter into adolescence and are no longer under the watchful eye of parents or a church. As literary scholar James Kincaid describes it, "Innocence is . . . not nurtured but enforced."

Today in America, young people tend to be between ten and fifteen when they are first exposed to online porn. This average age of first exposure is younger than decades past, especially for girls. All the educators, therapists, religious leaders, and activists I interviewed, regardless of their position on porn, agreed that it makes for bad sex education. Opponents pointed to mainstream commercial videos that teach all the wrong lessons: normalizing physical aggression and sexual acts like facial ejaculation or double penetration, which most women would find, at best, unpleasant and, at worst, abusive and traumatic. Even if aggression or violence stemmed from a consensual BDSM scene, antiporn advocates argued that young people are likely to lack the sexual knowledge to fully understand such nuance. Though most of my respondents saw no real difference between Pornhub and independent producers, those who did acknowledge the efforts among ethical and feminist pornographers like Erika Lust dismissed them by insisting that teenagers are not seeking out those sites and, instead, are finding free streaming "tube" sites. Teens are violating the terms of use on whatever porn they find online, given that websites require users to—through the click of a button—acknowledge that they are at least eighteen years of age. Still, it is much easier for teens to use sites like Pornhub, which does not require the user to enter credit card information or sign up as a member.

Pornography's sympathizers push back that porn is for entertainment, not education. "We don't take our kids to see *Fast and the Furious* and then expect them to learn how to drive like Vin Diesel. It's the exact same principle," Andre Shakti told me in an exasperated tone. As a sex worker who also frequently led workshops and conferences on topics related to sex and who contributed to teen and young adult magazines like *Cosmopolitan*, Andre Shakti felt strongly that pornography should not substitute for sex education. "Most of it is for pure entertainment purposes, and most of it should not be used for sex ed, and that's okay, because that's not its role. If your kids are learning about things like safe sex from pornography, then that means they're not getting it where they should, which is in the home. Like, you should be talking to your kids about these things." According to Andre Shakti's logic, teens are capable of understanding the difference between real life and action movies and should also be able to understand the difference between real sex and porn sex. But this requires open communication between parents and their children.

DEFEND YOUNG MINDS is an educational program that enables parents to do just that. "I felt compelled to start looking for a children's book to help explain that looking at pornography is dangerous. I thought I'd find several, but I couldn't find *even one*," Kristen Jenson, a Christian mother of three, recalled. And so, Jenson decided to write one herself. Sure that pornography was the direct line between children and violence, exploitation, and addiction, she started her own nonprofit organization to teach children about pornography's dangers.

For young children, she explained, the best approach is a simple memory exercise. If a child sees what Jenson calls a "bad picture," they should "turn, run, and tell!" Defend Young Minds offers a program that, like fire safety's "stop, drop, and roll," is meant to be practiced by parents with their young children, so that the children learn it by heart. First, turn around to stop looking at the image. "Seconds count," Jenson insists. Next, leave the room. Children learn they should run away to distance themselves from whoever exposed them to the "bad picture." Finally, Defend Young Minds teaches children that they must tell a trusted adult about what happened. As adamant as Jenson is that pornography is nothing but dangerous, she emphasized that parents should not regard children who watch it as being bad or perverted. "Responding with alarm, anger, or tears can lead a child to retreat in shame and silence." Always respond with compassion, Jenson instructs.

Beginning when children are six, she recommends reading aloud from her picture book, *Good Pictures, Bad Pictures: Porn-Proofing Today's Young Kids*. Told from the perspective of a child (presumably a white preteen boy, judging by the sketched illustration), the first chapter, "What's Pornography?," begins with the boy and his mother looking through a family photo album. The mother comments, "Our photo album is full of *good* pictures that remind us of how important our family and friends are. But did you know there are *bad* pictures, too?" The mother goes on to explain the difference. Images or drawings in science books, even if they are of naked people, are not bad. Our private parts are not bad, but taking pictures of them is. And looking at pornography is bad, even if it might temporarily feel good: "Pornography is tricky because it's designed to feel exciting to your body. In fact, pornography tricks the brain into releasing a big dose of chemicals that make your body feel really good—for a short time," the mother of the book's narrator tells him. "The problem is that pornography can hurt parts of your growing brain. Looking at pornography is dangerous."

Jenson calls porn a "poisonous bait" and uses the analogy of riding a bike. As the fictional mom tells her child, "I've taught you to wear a helmet when you ride your bike to protect your brain on the outside. But pornography gets inside your brain and hurts it." It does this in three ways, the book explains. First, pornography teaches that people are objects, not whole people. Pornography also teaches lies: like when men are mean to women, women act like it's fun. Third, pornography can become a bad habit "or even a serious addiction," as Jenson warns. This leads to the next chapter, "What's an Addiction?" The remainder of the book focuses on this point, pornography addiction, comparing porn to drugs and alcohol to explain the damage caused especially to adolescents' brains.

For older children, a more complex remedy than "turn, run, and tell" is in order. Jenson calls this the CAN DO Plan. Using these two acronyms, older children should: Close their eyes, Always tell a trusted adult, and Name it when they see it. If they find themselves thinking about bad pictures, they should: Distract themselves and Order their thinking brain to be the boss. The paranoia over early exposure to porn and the solutions Jenson offers mimic porn addiction recovery programs, and indeed, Defend Young Minds has been showcased at events that bring together antiporn activists alongside the porn addiction recovery movement, like NCOSE's annual summit.

In many ways, antiporn education programs align most closely with the "sexual risk avoidance," or abstinence, model of sex education. The emphasis is harm and making sure teens understand the dangers of pornography. Not all educators see it this way, though, and instead insist that by teaching about the harms of pornography, they in fact encourage teens toward a healthy and progressive sense of their sexuality. Feminist antiporn activist Gail Dines says "the goal is a safe, respectful, mutually pleasurable relationship" in the curricula provided by her nonprofit organization, Culture Reframed, which offers free online programs advertised for parents of tweens and teens. The organization's tagline is "Building resilience and resistance to hypersexualized media and porn." With her program's help, Dines tells parents they can develop effective communication with their children that will support sexual curiosity, which can include masturbation, fantasy, and nonheterosexual identities—unlike conservative Christian curricula.

The advice that Culture Reframed offers to parents is part practical, part ideological. The practical includes removing all electronic devices from children's rooms at bedtime and using technology's available parental restrictions. The ideological is the message that porn saturates our culture through more than porn sites. Children must learn to recognize how other media like television, movies, and music also endorse and perpetuate sexualization and porn culture. Still, the problem addressed most directly by Culture Reframed is young people's easy access to free porn websites. "If you have a boy, you have to assume that he's looked at porn by the age of thirteen or fourteen," Dines says bluntly. Much of the training provided by Culture Reframed rehashes the "brain battles" of porn addiction and, like Defend Young Minds, clearly sides with the perspective that pornography is biologically addictive, referencing resources by both Donald Hilton and Gary Wilson. One aspect of the curricula is a story of a hypothetical tween named Sam, who has a cell phone and thus is able to access porn videos discreetly and virtually at any time. "Habitual viewing was beginning to wire his brain to the type of sex he was seeing on pornography. Without intervention, Sam was on a path to a behavioral addiction." Girls, though they tend to look at porn at a later age, are not immune from pornography's damaging influence. They, too, may become addicted to pornography, or more likely, they will internalize "the messages of hypersexualization and objectification" that exploit and victimize women, Dines warns.

WHEREAS DINES'S SOCIOLOGICAL research on pornography is what led her to create a nonprofit to help families educate adolescents about sex and pornography, public health professor Emily Rothman's path was the opposite. She never set out to research or teach about pornography. Her research program has been focused on sexual violence for the bulk of her career. In particular, she sought a research-based approach to teach adolescents about dating and sexual violence and to reduce their incidents. She tells a story in her TED Talk, which has been viewed over three million times, about growing tired of seeing teenagers' eyes glazing over when they were presented with statistics about the prevalence of sexual and dating violence and noticing how they eagerly they pricked up their ears when she broached the topic of pornography.

Though the topic of porn for teens is a challenging one, Rothman sees it also as an opportunity. She describes it like a mom who hides shredded zucchini in the brownies she makes for her kids. Rothman wondered if she could do something similar: develop a curriculum that centered on pornography but also included messages about consent, healthy relationships, and intimacy. Her goal, as she described it in a training session I attended to learn more about her approach, was to "leverage the issue of porn" to talk about the real foundation that she believes will help reduce the prevalence of dating and sexual violence.

Rothman helped create a "pornography literacy" curriculum as a form of sex education that draws from a broader effort called "media literacy," which encourages students to use critical thinking when they consume everything from entertainment media to the news. Since 2016, she has helped lead this effort for the Boston Public Health Commission's Start Strong dating violence program. Its curriculum, called "The Truth About Pornography: A Pornography-Literacy Curriculum for High School Students Designed to Reduce Sexual and Dating Violence," gained national attention when it was the focus of a 2018 *New York Times* feature article, WHAT TEENAGERS ARE LEARNING FROM ONLINE PORN. Still, it is one of the only curricula of its kind in the United States.

Based on her review of empirical research, "all signs point to the idea that mainstream online pornography appears to negatively influence youth in several ways," as Rothman describes it. Studies find evidence that watching porn may contribute to teens' negative beliefs about women, mental health problems including depression and anxiety, and teens' willingness to engage in risky sexual behaviors like unprotected sex. Rothman sees pornography and sexual and dating violence as related, given that mainstream porn often depicts violence against women and both teenage boys and girls report pressure to perform sex acts seen in pornography. Still, Rothman and her collaborators, Jess Alder and Nicole Daley, do not cite pornography as the single source of these problems since teens see unhealthy messages about sex and dating in many sources beyond pornographic videos, including television, movies, and magazines. Porn cannot be an isolated cause of violence and unhealthy dating behaviors, these social science researchers insist. It is but one correlating variable.

Rothman mentions more than once, both in her training for the porn literacy curriculum and in her TED Talk, that she is the parent of two preteens. For that personal reason, she feels concerned about teenagers' easy access to free commercial porn through sites like Pornhub. But she also describes herself as "sex positive," and to her, this means that she "fully supports people's right to enjoy whatever kind of sex life and sexuality they find fulfilling, no matter what it involves, so long as it includes the enthusiastic consent of all parties involved." And so, she doesn't oppose pornography on principle, even the kind of pornography she might find unappealing or even offensive, so long as it was produced with the full consent of the actors. Rothman also agrees with pornography opponents that teens likely do not understand much nuance when it comes to porn, and this likely is one reason pornography causes negative outcomes among teenage viewers. This is where her program, the Truth about Pornography, comes in.

Unlike Defend Young Minds, which calls pornography "bad pictures" for its audience of young children, the Truth about Pornography does not cast value judgments on porn itself, but instead encourages teens to articulate their own moral beliefs about sex and to find ways that their behavior can match those values. Facilitators are instructed to offer no judgment, negative or positive, if teens share an interest in watching porn and, instead, to draw from empirical research to share consequences that are associated with porn consumption. This curriculum encourages teens to reflect on what sexual values hold true *for them* and to respect that these values may not be the same as those held by their parents or peers. One basic principle of the curriculum is that parents must give permission for their children to participate, but parents should not observe or participate in the classes, because this "would change some youths' capacity to express themselves freely." The only value pushed upon participants as a moral obligation is that which Rothman calls "enthusiastic consent," which is the best practice, according to her, when it comes to sex and dating. When youth do not understand or enact consent in their sex and dating practices, women are most likely to be victimized.

The curriculum does address the problems of porn—for example, gender double standards that cast women as submissive and men as dominant—but it also encourages empathy and nuanced understanding of porn performers: that they are workers in one facet of the entertainment industry. One of the activities in the curriculum intended for older adolescents is a game called "Fear Factor." The facilitator asks the group: would you be "willing to endure your toe being squeezed until you press a button to tap out. The person who lasts the longest gets the prize money." Typically, most of the teenage audience agrees that, yes, they would be willing to do this. The facilitator then poses a follow-up question: "How much prize money would need to be offered in order for you to participate?" Here, responses vary from one dollar to thousands. The second hypothetical scenario asks if the group would be willing to enter a televised challenge of climbing a wall with the possibility that the challenge could be changed at any point.

"You could technically say no to the change, but a lot of people would be angry at you for stopping filming," the facilitator says. This time, the group responds with more reservations, a response opposite to that for the toe-squeezing challenge. Why is there more reluctance? The group agrees it's because of the lack of control over the unknown. Finally, the teens are asked is they would be willing to kneel and have a goopy substance poured on their faces. For this scenario, reactions are mixed, with some teens sharing fond memories of watching the Nickelodeon channel on TV, which popularized the dumping of bright green slime, and saying this would be fun and no big deal. Others refuse.

The takeaway with "Fear Factor" is for teens to consider pornography within the broader circumstances under which it is made and the fact that viewers do not know or understand a performer's intent or interests. The facilitator acknowledges that pornography may depict "people experiencing painful things," and this could have a number of different backstories: a performer consented to do it, and they enjoyed it; they consented to it not because they enjoy it, but because of the payment they will receive; or they don't enjoy it and did not agree to it. Discussion questions then ask teens how the changed scenario changes the way they think about pornography itself and porn performers.

ACROSS EDUCATIONAL PROGRAMS that tackle porn, whether picture books for kids or group discussions among teenagers, sex educators empha-size two dominant themes: context and consent. For proponents of porn literacy, context is taught in a sociological and practical way. First, teens learn that their beliefs about dating and sex come from both their indi-vidual experiences (their family upbringing, for example) and from broader society. Second, teens learn to understand the context of pornography itself: that it is curated entertainment, quite different from real life sex. Consent means teaching young people that all sexual experiences and activities should prioritize enthusiastic consent from all parties involved.

For antiporn sex educators, context and consent are framed differently but are still dominant ideas. Context means that sexual feelings and activ-ities have different consequences in different settings: what is healthy and appropriate in a committed monogamous relationship (typically framed as heterosexual marriage) is not healthy or appropriate in the context of casual hookups. Educators here also emphasize that pornography is not real life. Consent means that young people must be informed of the harms of pornography so they can make informed choices about whether to consume it. For them, the answer is straightforward: the only healthy path is to avoid pornography completely.

But for the differences when it comes to pornography itself, watching or not watching porn are not really the stakes of these debates. Both sides are using the "broccoli under the cheese" strategy—as Rothman describes sneaking vegetables into her children's food—of promoting core sexual ethics and values underneath talk about pornography, because, ultimately, it matters less, for both sides, if young people do watch porn if they have the right values. For religious conservatives, the act of sin is part of the Christian journey. As previous chapters have described, Christians indeed expect and normalize that young men will in fact look at porn. So, while the surface message they send to young people is "Do not look at porn," the deeper message is "You should believe that pornography is wrong, and you should believe that heterosexual marriage is right." This cements boundaries between conservative Christians, believed to be normal and moral, and others, either those in the porn industry or sex work or those who believe looking at porn or engaging in casual sex is okay.

Secular programs like Gail Dines's Culture Reframed may appear to bridge the gap and provide a more centrist model between conservative Christian sex education and progressive porn literacy programs. Culture Reframed does not unequivocally condemn sex before marriage or mastur- bation, and the program also acknowledges teens who come out as lesbian, gay, bisexual, or transgender. The Culture Reframed curriculum endorses what it calls "sex-positive parenting," which means "facilitating healthy sexual development, and it includes being critical of pornography because today's mainstream porn portrays sex in negative, degrading, and violent ways." Culture Reframed falls in line with a clear antipornography feminist position, painting porn as a monolith that harms women.

Emily Rothman is sympathetic to this point of view. "We have a serious problem of misogyny and rape in this country, and pornography probably isn't helping with any of that." Rothman recalled how she felt "tremendous pressure to pick a side," as she began researching the relationship between pornography and teenage dating and sex. Because she does not take a firm antiporn stance, she has been accused of being "pro-porn," or part of what Gary Wilson of YourBrainOnPorn called the "Porn Science Deniers Alliance."

Whereas antiporn curricula leave out empathetic discussions about sex workers or the possibility that people can watch porn without experiencing harm, Rothman invites more nuance. A "pornography literacy" approach emphasizes the awareness of the viewer who, should they choose to watch porn, understands that scenes are being performed by paid professionals and the sex acts depicted may not be the same ones enjoyed by real-life partners. For sex educators like Rothman, it doesn't make sense to make sweeping declarations about pornography being "bad." For their approach, too, watching or not watching porn is not really the issue. Their perspective centers on informed individual choice to create openness and acceptance.

PART IV

Truce

The battles that divide the two sides in the pornography debate implicate more than pornography. These are fights over the lessons we teach our children; which scientific claims count as fact; how to negotiate the constraints of a capitalist economy; and what moral principles should guide us. In each of these arenas, pornography's opponents and sympathizers appear to land on opposing sides.

Over the course of my research, I came to understand that every person I interviewed or observed earnestly believed their position to be true and right. But what if we cast aside their many differences? Will anything be left? By investigating the deep stories surrounding porn, we can see how these social movements are not always in opposition to each other. Both sides, in fact, care about the same sorts of things: human rights, sexual consent, and living a fulfilling life. They believe that their reaction to porn (either to admonish or embrace it) places them on the path to achieving a real and authentic sexuality within the synthetic and virtual world that surrounds us. For all the polarizing rhetoric, the people fighting share many of the same goals.

CHAPTER 18

Faking It

The 1960s was a decade of scientific discoveries and confidence. The nation saw the invention of vaccines preventing measles, mumps, and rubella. America's space program sent astronauts to the moon. And in a laboratory at Washington University in St. Louis, Missouri, two sexologists believed they had eradicated the fake orgasm.

Dr. William Masters and Virginia Johnson began watching people have sex in their laboratory in 1957. The time was right. Masters had spent the last decade building his reputation within the university and medical community. Alfred Kinsey had just published two bestsellers on Americans' sex lives. But Kinsey, who had a Ph.D. in biology and whose training was mostly with invertebrates, had left many questions unanswered. It was time for an expert on the human body to provide an objective and medical account of human sexuality.

To his surprise, Masters found Johnson, originally hired as a research assistant, to be particularly insightful and bold. Twice married and twice divorced, Johnson had enrolled in college in the hope of achieving what women's liberationists idealized at the time: a fulfilling career that enabled financial independence. But as a single mother of two young children, she needed to make a living while pursuing her degree. She saw an ad calling for a student research assistant in the lab of Masters, whom she knew for his groundbreaking research on infertility. His project was not exactly made plain in the advertisement for the job, but Johnson was unintimidated. She went on to successfully recruit nearly seven hundred volunteers, who masturbated or engaged in partnered sex while their bodies were hooked up to various medical testing equipment and researchers took notes. Though written in dry, clinical language, Masters and Johnson's first coauthored book, *Human Sexual Response*, became an instant bestseller.

Having discovered the physiology of what they call "the orgasmic phase," Masters and Johnson declared the fake orgasm gone for good. With definitive satisfaction, they write, "the age-old practice of the human female dissimulating has been made pointless." In other words, because they discovered how women orgasm, we shouldn't have had to fake it anymore.

Today, though, the fake orgasm remains alive and well. Research suggests that the vast majority of women has faked it at some point over the course of a sexually active life. In one study, a United Kingdom–based survey of more than 450 heterosexual women ages nineteen to seventy-three, researchers found that 3 out of 4 women had faked an orgasm at least once and that most had faked an orgasm with their current partner. On average, the current fakers did so in about one out of every three sexual encounters. Researchers following in Masters and Johnson's footsteps have found that women are more likely to moan audibly during partnered sex than during masturbation, suggesting that there's nothing natural about the orgasm put on by Sally Albright in the deli scene of *When Harry Met Sally*. It's performance when it happens both on the screen and in real life.

The distinction between real and fake is often at the heart of contemporary pornography debates. Is the pleasure of performers *real*? Is pornography addiction *real*? What is *real* when it comes to sex? To answer these questions, we must confront the same obstacle that flummoxed Masters and Johnson fifty years ago. Why couldn't they rid the world of the fake orgasm? Because they didn't anticipate the power of fake sexual pleasure on our real lives. Too focused on the patterns and variations found in their medical testing equipment, they forgot about the greatest sexual force of all: society.

MARLA STEWART AND Kayla are acutely aware of the sneaky and persistent influence of society on sexuality. And they both see their mission as helping individuals, especially women, learn to overcome social messages that may shame or pathologize their feelings or desires, in order that they can experience authentic sexual pleasure. Both women see good sex as one way to achieve a good life.

Kayla emphasized this point when describing how to have a strong marriage. It's easy for couples to compartmentalize sex and intimacy, she explained to me, storing it away from other conflicts or "issues" within a relationship. But Kayla insisted that sex is actually a good barometer for how a marriage is going. A strong marriage can exist, Kayla said, only if you are able to truly let yourself be "physically and emotionally vulnerable" with your partner. Stewart agrees and told me that she sees her work as related not only to sex but also to overall self-improvement. "When you're able to use your creative sexual energy, it just sort of bleeds out to other aspects of your life. Your work life, your family life, whatever. When women have orgasms, it seems to be they are just much happier."

Yet, for what they have in common, Stewart and Kayla live and love in worlds that appear nearly opposite from each other. Stewart, who considers herself kinky, queer, nonmonogamist, and feminist, lives in a southern city, has a master's degree in sociology and women's and gender studies, and at the time of our interview, worked as a sex coach and sex educator. She is not religious, but she meditates daily and describes herself as "spiritual." When I asked whom she voted for in the 2016 presidential election, Stewart responded, "Uh, Clinton," as if the answer were so obvious I needn't have asked the question. Stewart is cofounder of the large annual Sex Down South conference, intended for "sex educators and sex enthusiasts" to teach and learn about a wide range of topics: BDSM, kink, and costume play; polyamory and nonmonogamy; sex work; sex and disability; trans, nonbinary, gender-nonconforming, and genderqueer sexualities; and lesbian, gay, bisexual, and queer sexualities. What these topics have in common, she explained, is that they can help individuals on their journey to sexual liberation. The guiding principles of the Sex Down South conference have remained the same since Stewart and her team organized the first one in 2015: prioritizing voices, feelings, and experiences of people of color; not assuming someone's gender identity; not shaming anyone's sexuality; respecting all consensual relationships, including those that are nonmonogamous; and creating a positive space for all bodies, no matter their shape or size.

Kayla, for her part, is a devoted Christian. She is active in her church in the small western town in which she lives, where she is a stay-at-home mom and works part time for the Christian organization True Intimacy. She is a registered Republican who paused when I asked whom she voted for in 2016. "Let's see. I don't really get involved in politics," she explained. I reminded her of the two major-party candidates, and this jogged her memory. "Trump? Yes, I'm pretty sure Trump." Kayla believes that sex is intended for marriage and that marriage should be between one man and one woman. After she explained that one of her biggest priorities was raising a daughter who didn't carry shame and secrecy when it came to sex, as Kayla herself did growing up, I asked if she would consider herself a feminist. She answered hesitantly, "No, I don't." She then paused and reconsidered. "I mean, I'm very assertive and opinionated, and I've had women say I'm probably more the director in the family, but I have a kind of old-school view of things. I'm protective of marriage and think the husband is the head, you know, that kind of viewpoint. I guess I'm more in the middle, where I just focus on Jesus, not whether something's a man's or woman's issue." After another pause, she came to her conclusion. "So, I guess I don't know, I'm not sure. Maybe you should ask me a bunch of questions and then let me know if you think I'm a feminist," she said with a little laugh. I didn't follow up with a list of questions. Her rejection of the label, while embracing contradictory viewpoints surrounding marriage and sexuality, was telling enough.

Both women wore a kind of "business sexy" style at the conferences where I met them—Kayla, a short, fitted skirt and high heels; Stewart, a one-piece jumpsuit that made visible a red bra. They both appeared onstage speaking to their respective audiences with confidence and ease. Stewart identifies as Black, and Kayla as Black-and-white biracial. Both women are in their thirties and are speakers and writers who draw from their own experiences overcoming their sexual baggage to teach and empower other women. They told jokes and personal stories and spoke with expertise about the topic at hand.

Both women also offered nearly parallel accounts for what motivated them: orgasms and the fact that many women don't know how to have them. Kayla described talking openly and frankly with women she worked with and with her friends and family. "It gets radical in the sense that I know there are so many women out there who need help. No woman struggling with an orgasm with her husband is going to bring that up. And so, I usually bring it up. I've asked my friends and my sister, 'Do you orgasm with your husband?'" she recalled with a laugh. In addition to her conference speaking circuit, Kayla leads support groups for women. In one group—she told me in a tone of *Can you believe this?*—none of the fifteen women who attended, all of whom had been married at least twelve years, said they enjoyed sex. "And I'm just blown away," Kayla confided. "How are you guys not having orgasms?" Similarly, Stewart answered my question about the motivation for her work by talking about the plight of women's pleasure. "I think about how many women in particular are not having orgasms and how because they are not having orgasms, they are not interested in having sex. I just feel compelled to help women, I mean people in general, but really helping women become better lovers."

Sex Down South, Stewart's event, regularly pays porn performers to teach workshops or provide the evening entertainment with live erotic shows. When I asked her to sum up her beliefs about pornography, she sighed audibly and then paused. "It's not a difficult thing for me personally," she began, "but I definitely think porn can be problematic because people are looking at it for education, not entertainment. That's not good. If people are saying, 'Well, I saw this in porn,' they are forgetting that I'm not like those actors and actresses, and those are, you know, film tricks, not real life. And I definitely believe in the ethical consumption of porn, I mean paying for your porn, so you're paying the people who are entertainers and who are making a living for what they're doing." Stewart also explained that she thought pornography addiction was a problem, especially for men. As a sex coach, she has worked with a couple of guys who, as she described it, "watched way too much porn," and it was getting in the way of more than their sex lives. "I worked with this one guy who was watching it seven, eight hours a day. Who could say that's not a problem?" she asked rhetorically. "He's twenty-four and is having trouble with erections. As for with any addiction, if it's affecting your everyday life and is affecting the people around you, then it's a problem." Her advice was not to avoid porn altogether, but to learn how to watch it in moderation. "Porn can be great to get ideas from every now and again."

Ultimately, she said she's neither "for or against pornography itself," but she saw it as a double-edged sword that can either encourage or inhibit what she called people's "sexual imagination."

In Kayla's part-time work, she writes curricula for and speaks at True Intimacy's conferences on sex and pornography addiction recovery. She has traveled to cities across the country to promote the message that masturbation, sex, and pornography can all become addictive behaviors and, thus, must be carefully controlled through accountability in church groups, open communication with one's spouse, and a prayerful relationship with God. Not only are any sexual actions other than sex between a married man and woman wrong and sinful, Kayla believes, but they are also unhealthy and physically damaging. Her religious convictions are strong and clear that viewing pornography is a sin in the eyes of God. But through her involvement with True Intimacy, she explained how she now understands more completely the problem with pornography. "Pornography is not healthy," she asserted, because it literally affects a person's brain and ability to connect with real-life partners. "But God tells us that we can be transformed by the renewing of our mind. By quitting porn and masturbation, the brain can gain blood flow back and can build back new pathways. Isn't that just incredible?" she said with reverence, and then offered her own story as evidence.

"My husband gave up porn and masturbation, and I gave up masturbation, and my sexual life just intensified and became better and better and better. I was retraining my brain to be one hundred percent aroused and stimulated by my husband, and even though sex was good before, it only got better." She doesn't feel like she's "standing on a soapbox" when she speaks at True Intimacy events about the harms of porn, she told me. "I just get to share my story."

Kayla and Stewart simultaneously embody and defy stereotypes. Kayla, whose job is to oppose pornography, fits the part with her conservative Christian beliefs. Yet she also openly and confidently talks about sexual desire and pleasure, topics normally discussed through euphemism or in hushed tones among evangelical women like her. Her vibe is sexy, not prudish, and she believes girls and women should understand and embrace their bodies, rather than feel shame about them. Stewart, for her part, is sympathetic to sex workers and those who work in the pornography industry, viewpoints that align with her political beliefs and queer identity. Yet she is also ambivalent about internet pornography's effects on individuals and their relationships, and she acknowledges porn addiction as a valid concern. And both Kayla and Stewart share the goal of helping women so they won't have to fake their orgasms anymore.

ACROSS BOTH SIDES of the porn wars, "real sex" is frequently touted as the opposite of "porn sex." Proponents use the distinction of "real versus fake" to point to pornography as a genre of entertainment, a fiction not intended to capture reality. Opponents say the problem with porn is that it gets in the way of people's authentic desires and relationships. Both agree that porn sex is a carefully curated performance, unlike the sex of real life, which can be awkward, mundane, and unglamorous. Despite all their differences, these sides have a shared goal. Though the paths to get there are not the same, they ultimately lead to the same place: an authentic sexual self that breaks away from the fake sex that surrounds us.

Gordon B., the XConfessions porn director, artist, and sex educator, told me that he thinks of sexual health as his ultimate goal. "I think about sexual health as not just condoms and HIV and STI prevention," he said. "I think about health holistically, in the sense that all of the ways in which we are sexual beings are being impacted by society. I think about sexual health as women's empowerment, as pushing back against bullying and homophobia." Similarly, Bryan, who is a member of a Christian pornography addiction recovery group, told me about his commitment to avoid pornography as representing something bigger about his life and his values. "I realized that I'm not going to run around and try to prop up all these fake, thin, flimsy little walls to make it look like I have a, like, a 3D, rich, full life. I just want to open up and live a real life with true connections and true relationships." Both Gordon B. and Bryan place sex and porn within a much broader landscape.

To be *real*, according to the *Oxford English Dictionary*, is to be "true rather than ostensible, nominal, or apparent." In the United States, experiencing realness operates as a widely shared cultural value, or at least a cultural goal. Despite, or perhaps because of, our saturation in airbrushed images, fictional media, and the virtual world, we chase after that which we believe to be true and authentic, actual not imaginary. The quest goes by various names, including "self-discovery," or "finding one's true self." It fuels a multibillion-dollar self-help industry, one reason that nearly 33 million American adults are in therapy and, indeed, what motivates many of those who participate in pornography debates.

Porn battlefields are littered with advice about self-improvement. Often it is unsolicited advice, but there are opportunities facilitated by coaches for individuals to ask and receive one-on-one feedback based on their specific situation. On both sides, the common story of how a person became a coach was the same. For people who are speakers or presenters on topics related to sex and pornography, it was common for them to have received follow-up questions from their audiences sent via email or direct message. For many who were already working the gig economy by piecing together various forms of work, they decided to monetize their personal advice and the time they would spend responding to individual people who wanted their expertise. "Most of the time, I'm invited to be a presenter at a conference or something," Elle, who is a sex educator who teaches about ethical porn, told me. "But sometimes people are looking for that one-on-one time, so that's when I do my intimacy and flirtation coaching."

Noah Church, a leader in the online pornography addiction recovery movement, similarly started charging for one-on-one sessions when he found he simply could not keep up with the number of emails he was receiving each day. He now offers coaching through phone calls or email consultation for recovering addicts. In his liability waiver, Church instructs clients, "If you have mental health issues, my coaching and these courses can help you achieve your goals *in addition to* professional treatment, but not *in place of* such treatment." His coaching is based on, as he puts it, "personal experience, knowledge gained from others' scientific research, and anecdotal reports in order to offer perspective and advice—no more."

Typically, coaches establish their credentials through a combination of personal biography, like Church, and sometimes through completion of training programs, either for general "life coaching" or coaching specific to their area of expertise. Betrayal Trauma Recovery, an organization that sees secret porn use as a form of marital abuse, offers a team of certified coaches to support women who join as members of the site. Their certifications range from the generic ("Professional Certified Coach" and "Certified Life Coach") to the specific ("Certified Divorce Coach" and "Certified Abuse Specialist"). As one coach on the site says, women benefit from coaching "by recovering and owning their true self, being present in their body, and incorporating a deeper level of self-care."

Coaching related to sex or pornography covers more than those topics alone. Tia, a sex worker and massage therapist I interviewed, has also worked as what she calls an "erotic healing coach" and as a client with her own coach. As a client, she developed what she called her "radical purpose." Tia believes eroticism is a kind of energy that helps people connect to and feel pleasure throughout their entire bodies. Similarly, Beth, who calls herself a "body worker," helps her coaching clients discover safe BDSM practices. "Literally, my job is to expose them to different kinds of kinks that they may enjoy, that they may just have some curiosity cultivated by, and I pretty much just teach them how to safely explore those." She wants to become a certified sex coach someday and is also actively working on a training program with the National Organization for Victim Assistance, which trains professionals who work with victims of violence, and she believes this will help her better understand trauma and triggers in the context of sexual desires, kink, and BDSM. Both Tia and Beth see their work with clients on the topic of sex as helping people improve their overall well-being physically, emotionally, and spiritually.

"I'M DOING THE work" is how Andre Shakti, the sex worker and porn performer, described her quest for self-improvement. She was seeing a therapist, journaling, and reading books on living authentically—for example, the bestsellers written by Brené Brown. After my interview with Andre Shakti, I wrote in my notes, "Brené Brown is everywhere!" Hers was the second interview in two weeks to mention the now famous writer and social worker. The other interview was with Lizzy, who worked for True Intimacy, the Christian antiporn organization. At the time, I happened to be reading *Rising Strong*, one of Brown's books. Needless to say, Brené Brown was not among the list of topics I asked about during interviews. But overcoming shame—the focus of Brown's work and the reason both interview participants were mentioning her—was an important part of Andre Shakti's and Lizzy's stories of how they became involved in the pornography debate. It is telling that a sociologist, sex worker, and conservative Christian are among Brown's readers and fans. Her work speaks to a desire that transcends political ideology, religious affiliation, and occupation. Like Marla Stewart and Kayla, Andre Shakti and Lizzy were women on different sides of the porn debate, but they had in common a commitment not to fake it anymore.

For Andre Shakti, overcoming shame meant accepting and embracing the fact that she was polyamorous. She told me about the shame she felt as she failed to be faithful in teenage relationships. She said that she was "faking it," pretending and promising to be monogamous. When she committed to monogamy, she failed. At the same time that she began reading and learning about polyamory, she began her career as a sex worker—first, as a stripper; then, as a porn performer; and eventually, as a professional dominatrix. Sex work, she recalled, helped her set relationship boundaries and feel more confident in her polyamorous identity. Her work enabled her to see this aspect of herself as honest and healthy.

Lizzy, who shared that she struggled with an addiction to masturbation, grew up amid the pressure to be a "good Christian girl." As a teenager and young adult, this meant she was supposed to pretend to not have sexual feelings at all. All the while, she was feeling a deep sense of shame because she was allowing herself to have sexual fantasies and to masturbate. Overcoming that shame years later meant learning that she was not a bad Christian, wife, or, mother because she had sexual desires and fantasies. But it did not mean that she indulged in such desires, either. Over eight years of marriage, she succumbed to the temptation to masturbate only once. She learned to "guard" her thoughts, as she described, by having strict limits on the kinds of TV and movies she watches, because sometimes sex scenes get stuck in her head. She had to quit watching *The Handmaid's Tale* after the first season, she told me. She needed tools for her journey to self-love and acceptance, and these included therapy, books like Brené Brown's, and True Intimacy's sex and pornography addiction recovery program.

If we look only at the ending of Andre Shakti's and Lizzy's stories, we see two women who appear to be opposites: a polyamorous queer sex worker and a Christian wife and mother who speaks out against pornography and masturbation. And yet, they both spoke to me of the pressure to "fake it," a pressure that came from a different side of a shared social world. For Andre Shakti, it was the pressure and accompanying shame of monogamy. For Lizzy, it was the pressure and accompanying shame surrounding women's sexuality. They both push back in their own way against social norms according to their distinct worldview.

The people who are immersed in pornography debates attempt to make room for alternatives beyond and outside dominant sexual scripts. Joan Price, for instance, collaborated with famed porn performer and director jessica drake on an explicit educational film, *jessica drake's Guide to Wicked Sex: Senior Sex*. Having already written sex advice books geared toward seniors, Price agreed to partner with drake because, as she told me, "Our society thinks that old, wrinkly bodies are not desirable and no one wants to know about them having sex, nobody wants to see it, or know what happens. And I'm fighting against that. I want us to acknowledge that sex is lifelong. Desirability is lifelong. I won't just sit back and let our society get away with marginalizing older people and seeing them not as sexual beings." Price has made it her mission to counter the assumption that good sex has an expiration date. She said that she is "pro porn" to the extent that anything that gives someone pleasure and involves consenting adults is fine with her.

At the other end of the age spectrum, Martha, whom I met at the Freedom from Sexual Slavery conference, sees cultural norms as getting in the way of girls experiencing the movement of their bodies as something other than a glamorized and sexualized performance for gawking spectators. Her mission is to reclaim girls' dance as a part of, not a preview for, their future sexuality. "There's so much joy to see a child make that connection of mind, body, and spirit in dance," she explained to me. "But I began to see little people—I'm talking as young as preschool—being dressed to look like adults. And I just felt this calling from God to work to protect children from hypersexualization in adult costumes, choreography, and music, and then to protect the art of dance." Martha created a nonprofit organization and what she calls a "dance ministry" to educate parents and offer a wholesome alternative to mainstream dance culture. She got pulled into the pornography debate as she began to see dance culture as an extension of what she described to me as "the public health crisis of pornography." Though on different ends of the porn spectrum, Martha and Joan Price see dominant cultural images and messaging surrounding sexuality as misleading and harmful.

These parallels do not mean that we must find the values that guide Andre Shakti and Lizzy or Price and Martha to be equally credible. It's not a difference of preference—one flavor of ice cream over another. When it comes to sex, there is no even playing field. The porn wars are fought within a broader context of American history, where people like Lizzy and Martha (white, straight, conservative Christians) have been calling the shots when it comes to norms and laws related to sexuality. Because their goals generally align with cultural standards of what is sexually normal and desirable, activists within the antipornography movement have not, for the most part, faced violence, discrimination, or mistreatment. Sex workers and their allies, especially queer people of color, have. And yet the shared commitment to strive for authenticity amid social pressures deserves recognition. Across all the interviews I conducted, the problem named was never simply or only pornography. The real challenge faced was much deeper and bigger: how to achieve an authentic and fulfilling life, which includes sexuality, in the modern world.

On the surface, most of the people I interviewed "toed the party line" with answers that aligned them with the broader beliefs we associate with antiporn or porn-positive positions. Respondents who were straight, religious, and politically conservative opposed porn. Those who were queer, not religious, and politically liberal were more sympathetic to it. But beneath the surface, there were more contradictions and more overlap than the polarizing rhetoric would have us presume. Recognizing the shared enemy of "faking it" and the shared goal of real and authentic sexual experience offers an opportunity for empathy and conversation across the battle lines. Without it, we are destined to the same battles, where no side is declared the victor. "Mobility for stasis," as historian Janet Jakobsen calls it. "The more it goes on, the less it goes anywhere," she said, invoking the lyrics from that Cinderella song or the phrase Jean-Baptiste Alphonse Karr made famous, *Plus ça change, plus c'est la même chose.*

CHAPTER 19

The Good Place

Early on in my research, I had a conversation with a friend who pastors a theologically conservative Protestant church popular among the mostly white twentysomethings in our city. He was affirming what I had been observing among young Christian men, explaining that the number one reason they seek his counsel is to talk about their struggles with pornography. I asked him what was most common advice solicited by women from his congregation, and his answer took me by surprise: Yoga, he said, and whether or not practicing it interferes with the Christian faith. What do you tell them? I asked. Well, he said, we talk about why they think it might interfere, which usually has to do with a fear that meditation or chanting would count as worship to something other than a Christian god.

Pornography debate outsiders may feel a little like those young Christian women. *Given my espoused beliefs, politics, and friendship circles, what am I* supposed *to believe about porn?* Those who watch porn have likely asked themselves the question *Is it okay to watch this? Should I be watching a different kind of porn? Is this normal?* People who don't watch it may ask themselves the opposite: *Everyone seems to be watching it. Should I?* Or, at least, *Should I* want *to?* For conservatives, their opposition to porn is contradicted by the constant reinforcement that all men look at it, by outspoken sex workers who insist they are not victims, and by political beliefs that are supposed to support the free market and oppose government intervention. For liberals, deciding what to think about porn may be complicated by progressive sexual attitudes that bump up against concerns over the internet's potential for abuse and exploitation and dismay over the misogyny and racism that are so prevalent in commercial porn.

But back to yoga. Its origins are ancient India and a Hindu practice uniting body, mind, and spirit. It came to the United States at the end of the nineteenth century, and over the next one hundred years, it lost most resemblance to its original form. Like Christmas, yoga has been so thoroughly integrated into American culture and subsumed by capitalism that it seems for most of us to have lost any authentic religious quality. I am among the 37 million Americans who regularly attend yoga classes, and I laughed out loud when my pastor friend told me his female parishioners' concerns. But when I paused to reflect on my own relationship to yoga, I saw that the differences between me and those Christian women were not so stark. I have my own wariness about the practice, though my concerns are sociological rather than spiritual: that I am but one of the overwhelmingly white, thin, able-bodied women who contribute to an enterprise that profits from an appropriation of a religion and culture that is not their own. I practice anyway, and have done so since my early twenties, often feeling that it is the only time in my day when I get outside what Buddhists call "the monkey mind."

Our lives are made up of any number of these seemingly small conflicts, as virtually everything we consume (be it food, clothes, media, or a fitness regime) is likely to have a fraught backstory. We reconcile such conflicts by seeking confirmation and validation that our choices and behaviors align with those of the social group of which we are a part. We all have the strong desire to "get it right" and not accidentally or mistakenly align ourselves with those we perceive to have opposing beliefs. Psychologists have found that most of us tend to believe that we have the ability to independently make moral choices and decisions, but in fact, we adapt and change our self-perception by comparing ourselves to others whom we perceive to be like us. Because both sides of the porn wars are able to distill their positions into discrete talking points (sex work is work; pornography is entertainment; sex workers are victims; pornography is addictive), we may get the impression that pornography (or any aspect of sexual politics, for that matter) is simple. You're either for it or against it. The result is that we think we know what we should believe about porn when the reality is more complicated.

My friend did not tell his parishioners whether yoga was permissible or off-limits. That wasn't the point, he told me. Both options could be true. The issue was not yoga in and of itself, but rather, how individuals related to the practice, what it meant for them. The same can be said of pornography.

Many of the feminist and queer-identified defenders of porn I interviewed insisted that it had made their lives better, not worse. Pornography helped them live a life of sexual freedom in the face of conservative regulations and controls that attempted to thwart and admonish their sexual identities and relationships. Indeed, qualitative studies consistently find that LGBTQ youth and adults in the United States and beyond report positive outcomes from looking at porn, including sexual identity exploration and learning sexual information that they perceive to be otherwise unavailable to them as a sexual or gender minority. For straight couples, national surveys suggest that when both partners view pornography together, or when women report pornography consumption, the porn use tends to be associated with higher levels of relationship quality and sexual satisfaction among both men and women.

On the antiporn side, those I interviewed insisted that pornography made their lives worse. And their experiences, too, are confirmed by existing research. When individuals believe that watching porn is wrong, but they continue to do it anyway—think of evangelical men who perceive themselves to be struggling with pornography addiction—they largely report negative outcomes, such as depression and low relationship satisfaction. Many studies find that men's pornography use correlates with relationship problems, including separation and divorce.

Inconsistent conclusions about pornography's harms or harmlessness are echoed in stories from the sex industry. Many sex workers insist that they choose their work over alternatives, that they enjoy it as much as they enjoy any job, and that they are not exploited or coerced. Others, including those who freely entered the industry as well as those who were forced into it, have experienced trauma, violence, and abuse. For some, leaving the sex industry is the only option for them to live a healthy and flourishing life. For others, the sex industry itself is what provides the financial security and flexibility for a healthy and flourishing life. The rallying cry of the feminist movement to "believe women" does not mean we should cherry-pick which women to believe.

Neither faction is eager to acknowledge that the other side proffers some truth. Instead, each side doubles down on its message that its position alone is the right one. Both sides achieve what psychologist Marilynn Brewer calls "optimal distinctiveness." They see themselves as pushing back against dominant norms, but also as part of a social movement. Thus, fighting over porn allows individuals to feel simultaneously unique and like they belong. These feelings fuel polarization, causing members to avoid, fear, or disparage the perspectives of outsiders.

But the reality is that people experience pornography differently based on their sexual identity, experiences, and beliefs about sex. There is, in other words, some truth to both antiporn and porn-positive claims. The difference lies in people's location within a complex and unequal social world, not in pornography itself.

Despite the polarizing rhetoric, common ground does exist. Both sides agree that it is a bad idea to keep porn habits hidden. It's easy to watch porn in secret, given our accessibility to smartphones and other personal devices, but it can also lead to what researchers call "moral incongruence," the mismatch among beliefs, attitudes, and behaviors. For the antiporn movement, the solution is to come clean about porn habits in order to overcome them and quit watching. For the porn-positive movement, coming clean is just as important to break the stigmas associated with sex work and alternative sexual desires and practices. For both sides, healthy sexuality is presented as honest sexuality.

A second lesson is the importance of talking to kids about sex and porn. Everyone involved in the porn debate agrees that parents should not let teachers, peers, TV shows, or other adults be the only ones to shape what their children learn about sex. The message is clear: don't avoid talk of porn out of fear, embarrassment, or ambivalence, because your children can be all but guaranteed to encounter it by the time they are teenagers. Educators across the divide encourage parents to take a look at sites like Pornhub, so they can understand the content their children will likely be exposed to. Prepare kids, in an age-appropriate way, to understand what pornography is and what you think about it. Offer resources for sex education so that students do not have to look to porn alone to make sense of sexual and gender identities, desires and interests, and safety and consent.

A third lesson: don't watch free porn. To this point there was near-universal agreement across all my interviews and observations. The solution, according to pornography's opponents, is to quit watching porn altogether, for pay or otherwise. Sex workers and their allies recommend sites that allow you to pay performers. Typically, this is indirect payment, through third-party sites such as OnlyFans or ManyVids, where a percentage goes to website overhead costs and the rest goes to the content creator. Some independent porn companies also offer memberships to stream content from their sites. Across the porn divide, many people agree that free streaming porn sites like Pornhub are doing us more harm than good.

That sexism and coercion are problems in the porn industry is another point of common ground, though these similarities are typically buried under broader disputes. For antipornography activists, all porn is sex trafficking and, thus, evidence of deep-seated sexism and coercion within the industry. Porn-positive activists push back against this assumption that trafficking and sex work are synonymous, but they do not pretend the porn industry is without serious flaws. A broad movement of performers and activists has pushed back against men within the industry (including performers, agents, and producers) who have been accused of harassment, abuse, and assault. Others create content that purposefully dismantles the racist and sexist stereotypes prevalent in commercial porn. Groups of industry insiders have worked to improve the lives of performers on and off porn sets. Though the antiporn and porn-positive movements have radically different ideas about sex work, they in fact share concerns over the safety, autonomy, and consent of those within the industry.

A final shared lesson: sex matters far beyond the private sphere in which it most often occurs. Debates over pornography teach us that sexual desires, experiences, and identities are connected to broader social systems, including capitalism, the law and criminal justice, the media, and beyond. Both sides understand sexuality to be simultaneously "pleasure and danger"—in other words, a combination of possibility, agency, and autonomy alongside social pressures, control, and restraint. The pornography wars are never about pornography alone. They are instead about navigating how we should best live and relate to one another in our shared social world.

WILL THE PORN wars ever end? *The Good Place*, the NBC sitcom that aired from 2016 to 2020, centered on a different question regarding endings: What happens when we die? By the final season, the show had pushed the most common ideal to its extreme. Immortality in the afterlife: consciousness, an everlasting body, our deceased loved ones as company, endless joys and pleasures, the ability to amend past wrongs and regrets. Yet we learn that an eternal afterlife is not so ideal. Once wrongs have been amended and family members reunited, all those infinite joys become less joyful, the pleasures no longer pleasurable. The never-endingness of any kind of heaven becomes a kind of hell in and of itself.

The same is true for any idealized ending to the pornography wars. If somehow pornography as we know it ceased to exist, society would just spawn new forms of cultural objects for us to get off on. If, however, we removed all restrictions regarding adult sexual behavior, the resulting freedom would create repression of its own, as sexual freedom for some can victimize others. The reality is that no one I interviewed or observed believed that either the complete elimination of pornography or complete sexual freedom was a feasible or even a desirable goal. This is a myth propagated by one side about the other. In fact, many antiporn activists insisted they were anticensorship, and many who were porn positive advocated for legal limits.

What I observed over five years of research for this book is that fighters in the porn wars do not assume that if they fight hard enough, the other side will wave its white flag in defeat. The porn wars are fought not because either side perceives imminent victory, but because individuals believe it is the right thing to do. This is not to say there are not tangible policy changes for which each movement strives. Sex workers and their allies have mobilized to overturn SESTA-FOSTA; to decriminalize prostitution; to hold corporations like MindGeek accountable for illegal activities, without punishing porn performers; to make it easier for sex workers to maintain bank accounts and to receive secure online payments for their services. Antipornography activists have lobbied for laws to make it harder for websites to post pornographic content or receive payment for such material. Many insist that hard-core pornography should be considered illegal under existing obscenity laws. As this book has described, both sides have celebrated successes and lamented setbacks for over a century. At times, each has framed their movement as gaining momentum and aligned with broader American society and, at other times, as swimming upstream, against the current of both norms and laws.

In the series finale of *The Good Place*, "Whenever You're Ready," we see "the good place" as the main characters believe it should be: a paradise for as long as you want it and then the ability to make the choice for it to end, to cease to exist on your own terms. The good place of the porn wars does not require self-annihilation, but it invites self-examination. If we push aside the dividing line, we can see the broader goal for which both sides strive: to make ethical decisions for ourselves, recognizing the constraints that surround us. That challenge is much bigger than internet porn, and the work is harder. But the ability to experience our lives, sexual and otherwise, with as much intention, freedom, and integrity available to us is where the good place resides.

ACKNOWLEDGMENTS

I wrote most of this book during the first year and a half of the Covid-19 pandemic. On weekdays between the hours of seven and nine A.M., I squeezed in my writing before my spouse left for work and I transitioned to either virtually teach college students or homeschool my then third grader. As was true for so many of us, my life was marked by disrupted routines and isolation from friends and colleagues. Yet as in all projects of significant undertaking, many people helped bring this project into the world.

Two groups had nothing to do with writing the book per se, but had a lot to do with preserving my sanity: Peloton instructors who motivated me to move my body before my writing began and the team I was able to hire to clean my house. Thank you.

Many more people directly supported the book. I'm grateful to all the individuals who participated in interviews and allowed me to observe their groups and events as part of my research. In particular, thanks to Josh Grubbs, David Ley, Sam Perry, Marla Stewart, and Inka Winter, who not only participated in interviews but also helped the project in other ways.

At the University of Nebraska–Lincoln, I received research support from the following grants: the Behavioral Health Project of Excellence (2021 and 2019); the Layman Seed Program (2019); and the College of Arts and Sciences ENHANCE Award (2016). Thank you to my UNL research assistants and student collaborators: Jordan Malzer, Alek Duncan, Claire Bartels, Trenton Haltom, and Alice MillerMacPhee. Special thanks are owed to Maia Behrendt for her newspaper archive digging, internet sleuthing, and attention to detail, as well as the time she spent wrestling my endnotes. Needless to say, any remaining errors are my own.

I am deeply indebted to my agent, Amy Bishop, for seeing early promise in the project and for continuing to be its champion. Thanks to the fantastic team at Bloomsbury, including Suzanne Keller, Lauren Ollerhead, Katya Mezhibovskaya, Jennifer Dolan, Tanya Heinrich, and especially my editor,

Grace McNamee, for her kindness and support, in addition to continually smart feedback that helped me see the forest for the trees.

Thanks to my wonderful colleagues, friends, and mentors who read drafts, had conversations, and gave much needed encouragement along the way: Rebecca Barrett-Fox, Kathy Blee, James Brunton, Ben Chan, Amy and Steve Dishman, Christina Falci, Katie Gaddini, Julia McMillan, Alaina Morales, Max Perry Mueller, Phil Schwadel, Arlene Stein, Matthew Tracy, Alexa Trumpy, Lisa Wade, and Andrew Whitehead. I'm particularly grateful to three dear friends: the ever-grounded and wise Emily Kazyak; my longtime comrade in studying and making sense of evangelicals Amy McDowell; and lay editor extraordinaire and fellow member of the depraved writers' club Alena Bruzas. Their friendships always give me just what I need, whether that's laughter, listening, cheerleading, or commiseration.

Thank you to my parents, Alan and Jody, who I know are proud of me even if they would rather I write books on other topics. Their steady support means the world. Thanks to the Lozier hive, especially John and Kitty, who helped care for me and my family so that I could write. This book is dedicated to my spouse, Jacob, and our two kids, Sylvie and Esme. For most of the time I was writing, it felt like the world was crashing down around us. And yet, we depended on one another, and our family managed to grow bigger (a few pets acquired along the way), stronger, and happier. When I think of writing this book, I think of them, with love, fondness, and gratitude.

NOTES

PREFACE

xiv   *Choose Your Own Adventure* books: Portions of this story were told in my 2021 Furfey Lecture at the Association for the Study of Religion annual meeting and later published in Kelsy Burke, "The False Dichotomy of Sex and Religion in America," *Sociology of Religion* (2022), https://doi.org/10.1093/socrel/srab062.

xv   Hochschild calls a "deep story": Arlie Hochschild, *Strangers in Their Own Land: Anger and Mourning on the American Right* (New York: New Press, 2016).

xvi   writes psychologist Paul Rozin: Paul Rozin et al., "The CAD Triad Hypothesis: A Mapping Between Three Moral Emotions (Contempt, Anger, Disgust) and Three Moral Codes (Community, Autonomy, Divinity)," *Journal of Personality and Social Psychology* 76, no. 4 (1999): 574.

xvi   Hochschild calls the "empathy wall": Hochschild, *Strangers in Their Own Land*, 5.

xvi   eulogy of the late Jerry Falwell: Larry Flynt, "Larry Flynt: My Friend, Jerry Falwell," *Los Angeles Times*, May 20, 2007, https://www.latimes.com/la-op -flynt20may20-story.html.

INTRODUCTION

1   expansive power included archaeology: Bettina Arnold, "'Arierdämmerung': Race and Archaeology in Nazi Germany," *World Archaeology* 38, no. 1 (2006): 8–31.

1   joined the Nazi army: "'Useless' Art: Why Did a Prehistoric Artist Make This Sculpture?," *Civilisations*, BBC, March 1, 2018, https://www.bbc.co.uk /programmes/articles/59hXxokKpv2mZKK3h6Z4dDl/useless-art-why-did -a-prehistoric-artist-make-this-sculpture.

2   Venus of Hohle Fels: Nicholas J. Conard, "A Female Figurine from the Basal Aurignacian of Hohle Fels Cave in Southwestern Germany," *Nature* 459 (2009): 248–52.

2   enticed readers with headlines: Eliza Strickland, "'Pornographic' Statue Could Be World's Oldest Piece of Figurative Art," *Discover Magazine*, May 13,

2009, https://www.discovermagazine.com/planet-earth/pornographic-statue -could-be-worlds-oldest-piece-of-figurative-art; Dale Allen, "God the Mother or Paleolithic Porn?," *HuffPost*, June 19, 2009, https://www.huffpost .com/entry/god-the-mother-or-paleoli_b_205259.

2   prehistory: Ian Moulton, *Before Pornography: Erotic Writing in Early Modern England (Studies in the History of Sexuality)* (Oxford, UK: Oxford University Press, 2000).

2   "Pornography names an argument": Walter Kendrick, *The Secret Museum: Pornography in Modern Culture* (Oakland: University of California Press, 1997), 31.

2   "obscenity existed in plenty": Kendrick, *The Secret Museum*, 31–32.

2   genre of sexually explicit media: C. Thi Nguyen and Bekka Williams, "Why We Call Things 'Porn': The Word Captures a New Way of Relating to Food, Real Estate and Even Moral Outrage," *New York Times*, July 26, 2019.

3   "I know it when I see it": Jacobellis v. Ohio, 378 U.S. 184 (1964).

3   *"Being pornography"*: Michael C. Rea, "What Is Pornography," *Noûs* 35, no. 1 (2001): 135.

3   Instagram account suspended: Stephanie Sarley, "About," https:// stephaniesarley.com/about/.

4   failure to remove hate speech: European Commission, "European Commission and IT Companies Announce Code of Conduct on Illegal Online Hate Speech," Press Release, May 31, 2016, https://ec.europa.eu /commission/presscorner/detail/en/IP_16_1937.

4   disinformation campaigns: Nancy Schola, "How Facebook, Google and Twitter 'Embeds' Helped Trump in 2016: A Study Reveals Employees the Companies Placed in the Trump Campaign Played a Surprisingly Active Role in Shaping Its Message and Targeting Voters," Politico, October 26, 2017, https://www.politico.com/story/2017/10/26/facebook-google-twitter -trump-244191.

4   Instagram suspended accounts in 2016: Alison Lynch, "Mum's Easter Simnel Cake Censored by Instagram for Looking Like a Boob," Metro (UK), April 5, 2016, https://metro.co.uk/2016/04/05/mums-easter-simnel-cake -censored-by-instagram-for-looking-like-a-boob-5796360/.

4   "destroying the lives of millions": "Republican Platform 2016," Committee on Arrangements for the 2016 Republican National Convention, Cleveland, OH.

4   IT'S O.K., LIBERAL PARENTS: Judith Shulevitz, "It's O.K., Liberal Parents, You Can Freak Out About Porn," *New York Times*, July 16, 2016.

4   "DOWNTON ABBEY" PORN PARODY: Alex Rees, "Everything You Need to Know About That 'Downton Abbey' Porn Parody," *Cosmopolitan*, April 2,

2014, https://www.cosmopolitan.com/sex-love/advice/a6263/downton-abbey
-porn-fails/.

5   Christian sex advice: Kelsy Burke, *Christians under Covers: Evangelicals and
     Sexual Pleasure on the Internet* (Oakland: University of California Press, 2016).

5   participants in porn addiction: Kelsy Burke and Trenton M. Haltom,
     "Created by God and Wired to Porn: Redemptive Masculinity and Gender
     Beliefs in Narratives of Religious Men's Pornography Addiction Recovery,"
     Gender and Society 34, no. 2 (2020): 233–58.

5   trail of bread crumbs I followed: These findings were also published in Kelsy
     Burke and Alice MillerMacPhee, "Constructing Pornography Addiction's
     Harms in Science, News Media, and Politics," *Social Forces* 99, no. 3 (2021):
     1334–62.

8   "big sort": Bill Bishop, *The Big Sort: Why the Clustering of Like-Minded America
     Is Tearing Us Apart* (New York: Houghton Mifflin Harcourt, 2008); Liliana
     Mason, *Uncivil Agreement: How Politics Became Our Identity* (Chicago:
     University of Chicago Press, 2018); Alan I. Abramowitz, *The Great Alignment:
     Race, Party Transformation, and the Rise of Donald Trump* (New Haven, CT:
     Yale University Press, 2019).

8   falling into one of two categories: Kristin Luker, *When Sex Goes to School:
     Warring Views on Sex—and Sex Education—Since the Sixties* (New York:
     W. W. Norton, 2006).

8   dichotomy is grounded in empirical evidence: *Political Polarization in the
     American Public: How Increasing Ideological Uniformity and Partisan Antipathy
     Affect Politics, Compromise, and Everyday Life*, Report, Pew Research Center,
     June 12, 2014, https://www.pewresearch.org/politics/2014/06/12/political
     -polarization-in-the-american-public/.

9   proposed a theory of culture: John Levi Martin, "Power, Authority, and the
     Constraint of Belief Systems," *American Journal of Sociology* 107, no. 4 (2002):
     861–904.

CHAPTER 1: COMSTOCKERY

14   publishers printed illicit stories: Donna Dennis, *Licentious Gotham: Erotic
     Publishing and Its Prosecution in Nineteenth-Century New York* (Cambridge,
     MA: Harvard University Press, 2009).

15   masculine camaraderie: Judith Giesberg, *Sex and the Civil War: Soldiers,
     Pornography, and the Making of American Morality* (Chapel Hill: University
     of North Carolina Press, 2017), 56–57.

15 seventeen sections of the law: "Thirty-Eighth Congress. Second Session. Senate," *New York Times*, February 8, 1865.

16 To break this law: Giesberg, *Sex and the Civil War*, 2.

16 describes in his diary: Amy Werbel, *Lust on Trial: Censorship and the Rise of American Obscenity in the Age of Anthony Comstock* (New York: Columbia University Press, 2018).

16 empty the saloon's barrels: Lakshmeeramya Malladi, *The Embryo Project Encyclopedia*, s.v. "Anthony Comstock 1844–1915."

17 the Comstock Act: Whitney Strub, *Obscenity Rules: Roth v. United States and the Long Struggle over Sexual Expression* (Lawrence: University Press of Kansas, 2013), 16.

17 Comstock estimated: Giesberg, *Sex and the Civil War*, 3.

17 Train was well known for attracting: "George Francis Train Touches Bottom—He Is Arrested for Publishing an Obscene Sheet," *San Francisco Daily Evening Bulletin*, December 30, 1872.

18 the arrests of women: Shirley J. Burton, "Obscene, Lewd, and Lascivious: Ida Craddock and the Criminally Obscene Women of Chicago, 1873–1913," *Michigan Historical Review* 19, no. 1 (1993): 12.

18 Ida Craddock was considered: Burton, "Obscene, Lewd, and Lascivious," 1–16.

18 Spiritualism appealed to American women: Molly McGarry, *Ghosts of Futures Past: Spiritualism and the Cultural Politics of Nineteenth Century America* (Berkeley: University of California Press, 2008).

19 "hoochie-coochie dance": Marsha Silberman, "The Perfect Storm: Late Nineteenth-Century Chicago Sex Radicals: Moses Harman, Ida Craddock, Alice Stockham and the Comstock Obscenity Laws," *Journal of the Illinois State Historical Society (1998–)* 102, no. 3/4 (2009): 324–67.

19 she took her own life: Burton, "Obscene, Lewd, and Lascivious," 14.

19 passed anti-obscenity laws: Werbel, *Lust on Trial*, 248.

20 justifying the arrest of the actors: Werbel, *Lust on Trial*, 243.

20 "Owning the right to look": Mireille Miller-Young, *A Taste for Brown Sugar: Black Women in Pornography* (Durham, NC: Duke University Press, 2014), 27.

20 "frenzy of the visible": Linda Williams, *Hard Core: Power, Pleasure, and the "Frenzy of the Visible"* (Berkeley: University of California Press, 1999), 36.

21 Early cinema, whose goal: Williams, *Hard Core*, 48.

21 Chicago was the first city: Jeremy Geltzer, *Dirty Words and Filthy Pictures: Film and the First Amendment* (Austin: University of Texas Press, 2016).

21 FBI discovered that: Douglas M. Charles, *The FBI's Obscene File: J. Edgar Hoover and the Bureau's Crusade Against Smut* (Lawrence: University Press of Kansas, 2012).

21 "surrogates for the male audience": Al Di Lauro and Gerald Rabkin, *Dirty Movies: An Illustrated History of the Stag Film, 1915–1970* (New York: Chelsea House, 1976), 26–27.

22 "money shot": Williams, *Hard Core*, 73.

22 *New York Times* described: "Mrs. Dennett Guilty in Sex Booklet Case," *New York Times*, April 24, 1929.

23 Dennett's case established: John M. Craig, "'The Sex Side of Life': The Obscenity Case of Mary Ware Dennett," *Frontiers: A Journal of Women Studies* 15, no. 3 (1995): 145–66.

23 Comstock sent three detectives: Werbel, *Lust on Trial*, 257.

23 Craddock called Comstock a "sex pervert": Vere Chappell, *Sexual Outlaw, Erotic Mystic: The Essential Ida Craddock* (San Francisco: Weiser Books, 2010), 238.

23 varying interpretations of Comstock's motives: Margaret A. Blanchard and John E. Semonche, "Anthony Comstock and His Adversaries: The Mixed Legacy of This Battle for Free Speech," *Communication Law and Policy* 11, no. 3 (2006): 317–66; Mark I. West, "The Role of Sexual Repression in Anthony Comstock's Campaign to Censor Children's Dime Novels," *Journal of American Culture* 22, no. 4 (1999): 49.

24 efforts like Comstock's as "symbolic crusades": Joseph R. Gusfield, *Symbolic Crusade: Status Politics and the American Temperance Movement* (Urbana: University of Illinois Press, 1963).

CHAPTER 2: OBSCENE FILES

25 For Hoover, this meant protecting the country: Charles, *The FBI's Obscene File*.

26 "merchants of filth": John Edgar Hoover, "Combatting the Merchants of Filth: The Role of the FBI," *University of Pittsburgh Law Review* 25, no. 3 (1964): 469.

26 In one of its first major raids: Charles, *The FBI's Obscene File*, 27.

26 personal life and his political position: Beverly Gage, "Were J. Edgar Hoover and Clyde Tolson Lovers?," *Slate*, November 10, 2011.

26 "social regulation": Charles, *The FBI's Obscene File*, 38.

27 titles themselves constituted the raciest content: Strub, *Obscenity Rules*, 73.

27 "a social document of the first order of importance": Strub, *Obscenity Rules*, 113.

28 "merchandising of razor blades": Strub, *Obscenity Rules*, 137.

29 *Roth v. United States*: Roth v. United States, 354 U.S. 476 (1957).

29 pair of nudist magazines: Sunshine Publishing Company v. Summerfield, 184 F. Supp. 767 (D.D.C. 1960).

30 deserves credit or blame: Strub, *Obscenity Rules*, 2.

30 In an 8–1 decision in 1963: Bantam Books, Inc. v. Sullivan, 372 U.S. 58 (1963).

30 *Mishkin v. New York*: Mishkin v. New York, 383 U.S. 502 (1966).

31 *Ginsberg v. New York*: Ginsberg v. New York, 390 U.S. 629 (1968).

31 The 1969 case centered: Stanley v. Georgia, 394 U.S. 557 (1969).

31 *Miller v. California*: Miller v. California, 413 U.S. 15 (1973).

32 justices boasted political affiliations: Richard F. Hixson, *Pornography and the Justices: The Supreme Court and the Intractable Obscenity Problem* (Carbondale: Southern Illinois University Press, 1996).

34 Nixon and Hoover found common ground: Charles, *The FBI's Obscene File*.

34 Citizens for Decent Literature: Whitney Strub, *Perversion for Profit: The Politics of Pornography and the Rise of the New Right* (New York: Columbia University Press, 2010).

35 Formerly a champion collegiate swimmer: Robert D. McFadden, "Charles Keating, 90, Key Figure in the '80s Savings and Loan Crisis, Dies," *New York Times*, April 2, 2014.

35 rhetoric of "radical liberals": Charles, *The FBI's Obscene File*, 82.

36 Nixon called the commission "morally bankrupt": Warren J. Weaver, "Nixon Repudiates Obscenity Report as Morally Void," *New York Times*, October 25, 1970.

CHAPTER 3: CHRISTIAN RIGHT V. AMERICA

37 divides his history of sexuality: Michel Foucault, *The History of Sexuality*, Vol. 1: *An Introduction*, trans. Robert Hurley (New York: Random House, 1978).

38 from religion to science: Frances Fitzgerald, *The Evangelicals: The Struggle to Shape America* (New York: Simon and Schuster, 2017).

38 Fundamentalists grounded their theology: Randall Balmer, *Evangelicalism in America* (Waco, TX: Baylor University Press, 2016).

38 Scopes Monkey Trial: Balmer, *Evangelicalism in America*, 126.

39 call "sexual liberalism": John D'Emilio and Estelle Freedman, *Intimate Matters: A History of Sexuality in America*, 3rd ed. (Chicago: University of Chicago Press, 2012), 239–42.

39 capitalist marketplace encouraged: Jonathan Ned Katz, *The Invention of Heterosexuality* (Chicago: University of Chicago Press, 2007).

39 American value and prerogative: M. E. Melody and Linda M. Peterson, *Teaching America About Sex: Marriage Guides and Sex Manuals from the Late Victorians to Dr. Ruth* (New York: New York University Press, 1999).

39 cinema a major American pastime: Jon Lewis, *Hollywood v. Hard Core: How the Struggle over Censorship Created the Modern Film Industry* (New York: New York University Press, 2002).

39 death of Virginia Rappe: "Roscoe Arbuckle Faces an Inquiry on Woman's Death," *New York Times*, September 11, 1921.

39 approach of the PCA: Lewis, *Hollywood v. Hard Core*, 149–50.

40 Catholics focused their attention locally: Gregory D. Black, *Hollywood Censored: Morality Codes, Catholics, and the Movies* (Cambridge, UK: Cambridge University Press, 1994).

40 Legion of Decency: D'Emilio and Freedman, *Intimate Matters*, 281.

40 *Howl*, his famed poem: D'Emilio and Freedman, *Intimate Matters*, 275.

40 legal battles over obscenity: Lewis, *Hollywood v. Hard Core*, 128–34.

40–41 death of the lesbian protagonist: Christopher Nealon, "Invert-History: The Ambivalence of Lesbian Pulp Fiction," *New Literary History* 31, no. 4 (2000): 745–64.

41 "liberated but compliant": Elizabeth Fraterrigo, *"Playboy" and the Making of the Good Life in Modern America* (Oxford, UK: Oxford University Press, 2009), 5.

41 marriage manual published: D'Emilio and Freedman, *Intimate Matters*, 267.

41 reality of racism: Patricia Hill Collins, *Black Sexual Politics: African Americans, Gender, and the New Racism* (New York: Routledge, 2004).

42 dating working-class girls: D'Emilio and Freedman, *Intimate Matters*, 263.

42 1953 radio sermon: Billy Graham, "The Bible and Dr. Kinsey," *Hour of Decision*, radio program, September 13, 1953.

42 Jewish and liberal Protestant leaders: R. Marie Griffith, *Moral Combat: How Sex Divided American Christians and Fractured American Politics* (New York: Basic Books, 2017), 141–47.

42 "affable crusader": "Affable Crusader—Billy Graham," *New York Times*, May 17, 1957.

43 religious leaders on the left: Jack Jenkins, *American Prophets: The Religious Roots of Progressive Politics and the Ongoing Fight for the Soul of the Country* (New York: HarperCollins, 2020).

43 civil rights movement: Anthea Butler, *White Evangelical Racism: The Politics of Morality in America* (Chapel Hill: University of North Carolina Press, 2021); Jesse Curtis, *The Myth of Colorblind Christians: Evangelicals and White Supremacy in the Civil Rights Era* (New York: New York University Press, 2021).

43 the word *evangelical* became shorthand: Balmer, *Evangelicalism in America*.

43 both preachers emphasized: Fitzgerald, *The Evangelicals*, 291–318.

44 oppose pornography using a wide range of tactics: Matthew Avery Sutton, *Jerry Falwell and the Rise of the Religious Right: A Brief History with Documents* (Boston: Bedford/St. Martin's, 2013), 20–26.

44 commission was a "balanced group": Philip Shenon, "Meese Names Panel to Study How to Control Pornography," *New York Times*, May 21, 1985.

45 commission declared definitively: Attorney General's Commission on Pornography, *Final Report of the Attorney General's Commission on Pornography* (Washington, D.C.: U.S. Department of Justice, 1986).

45 National Christian Network: Peter J. Boyer, "Falwell Buys a Cable TV Network," *New York Times*, January 16, 1986.

45 "upsets the abortionists, that upsets the pornographer": Samuel G. Freedman, "Mr. Falwell Meets an Outspoken Antagonist, Yale's Giamatti," *New York Times*, November 12, 1982.

45 conservative gender and sexual politics: Griffith, *Moral Combat*.

46 Falwell's chosen lawyer: Rodney A. Smolla, *Jerry Falwell v. Larry Flynt: The First Amendment on Trial* (Champaign: University of Illinois Press, 1988), 3.

46 Moral Majority sent out mailers: Hustler Magazine Inc. and Larry Flynt v. Jerry Falwell, 485 U.S. 46 (1988).

46 Flynt and Falwell had much in common: Smolla, *Jerry Falwell v. Larry Flynt*, 6–7.

46 "more of a politician than preacher": Smolla, *Jerry Falwell v. Larry Flynt*, 133–34.

47 "the caricature of the respondent": Hustler Magazine Inc. and Larry Flynt v. Jerry Falwell, 485 U.S. 46 (1988).

47–48 "most devastating moral influence": Jerry Falwell, *Listen, America!* (Garden City, NY: Doubleday, 1980), quoted in Sutton, *Jerry Falwell and the Rise of the Religious Right*, 123.

48 a relatively recent addition to antiabortion efforts: Andrew R. Lewis, *The Rights Turn in Conservative Christian Politics: How Abortion Transformed the Culture Wars* (Cambridge, UK: Cambridge University Press, 2017).

48 "God will judge the nation": Jerry Falwell, *How You Can Help Clean Up America* (Lynchburg, VA: Liberty, 1978), quoted in Sutton, *Jerry Falwell and the Rise of the Religious Right*, 107.

49 Abortion support among all Americans: Ted G. Jelen and Clyde Wilcox, "Causes and Consequences of Public Attitudes Toward Abortion: A Review and Research Agenda," *Political Research Quarterly* 56 no. 4 (2003): 489–500.

49 attitudes about homosexuality: Alan S. Yang, "The Polls—Trends: Attitudes Toward Homosexuality," *Public Opinion Quarterly* 61 (1997): 477–507.

49 believed pornography should be illegal: Tom W. Smith, Michael Hout, and Peter V. Marsden, General Social Survey, 1972–2016, Cumulative File, ICPSR36797.v1, Chicago, IL: National Opinion Research Center, Distributed by Ann Arbor, MI: Inter-university Consortium for Political and Social Research.

CHAPTER 4: PORNO CHIC

50 majority of Americans: Smith, Hout, and Marsden, General Social Survey.

50 Monroe later told close friend: George Barris, *Marilyn: Her Life in Her Own Words* (New York: Kensington, 1995), 83.

50 Hefner did not engage with: Martha Elizabeth Thorpe, "Making American: Constitutive Rhetoric in the Cold War" (Ph.D. diss., Texas A&M University, 2011).

50 cautious advocate of reforming: Carrie Pitzulo, *Bachelors and Bunnies: The Sexual Politics of Playboy* (Chicago: University of Chicago Press, 2011).

51 steady stream of films without the approval: Lewis, *Hollywood v. Hard Core*.

51 Jack Valenti: Lewis, *Hollywood v. Hard Core*, 138.

51 *Midnight Cowboy*: Lewis, *Hollywood v. Hard Core*, 151.

52 hard-core pornographic films: Lewis, *Hollywood v. Hard Core*, 153.

52 invited Hollywood's outcasts: David Friedman, "A History of the Adult Film Association of America," *The Rialto Report*, March 15, 1982.

52 "porno chic": Ralph Blumenthal, "'Hard-Core' Grows Fashionable—and Very Profitable," *New York Times*, January 21, 1973.

52   FBI sent agents: Charles, *The FBI's Obscene File*, 96–97.

53   "celebrities, diplomats, critics": Blumenthal, "'Hard-Core' Grows Fashionable."

53   sex therapist alongside Reems: Williams, *Hard Core*, 111.

53   two other feature-length pornos: Lewis, *Hollywood v. Hard Core*, 192.

53   "the best hard-core porn film": Roger Ebert, review of *The Devil in Miss Jones*, directed by Gerard Damiano, *Chicago Sun-Times*, June 13, 1973.

54   small screens in private booths: Lewis, *Hollywood v. Hard Core*.

54   "manufacturers are making a big mistake": Tony Schwartz, "The TV Pornography Boom," *New York Times*, September 13, 1981.

54   nearly 30 percent: Jonathan Takiff, "Report Finds VCR Becoming the Appliance of the 80s," *Chicago Tribune*, June 13, 1986.

54   American households owning a VCR: Julie Siebens, "Extended Measures of Well-Being: Living Conditions in the United States: 2011," U.S. Census Bureau, September 2013, https://www.census.gov/history/pdf/sipp-data -appliances.pdf.

54   Hail Mary pass: Timothy Egan, "EROTICA INC.—A Special Report.; Technology Sent Wall Street into Market for Pornography," *New York Times*, October 23, 2000.

55   pornography's silver era: Miller-Young, *A Taste for Brown Sugar*, 105.

55   founder, Bob Guccione: Robert D. McFadden, "Bob Guccione, Penthouse Founder, Dies at 79," *New York Times*, October 20, 2010.

56   Flynt ran for President: Bob Colacello, "Larry Flynt Hustling the American Dream," *Vanity Fair*, February 1984.

56   scenes from the Vietnam War: Nancy Semin Lingo, "Making Sense of Linda Lovelace," in Carolyn Bronstein and Whitney Strub, eds., *Porno Chic and the Sex Wars: American Sexual Representation in the 1970s* (Amherst: University of Massachusetts Press, 2016), 104–22.

56   iconic 1969 Stonewall Riots: Melinda Chateauvert, *Sex Workers Unite: A History of the Movement from Stonewall to SlutWalk* (Boston: Beacon Press, 2014).

56   "physique magazines": D'Emilio and Freedman, *Intimate Matters*, 280.

57   Court declared his magazines: Manual Enterprises, Inc. v. Day, 370 U.S. 478 (1962).

57   described the film in vivid detail: Charles, *The FBI's Obscene File*, 66.

57   Warhol befriended some: Bertram J. Cohler, "Memoir and Performance: Social Change and Self Life-Writing Among Men Who Are Gay

Pornography Producers and Actors," *Journal of Homosexuality* 47, no. 3–4 (2004): 21.

57 "most libertine period": Jeffrey Escoffier, "Sex in the Seventies: Gay Porn Cinema as an Archive for the History of American Sexuality," *Journal of the History of Sexuality* 26, no. 1 (2017): 21.

57 Gay porn stars: Michael Lucas, "On Gay Porn," *Yale Journal of Law and Feminism* 18 (2006): 299–302.

57 gay pornography changed: Evangelos Tziallas, "Between the Gothic and Surveillance: Gay (Male) Identity, Fiction Film, and Pornography (1970–2015)" (Ph.D. diss., Concordia University, Montreal, 2015), 224.

58 "soul porn": Miller-Young, *A Taste for Brown Sugar*, 66–67.

58 Black man who "ravages" her: Williams, *Hard Core*, 164.

58 career in the adult industry: Jennifer C. Nash, "Desiring Desiree," in Bronstein and Strub, *Porno Chic and the Sex Wars*, 83–103.

59 "Sex World rehearses a scenario": Miller-Young, *A Taste for Brown Sugar*, 96.

59 "black nationalist and black feminist": Miller-Young, *A Taste for Brown Sugar*, 100.

60 genre called "couple's porn": Carolyn Bronstein, "Mass-Market Pornography for Women," in Bronstein and Strub, *Porno Chic and the Sex Wars*, 125–53.

60 feminist porn movement: Constance Penley, Celine Parreñas Shimizu, Mireille Miller-Young, and Tristan Taormino, "Introduction: The Politics of Producing Pleasure," in Tristan Taormino et al., eds., *The Feminist Porn Book: The Politics of Producing Pleasure* (New York: Feminist Press at City University of New York, 2013), 9–22.

60 "true" keeper of feminism: Lisa Duggan and Nan D. Hunter, *Sex Wars: Sexual Dissent and Political Culture* (New York: Routledge, 2006).

CHAPTER 5: WOMEN AGAINST PORNOGRAPHY

61 "women's liberation movement": Nancy Moran, "9 Women Arrested in 5-Hour Sit-in at Grove Press," *New York Times*, April 14, 1970.

61 all arrested were acquitted: "9 Women Demonstrators at Grove Press Acquitted," *New York Times*, May 7, 1970.

61 "the first time feminists openly": Laura Lederer, "Women Have Seized the Executive Offices of Grove Press Because . . . ," in Laura Lederer, ed., *Take Back the Night: Women on Pornography* (New York: William Morrow, 1980), 268.

62   notoriety in the 1950s and '60s: Michael Rosenthal, *Barney: Grove Press and Barney Rosset, America's Maverick Publisher and His Battle Against Censorship* (New York: Arcade, 2017).

62   under the pseudonym "Pauline Reage": Geraldine Bedell, "I Wrote the 'Story of O,'" *Guardian*, July 24, 2004.

62   radical feminists coalesced: Carolyn Bronstein, *Battling Pornography: The American Feminist Anti-Pornography Movement, 1976–1986* (Cambridge, UK: Cambridge University Press, 2011).

63   "freedom to decline sex": Dana Densmore, "Independence from the Sexual Revolution," in Anne Koedt, Ellen Levine, and Anita Rapone, eds., *Radical Feminism* (New York: Quadrangle, 1973), 111.

63   radical feminist group: Cell 16, "No More Fun and Games," *A Journal of Female Liberation* (February 1969).

63   Black and Chicana feminists: Frances Beale, "Double Jeopardy: To Be Black and Female," *Meridians* 8, no. 2 ([1969] 2008): 166–76; see also Lorna N. Bracewell, *Why We Lost the Sex Wars: Sexual Freedom in the #MeToo Era* (Minneapolis: University of Minnesota Press, 2021), 148.

63   conservative women blamed: Gillian Frank, "'Think About That Special Man Who's on His Way Home to You': Conservative Women's Sexualization of Marriage in the 1970s," in Bronstein and Strub, *Porno Chic and the Sex Wars*, 178–95.

64   Christian sex advice was an emerging genre: Amy DeRogatis, *Saving Sex: Sexuality and Salvation in American Evangelicalism* (Oxford, UK: Oxford University Press, 2015); Burke, *Christians under Covers*.

65   "putting pornographers out of business": Tim LaHaye, *The Battle for the Family* (Ada, MI: Fleming H. Revell, 1984), 183.

65   organization for women who disagreed: Mary T. Schmich, "A Spokeslady for the Right Speaks Out," *Chicago Tribune*, March 23, 1986.

65   "not all women are feminists": George W. Cornell, "Not All Women are Feminists, Conservative Group Tells Public," *Daily Breeze* (Hermosa Beach, CA), August 25, 1984.

66   who opposed the Equal Rights Amendment: Leslie Dorrough Smith, *Righteous Rhetoric: Sex, Speech, and the Politics of Concerned Women for America* (Oxford, UK: Oxford University Press, 2014).

66   "common-sense distinction between the two sexes": George W. Cornell, "Conservative Women Mount Feminist Movement Challenge," *Paducah Sun* (KY), August 24, 1984.

66 feminists championed the message: Nancy Whittier, *Frenemies: Feminists, Conservatives, and Sexual Violence* (Oxford, UK: Oxford University Press, 2018).

67 two feminist positions: Duggan and Hunter, *Sex Wars*, 29–40.

67 groups were not actually collaborators: Whittier, *Frenemies*.

67 uniformly critiqued by many nonwhite feminists: Bracewell, *Why We Lost the Sex Wars*.

69 Christenson was found: Chuck Haga, "Peace Came at an Awful Price to a Soul Pained by Injustice," *Star Tribune: Newspaper of the Twin Cities* (MN), December 14, 1990.

69 Marchiano used the stage: Lingo, "Making Sense of Linda Lovelace," 104–22.

70 over the course of Applegate's short career: Howard Rosenberg, "'Death of Porn Queen': Stunning Storytelling," *Los Angeles Times*, June 9, 1987.

71 Vanessa Williams: Lili Anolik, "'A Felony Just to Own': The Sleazy Story Behind Penthouse's Most Controversial Issue," *Esquire*, September 15, 2020.

71 "I've let other women down": Brad Darrach, "Vanessa Fights Back: 'I Am Not a Lesbian and I Am Not a Slut, and Somehow I Am Going to Make People Believe Me,'" *People*, September 10, 1984.

71 Miss America pageant: D'Emilio and Freedman, *Intimate Matters*, 302.

71 Women Against Pornography: Elizabeth Kastor, "Miss America Resigns amid Controversy: Williams Resigns as Miss America," *Washington Post*, July 24, 1984.

71 Phyllis Schlafly: Sandi Wisenberg, "There She Is, Miss America: A Symbol or a Victim," *Miami Herald*, July 27, 1984.

72 Guccione's empire slowly crumbled: McFadden, "Bob Guccione, Penthouse Founder, Dies at 79."

CHAPTER 6: THE INTERNET IS FOR PORN

73 62 million of them: Jennifer Chessman Day, Alex Janus, and Jessica Davis, "Computer and Internet Usage in the United States: 2003," U.S. Census Bureau, October 2005, https://www.census.gov/prod/2005pubs/p23-208.pdf.

73 "All-pornography, all-the-time": Pamela Paul, *Pornified: How Pornography Is Transforming Our Lives, Our Relationships, and Our Families* (New York: Owl Books, 2005), 5.

73 pornography industry's profits at the turn: Frederick S. Lane, *Obscene Profits: Entrepreneurs of Pornography in the Cyber Age* (New York: Routledge, 2001); "How Big Is Porn?," *Forbes*, May 25, 2001.

74   owners of these sites were lamenting: John Schwartz, "New Economy: The Steamy Side of the Internet, Pervasive and Resilient to Recession, Is the Underpinning of a New Online Cash Venture," *New York Times*, April 9, 2001.

74   national sample of American adults: Susannah Fox, "Adult Content Online," Pew Research Center, August 18, 2005, https://www.pewresearch.org /internet/2005/08/18/adult-content-online.

74   similar to data reported by the *New York Times*: Schwartz, "New Economy."

74   Between 1973 and 1980: Joseph Price et al., "How Much More XXX Is Generation X Consuming? Evidence of Changing Attitudes and Behaviors Related to Pornography Since 1973," *Journal of Sex Research* 53, no. 1 (2016): 12–20.

74   men across all ages: Paul J. Wright, "U.S. Males and Pornography, 1973–2010: Consumption, Predictors, Correlates," *Journal of Sex Research* 50, no. 1 (2013): 60–71.

74   General Social Survey: Researchers analyzed a question asking about X-Rated movie viewership to compare trends over time. Between 2000 and 2004, the GSS also asked respondents if they used a pornographic website in the past 30 days, to which 21 percent of men said yes.

74   controlled for attitudes regarding pornography: Price et al., "How Much More XXX Is Generation X Consuming?"

75   lived in a "raunch culture": Ariel Levy, *Female Chauvinist Pigs: Women and the Rise of Raunch Culture* (New York: Free Press, 2005); Brian McNair, *Striptease Culture: Sex, Media and the Democratization of Desire* (New York: Routledge, 2002); Paul, *Pornified*.

75   growth of the pornography industry: Schwartz, "New Economy."

75   "Julia Roberts of Straight Porn": Jacob Bernstein, "How OnlyFans Changed Sex Work Forever," *New York Times*, February 9, 2019.

75   One porn industry mogul: Frank Rich, "Naked Capitalists," *New York Times*, May 20, 2001.

75   Entertainment Network: Schwartz, "New Economy."

75   one in four households: Eric C. Newburger, "Home Computers and Internet Use in the United States: August 2000," U.S. Census Bureau, September 2001, https://www.census.gov/prod/2001pubs/p23-207.pdf.

76   startling dangers of internet pornography: Philip Elmer-Dewitt, "Online Erotica: On a Screen Near You," *Time*, July 3, 1995.

76 study was an eighty-five-page undergraduate research paper: Peter H. Lewis, "Tech: On the Net; The Internet Battles a Much-Disputed Study on Selling Pornography on Line," *New York Times*, July 17, 1995.

76 public learned that Rimm: Todd Lapin, "Rimm Job," *Wired*, September 1, 1995.

76–77 "the information superhighway": Robert Cannon, "The Legislative History of Senator Exon's Communications Decency Act: Regulating Barbarians on the Information Superhighway," *Federal Communications Law Journal* 49, no. 1 (1996): 53.

77 FBI boasted 249 child pornography prosecutions: Whittier, *Frenemies*, 71.

77 CDA articulated this precedent and applied it to the internet: Telecommunications Act of 1996, 104 P.L. 104, 110 Stat. 56, 1996 Enacted S. 652, 104 (February 8, 1996).

77 Calling this the "blue book": Cannon, "The Legislative History of Senator Exon's Communications Decency Act," 64.

77 In Exon's personal testimony: Cannon, "The Legislative History of Senator Exon's Communications Decency Act," 57.

78 "Person of the Year": Lev Grossman, "You—Yes, You—Are TIME's Person of the Year," *Time*, December 25, 2006.

78 "The porn world was there for the taking": Jon Ronson, "A Nondescript Building in Montreal," audio podcast, *The Butterfly Effect*, November 2, 2017.

78 GEEK-KINGS OF SMUT: Benjamin Wallace, "The Geek-Kings of Smut," *New York Magazine*, January 28, 2011.

78 Its formal purpose: Manwin German GmbH, *DufaIndex*, Hamburg, Germany, November 14, 2012.

79 "awfully good thing to buy adult websites": Wallace, "The Geek-Kings of Smut."

79 "I bought pretty much everything": Ronson, "A Nondescript Building in Montreal."

79 also buy the leading pay subscription sites: Wallace, "The Geek-Kings of Smut."

79 some commercial porn studios hire out firms: "Corey D. Silverstein Speaks About Understanding Laws & Regulations Affecting Your Bottom Line," YouTube video, 47:48, Silverstein Legal, February 22, 2017.

79 company reported an annual revenue: BB, "Porn Empire Reports Half Billion Dollars in Revenue—But Ends Year with Loss," *Luxembourg Times*, March 23, 2018.

79 "A Leader in Web Design, IT, Web Development": MindGeek, "Industry-Leading Exclusive Technologies Driving Unparalleled Performance."

79 company owns 90 percent: Matt Blake, "UK Porn Is About to Change in a Way You're Not Going to Like," *Vice*, November 24, 2017.

CHAPTER 7: TRAFFICKING HUB

85 greater percentage of conservative Protestants: Samuel L. Perry, "Banning Because of Science or in Spite of It? Scientific Authority, Religious Conservatism, and Support for Outlawing Pornography, 1984–2018," *Social Forces* (2021), https://doi.org/10.1093/sf/soab024.

85 Miller test's subjective definition: Miller v. California, 413 U.S. 15.

85 laws against sex trafficking: Elizabeth M. Donovan, "Fight Online Sex Trafficking Act and Stop Enabling Sex Traffickers Act: A Shield for Jane Doe," *Connecticut Law Review* 52, no. 1 (2020): 85.

85 filed a civil suit against Backpage: Jane Doe No. 1 v. Backpage.Com, LLC, 817 F.3d 12 (1st Cir. 2016).

86 TVPA defines broadly: Victims of Trafficking and Violence Protection Act of 2000, H.R. 3244, 106th Cong. (2020), 114 STAT, 1470.

86–87 "Nothing in this section may be construed to authorize": Victims of Trafficking and Violence Protection Act, 1548.

87 nearly identical bills in the House and Senate: Allow States and Victims to Fight Online Sex Trafficking Act, H.R.1865, 115th Cong. (2018).

87 campaign against human trafficking: Jessica Kwong, "President Gives 'Credit to Ivanka Trump' at Signing for Online Sex Trafficking Crackdown Bill," *Newsweek*, April 11, 2018.

87 somber public service announcement supporting the bills: "PSA Featuring Seth Meyers, Amy Schumer, Josh Charles, Tony Shalhoub and others— SESTA," YouTube video, 2:26, January 11, 2018.

87 SESTA-FOSTA . . . amended the Communications Decency Act: Allow States and Victims to Fight Online Sex Trafficking Act, H.R. 1865.

87 antipornography efforts of the 1980s: Whittier, *Frenemies*, 49, 69.

87 federal law enforcement shut down Backpage: United States Department of Justice, "Justice Department Leads Effort to Seize Backpage.Com, the Internet's Leading Forum for Prostitution Ads, and Obtains 93-Count Federal Indictment," Department of Justice Office of Public Affairs, News Release, April 9, 2018.

88 the term *sex trafficking*: Sverre Molland, *The Perfect Business? Anti-Trafficking and the Sex Trade Along the Mekong* (Honolulu: University of Hawaii Press, 2012), 33.

88 White Slave Traffic Act: Charles, *The FBI's Obscene File*, 14–16.

88   "immoral purposes": Transportation for Illegal Sexual Activity and Related Crimes, 18 U.S. Code § 2421 (2009).

88   Antiporn and antitrafficking activists: Elizabeth Bernstein, *Brokered Subjects: Sex, Trafficking, and the Politics of Freedom* (Chicago: University of Chicago Press, 2018), 68–97.

89   movement led by conservative Christians: Similar commentary appeared in Kelsy Burke and Nancy Whittier, "Conservative Christians and Anti-Porn Feminists Want to Shut Down Online Pornography. That Doesn't Make Them Allies," *Washington Post*, October 4, 2021.

89   prayer group: Anton Carillo, "Woman Working with Christian Groups Lead Charge to End Porn and Sex Trafficking," *Christianity Daily*, July 23, 2021.

89   In a lengthy exposé: Nicholas Kristof, "The Children of Pornhub: Why Does Canada Allow This Company to Profit Off Videos of Exploitation and Assault?," *New York Times*, December 4, 2020.

89   job is called "content formatter": David Auerbach, "Vampire Porn: MindGeek Is a Cautionary Tale of Consolidating Production and Distribution in a Single, Monopolistic Owner," *Slate*, October 23, 2014.

90   forced to make pornographic videos: "Elizabeth Frazier: Sex Trafficking Survivor, Activist, and Entrepreneur," audio podcast, *Consider Before Consuming*, January 7, 2020.

91   investigation in 2014 about Somaly Mam: Simon Marks, "Somaly Mam: The Holy Saint (and Sinner) of Sex Trafficking," *Newsweek*, May 21, 2014.

91   "survivor and activist": "Our History," Somaly Mam Foundation, https://www.somaly.org/our-history/.

91   Mam was previously featured: Nicholas Kristof, "Fighting Back, One Brothel Raid at a Time," *New York Times*, November 12, 2011.

91   "rescue industry": Laura Augustin, "Somaly Mam, Nick Kristof, and the Cult of Personality," *Jacobin*, June 16, 2014.

91   Trump administration announced: Jeff Amy, "Barr Announces $100 Million More to Combat Human Trafficking," *NewsHour*, PBS, September 21, 2020.

91   "brokered subjects": Bernstein, *Brokered Subjects*.

91   series of new policies: "Our Commitment to Trust and Safety," Pornhub, https://help.pornhub.com/hc/en-us/categories/360002934613-Our-Commitment-to-Trust-and-Safety.

92   skeptical of the implementation: Nicholas Kristof, "An Uplifting Update, on the Terrible World of Pornhub: Young Heroes Lead in Confronting Pornography Companies that Monetize Rape and Child Abuse," *New York Times*, December 9, 2020.

92 worries porn performers and sex worker advocates: Melissa Gira Grant, "Nick Kristof and the Holy War on Pornhub: Having Declared Victory in Its War on Backpage and Sex Work, the Liberal-Conservative Coalition Has Pivoted to Porn," *New Republic*, December 10, 2020.

92 Visa and Mastercard announced: Gillian Friedman, "Mastercard and Visa Stop Allowing Their Cards to Be Used on Pornhub," *New York Times*, December 10, 2020.

92 One performer who used Modelhub: "Episode 78: Porn Performers Talk Pornhub and Payment Processing," audio podcast, *Peepshow Media*, December 21, 2020.

92 who has since blamed feminists: Adam Gabbatt, "Republican Senator Josh Hawley Worries Feminism Has Driven Men to 'Pornography and Video Games,'" *Guardian*, November 1, 2021.

92 allow individuals to sue Pornhub: Survivors of Human Trafficking Fight Back Act of 2020, S.4983, 116th Cong., 2nd Sess. (2020).

92 antitrafficking activists: Bernstein, *Brokered Subjects*.

93 legality of internet pornography: Woodhull Freedom Foundation v. United States of America, 334 F. Supp. 3d 185 (D.D.C. 2018).

93 sex workers who have turned to the internet: "SWOP-USA Stands in Opposition of [*sic*] Disguised Internet Censorship Bill SESTA, S. 1963," Sex Workers Outreach Project–USA, August 11, 2017.

94 as sex workers have pointed out: "Episode 78: Porn Performers."

94 study the unintended impacts of SESTA-FOSTA: SESTA/FOSTA Examination of Secondary Effects for Sex Workers Study Act, S. 3165, 116 Cong., 2nd Sess. (2020).

95 police departments in many cities: Alexandra Villarreal, "Side Effect of Trafficking Law: More Street Prostitution?," AP News, September 24, 2018.

95 autonomy and control over their work: Sean Bland and Benjamin Brooks, "Improving Laws and Policies to Protect Sex Workers and Promote Health and Wellbeing: A Report on Criminalization of Sex Work in the District of Columbia," Whitman-Walker Institute, O'Neill Institute for National and Global Health Law, and HIPS, Washington, D.C., June 9, 2020.

CHAPTER 8: SAFER SEX (WORK)

96 "sexual health": World Health Organization, "Education and Treatment in Human Sexuality: The Training of Health Professionals," Report of a WHO Meeting [Held in Geneva from 6 to 12 February 1974]," World Health

Organization Technical Report Series No. 572, World Health Organization, Geneva, 1975, 6.

97 Sociologists Steve Epstein and Laura Mamo: Steven Epstein and Laura Mamo, "The Proliferation of Sexual Health: Diverse Social Problems and the Legitimation of Sexuality," *Social Science and Medicine* 188 (2017): 176–90.

97 Weinstein mailed fifty-eight porn DVDs: Associated Press, "Unsafe Sex Begets Porn-film Co. Fines—Health: Cal-OSHA Acts After Spread of HIV Closed Industry Briefly This Year," *Long Beach Press-Telegram* (CA), September 18, 2004.

97 ballot initiative in Los Angeles County: Madison Pauly, "California's Fight over Condoms in Porn Is About to Climax—We Explore All the Positions on Prop 60," *Mother Jones*, October 21, 2016.

98 "public health resolution": Dennis Romero, "It Now Costs $1,671 for Permission to Film a Porno," *LA Weekly*, August 23, 2017.

98 industry had not adopted condom use: Sharif Mowlabocus, Justin Harbottle, and Charlie Witzel, "Porn Laid Bare: Gay Men, Pornography and Bareback Sex," *Sexualities* 16, no. 5–6 (2013): 523–47.

98 performer contracted HIV: Rong-Gong Lin II and Kimi Yoshino, "Porn Actress Tests Positive for HIV," *Los Angeles Times* (LATWP News Service) (CA), June 11, 2009.

98 companies halt production: Pauly, "California's Fight over Condoms in Porn."

98 legal battle with Weinstein's AHF: Dennis Romero, "Porn Clinic AIM Closes for Good: Valley-Based Industry Scrambles to Find New STD Testing System," *LA Weekly*, May 3, 2011.

98 media have sensationalized stories: Lin and Yoshino, "Porn Actress Tests Positive for HIV."

98 rates of STIs for porn performers: Binh Y. Goldstein et al., "High Chlamydia and Gonorrhea Incidence and Reinfection Among Performers in the Adult Film Industry," *Sexually Transmitted Diseases* 38, no. 7 (2011): 644–48.

98 "widespread transmission of sexually transmitted infections": County of Los Angeles Safer Sex in the Adult Film Industry Act, Los Angeles County (CA) Ordinance 181989 (2012).

98 one industry executive pointed: Steven Hirsch to Los Angeles County Voters, Vivid Entertainment LLC, quoted in Frank Girardot, "Vivid Entertainment Owner Says Condoms Bad for Porn Biz," blog post, *CrimeScene*, October 3, 2012, http://www.insidesocal.com/sgvcrime/files/import/62506-VividVideo XXX.pdf.

99   Free Speech Coalition: "What Is PASS?," PASS, https://www.passcertified
      .org/about-the-organization.

99   model for contact tracing: Michele C. Hollow, "Lessons on Coronavirus
      Testing from the Adult Film Industry: An Industry that Survived One
      Health Crisis Could Be a Model for Others Looking to Build Confidence,
      Experts Say," *New York Times*, June 18, 2020.

100   nine to eleven days after exposure: Leigh Cowart, "How Porn Isn't Protecting
      Its Stars from HIV—As California Votes Against Mandatory Condom Use
      in Porn, a New CDC Study Sheds Light on How One Gay Porn Star
      Managed to Infect a Coworker with HIV Despite the Industry's Routine
      Testing," The Daily Beast, February 20, 2016.

100   Shelley Lubben: Olsen Ebright, "Porn Industry Under Fire for Lack of
      Condoms," NBC Los Angeles, August 20, 2009, https://www.nbclosangeles
      .com/news/local/porn-industry-under-fire-for-lack-of-condoms/2102392.

100   Jan Merritt: Ebright, "Porn Industry Under Fire for Lack of Condoms."

100   Nina Hartley: Rhett Pardon, "Nina Hartley Discusses Myths, Rumors over
      HIV in Porn," *XBIZ*, September 16, 2013.

100   existing rigorous testing standards: Free Speech Coalition, "Measure B
      Decision Will Hurt Performers," Press Release, December 15, 2014, https:
      //www.businesswire.com/news/home/20141215006587/en/Free-Speech
      -Coalition-%E2%80%9CMeasure-B-Decision-Will-Hurt-Adult
      -Performers%E2%80%9D.

100   public letter to Los Angeles County voters: Steven Hirsch, "Public Letter to
      Los Angeles County Voters."

101   stopped all production for a short time: Shaya Tayefe Mohajer, "Positive HIV
      Test Halts Porn Shoots at Companies," Associated Press Archive, October 14,
      2010.

101   lawsuit against the Los Angeles County Department of Public Health: Vivid
      Entertainment, LLC v. Fielding, 774 F.3d 566 (2014).

101   law detailing regulations: Romero, "It Now Costs $1,671 for Permission to
      Film a Porno."

102   As the Measure B legal battles unfolded: Pauly, "California's Fight over
      Condoms in Porn."

102   ten largest California newspapers: "FSC: Prop 60 Now Opposed by over 55
      California Newspapers—Sacramento News & Review and East Bay Express
      Are the Latest to Say 'No on 60,' Joining the LA Times, San Francisco
      Chronicle, LA Opinion, Sacramento Bee and the over Fifty Other Papers

Opposing Controversial and Dangerous Proposition 60," GlobeNewswire (USA), November 5, 2016.

102 organizations for the adult industry: Pauly, "California's Fight over Condoms in Porn."

102 polls in the months preceding: Javier Panzar, "Most Californians Support Initiative to Require Adult Film Actors to Use Condoms," *Los Angeles Times*, September 15, 2016.

102 "CEO of HIV": Christopher Glazek, "The C.E.O. of H.I.V.," *New York Times*, April 26, 2017.

102 avoided collaboration even with organizations: Werbel, *Lust on Trial*, 234.

103 "the Koch brothers of public health": Glazek, "The C.E.O. of H.I.V."

103 Weinstein is virtually alone: Glazek, "The C.E.O. of H.I.V."

103 a "party drug": Associated Press, "Divide over HIV Prevention Drug Truvada persists," *USA Today*, April 6, 2014. Weinstein later clarifies his opposition to the implementation of PrEP in Michael Weinsten, Otto O. Yang, and Adam C. Cohen. "Were We Prepared for PreEP? Five Years of Implementation," *AIDS* 31, no. 16 (2017): 2303–2305.

103 Macro-level factors: "Addressing Violence Against Sex Workers," World Health Organization, October 18, 2013, 19–39, https://www.who.int/hiv/pub/sti/sex _worker_implementation/swit_chpt2.pdf; Susan G. Sherman et al., "Drivers of HIV Infection Among Cisgender and Transgender Female Sex Worker Populations in Baltimore City: Results from the SAPPHIRE Study," *Journal of Acquired Immune Deficiency Syndrome* 80, no. 5 (2019): 513–52; Kimberly A. Tyler and Katherine A. Johnson, "Trading Sex: Voluntary or Coerced? The Experiences of Homeless Youth," *Journal of Sex Research* 43, no. 3 (2006): 208–16.

103 interview study of sex workers in New York City: Juhu Thukral and Melissa Ditmore, *Revolving Door: An Analysis of Street-Based Prostitution in New York City*, Urban Justice Center, Sex Workers Project, 2003, https://www.nswp .org/ru/node/356.

105 2015 national survey of transgender respondents: Sandy James et al., *The Report of the 2015 U.S. Transgender Survey*, National Center for Transgender Equality, Washington, D.C., 2016.

106 In the New York City study: Thukral and Ditmore, *Revolving Door*.

106 Olivia Nova: Georgia Diebelius, "Porn Star Olivia Nova Died After Contracting Sepsis from Infection," Metro, January 20, 2018.

106 Olivia Lua: Maria Perez, "Who Is Olivia Lua? The Fifth Adult Actress Found Dead in Three Months," *Newsweek*, January 20, 2018.

106   Yuri Luv: Maria Vultaggio, "After August Ames, Yurizan Beltran Accidentally Overdosed on Prescription Pills, Friend Says," *Newsweek*, December 18, 2017.

106   Shyla Stylez: Frances Kindon, "Suicide, Sepsis and Killer Infections—Most Harrowing Porn Star Deaths Exposed: From Killer UTIs and Overdoses to Fatal Falls and Horrifying Accidents, the Stars of the Adult Entertainment Industry Have Lost Their Lives in Truly Tragic Circumstances," *Daily Star*, January 27, 2020.

106   "The reason this resource is so important": PleazeMe, "Face to Face with Pineapple Support Founder Leya Tanit," YouTube video, 49:54, September 23, 2020.

107   Shortly after Pineapple Support was established: Pornhub, "Pornhub Partners with Pineapple Support to Provide Mental Health Support to Adult Entertainment Industry Performers," Press Release, December 17, 2018, https://www.pornhub.com/press/show?id=1761.

CHAPTER 9: HOT GIRLS WANTED

108   Steinem's "A Bunny's Tale": Gloria Steinem, "A Bunny's Tale," *SHOW*, May 1, 1963, 66–68.

109   neither side is more or less feminist: Bernadette Barton, *The Pornification of America: How Raunch Culture Is Ruining Our Society* (New York: New York University Press, 2021), 17.

112   charged with twelve felony counts: State of California Department of Justice, "Attorney General Becerra Announces Criminal Charges in Alleged North Hollywood Prostitution Operation," Press Release, March 5, 2020, https://oag .ca.gov/news/press-releases/attorney-general-becerra-announces-criminal -charges-alleged-north-hollywood.

112   offered them escorting opportunities: Amelia McDonell-Parry, "Four Porn Performers Accuse Top Agent Derek Hay of Sex Abuse, Trafficking: The Women, Including Porn Performer Charlotte Cross, Also Accuse LA Direct Models Owner of Defrauding Them of Performance Fees by Overcharging Producers," *Rolling Stone*, July 11, 2018.

112   Hay has denied: "'They had their own cameras on me'—Louis Theroux on his Showdowns with US Extremists," *Guardian*, February 10, 2022.

112   Linda Marchiano: Daphne Merkin, "Pop-Porn: She Made Hard Core Acceptable to the Masses, Then Crusaded Against It," *New York Times*, December 29, 2002.

112 Shelley Lubben: Rick Elkins, "Former Actress Takes on Porn Industry," *Porterville Recorder* (CA), July 6, 2016.

112 Elizabeth Smart: "Elizabeth Smart's Heartbreaking Account of Porn's Role in Her Abuse," Fight the New Drug, April 3, 2019, https://fightthenewdrug .org/elizabeth-smart-speaks-for-the-first-time-about-pornographys-role-in -her-abduction-video/.

113 "fauxcest": "'Fauxcest:' The Disturbing Rise of Incest-Themed Porn," The Daily Beast, April 22, 2017.

114 Riley Reynolds: Tarpley Hitt, "Florida's Porn King Accused of Sexually 'Exploiting' Women," The Daily Beast, October 1, 2018, https://www .thedailybeast.com/floridas-porn-king-accused-of-sexually-exploiting -women.

117 "revealed a schism between the gay and straight communities": Tina Horn, "Death of a Porn Star: When August Ames Killed Herself Following Controversy on Twitter, It Revealed a Schism Between the Gay and Straight Communities in the Porn Industry," *Rolling Stone*, December 12, 2017.

117 *The Last Days of August*: Jon Ronson, host, *The Last Days of August*, audio podcast series, 2019.

118 EXXXOTICA Expo banned Jeremy: Mischa Pearlmen, "Ron Jeremy Banned from Adult Film Expo After Sexual Misconduct Allegations," LADbible, January 25, 2018.

118 *AVN* Awards followed suit: Hayley Miller, "Ron Jeremy Banned from Porn Awards After Admitting He's a 'Groper': The Adult Film Legend Allegedly Violated the Adult Video News Event's 'Zero Tolerance Harassment Policy,'" *HuffPost*, January 25, 2018.

118 250 years in prison: Lisette Voytko, "Adult Film Star Ron Jeremy Gets 20 More Sexual Assault Counts, Faces 250 Years in Prison," *Forbes*, August 31, 2020.

118 accused by nearly a dozen women: Melissa Gira Grant, "How Stoya Took on James Deen and Broke the Porn Industry's Silence," *Guardian*, December 4, 2015.

118 He has denied wrongdoing: Aurora Snow, "James Deen Breaks His Silence: 'I Am Completely Baffled' by Rape Allegations," The Daily Beast, June 26, 2017.

118 some companies refused to hire him: Aurora Snow, "James Deen Sexual-Assault Accuser Disgusted by His Porn Awards Nominations: 'Nobody Seemed to Care,'" The Daily Beast, December 7, 2019.

118 "Exclusive Contract Star": Marlow Stern, "The Rising Porn Actor Accused
     of Abuse and Harassment: 'He Put Me in a Suitcase,'" The Daily Beast,
     March 18, 2020.

119 agreed to work with Lux to take Reynolds to court: Amelia McDonell-Parry,
     "Prominent Porn Agent Sued by Adult-Film Actress: Actress Lenna Lux
     Claims that Riley Reynolds, Who Appeared in the 2015 Doc 'Hot Girls
     Wanted,' Was Not Properly Licensed to Work as Her Agent in Florida,"
     Rolling Stone, October 1, 2018.

119 applications to work with him: "We Talked to the Guy from 'Hot Girls
     Wanted' About What It's Like to Be a Porn Agent. Some People Think the
     Netflix Documentary Is a Condemnation of Sex Work. Riley Reynolds
     Thinks It's Good Business," Daily Dot, May 28, 2021.

119 "False consciousness": György Lukács, History and Class Consciousness: Studies
     in Marxist Dialectics (Cambridge, MA: MIT Press, 1971), 50–51; Karl Marx
     and Friedrich Engels, The German Ideology (1947; repr. New York: International,
     2004).

119 "I want to grow up to be a prostitute": Lola Davina, Thriving in Sex Work:
     Heartfelt Advice for Staying Sane in the Sex Industry (Oakland, CA: Erotic as
     Power Press, 2017), 256.

119 "not your typical strip joint": Davina, Thriving in Sex Work, 256.

119 chose to work in porn over alternatives: Alex Morris, "The Blue Devil in
     Miss Belle Knox: Meet Duke Porn Star Miriam Weeks, She's a Studious
     College Freshman—and America's Top New Adult-Film Actress," Rolling
     Stone, April 23, 2014.

120 "My heart just breaks": Morris, "The Blue Devil in Miss Belle Knox."

120 "I've got no moral hang-ups about what you do": Piers Morgan, Interview
     with Belle Knox, Piers Morgan Tonight, CNN, March 6, 2014.

120 accepted to New York University Law School: Joshua Rhett Miller, "What
     Comes Next for Belle Knox?," New York Post, March 12, 2018.

120 subjects of disturbing racist content in pornography: Miller-Young, A Taste
     for Brown Sugar, 46–47.

121 experiencing pressure, coercion, or outright violence: Debby Herbenick et al.,
     "Feeling Scared During Sex: Findings from a US Probability Sample of
     Women and Men Ages 14 to 60," Journal of Sex and Marital Therapy 45, no. 5
     (2019): 424–39; Mary P. Koss, Christine A. Gidycz, and Nadine Wisniewski,
     "The Scope of Rape: Incidence and Prevalence of Sexual Aggression and
     Victimization in a National Sample of Higher Education Students," Journal
     of Consulting and Clinical Psychology 55, no. 2 (1987): 162.

121 African Americans, Latinos, and Native Americans: Tyrone C. Cheng and
     Celia C. Lo, "Racial Disparities in Intimate Partner Violence and in Seeking
     Help with Mental Health," *Journal of Interpersonal Violence* 30, no. 18 (2015):
     3283–307.

121 "in homes, in cars, on beaches": Andrea Dworkin, *Our Blood: Prophecies and
     Discourses on Sexual Politics* (New York: Perigee Books, 1976), xvii, quoted in
     Jane Ward, *The Tragedy of Heterosexuality* (New York: New York University
     Press, 2020), 10.

121 gender pay gap: Amanda Barroso and Anna Brown, "Gender Pay Gap in U.S.
     Held Steady in 2020," Pew Research Center, May 25, 2021, https://www
     .pewresearch.org/fact-tank/2021/05/25/gender-pay-gap-facts/; Michael
     Bittman et al., "When Does Gender Trump Money? Bargaining and Time
     in Household Work," *American Journal of Sociology* 109, no. 1 (2003):
     186–214.

121 low rates of satisfaction: Mamadi Corra et al., "Trends in Marital Happiness
     by Gender and Race, 1973 to 2006," *Journal of Family Issues* 30, no. 10 (2009):
     1379–404.

121 against poor women and women of color: Beth E. Richie, *Arrested Justice*
     (New York: New York University Press, 2012); Jody Miller, *Getting Played:
     African American Girls, Urban Inequality, and Gendered Violence* (New York:
     New York University Press, 2008); Stephanie Wahab and Lenora Olson,
     "Intimate Partner Violence and Sexual Assault in Native American
     Communities," *Trauma, Violence, and Abuse* 5, no. 4 (2004): 353–66; William
     George Axinn, Maura Elaine Bardos, and Brady Thomas West, "General
     Population Estimates of the Association Between College Experience and
     the Odds of Forced Intercourse," *Social Science Research* 70 (2018): 131–43.

CHAPTER 10: HUSTLERS

122 conjures up an absurd scenario: Carol Leigh, "Inventing Sex Work," in Jill
     Nagle, ed., *Whores and Other Feminists* (New York: Routledge, 1997), 230.

124 "late-stage capitalism": Ernest Mandel, *Late Capitalism* (London: Verso, 1978).

125 "catastrophe and progress": Fredric Jameson, *Postmodernism, or, The Cultural
     Logic of Late Capitalism* (Durham, NC: Duke University Press, 1991), 47.

125 winner-take-all economy: Chrystia Freeland, *Plutocrats: The Rise of the New
     Global Super Rich and the Fall of Everyone Else* (New York: Penguin Books, 2012).

125 employment rate for people aged twenty-five to thirty-four: "Employment
     and Unemployment Rates by Educational Attainment," National Center for

Education Statistics, May 19, 2020, https://nces.ed.gov/programs/coe/pdf/coe_cbc.pdf.

125 "gig economy" has created jobs: Jeremias Prassl, *Humans as a Service: The Promise and Perils of Work in the Gig Economy* (Oxford, UK: Oxford University Press, 2018).

125 earnings of $97 billion: Geoffrey Fattah, "Porn Industry Is Booming Globally: Utah Study Says U.S. and China Dominate Markets," *Deseret News* (UT), March 17, 2007.

126 circulated among antiporn groups: "Porn Industry Archives," Enough Is Enough, https://enough.org/stats_porn_industry_archives.

126 national news: "Things Are Looking Up in America's Porn Industry," NBC News, January 20, 2015, https://www.nbcnews.com/business/business-news/things-are-looking-americas-porn-industry-n289431.

126 estimate annual earnings at $10 billion: "How Big Is Porn?"

126 the research firm IBIS World: "Adult & Pornographic Websites in the US—Market Size 2005–2026," IBISWorld, October 19, 2020, https://www.ibisworld.com/industry-statistics/market-size/adult-pornographic-websites-united-states/.

126 MindGeek has either bought out: Auerbach, "Vampire Porn."

126 users can watch porn for free online: David Cay Johnston, "Indications of a Slowdown in Sex Entertainment Trade," *New York Times*, January 4, 2007.

126 any content they create on their own: Angela Jones, *Camming: Money, Power, and Pleasure in the Sex Work Industry* (New York: New York University Press, 2020), 123–24.

128 NPR's *This American Life*: Ira Glass and David Hauptschein, "312: How We Talked Back Then, Act Two: Internet," audio podcast, *This American Life*, Chicago Public Media, May 12, 2006.

128 "It's not about exhibitionism": Glass and Hauptschein, "312: How We Talked Back Then."

128 closed her account for depictions of nudity: Kate Knibbs, "Jennicam: Why the First Lifecaster Disappeared from the Internet," Gizmodo, April 14, 2015.

128 "embodied authenticity": Jones, *Camming*, 7, 45.

128 "believe that it's a real woman": Jones, *Camming*, 46.

129 TV critic, comparing *The Real World*: "The Realer World," *New York Times*, July 6, 1997.

129 integrate new technologies: John Tierney, "Porn, the Low-Slung Engine of Progress," *New York Times*, January 9, 1994.

130 Teledildonics: Steve Diltea, "Virtual Reality: Within a Decade, You'll See It, Feel It, Manipulate It. You'll Use It at Home and at Work. You May Even Have Sex with It. Just One Thing—It Won't Be Real," *San Francisco Chronicle*, October 21, 1990.

130 OhMiBod: "Introducing OhMiBod™, the First Socially Acceptable Vibrator—The iPod® Accessory that Lets People Feel Their Music," PR Newswire (USA), November 14, 2006.

130 pay to control the sexual experience: Jones, *Camming*, 58.

130 a tool for safe sex: Katie Bishop, "Sex Robots, Teledildonics, and the Rise of Technosexuals During Lockdown," *New York Observer*, October 21, 2020.

130 dealt with "capping": Jones, *Camming*, 123–25.

130 flexible schedule and limited time: Jones, *Camming*, 91–97.

131 reported earning $257 in her first month: Bernstein, "How OnlyFans Changed Sex Work Forever."

131 OnlyFans made national headlines: Taylor Lorenz and Alyssa Lukpat, "OnlyFans Says It Is Banning Sexually Explicit Content: The Company Is the Latest Digital Platform to Crack Down on Such Material. The Site Became a Source of Income for Millions During the Coronavirus Pandemic," *New York Times*, August 19, 2021.

131 One of the groups that took credit: Similar commentary appeared in Kelsy Burke, "The OnlyFans Fight Isn't Over," *Slate*, August 25, 2021.

131 described by NCOSE: "The 2021 Dirty Dozen List: OnlyFans," National Center on Sexual Exploitation, https://endsexualexploitation.org/onlyfans/.

131 letter to the Department of Justice: "Congresswoman Ann Wagner Leads Bipartisan Coalition Calling for DOJ to Investigate OnlyFans for Child Exploitation," Congresswoman Ann Wagner, Press Release, August 10, 2021, https://wagner.house.gov/media-center/press-releases/congresswoman-ann-wagner-leads-bipartisan-coalition-calling-for-doj-to.

132 independent investigation conducted by the BBC: Noel Titheradge, "OnlyFans: How It Handles Illegal Sex Videos—BBC Investigation," BBC News, August 19, 2021.

132 criticism on behalf of sex workers: Samantha Cole, "'I Felt Betrayed': OnlyFans Creators Scramble to Adapt to Imminent Ban," *Vice*, August 20, 2021.

132 Bella Thorne: Mary-Ann Russon, "Bella Thorne, OnlyFans and the Battle over Monetising Content," BBC News, September 1, 2020.

132 A company statement: Ashley Carman, "OnlyFans Confirms New Caps on Tips and Pay-per-View Content, but Says the Changes Are Unrelated to Bella Thorne," *The Verge*, September 1, 2020.

132 cam models depended on the site's PPV: Amy Kaufman, "OnlyFans Denies that Bella Thorne Prompted New Spending Restrictions on Site," *Los Angeles Times*, August 28, 2020.

132 Thorne apologized on social media: Sonaiya Kelley, "Bella Thorne Apologizes After Sex Workers, Advocates Blast Her OnlyFans Work," *Los Angeles Times*, August 30, 2020.

133 have different structures: Jones, *Camming*, 66–68.

134 performed femininity in socially desirable ways: Jones, *Camming*, 158–73.

134 independent and amateur markets have grown: Shira Tarrant, *The Pornography Industry: What Everyone Needs to Know* (Oxford, UK: Oxford University Press, 2016), 28–32.

134 taking an interest in transgender porn: Sophie Pezzutto and Lynn Comella, "Trans Pornography: Mapping an Emerging Field," *Transgender Studies Quarterly* 7, no. 2 (2020): 152–71.

134 homicide suggest that transgender victims: Laurel Westbrook, *Unlivable Lives: Violence and Identity in Transgender Activism* (Oakland: University of California Press, 2021), 245.

134 commercial studios produce films: Jon Ronson, "Ep. 2: The Fallow Years Between Teen & MILF," audio podcast, *The Butterfly Effect*, November 3, 2017.

135 coronavirus pandemic eliminated: Jacob Serebrin, "'I Have a Mortgage to Pay': Sex Workers Banned from Small-Business Loans Under CARES Act Due to 'Prurient Sexual Nature,'" MarketWatch, May 24, 2020.

135 Pornhub, was boasting a record number: "Coronavirus Update—April 14," Pornhub Insights, Pornhub, April 14, 2020.

136 premium-access program: "Pornhub Offers Free Pornhub Premium to Users Worldwide for 30 Days During COVID-19 Pandemic," Pornhub, March 24, 2020.

136 successfully sued the government: DV Diamond Club of Flint, LLC, et al. v. United States Small Business Administration, et al., 459 F. Supp. 3d 943, (E.D. Mich. 2020).

136 excluded businesses that profited: DV Diamond Club of Flint, LLC, 459 F. Supp. 3d 943.

136 "precarity brings insecurity": Heather Berg, *Porn Work: Sex, Labor, and Late Capitalism* (Chapel Hill: University of North Carolina Press, 2021), 6.

CHAPTER 11: SHADES OF GREY

137   In a 2010 study: Ana J. Bridges et al., "Aggression and Sexual Behavior in Best-selling Pornography Videos: A Content Analysis Update," *Violence Against Women* 16, no. 10 (2010): 1065–85.

137   violence became less common: Eran Shor and Kimberly Seida, "'Harder and Harder'? Is Mainstream Pornography Becoming Increasingly Violent and Do Viewers Prefer Violent Content?," *Journal of Sex Research* 56, no. 1 (2019): 16–28.

137   violence is directed unevenly: Jennifer Lynn Gossett and Sarah Byrne, "'Click Here': A Content Analysis of Internet Rape Sites," *Gender and Society* 16, no. 5 (2002): 689–709.

138   most controversial scene from the film: Miller-Young, *A Taste for Brown Sugar*, 127.

138   Sahara, began producing fewer movies: Miller-Young, *A Taste for Brown Sugar*, 130.

139   *KKK Night Riders*: Miller-Young, *A Taste for Brown Sugar*, 59–65.

141   According to national surveys: "Summer Unrest over Racial Injustice Moves the Country, but Not Republicans or White Evangelicals," Public Religion Research Institute, August 21, 2020, https://www.prri.org/research/racial -justice-2020-george-floyd/.

141   Pornhub's BLM hashtag: Gail Dines and Carolyn M. West, "'White Girl Moans Black Lives Matter': Pornhub's #BLM Genre and the Industry's Brash Racism," *Slate*, July 9, 2020.

142   according to Kink.com's 2020 year in review: "Second Annual Kink.com Site Review 2020: A Kink.com Data Analysis, Trends in User Behavior," Kink .com, n.d., https://kink.zendesk.com/hc/en-us/articles/1260803327369-Second -Annual-Kink-com-Site-Review-2020.

143   one of the last major porn production sites: Benny Evangelista, "Porn Site Loosens Chains, Seeks to Change Direction," *San Francisco Chronicle*, May 11, 2018.

147   sale on Mission Street: Sam Levin, "'End of an Era': Porn Actors Lament the Loss of Legendary San Francisco Armory," *Guardian*, January 25, 2017.

147   brought the company out of the red: Evangelista, "Porn Site Loosens Chains."

148   "absolutely a feminist work": Bedell, "I Wrote the 'Story of O.'"

148   Sexuality is always both "pleasure and danger": Carol Vance, "Pleasure and Danger: Toward a Politics of Sexuality," in Wendy K. Kolmar and Frances

Bartkowski, eds., *Feminist Theory: A Reader* (1984; repr. New York: McGraw-Hill, 2013), 327.

149 Researchers of BDSM communities: Andreas A. J. Wismeijer and Marcel A. L. M. van Assen, "Psychological Characteristics of BDSM Practitioners," *Journal of Sexual Medicine* 10, no. 8 (2013): 1943–52; Ashley Brown, Edward D. Barker, and Qazi Rahman, "A Systematic Scoping Review of the Prevalence, Etiological, Psychological, and Interpersonal Factors Associated with BDSM," *Journal of Sex Research* 57, no. 6 (2020): 781–811.

149 historian and porn studies scholar: Miller-Young, *A Taste for Brown Sugar*, 129.

150 "Sahara's complicity does not condone white supremacy": Miller-Young, *A Taste for Brown Sugar*, 129.

150 "racialized eroticism into sexual media": Miller-Young, *A Taste for Brown Sugar*, 66.

150 "I never saw it": Nash, "Desiring Desiree," 84–85.

CHAPTER 12: COME AS YOU ARE

155 Feminist pornography developed as a brand: Constance Penley et al., "Introduction: The Politics of Producing Pleasure," 9–20.

156 "You have to pay for it": Paisley Gilmour, "Why Paying for Porn Makes You a Better Feminist," *Cosmopolitan*, March 18, 2019.

156 "Akin to climate change deniers": Carol Cadwalladr, "Editors of Sex Studies Journal Attacked for Promoting Porn," *Guardian*, June 15, 2013.

157 Peggy Orenstein: Peggy Orenstein, *Girls and Sex: Navigating the Complicated New Landscape* (New York: Harper, 2016), 34.

157 Bernadette Barton: Barton, *The Pornification of America*, 60.

157 dissonance between the messages Mattel sends: Erica Rand, *Barbie's Queer Accessories* (Durham, NC: Duke University Press, 1995).

160 "Together we are changing the rules of pornography": Erika Lust, "It's Time for Porn to Change," YouTube video, 12:55, TEDx Talks, December 3, 2014.

161 Feminist pornography is "hot": Bob Johnson, "The Power of Feminist Porn, What Retailers Need to Know," *XBIZ*, July 19, 2013.

161 "the people who are really ethical": Tracy Clark-Flory, "Is 'Feminist' Porn Getting Its #MeToo Moment?," Jezebel, September 20, 2018.

161 gender-neutral doll in 2019: Eliana Dockterman, "'A Doll for Everyone': Meet Mattel's Gender-Neutral Doll," *Time*, September 25, 2019.

161 resolved conflicts: "Joint Statement by Erika Lust Films & Hello Rooster," ErikaLust.com, June 12, 2021, https://erikalust.com/joint-statement.

162 "My politics and I are feminist": Stoya, "Feminism and Me," *Vice*, August 15, 2013.

162 Levy blames "raunch culture": Levy, *Female Chauvinist Pigs*.

163 In one of the largest surveys of sexual experience: Elizabeth A. Armstrong, Paula England, and Alison C. K. Fogarty, "Accounting for Women's Orgasm and Sexual Enjoyment in College Hookups and Relationships," *American Sociological Review* 77, no. 3 (2012): 446.

163 women are less sexually satisfied than men: Edward O. Laumann et al., *The Social Organization of Sexuality: Sexual Practices in the United States* (Chicago: University of Chicago Press, 2000); Laura M. Carpenter, Constance A. Nathanson, and Young J. Kim, "Physical Women, Emotional Men: Gender and Sexual Satisfaction in Midlife," *Archives of Sexual Behavior* 38, no. 1 (2009): 87–107.

163 Rates of self-reported rape and sexual assault: Jennifer Benner, "New Data— Sexual Assault Rates Doubled," National Sexual Violence Resource Center, October 10, 2019, https://www.nsvrc.org/blogs/new-data-sexual-assault -rates-doubled.

163 describing a "stalled revolution": Arlie Hochschild and Anne Machung, *The Second Shift: Working Families and the Revolution at Home* (New York: Penguin Books, 1989).

163 equal pay for equal work: Barroso and Brown, "Gender Pay Gap in U.S. Held Steady in 2020."

163 "to be imitating strippers and porn stars": Levy, *Female Chauvinist Pigs*, 27.

164 "[W]hat if you are a feminist who is pro-sex": Gail Dines, *Pornland: How Porn Has Hijacked Our Sexuality* (Boston: Beacon Press, 2010), x.

164 "But for some of us mainstream porn": Jane Ward, "Queer Feminist Pigs: A Spectator's Manifesta," in Taormino et al., *The Feminist Porn Book*, 130.

165 "sexual scripts": John Gagnon and William Simon, *Sexual Conduct: The Social Sources of Human Sexuality* (Chicago: Aldine, 1973).

PART III: THE BATTLE OVER WATCHING PORN

167 illicit literature was like a "deadly acid:" Giesberg, *Sex and the Civil War*, 12.

168 "crack babies of porn": Shmuley Boteach and Pamela Anderson, "Take the Pledge: No More Indulging Porn," *Wall Street Journal*, August 31, 2016.

CHAPTER 13: TO YOUR HEALTH

169 as he told the story: Matt Fradd and Noah Church, "26: Noah's Story of Recovering from Porn," audio podcast, *Love People Use Things*, May 28, 2018.

171 entrepreneurial possibilities: Executive Summary, *2020 ICF Global Coaching Study*, International Coaching Federation (ICF), https://coachingfederation .org/app/uploads/2020/09/FINAL_ICF_GCS2020_ExecutiveSummary .pdf.

171 "public health crisis": "Republican Platform 2016."

171 "public health hazard": Concurrent Resolution on the Public Health Crisis, S.C.R. 9, 61 Leg. 2016 Sess. (U.T. 2016).

171 "every warning it contained has come true": Pamela Atkinson, Orrin Hatch, and Todd Weiler, "We Must Work Together to Combat the Threat of Pornography," *Deseret News* (UT), August 7, 2016.

172 "address the pornography epidemic": U.T., S.C.R. 9.

172 National media covered the story: Corky Siemaszko, "Utah State Sen. Todd Weiler: Porn Is a Public Health Crisis," NBC News, February 9, 2016; Camila Domonoske, "Utah Declares Porn a Public Health Hazard," *The Two-Way*, NPR, April 20, 2016; Liam Stack, "Utah's War on Pornography Finds Skeptics," *New York Times*, April 21, 2016.

172 "unsolicited moral, religious, and political values": Matt Canham, "Penthouse Goes After Utah Governor, Mormon Church on Anti-porn Resolution— Anti-porn Pushback: Utah's Governor Makes the Publication's Cover— Without His Picture," *Salt Lake Tribune* (UT), August 3, 2016.

172 sending complimentary copies of *Hustler* magazine: Robert Gehrke, "Hustler Magazine Hits the Mailboxes of Utah Lawmakers," *Salt Lake Tribune* (UT), June 7, 2016.

172 based on a model drafted by leaders of NCOSE: No state resolution explicitly references NCOSE. As of 2018, NCOSE published its "model resolution" on its website but has since removed it.

172 nearly identical resolutions: Burke and MillerMacPhee, "Constructing Pornography Addiction's Harms."

172 It passed in Montana's legislature: Resolution on The Public Health Crisis of Pornography, H.R. 0005, 66th Legislature (M.T. 2019).

173 "The science is there": Gail Dines, "Is Porn Immoral? That Doesn't Matter: It's a Public Health Crisis," *Washington Post*, April 8, 2016.

173 Schlafly used the language of addiction: Wisenberg, "There She Is, Miss America."

173 critics have accused the organization: Samantha Allen, "'Porn Kills Love':
Mormons' Anti-Smut Crusade," The Daily Beast, April 13, 2017.

175 surveys consistently reveal a negative relationship: Samuel L. Perry,
"Pornography and Relationship Quality: Establishing the Dominant
Pattern by Examining Pornography Use and 31 Measures of Relationship
Quality in 30 National Surveys," Archives of Sexual Behavior 49, no. 4 (2020):
1199–213.

175 negative effects are the result of masturbation: Samuel L. Perry, "Is the Link
Between Pornography Use and Relational Happiness Really More About
Masturbation? Results from Two National Surveys," Journal of Sex Research
57, no. 1 (2020): 64–76.

176 married women who watch porn: Ana J. Bridges and Patricia J. Morokoff,
"Sexual Media Use and Relational Satisfaction in Heterosexual Couples,"
Personal Relationships 18, no. 4 (2011): 562–85; Cameron C. Brown et al., "A
Common-Fate Analysis of Pornography Acceptance, Use, and Sexual
Satisfaction Among Heterosexual Married Couples," Archives of Sexual
Behavior 46, no. 2 (2017): 575–84.

176 boys and men look at porn more frequently: Janis Wolak, Kimberly Mitchell,
and David Finkelhor, "Unwanted and Wanted Exposure to Online
Pornography in a National Sample of Youth Internet Users," Pediatrics 119,
no. 2 (2007): 247–57; Jason S. Carroll et al., "The Porn Gap: Differences in
Men's and Women's Pornography Patterns in Couple Relationships," Journal
of Couple and Relationship Therapy 16, no. 2 (2017): 146–63.

176 likelihood to commit acts of violence: Elizabeth Cramer et al., "Violent
Pornography and Abuse of Women: Theory to Practice," Violence and Victims
13, no. 4 (1998): 319–32; Gert Martin Hald, Neil M. Malamuth, and Carlin
Yuen, "Pornography and Attitudes Supporting Violence Against Women:
Revisiting the Relationship in Nonexperimental Studies," Aggressive Behavior:
Official Journal of the International Society for Research on Aggression 36, no. 1
(2010): 14–20.

176 correlation, not causation: Emily F. Rothman, Pornography and Public Health
(New York: Oxford University Press, 2021), 72–75.

176 exhibited antiwoman attitudes: John D. Foubert and Ana J. Bridges,
"Predicting Bystander Efficacy and Willingness to Intervene in College Men
and Women: The Role of Exposure to Varying Levels of Violence in
Pornography," Violence Against Women 23, no. 6 (2017): 692–706.

176 men who watch porn have more feminist views: Taylor Kohut, Jodie L. Baer,
and Brendan Watts, "Is Pornography Really About 'Making Hate to

Women'? Pornography Users Hold More Gender Egalitarian Attitudes than Nonusers in a Representative American Sample," *Journal of Sex Research* 53, no. 1 (2016): 1–11.

176   problem of acquiescence: Eric S. Knowles and Christopher A. Condon, "Why People Say 'Yes': A Dual-Process Theory of Acquiescence," *Journal of Personality and Social Psychology* 77, no. 2 (1999): 379.

176   discover potential benefits of porn use: Ilisha M. French and Lisa Dawn Hamilton, "Male-centric and Female-centric Pornography Consumption: Relationship with Sex Life and Attitudes in Young Adults," *Journal of Sex and Marital Therapy* 44, no. 1 (2018): 73–86; Gert Martin Hald, Derek Smolenski, and B. R. Simon Rosser, "Perceived Effects of Sexually Explicit Media Among Men Who Have Sex with Men and Psychometric Properties of the Pornography Consumption Effects Scale (PCES)," *Journal of Sexual Medicine* 10, no. 3 (2013): 757–67; Ingela Lundin Kvalem, Bente Træen, and Alex Iantaffi, "Internet Pornography Use, Body Ideals, and Sexual Self-Esteem in Norwegian Gay and Bisexual Men," *Journal of Homosexuality* 63, no. 4 (2016): 522–40.

176   General Social Survey: Smith, Hout, and Marsden, General Social Survey.

178   refining the scale: Joshua B. Grubbs et al., "The Cyber-Pornography Use Inventory: The Development of a New Assessment Instrument," *Sexual Addiction and Compulsivity* 17, no. 2 (2010): 106–26.

178   people who *perceived* themselves to be addicted: Joshua B. Grubbs, Shane W. Kraus, and Samuel L. Perry, "Self-Reported Addiction to Pornography in a Nationally Representative Sample: The Roles of Use Habits, Religiousness, and Moral Incongruence," *Journal of Behavioral Addictions* 8, no. 1 (2019): 88–93.

178   "moral incongruence": Samuel Perry, *Addicted to Lust: Pornography in the Lives of Conservative Protestants* (Oxford, UK: Oxford University Press, 2019).

178   experience depression associated with their porn use: Samuel L. Perry, "Pornography Use and Depressive Symptoms: Examining the Role of Moral Incongruence," *Society and Mental Health* 8, no. 3 (2018): 195–213.

179   TEDx Talk, "The Great Porn Experiment": Gary Wilson, "The Great Porn Experiment," filmed May 2012, video, TEDxGlasgow, 16:28.

179   receives nearly four hundred thousand visitors each month: Gary Wilson v. Privacy Inc. Customer 0154207478 / Daniel Burgess, Family Life Services / Dr. Nicole Prause, Liberos LLC, Case No. D2019-1544, World Intellectual Property Organization Arbitration and Mediation Center, Geneva, Switzerland, 2019.

179 Wilson insisted he was not antiporn: "About Us," Your Brain on Porn, https://www.yourbrainonporn.com/about/about-us/.

179 11,000 web pages: Donald L. Hilton Jr. v. Nicole Prause and Liberos LLC, 5:19-cv-00755-OLG (W.D. Tex. 2019).

179 Wilson authored two academic articles: Gary Wilson, "Eliminate Chronic Internet Pornography Use to Reveal Its Effects," *Addicta: The Turkish Journal on Addictions* 3, no. 2 (2016): 209–21; Brian Y. Park et al., "Is Internet Pornography Causing Sexual Dysfunctions? A Review with Clinical Reports," *Behavioral Sciences* 6, no. 3 (2016): 17.

179 national antipornography organization: "Your Brain on Porn: Gary Wilson's Online Guide to the Latest Science & Research," Fight the New Drug, March 29, 2018, https://fightthenewdrug.org/your-brain-on-porn-gary-wilsons-porn-fighting-ba-website-working/.

180 a "knowledge society": Karin Knorr Cetina, *Epistemic Cultures: How the Sciences Make Knowledge* (Cambridge, MA: Harvard University Press, 1999).

180 on the fringe of established science: Tom Waidzunas, *The Straight Line: How the Fringe Science of Ex-Gay Therapy Reoriented Sexuality* (Minneapolis: University of Minnesota Press, 2015).

180 parents who refuse to vaccinate: Jennifer A. Reich, *Calling the Shots: Why Parents Reject Vaccines* (New York: New York University Press, 2018).

180 science is always *sciences*: Donna Haraway, "The Biopolitics of Postmodern Bodies: Determinations of Self in Immune System Discourse," in Janet Price and Margrit Shildrick, eds., *Feminist Theory and the Body: A Reader* (New York: Routledge, 1999), 204.

180 Rhodes told the *New York Times*: Sridhar Pappu, "Internet Porn Nearly Ruined His Life. Now He Wants to Help," *New York Times*, July 6, 2016.

182 calls "healthism": Robert Crawford, "Healthism and the Medicalization of Everyday Life," *International Journal of Health Services* 10, no. 3 (1980): 365–88.

CHAPTER 14: IN RECOVERY

183 sheer magnitude of recovery culture: Trysh Travis, *The Language of the Heart: A Cultural History of the Recovery Movement from Alcoholics Anonymous to Oprah Winfrey* (Chapel Hill: University of North Carolina Press, 2010).

183 groups that used the AA model: Travis, *The Language of the Heart*, 56.

183   Sex and Love Addicts Anonymous: Janice M. Irvine, *Disorders of Desire: Sex and Gender in Modern American Sexology* (Philadelphia: Temple University Press, 2005), 166.

184   addiction not as a moral failing: Travis, *The Language of the Heart*; Scott Vrecko, "Birth of a Brain Disease: Science, the State and Addiction Neuropolitics," *History of the Human Sciences* 23, no. 4 (2010): 52–67.

184   graduate student in counseling education: Patrick James Carnes, "Educating Interactionally Impaired Adults: An Analysis of Curriculum Impact on Family Environment" (Ph.D. diss., University of Minnesota, 1980).

184   rerelease the book with a different title: Patrick J. Carnes, *Out of the Shadows: Understanding Sexual Addiction*, 3rd ed. (Center City, MN: Hazelden, 2001).

184   the "SAFE" formula: Carnes, *Out of the Shadows*, 189.

184   pornography as one of the many behaviors: Carnes, *Out of the Shadows*, 65–68.

185   New York tournament for Atari's *Space Invaders*: Dudley Clendinen, "4,000 Line Up to Join Battle Against Electronic Invader," *New York Times*, June 30, 1981.

185   founded On-Line Gamers Anonymous: Martha Irvine, "A Troubled Gaming Addict Takes His Life," Associated Press, May 22, 2002.

185   internet pornography addiction emerged: Madita Oeming, "A New Diagnosis for Old Fears? Pathologizing Porn in Contemporary US Discourse," *Porn Studies* 5, no. 2 (2018): 213–16; Jamie Stoops, "Just Like Heroin: Science, Pornography, and Heteronormativity in the Virtual Public Sphere," *Porn Studies* 4, no. 4 (2017): 364–80.

185   Pornhub's own boastful statistics: "The 2019 Year in Review," Pornhub Insights, Pornhub, December 11, 2019, https://www.pornhub.com/insights /2019-year-in-review.

189   earnings of over $26 million: Independent NewsGroup, "Covenant Eyes Again Named One of America's Fastest Growing Private Companies," *Independent Newsgroup* (MI), August 17, 2020.

189   CEO of Covenant Eyes: Greyson Steele, "Accountable to Themselves," *Argus-Press* (MI), June 21, 2020.

189   "I did not have anything left": Independent NewsGroup, "Covenant Eyes Again Named."

189   fastest-growing private companies: "Introducing the *Inc.* 5000 Fastest-Growing Private Companies in America," *Inc.*, 2021, https://www.inc.com/inc5000/2021.

189   staff of more than two hundred: Steele, "Accountable to Themselves."

190   Pastor Gross publicly debated: "Yale Student: 'I'm Here 'Cause I Love Porn': Porn Stars and Porn Preachers Engage in Fiery 'Face-Off' During Sex Week," ABC News, February 5, 2008.

191 Evangelicals are "cultural innovators": Shayne Lee and Phillip Luke Sinitiere, *Holy Mavericks: Evangelical Innovators and the Spiritual Marketplace* (New York: New York University Press, 2009).

191 Sociologist Jeremy Thomas: Jeremy N. Thomas, "Outsourcing Moral Authority: The Internal Secularization of Evangelicals' Anti-Pornography Narratives," *Journal for the Scientific Study of Religion* 52, no. 3 (2013): 457–75.

192 Sex scandals involving televangelists: Richard N. Ostling, "Jim Bakker's Crumbling World," *Time*, December 19, 1988.

192 a shift from offense to defense: Perry, *Addicted to Lust*, 36.

192 watch less porn than their nonevangelical counterparts: Joshua B. Grubbs, Justin Tosi, and Brandon Warmke, *Status Seeking and Public Discourse Ethics: A Nationally Representative Sample with Longitudinal Follow-up*, distributed by Open Science Framework, updated April 4, 2021),

192 religious commitment is a better predictor: Joshua B. Grubbs and Samuel L. Perry, "Moral Incongruence and Pornography Use: A Critical Review and Integration," *Journal of Sex Research* 56, no. 1 (2019): 29–37.

193 "assertion that sex is 'natural'": Irvine, *Disorders of Desire*, 88.

193 multitude of "sexual dysfunctions": Irvine, *Disorders of Desire*, 167.

193 Gentle Path at the Meadows: "Amid Harvey Weinstein, Kevin Spacey Scandals, Founder of Sex Rehab Center Defends Program," *CBS This Morning*, CBS, November 13, 2017.

194 *The Myth of Sex Addiction*: David J. Ley, *The Myth of Sex Addiction* (Lanham, MD: Rowman and Littlefield, 2012).

196 The man who murdered: Similar commentary appeared in Kelsy Burke, "The Dark Tales of the Christian Sex Addiction Industry," *Slate*, March 23, 2021.

196 According to police accounts: Richard Fausset, "Suspect in Atlanta-Area Spa Shootings Pleads Guilty to 4 Counts of Murder: Robert Aaron Long Also Faces Four Murder Charges in a Neighboring County, Where the Prosecutor Is Seeking the Death Penalty," *New York Times*, July 27, 2021.

196 remove "temptation": Nicholas Bogel-Burroughs, "The Suspect Had Sought Treatment for Sex Addiction, a Former Roommate Says," *New York Times*, March 18, 2021.

197 white nationalist groups: Jessica Warner, *All or Nothing: A Short History of Abstinence in America* (Toronto, Ontario: McClelland and Stewart, 2008).

197 Rhodes argued: Alexander Rhodes v. Nicole Prause and Liberos LLC (W.D. PA 2019).

197 self-described chauvinists: "Proud Boys," Southern Poverty Law Center, https://www.splcenter.org/fighting-hate/extremist-files/group/proud-boys.

198 Twitter accounts that use the NoFap hashtag: Scott Burnett, "The Battle for 'NoFap': Myths, Masculinity, and the Meaning of Masturbation Abstention," *Men and Masculinities*, 2021, https://doi.org/10.1177/1097184X211018256.

198 one survey of more than a thousand users: Felix Zimmer and Roland Imhoff, "Abstinence from Masturbation and Hypersexuality," *Archives of Sexual Behavior* 49, no. 4 (2020): 1333–43.

198 Protestant beliefs about sex: Janet Jakobsen and Ann Pellegrini, *Love the Sin: Sexual Regulation and the Limits of Religious Tolerance* (New York: New York University Press, 2003).

198 exalt heterosexuality, marriage, monogamy: Burke, *Christians under Covers.*

CHAPTER 15: BRAIN BATTLES

199 filed a ten-million-dollar lawsuit against Prause: Donald L. Hilton Jr. v. Nicole Prause and Liberos LLC (W.D. Tex. 2019).

201 expert on sexual harassment laws: Jacob Sullum, "Prominent Pornography Researcher Frames Defamation Claims as Sexual Harassment, Prompting a Defamation Suit by Her Target," *Reason*, July 3, 2019.

201 immoral and perverse sexologists: "Nicole Prause's Unethical Harassment and Defamation of Gary Wilson & Others," Your Brain on Porn, https://www .yourbrainonporn.com/relevant-research-and-articles-about-the-studies /critiques-of-questionable-debunking-propaganda-pieces/nicole-prauses -unethical-harassment-and-defamation-of-gary-wilson-others/.

201 data came from adult respondents: Joseph E. Davis, *Accounts of Innocence: Sexual Abuse, Trauma, and the Self* (Chicago: University of Chicago Press, 2005), 25–55.

201 Rex King: Caleb Crain, "Alfred Kinsey: Liberator or Pervert?," *New York Times*, October 3, 2004.

201 Kinsey remains a vilified figured: Daniel Radosh, "Why Know?," *New Yorker*, November 28, 2004.

202 According to Hilton's lawsuit: Donald L. Hilton Jr. v. Nicole Prause and Liberos LLC.

202 mentioned the phrase "pornography addiction": Burke and MillerMacPhee, "Constructing Pornography Addiction's Harms."

202 I kept hearing about one research study in particular: Nikolaas Tinbergen, "Social Releasers and the Experimental Method Required for Their Study," *Wilson Bulletin* 60, no. 1 (1948): 6–51.

203 "the enhanced novelty (internet porn) provides": Donald L. Hilton Jr., "Pornography Addiction a Supranormal Stimulus Considered in the Context of Neuroplasticity," *Socioaffective Neuroscience and Psychology* 3, no. 1 (2013): 20767.

203 even of listening to our favorite music: Line Gebauer, Morten L. Kringelbach, and Peter Vuust, "Ever-Changing Cycles of Musical Pleasure: The Role of Dopamine and Anticipation," *Psychomusicology: Music, Mind, and Brain* 22, no. 2 (2012): 152.

203 anticipate and experience pleasure: Kent C. Berridge and Morten L. Kringelbach, "Pleasure Systems in the Brain," *Neuron* 86, no. 3 (2015): 646–64.

204 "a dopaminergic reward": Donald L. Hilton Jr., Stefanie Carnes, and Todd L. Love, "The Neurobiology of Behavioral Addictions: Sex Addiction," in Alan C. Swann, F. Gerard Moeller, and Marijn Lijffijt, eds., *Neurobiology of Addictions* (Oxford, UK: Oxford University Press, 2016), 182.

204 "a powerful neuroplastic response": Hilton, Carnes, and Love, "The Neurobiology of Behavioral Addictions," 183.

204 distinct "addiction cycle": Nora D. Volkow, George F. Koob, and A. Thomas McLellan, "Neurobiologic Advances from the Brain Disease Model of Addiction," *New England Journal of Medicine* 374, no. 4 (2016): 363–71.

204 addiction cycle to compulsive sexual behavior: Todd Love et al., "Neuroscience of Internet Pornography Addiction: A Review and Update," *Behavioral Sciences* 5, no. 3 (2015): 388–433.

204 use brain scans to compare respondents: Matthias Brand et al., "Ventral Striatum Activity When Watching Preferred Pornographic Pictures Is Correlated with Symptoms of Internet Pornography Addiction," *Neuroimage* 129 (2016): 224–32; Mateusz Gola et al., "Can Pornography Be Addictive? An fMRI Study of Men Seeking Treatment for Problematic Pornography Use," *Neuropsychopharmacology* 42, no. 10 (2017): 2021–31; Simone Kühn and Jürgen Gallinat, "Brain Structure and Functional Connectivity Associated with Pornography Consumption: The Brain on Porn," *JAMA Psychiatry* 71, no. 7 (2014): 827–34; Pukovisa Prawiroharjo et al., "Impaired Recent Verbal Memory in Pornography-Addicted Juvenile Subjects," *Neurology Research International* (2019): 1–5.

204 CSB respondents react more strongly: Paula Banca et al., "Novelty, Conditioning and Attentional Bias to Sexual Rewards," *Journal of Psychiatric Research* 72 (2016): 91–101.

204 evidence of habituation: Kühn and Gallinat, "Brain Structure and Functional Connectivity."

204 examined withdrawal and negative effects: Rudolf Stark and Tim Klucken, "Neuroscientific Approaches to (Online) Pornography Addiction," in Christian Montag and Martin Reuterpp, eds., *Internet Addiction: Neuroscientific Approaches and Therapeutical Implications Including Smartphone Addiction* (Cham, Switzerland: Springer, 2017), 109–24; Valerie Voon et al., "Neural Correlates of Sexual Cue Reactivity in Individuals with and Without Compulsive Sexual Behaviours," *PLOS One* 9, no. 7 (2014): e102419.

204 *He Restoreth My Soul*: Donald L. Hilton Jr., *He Restoreth My Soul: Understanding and Breaking the Chemical and Spiritual Chains of Pornography through the Atonement of Jesus Christ* (San Antonio, TX: Forward Press, 2009).

205 Hilton quotes Mormon elder Bruce Hafen: Elder Bruce C. Hafen, "The Atonement: All for All," Ensign of the Church of Jesus Christ of Latter-day Saints, May 2004, https://www.churchofjesuschrist.org/study/general -conference/2004/04/the-atonement-all-for-all?lang=eng.

206 addiction science was a marginal field: Scott Vrecko, "Birth of a Brain Disease: Science, the State and Addiction Neuropolitics," *History of the Human Sciences* 23, no. 4 (2010): 52–67.

206 psychedelics like LSD: Matthias E. Liechti, "Modern Clinical Research on LSD," *Neuropsychopharmacology* 42, no. 11 (2017): 2114–27.

206 coined the "neurochemical self": Nikolas Rose, *The Politics of Life Itself: Biomedicine, Power and Subjectivity in the Twenty-first Century* (Princeton, NJ: Princeton University Press, 2007).

206 revealed the brain as the center: Eric Vance, "The Drugs Inside Your Head," interview by Krista Tippet, audio podcast, *On Being with Krista Tippet*, September 19, 2019.

207 "fundamental role that your brain has": Vance, "The Drugs Inside Your Head."

207 discovery of "brain plasticity": Bryan Kolb and Ian Q. Whishaw, "Brain Plasticity and Behavior," *Annual Review of Psychology* 49, no. 1 (1998): 43–64.

207 activates the brain's dopamine system: Kent C. Berridge and Terry E. Robinson, "Liking, Wanting, and the Incentive-Sensitization Theory of Addiction," *American Psychologist* 71, no. 8 (2016): 670–79.

207 Rats have been used in scientific experiments: Sam Schipani, "The History of the Lab Rat Is Full of Scientific Triumphs and Ethical Quandaries," *Smithsonian Magazine*, February 27, 2019.

208 tested the effects of cocaine on rats: Suzanne H. Gage and Harry R. Sumnall, "Rat Park: How a Rat Paradise Changed the Narrative of Addiction," *Addiction* 114, no. 5 (2019): 917–22.

208 an estimated 22 million adult Americans: Volkow, Koob, and McLellan, "Neurobiologic Advances."

208 positive social environments: James McIntosh and Neil McKeganey, "Addicts' Narratives of Recovery from Drug Use: Constructing a Non-Addict Identity," *Social Science and Medicine* 50, no. 10 (2000): 1501–10.

208 One interview study emphasized employment: Paul Duffy and Helen Baldwin, "Recovery Post Treatment: Plans, Barriers and Motivators," *Substance Abuse Treatment Prevention Policy* 8, no. 6 (2013): 1–12.

208 a series called Rat Park: Gage and Sumnall, "Rat Park."

208 skewed by a "couch potato effect": Schipani, "The History of the Lab Rat."

209 stimulate the dopamine system: Berridge and Robinson, "Liking, Wanting, and the Incentive-Sensitization Theory of Addiction."

209 words of medical sociologist: Jules Netherland, "'We Haven't Sliced Open Anyone's Brain Yet': Neuroscience, Embodiment and the Governance of Addiction," in Martyn Pickersgill and Ira Van Keulen, eds., *Sociological Reflections on the Neurosciences* (Bingley, UK: Emerald Group, 2011), 153–57.

209 an increase of over 800 percent: Netherland, "'We Haven't Sliced Open Anyone's Brain Yet,'" 154.

209 "have to tell morality from non-morality": Gabriel Abend, "What Are Neural Correlates Neural Correlates Of?," *BioSocieties* 12, no. 3 (2017): 416.

209 no evidence that pornography: Rory C. Reid, Bruce N. Carpenter, and Timothy W. Fong, "Neuroscience Research Fails to Support Claims that Excessive Pornography Consumption Causes Brain Damage," *Surgical Neurology International* 2 (2011); Gilles N. Stormezand et al., "No Evidence for Decreased D2/3 Receptor Availability and Frontal Hypoperfusion in Subjects with Compulsive Pornography Use," *Psychiatry Research: Neuroimaging* 311 (2021): 111284.

210 people have differing sex drives: Vaughn R. Steele et al., "Sexual Desire, Not Hypersexuality, Is Related to Neurophysiological Responses Elicited by Sexual Images," *Socioaffective Neuroscience and Psychology* 3, no. 1 (2013): 20770.

210 viewing pornography triggers: Serge Stoléru et al., "Functional Neuroimaging Studies of Sexual Arousal and Orgasm in Healthy Men and Women: A Review and Meta-analysis," *Neuroscience and Biobehavioral Reviews* 36, no. 6 (2012): 1481–509.

210 problematic pornography use: Meghan E. Maddock et al., "What Is the Relationship Among Religiosity, Self-perceived Problematic Pornography Use, and Depression over Time?," *Sexual Addiction and Compulsivity* 26, no. 3–4 (2019): 211–38; Perry, "Pornography Use and Depressive Symptoms."

210 treat pornography itself: Mateusz Gola et al., "Visual Sexual Stimuli—Cue or Reward? A Perspective for Interpreting Brain Imaging Findings on Human Sexual Behaviors," *Frontiers in Human Neuroscience* 10 (2016): 402.

211 a series of negative outcomes: Voon et al., "Neural Correlates," 4.

211 based on a national survey: Janna A. Dickenson et al., "Prevalence of Distress Associated with Difficulty Controlling Sexual Urges, Feelings, and Behaviors in the United States," *JAMA Network Open* 1, no. 7 (2018): 1–10.

212 Prause's name has appeared: Gary Wilson v. Privacy Inc. Customer 0154207478.

213 WIPO sided with Prause: Gary Wilson v. Privacy Inc. Customer 0154207478.

213 A spokesperson for xHamster: Samantha Cole, "Let This Be the Last No Nut November," *Vice*, November 30, 2018.

214 Rhodes filed a similar lawsuit: Alexander Rhodes v. Nicole Prause and Liberos LLC.

214 "The world is not a solid continent of facts": Bruno Latour, *Reassembling the Social: An Introduction to Actor-Network Theory* (Oxford, UK: Oxford University Press, 2005), 245.

CHAPTER 16: OPPOSITE SEXES

216 Historian Margaret Thickstun argues: Margaret Olofson Thickstun, *Fictions of the Feminine: Puritan Doctrine and the Representation of Women* (Ithaca, NY: Cornell University Press, 1988).

217 "passionlessness": Nancy F. Cott, "Passionlessness: An Interpretation of Victorian Sexual Ideology, 1790–1850," *Signs: Journal of Women in Culture and Society* 4, no. 2 (1978): 219–36.

217   Men and Religion Forward Movement: Gail Bederman, "'The Women Have Had Charge of the Church Work Long Enough': The Men and Religion Forward Movement of 1911–1912 and the Masculinization of Middle-Class Protestantism," *American Quarterly* 41, no. 3 (1989): 432–65.

217   gendered nature of conservative evangelicalism: Margaret Lamberts Bendroth, *Fundamentalism and Gender: 1875 to the Present* (New Haven, CT: Yale University Press, 1993).

218   *Introduction to Psychology* textbook: Richard A. Griggs, "Coverage of the Stanford Prison Experiment in Introductory Psychology Textbooks," *Teaching of Psychology* 41, no. 3 (2014): 195–203.

218   tactics of coercion, degradation, and humiliation: Claudia Dreifus, "Finding Hope in Knowing the Universal Capacity for Evil," *New York Times*, April 3, 2007.

218   convinced him to call off the experiment: Kathleen O'Toole, "The Stanford Prison Experiment: Still Powerful After All These Years," *Stanford News*, January 8, 1997.

218   "guys aren't interested in maintaining": Philip Zimbardo, "The Demise of Guys: In Record Numbers, Guys Are Flaming Out," *Psychology Today*, May 23, 2012.

218   "what it means to be male": Nikita Coulombe and Philip Zimbardo, *Man Disconnected: How Technology Has Sabotaged What It Means to Be Male* (London: Rider, 2015).

218   in his book *Cheap Sex*: Mark Regnerus, *Cheap Sex: The Transformation of Men, Marriage, and Monogamy* (Oxford, UK: Oxford University Press, 2017).

218   children of straight married parents: Mark Regnerus, "How Different Are the Adult Children of Parents Who Have Same-Sex Relationships? Findings from the New Family Structures Study," *Social Science Research* 41, no. 4 (2012): 752–70.

219   supporting same-sex marriage: Brief for the American Sociological Association as Amicus Curiae, i–28, Obergefell v. Hodges, 576 U.S. 644 (2015); Brief for the American Psychological Association as Amicus Curiae, iii–33, Obergefell v. Hodges, 576 U.S. 644 (2015).

219   "the cheapest sex": Regnerus, *Cheap Sex*, 107.

219   "is rooted in stable realities": Regnerus, *Cheap Sex*, 44.

219   "Male brains separate sex and romance": Philip Zimbardo and Nikita D. Coulombe, *Man, Interrupted: Why Young Men are Struggling and What We Can Do About It* (Newburyport, MA: Conari Press, 2016), xx.

219   coined the term *neurosexism*: Cordelia Fine, *Delusions of Gender: How Our Minds, Society, and Neurosexism Create Difference* (New York: W. W. Norton, 2010).

219 Fine debunks the research: Cordelia Fine, *Testosterone Rex: Myths of Sex, Science, and Society* (New York: W. W. Norton, 2017), 29.

220 how men's and women's brains are wired: Cliodhna O'Connor and Helene Joffe, "Gender on the Brain: A Case Study of Science Communication in the New Media Environment," *PLOS One* 9, no. 10 (2014): e110830.

220 "none could be described as fully male or female": Gina Rippon, "How 'Neurosexism' Is Holding Back Gender Equality—and Science Itself," *The Conversation*, October 27, 2016.

220 "Brains reflect the lives that they have lived": Gina Rippon, *Gender and Our Brains: How New Neuroscience Explodes the Myths of the Male and Female Minds* (New York: Pantheon Books, 2019), xvi.

220 "simply not participating in the same experiment": Barbara J. King, "The Science of Gender: No, Men Aren't From Mars and Women from Venus," Cosmos & Culture, NPR, January 26, 2017.

220–21 insists that his critique of porn: Regnerus, *Cheap Sex*, 6.

221 more plausible explanations: Paula England, "Book Review: 'Cheap Sex': The Transformation of Men, Marriage, and Monogamy," *Men and Masculinities* 20, no. 1 (2018): 152–54.

221 "there's no convincing evidence to suggest": Barbara J. King, "Book Review: Cheap Sex: The Transformation of Men, Marriage, and Monogamy," *Men and Masculinities* 21, no. 1 (2018): 154–56.

222 "God's superglue": Stacy Schiff, "Sex and the Single-Minded," *New York Times*, January 20, 2007.

222 prohibit attachments later in life: Alliant International University, "Dr. Rebecca Turner Issues Statement Rebutting 'Pseudoscience,'" Newswise, November 20, 200, https://www.newswise.com/articles/dr-rebecca-turner-issues-statement-rebutting-pseudoscience.

222 wide range of relational contexts: Nicole M. Else-Quest, Janet Shibley Hyde, and Roseanne Clark, "Breastfeeding, Bonding, and the Mother-Infant Relationship," *Merrill-Palmer Quarterly* 49, no. 4 (2003): 495–517; Suzanne C. Miller et al., "An Examination of Changes in Oxytocin Levels in Men and Women Before and After Interaction with a Bonded Dog," *Anthrozoös* 22, no. 1 (2009): 31–42.

222 men's brains are "wired": Portions of this chapter presenting interview data and analysis of religious participants in pornography addiction recovery groups were previously published in Kelsy Burke and Trenton M. Haltom, "Created by God and Wired to Porn: Redemptive Masculinity and Gender Beliefs in Narratives of Religious Men's Pornography Addiction Recovery,"

Gender and Society 34, no. 2 (2020): 233–58. Similar commentary appeared in Kelsy Burke, "Sinning Like a Man: The Christian Porn Addiction Industry is Selling a Lucrative, Dangerous Idea," *Slate*, May 18, 2020.

222 garnered sympathy and understanding: Perry, *Addicted to Lust*, 115.

224 "podcast bros": Molly Worthen, "The Podcast Bros Want to Optimize Your Life: Don't Dismiss Them as Hucksters Promoting Self-help Books and Dubious Mushroom Coffee," *New York Times*, August 3, 2018.

224 preface to *The Mask of Masculinity*: Lewis Howes, *The Mask of Masculinity: How Men Can Embrace Vulnerability, Create Strong Relationships, and Live Their Fullest Lives* (Emmaus, PA: Rodale, 2017), xvi.

224 Howes interviewed Terry Crews: Lewis Howes, "Ep. 760: Terry Crews—Success, Accountability, and Toxic Masculinity," audio podcast, *Lewis Howes*, February 18, 2019.

226 "sinning against their gender": Perry, *Addicted to Lust*, 90.

226 "I thought I was the only one": Anne Jackson, foreword to Crystal Renaud, *Dirty Girls Come Clean* (Chicago: Moody, 2011), 9.

226 "exposed my heart, my mind, and my body": Renaud, *Dirty Girls Come Clean*, 23.

227 "emotional trauma": Renaud, *Dirty Girls Come Clean*, 23.

227 "meets her emotional needs": Renaud, *Dirty Girls Come Clean*, 26.

229 "white racial project": Howard Winant, *The New Politics of Race: Globalism, Difference, Justice* (Minneapolis: University of Minnesota Press, 2004), 55.

229 men watch porn more often: Grubbs, Tosi, and Warmke, *Status Seeking and Public Discourse Ethics*.

229 pornography's gendered audience: Steve Garlick, "Taking Control of Sex? Hegemonic Masculinity, Technology, and Internet Pornography," *Men and Masculinities* 12, no. 5 (2010): 597–614.

229 Christian pornography addiction recovery: Burke and Haltom, "Created by God and Wired to Porn."

CHAPTER 17: PROTECT THE CHILDREN

231 Mary Ware Dennett's: Craig, "'The Sex Side of Life.'"

231 solving society's sexual problems: Luker, *When Sex Goes to School*, 39–44.

232 Between the 1960s and '80s: Luker, *When Sex Goes to School*, 66.

232 dissemination of the birth control pill: Luker, *When Sex Goes to School*, 74–75.

232 the Supreme Court ruled: Griswold v. Connecticut, 381 U.S. 479 (1965); Eisenstadt v. Baird, 405 U.S. 438 (1972).

232 "caring" and "nonexploitative": Luker, *When Sex Goes to School*, 86.

232 two broad branches of sex education: Pamela K. Kohler, Lisa E. Manhart, and William E. Lafferty, "Abstinence-Only and Comprehensive Sex Education and the Initiation of Sexual Activity and Teen Pregnancy," *Journal of Adolescent Health* 42, no. 4 (2008): 345.

232 Both approaches have taken credit: Luker, *When Sex Goes to School*, 26.

232 Today in America: Gladys Martinez, Joyce Abma, and Casey Copen, "Educating Teenagers about Sex in the United States," *NCHS Data Brief* No. 44, National Center for Health Statistics, Hyattsville, MD, 2010.

232 states have passed laws: "SIECUS State Profiles: Sex Ed State Law and Policy Chart," SIECUS: Sex Ed for Social Change, https://siecus.org/wp-content/uploads/2020/03/SIECUS-2019-Sex-Ed-State-Law-and-Policy-Chart-Final.pdf.

233 "chastity and self-discipline": Rebekah Saul, "Whatever Happened to the Adolescent Family Life Act?," *Guttmacher Report on Public Policy* 1, no. 2 (1998): 5–10.

233 "sexual risk avoidance": Jesseca Boyer, "New Name, Same Harm: Rebranding of Federal Abstinence-Only Programs," *Guttmacher Policy Review* 21, no. 6 (2018): 11–16.

233 secondary school health teachers: David J. Landry et al., "Factors Associated with the Content of Sex Education in US Public Secondary Schools," *Perspectives on Sexual and Reproductive Health* 35, no. 6 (2003): 261–62.

234 no state requires specific credentials: Marla E. Eisenberg et al., "'Am I Qualified? How Do I Know?' A Qualitative Study of Sexuality Educators' Training Experiences," *American Journal of Health Education* 41, no. 6 (2010): 337–44.

234 1,100 professionals have completed the certification: "About Us: Our History," American Association of Sexuality Educators, Counselors, and Therapists (AASECT), https://www.aasect.org/about-us.

234 "it will teach them things they never thought of": "My Children Shall Not Read It—It Will Teach Them Things They Never Thought Of," *Illuminator* (Boston), August 31, 1836, 162.

234 "albeit without much evidence": Strub, *Obscenity Rules*, 118–19.

235 (WAP) conflated pornography's harm: Gillian Frank, "Save Our Children: The Sexual Politics of Child Protection in the United States, 1965–1990" (Ph.D. diss., Brown University, 2008).

235 Newspaper and magazine article titles: Burke and MillerMacPhee, "Constructing Pornography Addiction's Harms."

235   "the narrative inevitability of a normative adulthood": Gabrielle Owen, *A Queer History of Adolescence: Developmental Pasts, Relational Futures* (Athens: University of Georgia Press, 2020), 3–6.

235   "not nurtured but enforced": James Kincaid, *Child-Loving: The Erotic Child and Victorian Culture* (New York: Routledge, 1992), 73.

235   are first exposed to online porn: Rothman, *Pornography and Public Health*, 131.

235   younger than decades past: W. Cody Wilson and Herbert I. Abelson, "'Experience with and Attitudes toward Explicit Sexual Material," *Journal of Social Issues* 29, no. 3 (1973): 19–39.

236   Defend Young Minds: Similar commentary throughout this chapter was published in Kelsy Burke, "Billie Eilish's Brain on Porn," *Slate*, December 17, 2021.

236   For young children: Kristen A. Jenson, *Good Pictures Bad Pictures, Jr.: A Simple Plan to Protect Young Minds* (Kennewick, WA: Glen Cove Press, 2017).

237   Beginning when children are six: Kristen A. Jenson, *Good Pictures Bad Pictures: Porn-Proofing Today's Young Kids*, 2nd ed. (Kennewick, WA: Glen Cove Press, 2018).

238   Culture Reframed offers to parents: "Enrichment 1: Porn & the Brain," Culture Reframed Parents Program—Building Resilience & Resistance to Hypersexualized Media & Porn, https://parents.culturereframed.org/.

239   tells a story in her TED Talk: Emily F. Rothman, "How Porn Changes the Way Teens Think About Sex," filmed November 2018, video, TEDMED, 15:26.

240   2018 *New York Times* feature article: Maggie Jones, "What Teenagers Are Learning from Online Porn," *New York Times*, February 7, 2018.

240   one of the only curricula of its kind: Jessica Alder, Nicole Daley, and Emily F. Rothman, "The Truth About Pornography: A Pornography-Literacy Curriculum for High School Students Designed to Reduce Sexual and Dating Violence," Start Strong: Building Healthy Teen Relationship Initiative at the Boston Public Health Commission, 2016.

240   "negatively influence youth": Rothman, *Pornography and Public Health*, 135.

240   Porn cannot be an isolated cause: Rothman, *Pornography and Public Health*, 130.

CHAPTER 18: FAKING IT

247   began watching people have sex: Thomas Maier, *Masters of Sex: The Life and Times of William Masters and Virginia Johnson, the Couple who Taught America How to Love* (New York: Basic Books, 2009), 87–102.

248 but Johnson was unintimidated: Maier, *Masters of Sex*, 89–90.

248 successfully recruit nearly seven hundred volunteers: William H. Masters and Virginia E. Johnson, *Human Sexual Response* (Boston: Little, Brown, 1966), 13–15.

248 "human female dissimulating": Masters and Johnson, *Human Sexual Response*, 134.

248 most had faked an orgasm: Emily A. Harris et al., "Beliefs about Gender Predict Faking Orgasm in Heterosexual Women," *Archives of Sexual Behavior* 48, no. 8 (2019): 2419–33.

248 women are more likely to moan audibly: Gayle Brewer and Colin A. Hendrie, "Evidence to Suggest that Copulatory Vocalizations in Women Are Not a Reflexive Consequence of Orgasm," *Archives of Sexual Behavior* 40, no. 3 (2011): 559–64.

254 nearly 33 million American adults are in therapy: Emily P. Terlizzi and Benjamin Zablotsky, "Mental Health Treatment Among Adults: United States, 2019," *NCHS Data Brief* No. 380, National Center for Health Statistics, Hyattsville, MD, 2020, 1–8.

255 Brené Brown is everywhere: Findings from this chapter were shared in my 2021 Furfey Lecture at the Association for the Study of Religion annual meeting and later published in Burke, "The False Dichotomy of Sex and Religion in America."

255 happened to be reading *Rising Strong*: Brené Brown, *Rising Strong: How the Ability to Reset Transforms the Way We Live, Love, Parent, and Lead* (New York: Random House, 2015).

258 there is no even playing field: Jakobsen and Pellegrini, *Love the Sin*.

258 Sex workers and their allies: Georgina Voss, *Stigma and the Shaping of the Pornography Industry* (New York: Routledge, 2015).

258 "Mobility for stasis": Janet R. Jakobsen, *The Sex Obsession: Perversity and Possibility in American Politics* (New York: New York University Press, 2020), 3.

CHAPTER 19: THE GOOD PLACE

260 a Hindu practice: Alistair Shearer, *The Story of Yoga: From Ancient India to the Modern West* (New York: Oxford University Press, 2020).

260 adapt and change our self-perception: Leon Festinger, "A Theory of Social Comparison Processes," *Human Relations* 7, no. 2 (1954): 117–40; Jerry Suls, Rene

Martin, and Ladd Wheeler, "Social Comparison: Why, with Whom, and with What Effect?," *Current Directions in Psychological Science* 11, no. 5 (2002): 159–63.

261   sexual identity exploration: Renata Arrington-Sanders et al., "The Role of Sexually Explicit Material in the Sexual Development of Same-Sex-Attracted Black Adolescent Males," *Archives of Sexual Behavior* 44, no. 3 (2015): 597–608; Penny Harvey, "Let's Talk About Porn: The Perceived Effect of Online Mainstream Pornography on LGBTQ Youth," in D. Nicole Farris, D'Lane R. Compton, and Andrea P. Herrera, eds., *Gender, Sexuality, and Race in the Digital Age* (Cham, Switzerland: Springer, 2020), 31–52.

261   higher levels of relationship quality: Ana J. Bridges, Raymond M. Bergner, and Matthew Hesson-McInnis Bridges, "Romantic Partners' Use of Pornography: Its Significance for Women," *Journal of Sex and Marital Therapy* 29, no. 1 (2003): 1–14; Amanda M. Maddox, Galena K. Rhoades, and Howard J. Markman, "Viewing Sexually-Explicit Materials Alone or Together: Associations with Relationship Quality," *Archives of Sexual Behavior* 40, no. 2 (2011): 441–48.

261   report negative outcomes: Joshua B. Grubbs et al., "Pornography Problems Due to Moral Incongruence: An Integrative Model with a Systematic Review and Meta-analysis," *Archives of Sexual Behavior* 48, no. 2 (2019): 397–415; Massimiliano Sommantico et al., "Body Image, Depression, and Self-Perceived Pornography Addiction in Italian Gay and Bisexual Men: The Mediating Role of Relationship Satisfaction," *Mediterranean Journal of Clinical Psychology* 9, no. 1 (2021).

261   separation and divorce: Samuel L. Perry and Joshua T. Davis, "Are Pornography Users More Likely to Experience a Romantic Breakup? Evidence from Longitudinal Analysis," *Sexuality and Culture* 21, no. 4 (2017): 1157–76.

262   "optimal distinctiveness": Marilynn Brewer, "The Social Self: On Being the Same and Different at the Same Time," *Personality and Social Psychology Bulletin* 17, no. 5 (1991): 475–82.

262   experience pornography differently: Kate Dawson, Saoirse Nic Gabhainn, and Pádraig MacNeela, "Toward a Model of Porn Literacy: Core Concepts, Rationales, and Approaches," *Journal of Sex Research* 57, no. 1 (2020): 1–15.

264   "pleasure and danger": Vance, "Pleasure and Danger," 327.

INDEX

A NOTE ON THE AUTHOR

Kelsy Burke is an award-winning sociologist and author of *Christians under Covers*. She has spent the last decade studying how sex and religion collide in America and is currently an associate professor of sociology at the University of Nebraska–Lincoln. Her work has been supported by multiple grants and fellowships, including an award from the National Science Foundation. Her writing has appeared in the *Huffington Post*, the *Guardian*, *Newsweek*, *Slate*, and the *Washington Post*.